MW00479226

MERIDIAN

Crossing Aesthetics

Werner Hamacher

& David E. Wellbery

Editors

*Stanford
University
Press*

———

*Stanford
California
1995*

TOPOGRAPHIES

J. Hillis Miller

Stanford University Press
Stanford, California

© 1995 by the Board of Trustees of the
Leland Stanford Junior University

Printed in the United States of America

CIP data appear at the end of the book

Stanford University Press publications
are distributed exclusively by
Stanford University Press within
the United States, Canada, and Mexico;
they are distributed exclusively by
Cambridge University Press
throughout the rest of the world.

Acknowledgments

Parts of this book have been previously published. All have been revised for publication here. I am deeply grateful to all those who have permitted me to reuse this material. Part of chapter 1 was published in an earlier form as "Topography in *The Return of the Native*," in *Essays in Literature* 8, no. 2 (Fall 1981): 119–34. Earlier versions of parts of chapter 2 were included in "Face to Face: Plato's *Protagoras* as a Model for Collective Research in the Humanities," in *The States of Theory*, ed. David Carroll (New York: Columbia University Press, 1990), pp. 281–95. Chapter 3 was published as "Laying Down the Law in Literature" in *Deconstruction and the Possibility of Justice, Cardozo Law Review* 11, nos. 5–6 (July/August 1990): 1491–514. Chapter 4 will appear as "Sam Weller's Valentine" in *Literature in the Marketplace*, ed. John O. Jordan and Robert L. Patten (Cambridge, Engl.: Cambridge University Press, 1994). Chapter 5 has been published as "Temporal Topographies: Tennyson's Tears," in *Victorian Poetry* 30, nos. 3–4 (Autumn-Winter 1992): 277–89, as well as in the Republic of China in *EurAmerica* 21, no. 3 (September 1991): 29–45, and in Chinese translation in the Republic of China by Chen Tung-jung in *Chung-Wai Literary Monthly* 22, no. 1 (September 1993). Chapter 6 was published as "Naming and Doing: Speech Acts in Hopkins's Poems" in *Religion & Literature* 22, nos. 2–3 (Summer–Autumn 1990): 173–91. Part of chapter 7 was published as "Nietzsche in Basel: Writing Reading," *Journal of Advanced Composition* 13, no. 2 (Fall 1993): 311–28. Chapter 10 was published in Chinese, trans. Lin-Su-ying, in *Chung-Wai Literary Monthly* 22 (January 1994): 74–105. Chapter 11 has been published in *South Atlantic Review* (Spring 1994), 1–25. A version has been published in French as "Les Topographies de Derrida," trans. Marie Pierre-Baggett, in *Le Passage des frontières: Autour du travail de Jacques Derrida*, Colloque de Cerisy (Paris: Galilée, 1994), 193–201. Chapter 12 was published in the Republic of China as "Border Crossings: Translating Theory" in *EurAmerica* 21, no. 4 (December 1991): 27–51, and in Spanish translation by Mabel Richart as *Cruce de Fronteras: Traduciendo Teoría* (Valencia: Amós Belinchón, 1993). A Chinese translation of "Border Crossings," trans. Shan Te-hsing, was published in *Con-Temporary Monthly* 75 (July 1992): 28–47. A later English version was published in *Selected Essays of the Third Conference on American Literature and Thought: The Literary Section*, ed. Shan Te-hsing (Taipei: Institute of European and American Studies, Academia Sinica, 1993), 1–27. Chapters 5, 10, and 12 have been published for distribution in the Republic of China in *New Starts: Performative Topographies in Literature and Criticism* (Taipei: The Institute of European and American Studies, Academia Sinica, 1993).

I am also grateful to all those who invited me to give various parts of this book as lectures and to those audiences whose comments and questions greatly helped me in revising the lectures for inclusion in this book.

Chapter 1 in a much earlier form was originally given, at the invitation of Murray Krieger, as seminars at the School of Criticism and Theory at the University of California, Irvine, in the summer of 1979. Those seminars were the germ of the topographies project that ultimately led to this book. Subsequently the material was presented as seminars to the participants in a Summer Seminar for College Teachers on "New Directions in the Interpretation of English and American Fiction," sponsored by the National Endowment for the Humanities and held at Yale University in the summer of 1980. A member of that seminar, Thomas Joswick, sponsored the publication of a section of my presentations on Hardy, along with other papers written for the seminar, in *Essays in Literature*, of which he was then Associate Editor.

A different version of chapter 2 was presented in 1987 at the University of California, Irvine, at the symposium "The States of Theory," sponsored by the Critical Theory Institute at UC Irvine, directed by David Carroll.

Chapter 3 was presented in October 1989 at the Cardozo Law School at the conference "Deconstruction and the Possibility of Justice," chaired by Drucilla Cornell.

Chapter 4 was presented in the summer of 1992 at the Dickens Universe, University of California, Santa Cruz, at the invitation of John Jordan, Director of the Dickens Project there.

Chapter 5 was presented in Taiwan at National Sun Yat-sen University in October, 1991, at the invitation of Shan Te-hsing.

Chapter 6 was given in March 1989 at Boston College, at the invitation of Francis Sweeney, SJ. It was given again at Loyola Marymount College in Los Angeles in April 1989, at the invitation of Robert Caro, SJ, as part of a series marking the centenary of Gerard Manley Hopkins's death.

Versions of parts of chapter 7 in earlier forms were given as lectures at a conference on rhetoric at the University of Chicago, chaired by Samuel Jaffe, at the University of South Florida at the invitation of Gary Olson, at the Claremont Graduate School at the invitation of Marc Redfield, and at the University of Washington as part of my presentations as Walker Aames Professor there in November 1992, at the invitation of Richard Dunn and Gene Woodruff.

Chapter 8 was originally given at the invitation of Evans Harrington as a lecture at the nineteenth annual Faulkner and Yoknapatawpha Conference at the University of Mississippi in August 1992. It was given again in November 1993 at the University of Zaragoza, at the invitation of Susana Oñega, and then again at the University of Madrid.

Chapter 10 was presented in October 1991 as a lecture in Taiwan at National Taiwan University, at the invitation of Shan Te-hsing, then subsequently that month at the Center for Literary Studies of the Hebrew University of Jerusalem, at the invitation of Lawrence Besserman, then in November 1991 at the University of Lausanne, at the invitation of Peter Halter, and at the University of Zurich, at the invitation of Peter Hughes, then again as a public lecture at the invitation of Michael Riffaterre at the Dartmouth School of Criticism and Theory in July 1992, and at the University of Zaragoza in November 1993, at the invitation of Susana Oñega.

Chapter 11 was originally presented in French, at the invitation of Marie-Louise Mallet and Jean-Michel Rabaté, at a "Décade" honoring the work of Jacques Derrida, in July 1992. It was subsequently given in English in the spring of 1993 at the Comparative Literature Works in Progress at the University of California, Irvine. Part of it was presented in October 1993, at a conference on "Deconstruction IS / IN America" at The Center for French Civilization and Culture and The Poetics Institute of New York University, at the invitation of Thomas Bishop and Anselm Haverkamp, and it was then presented in November 1993 in Atlanta at the meeting of the South Atlantic Modern Language Association, at the invitation of Robert Bell.

Chapter 12 was initially given as a lecture at the Third Conference on American Literature and Thought in Taipei held at the Academia Sinica, at the invitation of Shan Te-hsing. It was subsequently presented in October 1991 at the Center for Literary Studies, Hebrew University of Jerusalem, at the invitation of Sanford Budick and Wolfgang Iser, in December 1991 at the conference "Traveling Theory" at the University of California, Irvine, at the Chinese Comparative Literature Conference at the University of California, Los Angeles, in March 1992, at the invitation of Leo Ou-fan Lee, at the University of Cincinnati in January 1993 as the Taft lecture, at the invitation of Robin Sheets and James Hall, at the University of Oslo in October 1992, at the invitation of Arne Melberg, and in August 1993, at the invitation of David Wells, Peter Horvath, Roger Sell, and Danilo Lôbo at a Congress of the Fédération Internationale de Langages et Littératures Modernes held in Brasilia (a version of which will be published in the Congress volume in 1994).

I thank all these persons for their generosity and kindness.

Helen Tartar, Humanities Editor of Stanford University Press, was not only a wonderfully helpful editor but also did me the honor of copyediting the book herself. Finally, I thank my assistant, Senior Editor Barbara Cohen, for all her invaluable help with this book.

Contents

Contents

TOPOGRAPHIES

Introduction

Marcel Proust is one of the great topographical poets, taking poet in its wider sense of "maker with words." The important questions about topography are raised by the attempt to read certain sections of *Remembrance of Things Past.* One section of "Swann's Way" is called "Place-Names: The Name." A section of "Within a Budding Grove" is called "Place-Names: The Place." As these titles suggest, Proust knows that topographical considerations, the contours of places, cannot be separated from toponymical considerations, the naming of places. An admirable paragraph in "Place-Names: The Place" shows Marcel (not Proust himself, the reader should remember) thinking he can tell what a place is like from its name. He wanted, Marcel says, just once to take that 1:22 train from Paris to Balbec, "in order to become acquainted with the architecture of Normandy or Brittany."[1] Marcel thinks he knows what the stops along the rail line must be like from their names on the train schedule. Marcel's mistake, if it is a mistake, is not unlike the error the young Pip makes, in Dickens's *Great Expectations.* Pip thinks he can tell what his dead parents were like from the form of the lettering on their tombstone: "Philip Pirrip, Late of This Parish" and "Also Georgiana Wife of the Above." The paragraph in "Place Names: The Name" is a glorious exercise in Cratylean topographical poetry:

Vitré, whose acute accent barred its ancient glass with wooden lozenges [*vitré*, of course, means "glazed" in French]; gentle Lamballe,
whose whiteness ranged from egg-shell yellow to pearl grey; Coutances, a Norman cathedral which its final consonants, rich and
yellowing, crowned with a tower of butter [*que sa diphthongue finale,
grasse et jaunissante, couronné par une tour de beurre*]; Lannion with the
rumbling noise, in the silence of its village street, of a coach with a fly
buzzing after it [*du coche suivi de la mouche*; possibly an allusion is
made here to one of the fables of La Fontaine in which a fly does buzz
after a coach, though a "fly" is also a kind of vehicle for carrying
luggage attached to a coach], . . . Quimperlé, more firmly anchored,
ever since the Middle Ages, among its babbling rivulets threading their
pearls in a grey iridescence [*entre les ruisseaux dont il gazouille et
s'emperle en une grisaille*]. (E422; F389)

Marcel performs here a complex rhetorical operation of performative projection on the basis of the contingent material qualities
of the names. This is analogous to Swann's falling in love with
Odette because of the similarity of her face and body to a painting
by Botticelli, because of a flower, a note from her, and other such
signs. He assumes these signs indicate what she is like within
herself. Such readings are shown to be always false, but also always
unavoidable. They are posited on the assumption that each sign or
cluster of signs corresponds to a unique, individual person or place
behind the sign, to which the sign gives access. If Odette looks like
the Botticelli woman, she must be like what Swann imagines that
lady to have been, with all the aesthetic resonances Swann associates with the Renaissance. Vitré must have lots of old glass barred
with wooden lozenges, Coutances must be buttery, just because the
names sound like that. The name Venice gives access to that city: "I
did not then represent to myself cities, landscapes, historical mon-
uments, as more or less attractive pictures, cut out here and there of
a substance that was common to them all, but looked on each of
them as on an unknown thing, different in essence from all the rest,
a thing for which my soul thirsted and which it would profit from
knowing. How much more individual still was the character they
assumed from being designated by names, names that were for

themselves alone, proper names such as people have!" (420–21). This sounds so plausible, it is presented so persuasively, that it takes an effort to go on remembering that Proust is presenting here with loving irony an absurd infatuation. It is not that he does not say in so many words that these readings are false, but even so, we easily forget, no doubt because we do exactly the same thing in our own daily personal, social, and political life. There must be lots of deer, one thinks, on Deer Isle, Maine, and Irvine, California, must be a serious and earnest place where they grow grapes.

"Topography": the word combines the Greek word *topos*, place, with the Greek word *graphein*, to write. I speak above as though the word names solely the contours of a given place, but "topography" is in fact a complex word. Etymologically, it means the writing of a place. The English word "topography" has today three meanings, one obsolete. The obsolete meaning is the most literal: "the description of a particular place." Now the word means either "the art or practice of graphic and exact delineation in minute detail, usually on maps or charts, of the physical features of any place or region," or, by metonymy, "the configuration of a surface, including its relief, the position of its streams, lakes, roads, cities, etc."[2] At first the word meant just what it says: a description in words of a place. That meaning became obsolete. The word then came to mean the art of mapping by graphic signs rather than words. Hardly any map, however, is without inscriptions in two different kinds of words: general terms ("mountain," "river," "coral reef") and proper place names ("Mt. Chocorua," "Swatara River," "Key West," to take examples from Wallace Stevens's poetry). By a further sideways slippage "topography" has come to be the name for what is mapped, apparently without any reference to writing or other means of representation. General names and proper names, however, seem so much a part of the topography of a given region that it is difficult to think of the region without them. What would Key West be without its name? This third usage, in any case, is now the most common. It is the product of a triple figurative transference. "Topography" originally meant the creation of a metaphorical equivalent in words of a landscape. Then, by another transfer, it came to mean representation of a landscape according to the conventional signs of some system of mapping. Finally, by a third transfer, the name of the map was carried over to name what is mapped. Today we might say, "We must make a topographical map of the topography of Key West," using the word in two different ways in the same sentence. The implications of this third figurative transfer are subtle and far-reaching. The power of the conventions of mapping and of the projection of place names on the place are so great that we see the landscape as though it were already a map, complete with place names and the names of geographical features. The place names seem to be intrinsic to the places they name. The names are motivated. By a species of Cratylism they tell what the places are like. The place is carried into the name and becomes available to us there. You can get to the place by way of its name. Place names make a site already the product of a virtual writing, a topography, or, since the names are often figures, a "topotropography." With topotropography, the act of mapping, goes topology, the knowledge of places, or as the dictionary puts it, topology is "topographical study of a particular place; specif., the history of a region as indicated by its topography." Toponymy, finally, is "the place names of a region or language."[3]

This book investigates a cluster of related concepts as they gather around the central question of topography. How do topographical descriptions or terms function in novels, poems, and philosophical texts? Just what, in a given text, is the topographical component and how does it operate? The other topics in the cluster include the initiating efficacy of speech acts, responsibility, political or legislative power, the translation of theory from one topographical location to another, the way topographical delineations can function as parable or allegory, the relation of personification to landscape, or, as Thomas Hardy puts it, "the figure in the landscape." There is always a figure in the landscape. The way speech acts operate in literature and in life is the most pervasive of these additional topics. All are approached from the perspective of topography. Though they may not all seem at first to be connected to mappings of some landscape, imaginary or real, it is easy to see, for example, that the question of speech acts comes up in investigating what is involved in the naming of places. This, in turn, is related to the politics of nationalism as they involve border demarcations and territorial appropriations. Deciding whether to have street signs in French in Montreal or in Welsh in Wales is not a trivial issue. The question of transporting or translating theory from one country to another raises the question of the degree to which a given theory is rooted in one particular culture, able to function only in a specific place. The approach is made throughout by way of the reading of examples. In each reading I have allowed the text to dictate the paths to be followed in raising and answering one or another set of my topographical questions. This means that each chapter provides a particular perspective on the presupposed conceptual landscape, a perspective allowed by that text alone. Or it may be that each chapter contributes to the creation of that landscape. This tension between creating and revealing is one of my topics.

Though the chapters, with the exception of the first and the last, are organized according to conventional generic and historical progressions, they do not provide a conceptual progression or argument. Putting Nietzsche after Plato may indicate no more than that Nietzsche had read Plato, while Plato had no way of reading Nietzsche. But that does not mean that Nietzsche is more "advanced" than Plato. Far from it. Without doubting the overdetermined distinctions that separate philosophy from literature in their intellectual, disciplinary, and social uses, the readings attempt to take each text at its word without presuming to know beforehand how its generic placement ought to impose a way of reading. This is signaled by the interweaving of chapters in a roughly chronological sequence on novels, poems, and philosophical texts. Each chapter, then, contributes a new view of a terrain that always seems to have been there already when we move into it, though the text and its reading, it may be, are performative speech acts bringing the terrain into existence. It is impossible to make a decision about that, since the only way to approach the terrain is through the readings. About this strange feature of speech acts, that they may create that in the name of which they speak, though it is impossible to be sure about that, and in spite of the urgent need to know, the chapters themselves have more to say.

To propose another figure for the way the chapters are arranged: all of them taken together may be thought of as like the transparencies superimposed in palimpsest on a map, each transparency charting some different feature of the landscape beneath: annual rainfall, temperature distribution, altitudes and contours, forest cover, and the like. The landscape "as such" is never given, only one or another of the ways to map it. That, as I have said, is what topography means, or at any rate that is one of its meanings: the mapping by way of conventional signs of some terrain. Since another meaning of "topography" is the preexisting configuration and nature of a given region, the word "topography" contains the alternation between "create" and "reveal" I shall investigate.

A final figure for the organization of this book would see it as a virtual hypertext, presented in a somewhat arbitrary sequence through the necessity of the printed book. All but the first of the chapters were written on the computer, and that one has been transferred there and revised. All were written with a certain set of topographical questions in mind. The chapters when called up into the RAM or "random access memory" of a computer do not exist as a linear sequence. They exist rather as a strange spatial array in which the chapters can easily be arranged in different orders and through which various lines of exploration, in a different way in each case, are possible by following different paths of relation. Each chapter can be related to the others by a multitude of different conceptual and figurative links. The order of the chapters in the printed version is a somewhat arbitrary sequence that signals certain relations but hides others.

This book began with what seem easy questions to answer: What is the function of landscape or cityscape descriptions in novels and poems? What is the function of topographical terms in philosophical or critical thinking? The answers seem obvious. Landscape or cityscape gives verisimilitude to novels and poems. Topographical setting connects literary works to a specific historical and geographical time. This establishes a cultural and historical setting within which the action can take place. In philosophy and criticism, topographical terms (such as "method," which means "according to the way," in Descartes, or Kant's account of "symbols" like "ground," "flow," and "substance," in paragraph 59 of the third *Critique*) are subordinated to logical and rational thinking. Overtly topographical terms in philosophy and criticism are, so to speak, transparent illustrative metaphors, handy ways of thinking. Their original spatial and material reference has been eroded as they have been turned into conceptual terms. *Grund* in Kant has nothing to do with the ground Kant walked across every day in Königsberg to get from his house to the university. But is this really so? *Topographies* attempts to think this question out through the reading of examples in which landscape "description" (I use the blandest word for it) occurs—place names in both the generic and proper sense: river, stream, mountain, house, path, field, hedge, road, bridge, shore, doorway, cemetery, tombstone, crypt, tumulus, boundary, horizon, "Key West," "Egdon Heath," "The Quiet Woman Inn," "Balbec," "Quimperlé," "Sutpen's Hundred," "the old bridge at Heidelberg," and so on. Do they, I have asked, have a function beyond that of mere setting or metaphorical adornment? In reading each text I have allowed the text to dictate the paths to be followed.

In attempting to investigate my question I have found myself encountering in different ways within each topography the atopical. This is a place that is everywhere and nowhere, a place you cannot get to from here. Sooner or later, in a different way in each case, the effort of mapping is interrupted by an encounter with the unmappable. The topography and the toponymy in each example, in a different way in each case, hide an unplaceable place. It was the locus of an event that never "took place" as a phenomenal happening located in some identifiable spot and therefore open to knowledge. This strange event that took place without taking place cannot be the object of a cognition because it was a unique performative event. This strange locus is another name for the ground of things, the preoriginal ground of the ground, something other to any activity of mapping. The atopical inhabits the individual psyche. Why can desire not be satisfied in a happy coincidence of consciousness with the hidden other within the self? It haunts language. Why cannot language ever be wholly clear? It interferes with interpersonal relations, relations with the "other." Why can they never be wholly satisfactory or fulfill desire? It underlies society and history. Why are they so often a panorama of violence and injustice? It generates the opacities of storytelling. Why can no story ever bring the things it narrates wholly into the open? The encrypted place generates stories that play themselves out within a topography. Narration is a way to talk about it, which means personifying it. Such personifications, like prosopopoeias in general, seem a form of knowledge but are in fact potent speech acts. They have to do with doing rather than knowing. Whether or not all this can be clearly known and shown in critical readings the readings themselves will investigate.

Deer Isle, Maine
July 9, 1993

§ 1 Philosophy, Literature, Topography: Heidegger and Hardy

tout fleurira au bord d'une tombe désaffectée
— Jacques Derrida[1]

It seems to me an interesting idea: that is to say, the idea that we live in the description of a place and not in the place itself, and in every vital sense we do. — Wallace Stevens[2]

A spot whereon the founders lived and died
Seemed once more dear than life; ancestral trees
Or gardens rich in memory glorified
Marriages, alliances, and families,
And every bride's ambition satisfied.
Where fashion or mere fantasy decrees
Man shifts about—all that great glory spent—
Like some poor Arab tribesman and his tent.
— W. B. Yeats[3]

The notion that landscape provides grounding for novels has hardly given rise to a distinct mode of the criticism of fiction, as has the criticism of character, or of interpersonal relations, or of narrators and narrative sequence. Nevertheless, certain once-influential forms of criticism, for example, the phenomenological criticism of Gaston Bachelard, Georges Poulet, and Jean-Pierre Richard, base themselves on the space, inner or outer, constituted by works of literature. This sometimes means, in such criticism, attention to landscape as such in literature. Richard's essays on Stendhal and Flaubert in *Literature and Sensation* are cases of this, as is the guiding metaphor of Poulet's *The Interior Distance* or of Bachelard's *The Poetics of Space*. An important branch of modern geography investigates the mental mappings we make of our environments, whether "we" are aborigines or dwellers in modern cities. Topology

9

is, of course, a branch of mathematics, the science of the placement of places. One subbranch of topology is the theory of knots, of looped lines that turn back on themselves. Jacques Lacan has used the theory of knots as a powerful image for intra- and interpersonal relations. For him, semiotic lines tie the self to hidden regions of the self, to others, and to that Other who is always presupposed within the self as outside the self. One part of the traditional study of rhetoric is the location of places (*topoi*) and commonplaces. Modern anthropology studies the human space men and women create for themselves in their cultures, for example, the way the placement of houses, fields, and paths in a village reflects totemic structures and kinship taboos, the licit and the illicit in the drawing of genealogical lines. Martin Heidegger is a philosopher for whom topographical figures are more than merely figures. Examples are the image of the bridge in "Building Dwelling Thinking," or the governing figures of *On the Way to Language* and *Forest Paths*, or the topographical framework of "The Origin of the Work of Art."

Among these diverse forms of spatial mapping, the use of topography in narrative takes its place. Every narrative, without exception, even the most apparently abstract and inward (the stories of Maurice Blanchot or of Franz Kafka, for example), traces out in its course an arrangement of places, dwellings, and rooms joined by paths or roads. These arrangements could be mapped. They tend in fact to be mapped, at least implicitly, in the mind of the reader as he or she reads the novel. This chapter attempts to explore the implications of this aspect of narrative in one salient example of it: Thomas Hardy's *The Return of the Native*. The reading of this novel will be made against a background of all the other disciplinary uses of spatial mappings I have listed. Later chapters will map other features of the topography of topography.

～

Perhaps Martin Heidegger, in "The Origin of the Work of Art," in "Building Dwelling Thinking," in "The Thing," and in associated essays (which include ultimately, of course, all his work, even *Being and Time*), has established what looks like the firmest conceptual foundation for a notion that novels ground themselves on the landscape. A later chapter on Heidegger will identify what is shaky about this foundation.

Heidegger's work, insofar as it focuses on the human relation to the landscape, turns, like the passage from Yeats cited as an epigraph, on the distinction between being at home and homelessness, *Heimatlösigkeit.* Being rooted in one dear particular place, like a tree or a house, is the proper condition of Dasein, but modern "man" (*das Man,* as Heidegger puts it) is uprooted. He drifts from place to place, like the poor Arab tribesman and his tent. The first state would correspond, as Yeats's poem makes clear, to a condition of language in which words, even figurative words, are grounded in their referential function and in literary tradition. In the novel this might be the basis of a mimetic, referential, or "realistic" theory of fiction. The state of homeless drifting would correspond to an uprooted condition of language. In such a condition, the reference of each word is only another word, the meaning of that word yet another word, and so on. Language moves from word to word in a perpetual drifting, never being pinned down to anything outside language. In narrative theory this might lead to the notion of "fiction about fiction." In "Coole Park and Ballylee," the opposition is between Homer, or one of his descendants, seated in the saddle of Pegasus, and the "high horse riderless, . . . Where the swan drifts upon a darkening flood." Yeats's phrase, in its incoherent mixing of two incompatible metaphors, the horse and the swan, manifests the groundless drifting it names. Two orientations, toward the sun of the "Logos" and toward the mock northern sun, Hyperborean, white, cold, factitious (to borrow Pater's opposition in *Apollo in Picardy*), govern in one way or another much narrative theory. But no purely mimetic theory of fiction exists, nor any purely self-referential one either. The two apparently opposing orientations have a way of turning into one another, as this chapter may show.

Heidegger's essays can be taken as a brilliant interrogation of what is presupposed when we assume that novels ground themselves in a landscape. At a crucial point in each of the essays I have mentioned, a different linear image emerges as necessary to thinking through the relation of man and his artifacts (including implicitly works of art like novels) to the earth on which he dwells. In "The Origin of the Work of Art" the linear figure is the *Riß,* or cleft. In "Building Dwelling Thinking" it is the bridge joining bank to bank over a stream. In "The Thing" it is the ring encompassing earth and sky, mortals and divinities, in a round pulled tight. Taken together these three—dividing fissure, conjoining bridge, encircling ring—provide the rudimentary outlines of an implicit map. This is Heidegger's map of man's (*sic*) proper dwelling on the earth and under the sky when he and what he produces are at home there and in proximity to the gods. At the same time the three, *Riß, Brücke,* and *Ring,* provide images for Heidegger's sense of what is most problematic about this picture of man as at home in the world of what he barbarously calls "the fouring of the four." If Heidegger has reaffirmed in these essays the traditional, archaic, metaphysical, or religious concepts of being at home in the universe, rooted there, at the same time he has put these concepts in question. His thought has been the ground of an important form of twentieth-century religious philosophy. At the same time he has, of course, been influential in literary criticism of diverse sorts, most fruitfully when what he says has been patiently put in question, for example, by Jacques Derrida, Paul de Man, and others. Far from "basing itself" on Heidegger, so-called deconstruction has depended on a circumspect putting in question of Heidegger, as does this discussion here, in part through the reading of Hardy's novel, and as does the more extended reading of Heidegger in chapter 9.[4]

Heidegger's thinking on this topic is governed by double antithetical concepts. These concepts affirm the identity in difference of gathering and dispersal, being and nothing, proximity and distance, appropriation and expropriation. *Riß, Brücke,* and *Ring* are such image-concepts.

The *Riß* as line makes a path joining one place to another, like the straight white line of the old Roman road that runs across the heath in *The Return of the Native.* At the same time, the *Riß* is a furrow, fissure, or chasm dividing this side from that in an uncrossable abyss. The *Riß* sets one bank against the other in antagonistic opposition. The *Riß* is also the furrow cut by the plough, grave of the seed or grain, but source of all the living things that reappear above the earth, in a familiar resurrection: "unless the grain dies . . . ." At the same time, again, the *Riß* is the "trait" or carved line that engraves the earth, making its dumb surface into a sign, as in the act of engraving, in the sense the word is used in the graphic arts. Heidegger brings engraving up elsewhere in "The Origin of the Work of Art" by way of the example of Dürer. Wherever the word *Riß* or its cognates occur in this essay, Heidegger is playing on the multiple meanings of the word and its compounds, on *Riß* as cleft, as trait, as outline, as design, on *reissen* as wrest, on *Grundriß* as groundplan, on *Umriß* as outline, *Aufriß* as sketch, *Durchriß* as breach, *Reiz* as attraction, and so on. Here is an extravagant example: "Reißen heißt hier Herausholen des Risses und den 'Riß' reißen mit der Reißfeder auf dem Reißbrett." (" 'Wrest' here means to draw out the rift and to draw the design with the drawing-pen on the drawing-board.")[5]

The family of words built on *Riß* and *reißen* is intermarried, crossed in Heidegger's thought, with the family of words in *Zug* ("feature, trait, something drawn") and *ziehen* ("draw, attract"). According to an undecidability between active and passive, to draw is to be drawn, to inscribe a cleft or a *Riß* is to be drawn along it, and ultimately perhaps drawn into a gulf or abyss. An example is Eustacia in *The Return of the Native*, to be discussed in more detail later. Eustacia is fearless and active. She makes her way by day or night across the paths of Egdon Heath. Nevertheless, she is drawn by an unassuageable desire back to dance with Wildeve and ultimately drawn to her death in Shadwater Weir.

Dance, path, an action that is passive, a passion that is active, doing and suffering at once, the drawing of a line that is also allowing oneself to be drawn: these figures are present in Heidegger, too. Here is the crucial passage in "The Origin of the Work of Art" on the *Riß*:

As the world opens itself, it submits to the decision [*zur Ent-schiedung*] of a historical humanity the question of victory and defeat, blessing and curse, mastery and slavery. The dawning world brings out [*zum Vorschein*] what is as yet undecided and measureless, and thus discloses the hidden necessity of measure and decisiveness [*von Maß und Entschiedenheit*].

But as a world opens itself the earth comes to rise up. It stands both as that which bears all, as that which is sheltered in its own law and always wrapped up in itself. World demands its decisiveness and its measure [*ihre Entschiedenheit und ihr Maß*] and lets beings attain to the Open of their paths [*in das Offene ihrer Bahnen*]. Earth, bearing and jutting, strives to keep itself closed and to entrust everything to its law. The conflict is not a rift as a mere cleft is ripped open [*Der streit ist kein Riß als das Aufreißen einer bloßen Kluft*]; rather, it is the intimacy with which opponents belong to each other. This rift carries the opponents into the source [*die Herkunft*] of their unity by virtue of their common ground [*aus dein einigen Grunde*]. It is a basic design [*Er ist Grundriß*], an outline sketch [*Auf-riß*], that draws the basic features of the rest of the lighting of beings [*der die Grundzüge des Auf-gehens der Lichtung das Seienden zeichnet*]. This rift does not let the opponents break apart; it brings the opposition of measure and boundary into their common outline [*in den einigen Umriß*]. (E63; G51)

This extraordinary passage, as the reader can see, plays on the various forms of *Riß*: *Aufreißen, Aufriß, Grundriß, Umriß*. Chapter 9 will identify the political implications of such texts. A play on *Grund* also runs through the citation and overlaps with the resonances of the words in *Riß. Grund* is "ground," or "base," but *Grundriß* is "basic design," while *Grundzüge*, one of the *Zug* words, is "basic features," the result of the sharp drawing of lines making a fundamental design. World is set in antagonism against earth, but both are opposed to the common ground that supports both. Earth closes itself in on itself and hides the ground. World is what men and women in their living together make, for example in cutting paths through a forest or across a heath. Such paths are decisive fissures setting boundaries, dividing this side from that side. Paths give the world edges and measures. They also join this place to that place. They establish a place where the opposition between earth in its self-enclosure and world in its openness can be brought out, in an intimacy of proximity and distance. The paths are also clefts. The paths on a given terrain form a rudimentary design. They make a legible pattern like the features of a face or like the preliminary sketch for a building or a painting. In short, the design made by the paths is already a work of art, combining outline and matter in the violence done matter to make it a sign or a design. Any work of art as such, poem, painting, song, statue, or temple, is only an extension of the work of art made when roads are laid out: "The rift-design is the drawing together, into a unity, of sketch and basic design, breach and outline" (*Der Riß ist das einheitliche Gezüge von Aufriß und Grundriß, Durch- und Umriß*) (E63; G51). Out of this conflict on earth and world all things and beings (people and objects, for example, not just works of art) rise out of obscurity, appear in the light, and come into the open, as the sun rises, seemingly out of the earth, each morning.

What is undecidable in this act of decision and measuring is, as always in Heidegger, the question of whether the design is imposed superficially on the earth by man, laid out over the earth's skin, so to speak, or whether it brings out a hidden design already there but covered over. About this no decision is possible, since any decision only makes the *Riß* once more and returns once more to the unanswerable question of whether historical humanity gives measure and decisiveness or finds it. All Heidegger's political orientation hangs in the balance too between these opposing tensions of his thought, as chapter 9 will show.

～

Insofar as the *Riß* is a fissure, a gorge, or gulf, man needs a bridge to cross it. In "Building Dwelling Thinking" Heidegger interprets the bridge. The bridge is introduced initially as an apparently casual example of a man-made thing. A bridge is one of the things a man builds in his activity of constructing a dwelling on the earth and thereby making himself a world. As in the analysis of the *Riß* in "The Origin of the Work of Art," Heidegger's conception of the *Brücke* in this essay turns on opposites that are held together and kept apart by the line that joins them. Here he makes explicit the idea of a gathering that turns the wild earth into a landscape. Building turns earth into a coherent configuration of places with lines of communication between them. A boundary or perhaps a horizon (they are not the same) now surrounds the whole.

What is problematic about Heidegger's thinking here will be explored in detail in chapter 9. It is easy to see, however, that his concepts of the landscape as something made by man in his living on the earth, and of space not as something pre-existent, neutrally lying out there, but as something brought into existence by the building of houses, bridges, and roads, could form the foundation of an interpretation of landscape in narrative. Insofar as men and women are among the beings who are brought into what the translation just quoted calls "presencing" by the building of bridges and the setting of boundaries, the landscape in a novel is not just an indifferent background within which the action takes place. The landscape is an essential determinant of that action. No account of a novel would be complete without a careful interpretation of the function of landscape (or cityscape) within it.

The writing of novels would be included as a form of artwork within the activity of bringing forth described by Heidegger in "The Origin of the Work of Art." The writing of a novel is an example of the origin of the work of art "as the outlining which brings into the light." This means that novels do not simply ground themselves on landscapes that are already there, made by prior activities of building, dwelling, and thinking. The writing of a novel, and the reading of it, participate in those activities. Novels themselves aid in making the landscapes that they apparently presuppose as already made and finished. Mississippi is partly what it is because of Faulkner's Yoknapatawpha novels. Dorset has been made what it is in part by way of Hardy's Wessex, Salisbury by way of Trollope's Barset novels, London by Dickens, Paris by Balzac and Proust, and so on.

This making is, however, ambiguous. It is both a making and a discovering, as in the doublet that runs through Yeats's essays in *Ideas of Good and Evil*: "create or reveal." Heidegger's form of these alternatives is "admit or install" (E158; G33). There is no way to decide which of these it is, yet nothing could be more important for thinking and action than to decide. No one has more scrupulously than Heidegger recorded this crucial fork in the road. The choice between forks involves the meaning of real forks and real roads as well as any conceivable use of these as figures, for example, in the motif of Hercules at the crossroads or in the story of Oedipus's murder of Laius at the place "where three roads cross." One fork would lead to such "deconstructive" branchings from Heidegger as the work of Jacques Derrida or Paul de Man. The other would lead to more "logological" or even strictly religious Heideggerianism and phenomenology: Rudolf Bultmann or Paul Ricoeur.

~

The fourfold that is at the same time a simple onefold—earth, sky, divinities, mortals—gathered by the *Riß* or the *Brücke* reappears in the image of the *Ring* in "The Thing." This gives rise to one of Heidegger's most exuberant passages of wordplay. It is wordplay that is not simply wordplay. Heidegger's own words participate, as much as any literary work could, in the activity of making the landscape that the words describe. The ring, as it circles the rift and the bridge, enclosing them and gathering their outlines tight, completes the groundplan of a fundamental human landscape:

> The fouring, the unity of the four, presences [*west*] as the appropriating mirror-play [*das ereignende Spiegel-Spiel*] of the betrothed, each to the other in simple oneness [*der einfältig einander Zugetrauten*]. The fouring presences as the worlding of world. The mirror-play of world is the round dance of appropriating. [*Das Spiegel-Spiel von Welt ist der Reigen des Ereignens.*] Therefore, the round dance does not encompass the four like a hoop. The round dance is the ring that joins while it plays as mirroring. . . . The mirror-play of the worlding world, as the ringing of the ring, wrests free the united four into their own compliancy, the circling compliancy of their presence. Out of the ringing mirror-play the thinging of the thing takes place. [*Aus dem Spiegel-Spiel des Gerings des Ringen ereignet sich das Dingen des Dinges.*] (E180; G53)

The image of the ring is only one of the elements at play within this passage, but it is the overtly topographical one. It will also be seen how difficult it is to translate these passages adequately into English. The *Ring* adds to the figures of the bridge and the rift the notion that the outline is not a mere encompassing circle. It is something that develops from the interplay of earth, sky, mortals, and divinities. Heidegger's figures for this are four: the ringing of the ring that joins multiplicity into unity, betrothal, the round dance, and the mirror. These figures unostentatiously personify or even sexualize a universal and impersonal process. They make it human, like the engagement of a man and a woman to be true to one another, or like men and women dancing in a ring, or like a man seeing his image in his beloved's eyes. It is as though human figures, along with an incipient story for them of courtship and marriage, were somehow generated by the intimate interaction, a sort of caressing interchange among the four. Out of this the ring rings: "Nestling, malleable, pliant, compliant, nimble—in Old German these are called *ring* and *gering.*" [*Schmiegsam, schmiedbar, geschmeidig, fügsam, leicht heißt in unserer alten deutschen Sprache "ring" und "gering"*] (E180; G53). Human figures rise out of the landscape, ringed by it, to swear allegiance, to dance, to make love, to be married by rings, and to see themselves mirrored in one another, as they do, for example, in *The Return of the Native.*

Heidegger elsewhere in the same essay says a man is not a thing, though a young maiden is a thing. Even so, a sexual prosopopoeia somewhat overtly appears, as if in obedience to some strong force, in Heidegger's description of the universal landscape of the world. This would seem to justify including men and women both among the things that manifest themselves in what he calls the thinging of the things that arise in the midst of the ring.

Heidegger's discussion of *Riß*, *Brücke*, and *Ring* suggests that there is no landscape without its story. One thing novels do is to tell such stories. These stories are not so much placed against the background of the scene as generated by it. One task of the following discussion of *The Return of the Native* will be to set Hardy against Heidegger to see to what degree they are congruent. Heidegger, it may be, though he clearly recognizes the opposition between installing and admitting, leans a little too easily toward the implication that Being with a capital "B" lies ready to be brought momentarily into the light by this activity of path- and bridge-making, courtship and marriage. Where Hardy stands on this issue my reading of *The Return of the Native* will attempt to show.

What is at stake in the assumption that a novel arises from the landscape in which the action takes place? The attachment of "realism" in the novel to referential assumptions is reinforced by this grounding. The landscape of a particular region is really there, with its hills, towns, roads, rivers, paths, its particular forms of cultivation and building, its special local customs. That culture is rooted in the earth. Its landscape may be visited, photographed, mapped. A novel may be the transposition of such a real country into a country of the mind or into a country of literature, an interior space or a literary space. Nevertheless, that real country remains as a solid base giving a grounding in material reality to the act of transposition. The reader may visit "the Hardy country" or "the Faulkner country" and see the "originals" of this or that place in the novels of each.

The text of the novel and the real landscape may be thought of as elements in a series. The actual landscape exists not only in itself but as if it has already been transposed into photographs or maps, for example, into official topographical survey maps of Mississippi or of Dorset, or into the photographs of "originals" that illustrated the Wessex and Anniversary editions of Hardy's novels. The real maps are in turn remapped in the texts of the novels that are "based on" those scenes and on the psycho-socio-economic realities of ways of life there—modes of transportation, agriculture, kinds of houses, roads, paths, walls, marriage customs, kinship systems, the annual round of local observances—for example, the Maypole, the Fawkes Fires, and the Mummers' Play in *The Return of the Native*.

A novel is a figurative mapping. The story traces out diachronically the movement of the characters from house to house and from time to time, as the crisscross of their relationships gradually creates an imaginary space. This space is based on the real landscape, charged now with the subjective meaning of the story that has been enacted within it. The houses, roads, paths, and walls stand not so much for the individual characters as for the dynamic field of relations among them. This is a complex form of the metonymy whereby environment may be a figure for what it environs, in this case the agents who move, act, and interact within the scene. All novels, even those that are least visual, create one form or another of this inner space. The *topoi* within this topography are powerful but sometimes unnoticed bearers of much meaning in the novel. Perhaps this can work so unostentatiously because we readers of novels live our own lives in the material world that way. We take this process unreflectingly for granted. We charge houses with our feelings for the personalities of those who live there or divide our lives, as Proust's Marcel did, between a Guermantes' Way and a Swann's Way. A great many Victorian novels presuppose in their readers an intimate knowledge of the socio-economic topography of London. The same thing may be said of Balzac's novels and Paris.

The process whereby meanings are projected on the landscape may be easier to see in novels that obey unity of place. It may be easiest of all when the novelist has produced a map of the imaginary country of his novels. This map records a transformation of the real landscape effected by writing the novels. This transformation renames towns, places, houses. It rearranges rivers and roads, and in other ways disarranges the actual landscape. Examples of this would be Faulkner's map of Yoknapatawpha County, Trollope's map of Barset, and Hardy's map of Wessex. These maps may be thought of as the last element in the series going from the real landscapes to the maps or photographs of them, to the texts of the novels, to the maps based on the novels. The latter are the traces left by the characters' movements as they go through life meeting and parting and meeting again, drawing out a design that the cartographer can engrave. The map may seem to show what is presupposed by the action of the novel, but in fact it is the product of the novel and impossible without it. The map is what remains after the characters are dead or happily married, like a tumulus or like a house with its gardens, fences, and paths, which have been gradually produced by the family living there.

The series is a relatively complex example of the logic or alogic of text and context, figure and ground, work and "hors d'oeuvre."

This series is a chain, a reversible concatenation. Any link may be placed at any point in the sequence. Any link presupposes the others as its determining causes, but in its turn is cause of the others. The landscape is not a pre-existing thing in itself. It is made into a landscape, that is, into a humanly meaningful space, by the living that takes place within it. This transforms it both materially, as by names, or spiritually, as by the ascription of some collective value to this or that spot. We say, for example, "This is Hart-Leap Well," and this speech act memorializes for generations an event that occurred there.

Among such transformations making the brute X-ignotum of the earth (if that is what it is) into a human landscape are the making of a map or of a picture, the telling of a story, the writing of a novel located at that place. The placing of a story in a certain setting, like the building of a house, a wall, or a road, makes that place habitable, but the place gives solidity, continuity, and per-durability to the life that is lived within it, as well as to the records of that life. According to the alogic of figure and ground relations, the landscape around, behind, or beneath the novel must both pre-exist the novel as what is outside it, prior to it, giving it solidity, and be incorporated within it. The landscape exists as landscape only when it has been made human in an activity of inhabitation that the writing of the novel repeats or prolongs. Causer and caused, first and second, change places in a perpetually reversing meta-lepsis. If the landscape is not prior to the novel and outside it, then it cannot be an extratextual ground giving the novel referential reality. If it is not part of the novel, in some way inside it as well as outside, then it is irrelevant to it. But if the landscape is inside the novel, then it is determined by it and so cannot constitute its ground. The same thing may be said of the relation of any two members of the series: novel and map; real map and imaginary map; landscape and map. Each is both prior to the other and later than it, causer and caused, inside it and outside it at once.

To investigate more specifically this strange, reversible relation of interiority and exteriority, priority and posteriority, I choose Thomas Hardy's *The Return of the Native*. All the requisite ele-ments are present here: the real landscape of Dorset in which

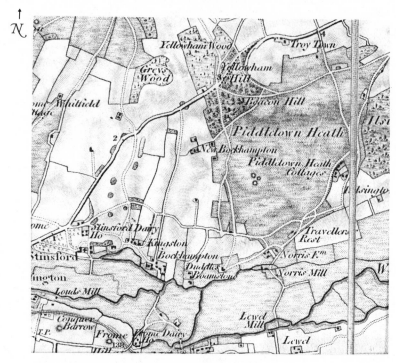

Fig. 1. Segment of Map 17, Dorchester, 1873, of Ordnance Survey of England and Wales. Courtesy Map Collection, Yale University Library.

Hardy dwelt at Max Gate, maps and photographs of Dorset (see fig. 1), the text of the novel, the general map of Wessex prepared for the Wessex Edition of Hardy's work, and "A Sketch Map of the Scene of the Story" included in the first edition of *The Return of the Native* (1878; see fig. 2). One might even include certain odd topographical drawings Hardy put in the pocket edition of his poems, since they are also representations of the scene of *The Return of the Native.*

∼

Any discussion of *The Return of the Native* is likely to begin and end with Egdon Heath, the "vast tract of unenclosed wild"[6] de-

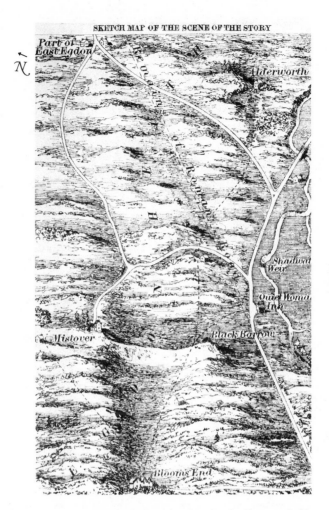

Fig. 2. Map included in the first book edition of *The Return of the Native* (1878). Reproduced from a copy in the Beinecke Rare Books and Manuscripts Library of Yale University, with their kind permission.

scribed in the first chapter. The characters trace out the courses of their lives as they cross back and forth, transversing the heath on the paths and roads Hardy drew on his map. These paths and roads are said to be like the white parting of hair across a scalp: "the long, laborious road, dry, empty, and white . . . was quite open to the heath on each side, and bisected that vast dark surface like the parting-line on a head of black hair, diminishing and bending away on the furthest horizon" (37), or like threads of glistening stones catching the light of the sun: "the white flints of a footpath lay like a thread over the slopes" (312). The first of these figures cooperates in the personifying of the heath that is this novel's generative prosopopoeia. The image of the parted head of hair lies over the heath, just as a thread lies on the surface of a table. These roads and paths join this place with that place, but they also divide this side from that side with a miniature fissure or seam.

The houses of the various characters in *The Return of the Native* are located, in the map Hardy drew, around the periphery of the heath. That is a ripple of ribbed hills behind hills, black against white or white against black in Hardy's drawing. Blooms-End, where the Yeobrights live, is at the bottom, Wildeve's Quiet Woman Inn at the right side, Mistover Knap, Eustacia Vye's house, at the left, and East Egdon is way at the top, beyond which, off the map, lies the cottage Clym Yeobright takes for his wife Eustacia. Off to the right, running down the margin of the map, is the river with Shadwater Weir, where Eustacia and Wildeve drown. In the midst of the map is Black Barrow or Rainbarrow, the prehistoric tumulus where the Fawkes Fires are burned, layer on layer over the centuries above the immolated remains of the forgotten dead. There the Guy Fawkes celebrants dance in the ashes, and there Eustacia meets Wildeve in the night:

> It was as if these men and boys had suddenly dived into past ages, and fetched therefrom an hour and deed which had before been familiar with this spot. The ashes of the original British pyre which blazed from that summit lay fresh and undisturbed in the barrow beneath their tread. The flames from funeral piles long ago kindled there had shone down upon the lowlands as these were shining now. Festival fires to Thor and Woden had followed on the same ground and duly had their day. Indeed, it is pretty well known that such blazes as this the heathmen were now enjoying are rather the lineal descendants from jumbled Druidical rites and Saxon ceremonies than the invention of popular feeling about Gunpowder Plot. (44–45)

The map made of all these elements combining vertical depth and surface pattern seems almost to make a picture. This picture is a residue, tracery, or hologram of the repeated action enacted and reenacted from time immemorial on a place of death that is also a place of dancing, trysting, and lovemaking, a place where fires are kindled. The picture is outlined by the roads: a blunt, polelike object with a conical peak, cap, or head, or perhaps a hollow-ribbed cylindrical cavity. The map, like a Gestaltist drawing, alternates between being seen as inside out and as outside in, between convexity and concavity. Or perhaps it may look as if the pole is within the hollow, male and female together. The heath, in this novel, is androgynous. It gives rise equally to Eustacia and to Wildeve, Clym, and Diggory Venn.

In order to make this map, which also seems vaguely to be a picture, Hardy has somewhat rearranged the actual topographical features of Dorsetshire. He has gathered features that are dispersed, so they make a configuration, a design, a sign. He has twisted the whole so east comes at the top of the map. This may be verified by setting Hardy's map against the official topographical map of the region. It is also verified by what Hardy says in the Postscript to the Preface, dated 1912: "though the action of the narrative is supposed to proceed in the central and most secluded part of the heaths united into one whole . . . , certain topographical features resembling those delineated really lie on the margin of the waste, several miles to the westward of the center. In some other respects also there has been a bringing together of scattered characteristics" (29). This gathering of the dispersed is necessary to make the topographical features into a design—the heath, ribbed ridge behind the ridge, with the prehistoric barrow in the center, encircled, or framed by the dwellings of the major characters and by the peripheral roads from each one to the others. The heath is crossed by paths and by the old Roman Road, a branch of Ikenild Street, that divides the heath like a parting of hair on a scalp. Another path crosses the Roman Road roughly from the lower left to the upper right, indicated by a dotted line, making the whole design a peripheral encircling ring crisscrossed, a kind of rudimentary labyrinth. Along these roads and paths, around the edge or across the center, the characters move in the slow dance of their approaches and withdrawals. In their movements they repeatedly encounter a crossroads or a fork in the path, the intersection in the journey through the maze of life that figures so powerfully the moment of choice.

If Hardy's gathering changes the real topography, rotating it to the left so up is not north but northeast, bringing things separated in reality closer together, making the roads and paths almost into a design or a picture, this gathering is never complete. The house Clym rents for his new bride has no place on the map Hardy drew. It is left out of its enclosing lines or margins. About the unplaced, more remains to be said. It will be necessary first to specify more exactly the relation between the characters and the heath.

⌒

The opening chapter ("A Face on which Time makes but Little Impression") is an extended prosopopoeia. The heath is personified as a great brooding creature, neither male nor female, beyond sexual difference. This giant person gathers the darkness to itself and exhales darkness out again, as though each night all the light had been entombed forever within its rough swarthy face:

> The place became full of a watchful intentness now; for when other things sank brooding to sleep the heath appeared slowly to awake and listen. Every night its Titanic form seemed to await something; but it had waited thus, unmoved, during so many centuries, through the crises of so many things, that it could only be imagined to await one last crisis—the final overthrow.
>
> . . .
>
> It was at present a place perfectly accordant with man's nature— neither ghastly, hateful, nor ugly: neither commonplace, unmeaning, nor tame; but, like man, slighted and enduring; and withal singularly colossal and mysterious in its swarthy monotony. As with some persons who have lived long apart, solitude seemed to look out of its countenance. It had a lonely face, suggesting tragical possibilities. (34, 35)

What is the justification for this personification? Does Hardy or the narrator really believe the heath is a person? That seems unlikely, knowing what Hardy says elsewhere about the indifference and unconsciousness of nature. Even the famous phrase at the end of *Tess of the d'Urbervilles* about how "the President of the Immortals had had his sport with Tess" was said by Hardy to be a personification of impersonal forces that rule man cruelly without cruel intent. The "tragical possibilities" expressed by the lonely face of the heath are made realities in the novel as they are embodied in the various characters' lives. The characters rise up from here and there over the heath as the personification of its personification. That initial personification seems to be the reflex of the narrator's personality. It is projected on the landscape along with his presuppositions about man's nature as "slighted and enduring," almost always lonely. It is expanded from the narrator's own brooding, watchful intentness. A cool, effaced, ironic looking-on characterizes the storyteller here as in Hardy's fiction generally. The personification of the heath is the covert manifestation of the ubiquitous presence of the narrator's consciousness, even when he seems least there as a person. The characters in the novel are, insofar as they are embodiments of the heath, therefore also indirectly representatives of the narrator. They represent his sense of the tragical possibilities of life. The narrator, in his turn, has got his sense of his own personality, it may be, from the heath. He does not exist as a character with a preformed selfhood and a life story. He speaks for the heath. It is as though the heath were telling one of the innumerable stories that had been enacted on its surface.

Whichever element in this system of projected persons is chosen draws its personality from the others and is secondary to them. This is a reciprocal displacement from landscape to person that is the reverse of the one in George Meredith's *The Egoist.* There the use of landscape terms to define selfhood is essential to the presentation of character. Here the counter-truth emerges. If there is no presentation of character without terms borrowed from the landscape, so there is no presentation of landscape without personification. Since there is no "literal" person on either side of this criss-cross substitution of properties, the words used for both character and landscape must be defined as catachreses. They are terms neither literal nor figurative, placeholders for missing literal words. Hardy's elaborate personification of the heath is no more than an unfolding of one basic catachresis for topographical features, "face," as when one says "face of the mountain" or "face of the heath": "it had a lonely face, suggesting tragical possibilities." The "face" is not literally a face, but the word does not substitute for some more normal literal term. If the narrator is effaced, he gives himself a face and a story by giving the heath a face and a story and then by incarnating those in the names, faces, and stories of the various characters—Eustacia Vye, Diggory Venn, Clym Yeobright, Mrs. Yeobright, and the rest. These rise up from the heath to move back and forth across it, acting out one version or another of the tragical possibilities it suggests. The characters trace the outline of those possibilities on the heath in their comings and goings, as a casual track across the heath gradually becomes a well-delineated path.

The peculiarity of *The Return of the Native*, as opposed to other novels by Hardy—for example, *The Mayor of Casterbridge, Tess of the d'Urbervilles, Jude the Obscure*, or *The Well-Beloved*—is that the drama is much more evenly distributed among the several main characters. All Hardy's novels do this to some extent. *Jude the Obscure* is Sue Bridehead's story as well as Jude's. *The Mayor of Casterbridge* focuses on Elizabeth-Jane as well as on Henchard. Nevertheless, these novels concentrate mainly on one character: on Henchard, Tess, Jude, or Jocelyn. *The Return of the Native* has a multiple focus. Its action is much more evenly distributed among the whole group of major characters, including, in addition to those listed above, Wildeve and Thomasin. Different persons arise from places scattered across the face of the heath and around the periphery that rings it, like the multiple Fawkes Fires that dot the dark landscape in chapter 3: "Red suns and tufts of fire one by one began to arise, flecking the whole country round" (43). The heath literally takes face and figure in these characters, but their dramas,

as so often in Hardy, are stories of effacement, defacing, disfigure-
ment, even of beheading.

~

If the story in *The Return of the Native* is distributed among the
various characters, as though not one sun but many should arise
some fine morning, a single drama is enacted differently over and
over in the knotted configurations of Hardy's language in this
novel. Any one of dozens of passages would do to exemplify this
drama. Among the many I choose one, Eustacia's dream:

> Such an elaborately developed, perplexing, exciting dream was
> certainly never dreamed by a girl in Eustacia's situation before. It had
> as many ramifications as the Cretan labyrinth, as many fluctuations as
> the Northern Lights, as much colour as a parterre in June, and was as
> crowded with figures as a coronation. . . .
> There was, however, gradually evolved from its transformation
> scenes a less extravagant episode, in which the heath dimly appeared
> behind the general brilliancy of the action. She was dancing to won-
> drous music, and her partner was the man in silver armour who had
> accompanied her through the previous fantastic changes, the visor of
> his helmet being closed. The mazes of the dance were ecstatic. Soft
> whispering came into her ear from under the radiant helmet, and she
> felt like a woman in Paradise. Suddenly these two wheeled out from
> the mass of dancers, dived into one of the pools of the heath, and came
> out somewhere beneath into an iridescent hollow, arched with rain-
> bows. "It must be here," said the voice by her side, and blushingly
> looking up she saw him removing his casque to kiss her. At that
> moment there was a cracking noise, and his figure fell into fragments
> like a pack of cards.
> She cried aloud, "O that I had seen his face!" (142–43)

This passage can be taken as an emblem for the whole terrain of
the novel, both for its expanse as an inner space the reader builds as
it is read, and for the narrative structure as a curriculum of criss-
crossing narrative lines running their course on the heath. The
passage is not an emblem in the sense that it is the central topos
around which everything in the novel organizes itself. There is no
such place, neither in the text thought of as a sequence of words,

passages, places, chapters, episodes, nor in the heath thought of as a featured expanse crossed by paths and roads. There are only multitudinous places, topoi in both the rhetorical and topographical senses, each one regathering in a different way the same configuration of elements.

One of the features of Eustacia's dream that makes it a good emblem for the whole novel is the multiplicity of its figures and the number of its ramifications. It has corridors or story lines as numerous as those of the Cretan labyrinth. Hardy indicates this not by telling all the stories but by a coruscation of incompatible figures, meaning "figures" in the tropological rather than the narrative sense. Eustacia's dream was like a labyrinth. No, it was like the Northern Lights. Or rather it was like a parterre. Or like a coronation. Figures, colors, fluctuating lights, branching ramifications— the dream, like the novel, is made of visible images, open in the sunlight, but derived from the sun and secondary to it, as the Northern Lights are generated in the darkness by invisible rays from the hidden sun.

The scenes of the dream that are not told, but only indirectly given in figure, are then replaced by the dream episode that *is* told. This stands by synecdoche for them all. Such a substitution is rather like Catherine Linton's second dream in *Wuthering Heights*. The dream she does tell replaces the one to which Nellie refuses to listen. It is a characteristic of dreams not only that each detail is a figure for what cannot be given literally, but that the episodes in a dream multiply themselves in lateral resemblances. Each episode figures what are only more figures. Basic features of the story repeated over and over in different ways in *The Return of the Native* are given in the episode of Eustacia's dream that separates itself out from the others and is enacted against the "realistic" background of the heath. I have said "basic features." Among the most salient of these is a lack of feature, as can be seen, or rather not seen. It can be seen as the impossibility of seeing.

The salient motif of the dream episode that is told is the dance. Dances also exist on the literal level of the story. Examples are the strange dance of the heathfolk in the dying embers of the Fawkes Fire on Rainbarrow, embers over ashes in layers down to the remains of the long-dead corpse in the tomb, or the dance at Mrs. Yeobright's house after the Mummers' Play, or the strange, moonlight dance that precipitates Eustacia back into Wildeve's arms. As in the dream, so in the last, "the mazes of the dance were ecstatic": "The dance had come like an irresistible attack upon whatever sense of social order there was in their minds, to drive them back into old paths which were now doubly irregular" (284). These dances remind the reader that all human relations in this novel are primarily erotic. The dances express the search for a partner of the other sex who will complete what is lacking in the searcher. In Eustacia's dream, as in all the love stories of the novel, this search is unsuccessful. Only the marriage of Thomasin and Diggory Venn, added as a capitulation to public taste and in contradiction to the main momentum of the novel, disobeys this law.

In her dream Eustacia and her visored lover dive into one of the pools of the heath. This anticipates not only her drowning but also a strange detail in the conversation between Mrs. Yeobright and the boy who accompanies her on her journey to death across the sunscorched heath. The exchange, in its connections to Eustacia's dream and to many other passages in the novel, is a good example of the overdetermined significance of what may seem casual elements put in for verisimilitude. Almost every sentence in this novel is motivated by its connections to a basic configuration of elements:

[The boy asks:] "What have made you so down? Have you seen a ooser?"[7]

"I have seen what's worse—a woman's face looking at me through a window-pane."

"Is that a bad sight?"

"Yes. It is always a bad sight to see a woman looking out at a weary wayfarer and not letting her in."

"Once when I went to Throope Great Pond to catch effets[8] I seed myself looking up at myself, and I was frightened and jumped back like anything." (306)

Mrs. Yeobright saw Eustacia's face, not her own, but Eustacia is Mrs. Yeobright's destructive double. Clym's love for her is a displacement of his love for his mother. Clym and his mother were so close, the narrator tells the reader, that they were like two halves of the same person: "he was a part of her—. . . their discourses were as if carried on between the right and left hands of the same body" (212). The face of the other is for Hardy always seen narcissistically. It is one's own face in the mirror. But it is seen by a narcissist frightened by his own image, as the boy was frightened by his reflection in Throope Great Pond.

The face of the other, moreover, Eustacia's dream tells the reader, is always, like the reflected colors of the rainbow, the displaced image of a lost and unattainable sun. If the heath's face may be seen, the desired other's face can never be encountered directly. It can only be seen as disfigured or decapitated. When he removes his casque to kiss her, the armored lover in Eustacia's dream falls into fragments like a pack of cards. She is left to cry out: "O that I had seen his face!" That face can never be seen, nor, for Hardy, can the promise of possession and satisfaction here and now ("It must be here," says the dream figure) ever be fulfilled. It can only perhaps be fulfilled beyond death or in death. There is no "here" there on the heath, only the signs of an unattainable elsewhere.

Again and again, at different places all over the heath or beyond its border, are enacted new versions of the drama of Eustacia's dream: something or someone appears in the sunlight, marked in one way or another by the sun or by one of the sun's surrogate lights. This something or someone seems to be a figure of the desired absent other. What marks the apparition as such a figure, however, is registered textually by accompanying figures of speech. These disfigure the figure, implicitly behead it, as happens to the armored lover in Eustacia's dream. This makes what appears a figure not of presence but of absence. It figures what could never be present except in such defaced figures, figures without figure. After its appearance the defaced figure sinks back into the ground, in the movement the title ironically names: the return of the native to what it was born from, some cleft in the dark earth. For Hardy as for Derrida in one of the epigraphs to this chapter, everything will flower at the edge of a neglected tomb.

When Diggory Venn, to give an example, spies on one of the

nighttime meetings of Eustacia and Wildeve at the base of the barrow, he creeps along the ground nearer and nearer to them, hidden under two large turves, "as though he burrowed underground" (108). It is an extraordinary fantasy. Diggory is here clothed in the heath itself, only half emerged from it. He is an embodiment of its obscure watchfulness. Eustacia and Wildeve too are figures of its life, put forth from it and then withdrawn again as Diggory watches: "Their black figures sank and disappeared from against the sky. They were as two horns which the sluggish heath had put forth from its crown, like a mollusc, and had now again drawn in" (112). Human figures in their erotic dramas are, these images suggest, only one among the many forms of life that rise up from the obscure vitality of the heath and then sink back into it, like a flower or a snail, or like the drop of blood that appears on Mrs. Yeobright's foot as a sign of the adder bite: "a scarlet speck, smaller than a pea, . . . a drop of blood, which rose above the smooth flesh of her ankle in a hemisphere" (314), or like the presents from the heath, each another figure or shape appearing from the depths on the surface, shining in red or white, that Charley brings to Eustacia to distract and please her after her attempt at suicide: "curious objects which he found in the heath, such as white trumpet-shaped mosses, red-headed lichens, stone arrow-heads used by the old tribes on Egdon, and faceted crystals from the hollows of flints" (355).

~

With beheading, as in Eustacia's dream figure's facelessness, goes emasculation. The motif of emasculation is unexpectedly present in *The Return of the Native*, both directly and somewhat covertly. It is present somewhat covertly in the remarkable absence of fathers for the main characters. Neither Clym, nor Thomasin, nor Diggory, nor Wildeve has a father. Eustacia has a substitute father in her somewhat weak and ineffectual grandfather. The theme of emasculation is also covertly present in the scene of Eustacia as a transvestite in the Mummers' Play. She appears dressed as the Turkish knight, complete with sword, a woman pretending to be a man. The Turkish knight in the play is defeated by Saint George and dies by "a gradual sinking to the earth" (114). Another emblem of emasculation, here displaced to the beheading of a woman, is the name and signboard Hardy chooses for Wildeve's inn. The inn is called "The Quiet Woman," "the sign of which represented the figure of a matron carrying her head under her arm, beneath which gruesome design was written the couplet so well known to frequenters of the inn:—

SINCE THE WOMAN'S QUIET
LET NO MAN BREED A RIOT" (69)

The only quiet woman is a beheaded woman. With such a woman no man need be tempted to a violence that the word "breed" makes obscurely sexual.

In one scene, that of the Fawkes Fire dance, the topic of castration comes up directly, an unusual event for a Victorian novel. The rather wandering conversation of the country people as they keep up their fire on Rainbarrow makes its way through the scandalous local story of Mrs. Yeobright's forbidding the banns between Thomasin and Wildeve. The talk then comes around to the question of whether there is any man "that no woman at all would marry" (51–52). Christian Cantle, Grandfather Cantle's grandson, "a faltering man, with reedy hair, no shoulders, and a great quantity of wrist and ankle beyond his clothes," advances into the firelight, and says, "I'm the man" (52). This is followed by a discussion of the causes of Christian's impotence. The talk leads ultimately to the assertion that single men who lie alone are more likely to see ghosts than married folks. They are likely, for example, to see the strange, bloodred ghost that has been glimpsed lately on the heath:

"Yes, 'No moon, no man.' 'Tis one of the finest sayings ever spit out. The boy never comes to anything that's born at new moon. A bad job for thee, Christian, that you should have showed your nose then of all days in the month."

. . .

"I'd sooner go without drink at Lammas-tide than be a man of no moon," continued Christian, in the same shattered recitative. " 'Tis

said I be only the rames⁹ of a man, and no good for my race at all; and I
suppose that's the cause o't."

. . .

"Well, there's many just as bad as he," said Fairway. "Wethers must
live their time as well as other sheep, poor soul."
"So perhaps I shall rub on? Ought I to be afeared o' nights, Master
Fairway?"
"You'll have to lie alone all your life; and 'tis not to married couples
but to single sleepers that a ghost shows himself when 'a do come. One
has been seen lately, too. A very strange one." (53–54)

No moon, no man. Virility is dependent upon the presence of
the reflected light of the sun and is itself a representation of the
sun's masculine force, the force that continues the race. A wether is
a castrated male sheep. Wethers must endure like other sheep, "rub
on" alone as best they may, but the fate of human wethers is not
only to lie alone but to see ghosts. Lack and the desire to fill that
lack make one especially prone to visitations of another form of the
missing sun.

As it turns out, the strange apparition is not a bloodred ghost, as
the country people think, but Diggory Venn the reddleman. Diggory rises more than once in the novel out of the nook or hollow in
the heath where he keeps his van, like the red ghost of the sun: "she
[Eustacia] beheld a sinister redness arising from a ravine a little way
in advance—dull and lurid like a flame in sunlight, and she guessed
it to signify Diggory Venn" (172). In Hardy's odd locution, Diggory, who is certainly virile, though passively so, does not present
himself as himself but as a sign, a mock red sun, eclipsed by the real
sun, a token appearance that stands for Diggory. The impotent
single man is, ironically, more likely than married couples to see a
"ghost" that manifests the sun's masculinity, necessary in the reflected form of moonlight to the virility of the newborn.

⁓

In the tightly woven texture of Hardy's prose in this novel,
passage after passage draws together in a knot another version of a
basic configuration. This configuration is open to interpretation
both laterally, in relation to all the passages before and after that

repeat it with a difference, and also vertically, in relation to the
hidden father beneath all the layers piled one on top of another on
Rainbarrow. That "father" is the unknown X that can only be
manifested or named in figure, therefore always as emasculated,
disfigured, or displaced. Even the sun is only a figure for this "it" or
"thing." The discussion by the country folk of men who are no
men takes place over the layers of ashes leading down to the bones
of the warrior immolated in the barrow in that "first" fire of time
immemorial. The text of the novel is a covering or series of
coverings, a translation of what can never be given in the original.
Any critical reading adds one more layer of ashes to the stratified
series. The image of similar configurations appearing one by one
here and there on the heath and the image of layers superimposed
come to the same thing. A "second" passage acts as an interpretation of the "first" passage, an uncovering of its meaning. At the
same time it covers the first passage over with a new manifestation
of the old enigma, the new replacing and hiding the old, as the new
ashes cover the old on Rainbarrow.

To put this in another way, the novel moves forward from
episode to episode, knotting and reknotting itself in nodes. Each
brings together a new version of the same features. These glow for a
moment like ignited filaments and then are extinguished, to be
replaced by the next textual layer of knotted lines. These light up
momentarily, to burn out in their turn. Each is like "that moth
whose skeleton is getting burned-up in the wick of the candle" that
in one episode distracts Eustacia from attending to what her husband Clym is saying. The moth serves as a prophetic emblem of
Wildeve's fatal return to Eustacia. He is attracted again by her glow
of life. This irresistibly attractive life force drawing one person to
another across the surface of the heath is also symbolized by the
signal fires Eustacia and Wildeve light for one another. These are
little, anachronistic Fawkes Fires that call the lover up as though he
were rising out of the ground. "I merely lit that fire because I was
dull," Eustacia tells Wildeve during one encounter early in the
novel, "and thought I would get a little excitement by calling you
up and triumphing over you as the Witch of Endor called up

Samuel" (91). Later, when Fawkes Day comes around again and Charley is once more about to light the Vyes' Fawkes Fire beside the pond (fire next to water, two of the basic elements of the novel, earth being the third), Eustacia thinks of "some other form which that fire might call up" (357). Sure enough, the splash of a pebble in the pond soon indicates the presence of Wildeve.

Sometimes the knotted elements are literal objects or topographical features. Sometimes they are figures of speech woven into the language by the narrator. Sometimes they are human features or lines of interconnection between one person and another, for instance, Eustacia's sunlike vitality. A scene in which Eustacia and Clym watch an eclipse of the moon, for example, is immediately preceded by a series of scenes that prepare for it. Each also echoes in its own way Eustacia's dream or the discussion beside the Fawkes Fire. In this section I shall follow this sequence in detail as a synecdochic example of the textual richness of *The Return of the Native*.

First comes the scene in which Clym helps raise the lost bucket out of Captain Vye's well. Again something rises from the deep, appears on the surface, and is marked by the sun. The sun on the bucket is echoed by Eustacia's look at Clym: "With the glance the calm fixity of her features sublimed itself to an expression of refinement and warmth: it was like garish noon rising to the dignity of sunset in a couple of seconds" (207).

This episode is followed by a day in which Clym reads all day and then at sunset has the first symptoms of the incipient blindness that is to incapacitate him: "Just when the sun was going down his eyes felt weary" (210). His blindness is always associated with the sun: "The sun was shining directly upon the window-blind, and at his first glance thitherward a sharp pain obliged him to close his eyes quickly" (270). The failure of Clym's eyesight after his marriage to Eustacia and his aspiring intellectual attempt turns him into a furze-cutter. He becomes so nearly the color of the heath, it seems as if he is being absorbed back into it.

Clym, it appears, is punished by blindness, a symbolic castration, as we hardly need Freud to tell us. He is punished for attempting to rival the sun and rise too far above his source. His punishment is mirrored by his mother's. She has a wide scope of vision the other characters lack, except for the detached and effaced narrator. She is killed by the heat of the sun, dying in "the great valley of purple heath thrilling silently in the sun" (305). She is killed also by that dark brother of the sun, the adder that does not "die till the sun goes down" even when it has been killed (315). If Mrs. Yeobright is killed by being "overlooked" by an adder, after having been bitten by one, Clym is punished by being blinded in an excess of light and by being forced to return to his native heath. As Eustacia says, "His complexion is by nature fair, and that rusty look he has now, all of a colour with his leather clothes, is caused by the burning of the sun" (301). Already, at the end of the chapter in which Clym's eyes first show their weakness, Clym's mother accuses him of being "blinded" by his love for Eustacia: "It was a bad day for you," she says, "when you first set eyes on her" (216). Clym responds by a "redden[ing]" like fire (216).

Earlier in the chapter, a brief episode gives "the next slight touch in the shaping of Clym's destiny" (213). A barrow in the heath is opened and burial urns discovered. One is given to Clym. The urns are, Christian Cantle says, "things like flower-pots upside down" and filled with "real skellington bones" (213). Clym at first intends the urn for his mother but then gives it to Eustacia. "The urn you had meant for me you gave away," she says reproachfully (213). Here again something from beneath the surface appears in the open, a representative of the absent father or masculine solar force, now only dead bones in a pot that would sponsor growth, if at all, in the wrong direction, down instead of up, like an upside-down flower pot. On the same page the narrator tells how Clym, some weeks later, returns home with "his face flushed and his eye bright," after having been kissed for the first time by Eustacia. The kiss is "like a seal set" upon his lips, the mark, brand, or "impress" of the life force most represented, for Hardy, by the sun. Clym half expects his mother to say: "What red spot is that glowing upon your mouth so vividly?" (214).

The description of the eclipse of the moon, the last episode in this series, picks up many of the same motifs once more, weaving them again into another textual knot. Before its eclipse the moon illuminates on the heath only places where "paths and water-courses had laid bare the white flints and glistening quartz sand, which made streaks upon the general shade" (217). The moon also shines on Clym Yeobright's face and "depict[s] a small image of herself [Eustacia] in each of his eyes" (217). As the eclipse gradually effaces the surface of the moon, Clym and Eustacia argue about the fragility and evanescence of love. Clym, at her insistence, describes the Paris for which she longs, the Gallerie D'Apollon of the Louvre, which faces east so that "in the early morning, when the sun is bright, the whole apartment is in a perfect blaze of splendour. The rays bristle and dart from the incrustations of gilding to the magnificent inlaid coffers, from the coffers to the gold and silver plate, from the plate to the jewels and precious stones, from these to the enamels, till there is a perfect network of light which quite dazzles the eye" (220). Here is another emblem both for the whole novel, which is made up of a multitude of objects and persons distributed on a topographical surface connected by a reticulation of lines. Each object or person is illuminated by the sun and shines in its turn like a little substitute sun.

In this episode the shadow of that sun gradually eclipses the moon's face and its rough features. The latter, though the narrator does not say so, are a version of the topography of the heath, with its ring around a central plane. The topography of Eustacia's dream has the same configuration. It is a labyrinthine dance floor adjacent to a hidden cave beneath a pond. As he looks at the moon Clym's eye "travel[s] over the length and breadth of that distant country— over the Bay of Rainbows, the sombre Sea of Crises, the Ocean of Storms, the Lake of Dreams, the vast Walled Plains, and the wondrous Ring Mountains" (217–18). As the moon's countenance is covered, Clym and Eustacia look in one another's faces. "Let me look right into your moonlit face," cries Clym, "and dwell on every line and curve in it!" (219). A little later Eustacia says: "Clym, the eclipsed moonlight shines upon your face with a strange foreign colour, and shows its shape as if it were cut out in gold" (221). If there is no man when there is no moon, Clym's infatuation with Eustacia, "the first blinding halo kindled about him by love and beauty" (223), as well as hers with him, is part of a network of lines of light and force that goes from the sun to the moon and then to the faces of the lovers. This reflected light is gradually obscured by that same sun. It seems as if the sun not only generates life and love, but then also jealously puts out all those smaller, displaced images of itself. It extinguishes them as love is always extinguished for Hardy: "Love lives on propinquity, but dies of contact."[10] What is given by the sun is in the same act taken away by it. The momentary glimpse of light and love is eclipsed in a movement that is effacement, disfiguration, or emasculation.

$\sim$

Everywhere the reader moves across the text of *The Return of the Native*, going from feature to feature across its surface, she encounters more versions of this drama of the sun that seals objects or people with its brand. The act of sealing makes the object or person only a sign, therefore the manifestation of an absence, something without power to satisfy desire. Eustacia quickly tires of Clym and returns to Wildeve, who had already come to bore her. The remarkable poetry, as it might be called, of *The Return of the Native*, as of much of Hardy's work in fiction and in verse, is topographical poetry. Or rather it is a poetry of the exchanges between human beings and the landscape. Each personifies and at the same time depersonifies the other. It would be almost as true to say that *The Return of the Native* is a prose poem about topography of the heath, the people in their tangled relations standing for this, as it would be true to say that it is a novel in which the human relationships are symbolized by the features of the heath. People are only one mode among many of the manifestations of the long-dead warrior in his barrow.

The reader's task is to decipher all those topographical signs of the encrypted source of meaning. For this hidden source even the "real sun" itself is only another cryptic sign. The sun, moreover, is a sign that cannot be looked in the face. It can only be seen in the marks it makes on objects on which it shines. From the first appearance of Eustacia as "the figure against the sky" (80) in one of her trysts with Wildeve on top of Rainbarrow, through the carefully noted two-and-a-half-year round of the seasons, as the sun rises and sets, swings northward and then south again in its diurnal and annual circuits, to the final appearance of Clym preaching his humanist gospel from the summit of the barrow as the unwitting double of his now-dead wife, the novel offers the reader example after example of such figures to decrypt.

The reader might note, for example, that Eustacia is initially represented as a male figure, as a phallic spike on a helmet. She is a sort of "last man," a last man missing any companions or mate (41). Eustacia does indeed appear in man's clothing at the Mummers' Play. Who or what would be a fit mate for her? Her inability to find anyone who satisfies her need, short of the final embrace of death, is one primary focus of the novel. The same drama, however, is repeated for all the other characters, too. It is as if, for Hardy, the sun, or rather the black sun behind the visible sun, the dark sun, the somber face the heath "personifies," had put each of us forth to seek unsuccessfully for something we lack. This something is possessed only by that always-invisible sun, the hidden sun without location or figure, the sun that never rises. Only the dead warrior in his barrow would satisfy desire, he or his equivalent, the mailed figure of Eustacia's dream. But he is without place or face. What can appear is never the figure himself but only figures for it, scattered everywhere across the heath and shining under the sun.

An emblematic expression for this is one extraordinary passage, a splendid example of the topographical poetry of *The Return of the Native*. The passage describes the landscape as Clym and Eustacia, at the height of their prenuptial love, walk hand in hand across the heath at dusk: "the sun [was] sloping down on their right, and throwing their thin spectral shadows, tall as poplar trees, far out across the firs and fern" (228). What Clym and Eustacia then see is foreshadowed by a long line of precursor passages in the Bible, in Dante, in Keats's "To Autumn," but most of all, for Hardy, in Shelley's "The Triumph of Life." In all these passages sparks of fire or insects are taken as emblems of the ephemerality of human life.

Each life is something that shines under the sun and contains some of the sun's vitality, though it is also destroyed by the sun after a brief transit: "The sun, resting on the horizon line, streamed across the ground from between copper-coloured and lilac clouds, stretched out in flats beneath a sky of pale soft green. All dark objects on the earth that lay towards the sun were overspread by a purple haze, against which groups of wailing gnats shone out, rising upward and dancing about like sparks of fire" (228–29).

Rising upward and dancing about like sparks of fire, and then like sparks of fire going out, leaving dead ash as trace behind—this exactly describes human life in *The Return of the Native* or in Hardy's work generally. The sun, like Dionysus or like that dark brother of the sun, the heath, is contradictory in its sexuality. It is both virile and effeminate.[11] The sun is a jealous power, but its power is a double bind imposed by its contradictory sexuality. On the one hand, as virile, the sun is a model for maleness, but, like a jealous father, it punishes those who attempt to appropriate that power. It punishes them by unmanning them. On the other hand, as effeminate, the sun is the model for feminine detachment and broad vision, like that possessed by Mrs. Yeobright or Clym. The sun effeminizes. It mocks any attempts to claim male power. So it might seem safer to efface yourself and not make any claims to power. The way of detachment, however, also asserts a kind of sovereignty. It is like the sun's vision at noon of all the landscape. That too is remorselessly punished, in this case by blinding or death. Either way, both men and women have had it. The heat of the sun is destructive both ways, as male and as female.

A moment after the passage describing the wailing gnats in the setting sun, after Clym and Eustacia have set their wedding day, she leaves him. He watches her as she "retire[s] toward the sun." The sight of her against the "dead flat of the scenery" gives him "a sense of bare equality with, and no superiority to, a single living thing under the sun" (230). Clym shares this broad perspective, which reduces all things to bare equality, with his mother, with the narrator, and with the patient, watching, personified presence of the heath. This detachment is the opposite of Eustacia's eager longing and expectation.

Clym's mother, for example, is, in a curious passage, compared to two famous blind men, Blacklock, the blind poet who described the visible world, and Professor Sanderson, the blind theorist of color. Once again blindness is associated with an ability to see and as punishment for seeing too well. Mrs. Yeobright too sees the whole world as like a dancing throng of fiery gnats: "Communities were seen by her as from a distance; she saw them as we see the throngs which cover the canvasses of Sallaert, Van Alsloot, and others of that school—vast masses of beings, jostling, zigzagging, and processioning in definite directions, but whose features are indistinguishable by the very comprehensiveness of the view" (212). For this wide vision Mrs. Yeobright is remorselessly punished, though her way of seeing matches that of Hardy himself, as expressed, for example, in similar images in the "Forescene" to *The Dynasts*. The accurate, comprehensive view is even more remorselessly punished than Eustacia's eager expectation. It is the supreme Promethean temerity of claiming the sun's wide, inclusive vision of things. Such vision is, in fact, its own punishment, since it is blind to the distinct features of things that make them seem uniquely valuable and uniquely desirable. The wide vision sees things as all equal in their featurelessness, as Clym, even at the moment of his greatest infatuation with Eustacia, sees her in her bare equality with everything under the sun. He thereby hollows out his desire and presages its end, his literal blindness and his loss of Eustacia.

All things are on a level of featureless equality because all are equally incapable of being an adequate figure for the always-absent source of value we would have them embody for us, so that, possessing them, we would be satisfied and complete. What Clym knows and Eustacia does not quite know is that this is impossible. If Clym is punished so cruelly for trying to raise himself above the heath to become sunlike in knowledge and broad vision, and if that vision corresponds to the vision of the narrator and then to that of the reader, when he or she has comprehended the novel, how, it might be asked, is that dangerous vision of the narrator and the reader also punished? Is our knowledge too its own punishment? Is there in some way mortal danger involved in the apparently innocuous act of reading Hardy's novel?

That reading is the tracing out of knot after knot of solar signs. I now continue with a final version of this, though with a somewhat uneasy feeling that confronting these may be as dangerous as trying to look the sun in the face or as watching an eclipse of the sun, even though what I am seeing is not the sun but disfaced signs that cover the sun. I leave it to the clear-seeing reader of the novel to identify all the examples of the solar drama I have left out, for example the many passages associating Wildeve, Clym, and Diggory with the sun. A network of solar images of the sun defines Eustacia's shifting relations to Wildeve, to Clym, and to Diggory. As Eustacia shifts from Wildeve to Clym and then back again to Wildeve, Diggory is a blocking agent who rises from the heath as a red mock sun to forbid Eustacia's access to Clym. Thomasin is also frequently associated with the sun, for example, in the late episode of the Maypole that rises in the early morning outside her window, encircled by flowers—another erotic emblem that appears as if from below—or in the description of the sun marking her with a solar caress. When she goes up into the loft where her aunt's apples are stored, "the sun [shines] in a bright yellow patch upon the figure of the maiden" (136) through a semicircular pigeonhole "which admit[s] the sunlight so directly upon her brown hair and transparent tissues that it almost seem[s] to shine through her" (136). An indirect omnipresence of the sun's all-seeing eye is evident also in the repeated motif of the ring of watchers. This is most admirably embodied in the heath ponies that stand in a vigilant ring in the darkness as Diggory and Wildeve dice by the illumination of glowworms for Mrs. Yeobright's hundred bright guineas (253–55). The motif of peripheral watching is also present in a curious way in the episode of the dance that brings Eustacia back to Wildeve. As the sunlight fades, the blushes of the dancing girls rise as the full moon rises. The darkness makes visible the image of the musicians "in outline against the sky": "the circular mouths of the trombone, ophicleide [from *ophus*, snake and *kleis*, key], and French horn gleamed out like huge eyes from the shade of their figures" (283). To see these brass mouths as eyes—it is a characteristically brilliant Hardyan personifying trope. The pleasure of this text, though perhaps a dangerous pleasure, since it involves us more deeply in what we read, is to follow this elaborate play of figuration. This verbal play transforms apparently casual details into a complex solar poetry sustaining like a ground bass the melodies of dramatic action in the novel.

∼

My final example of this has to do with names. Perhaps the most covert versions of the novel's basic elements are the names of the chief characters and places. With topography goes toponymy. Both are a form of poetry in *The Return of the Native*, as are the anagrammatic secrets in the names of the characters. This novel, as I have said, is unusual among novels by Hardy in the way his story of unappeasable desire is dispersed from character to character, rather than being centered in a single one. Each character is a new version of the heath's personification, a new little sun that rises from some place or point upon it, like the Fawkes Fires or like the signal fires Eustacia and Wildeve light. The personification of the heath, in turn, is a representation of the narrator's consciousness. He in turn is a prosopopoeia for the author. The narrator is a mask giving indirect expression to the author.

The author remains absent, effaced, unable or unwilling to speak in his own person, except in the author's note and in the footnotes added afterwards. These are adjacent to the main text, not fully part of it. In the novel itself the person of the author is dispersed, broken, and diffused around his imagined topography. He is present in the lives of his invented characters and in the places where they live out those lives. These characters are a sort of *corps morcelé*, scattered fragments of a single body. Like the shattered bits of the armored lover in Eustacia's dream, these characters are like a pack of cards with which innumerable games may be played, new configurations made.

If Thomas Hardy signed his name to *The Return of the Native*, that name, like every proper name, is an enigmatic sentence, a cryptic story. Hardy signs his name in another way in writing the text of the novel. The text is a version of his own secret story writ large over the imagined surface of the heath, like the name in large letters on a map. All the place names on a map in their systematic interrelation tell obscurely the story of the generations that have inhabited that place. In living they have left the traces of their lives behind in tombstone inscriptions and in names given to houses, villages, fields, roads, or streams. *The Return of the Native* is the reading of such a map, the retelling of a story latent in it. A critical essay on the novel, such as this one, is another text over the layers of texts, like the layers of ashes on Rainbarrow. In the end all this reading may be a way to decipher the name "Thomas Hardy" written large across the map. Such a name may be almost invisible, as Dupin, in Poe's "The Purloined Letter," says a name in large letters on a map will be almost invisible. The words "Egdon Heath" are written out in this way almost illegibly on Hardy's map of 1878.

All the characters' names in *The Return of the Native* are plausibly realistic and even authentically local to Hardy's Dorset. Nevertheless, they are secretly motivated and are all permutations of one another. All in one way or another are anagrams of parts of Hardy's own name. Hardy's name and story are broken and diffused among the main characters and in the place names—Diggory Venn, Clym Yeobright, Mrs. Yeobright, Eustacia Vye, Damon Wildeve, Thomasin Yeobright, Rainbarrow or Blackbarrow, Egdon Heath, Blooms-End, The Quiet Woman Inn, Shadwater Weir. Can the reader crack this code? Like all place names and proper names, in real life or in fiction, the names in *The Return of the Native* are somewhere on the scale between total arbitrariness and total motivation. A name wholly idiomatic, entirely "proper," altogether special to the person or place in question, would be idiotic, incomprehensible. Even so, it might still be secretly motivated according to some uncrackable code or private language. A name wholly arbitrary, a mere insertion of the place or person into a public code, would have nothing to do with the person or places. It would tell us nothing about its referent. To work, the name must be both arbitrary and motivated. It must take values from the public domain and twist them so they function in a way that corresponds, however obscurely, to the nature of the person or place named or to its function in a system of relationships making a story, the story, for example, of *The Return of the Native.*

Among names in the novel, "Thomasin" is perhaps easiest to decode. It is a feminine version of Thomas Hardy's own first name. That makes explicit the way he has, once more and characteristically, projected into a female protagonist his sense of himself as one who is patient, watchful, effaced, unhopeful, "feminine" in his lack of masculine self-assertion, but strong and enduring nevertheless. Perhaps ultimately, he hopes, he will be victorious as Thomasin is, as Elizabeth-Jane in *The Mayor of Casterbridge* is, but as Tess is not.

But why "Eustacia"? Why "Vye"? Why "Yeobright"? Why "Venn"? Why "Diggory"? Why "Wildeve"? Do they not make a cryptic sentence telling the story of the trajectory of the sun and of passion for the darkness or for what it hides? This would be the story of the native's return over again. All these names in one way or another combine the hard consonance of the first part of "Hardy" with some version, orthographic or acoustic, of the final "y," an "e" or "i" or "y" or "u." If the names are permutations of one another, they are also permutations of Hardy's own name. Vye: "eye." Yeobright: bright eye, egg, or yolk, as in the yellow yolk of the sun. Diggory: to dig as in the digging up of a barrow. Diggory is of the heath, heathy. Venn: van, the gypsy cart or van where Diggory hides in some brambled nook of the heath, so he can rise out of it like the sun out of the earth. Wildeve? Obviously, the wild deed of evening, the beast with two backs. This is what Wildeve has made with Eustacia here and there on the heath before the novel ever begins, the act that can never be named directly in the text, though it is the unnamed presupposition of all the action. Damon: demon. Wildeve is repeatedly associated with the devil. Like Diggory, he emerges from the heath as an uncanny and somehow dangerous masculine force. Vye: eye that vies, as in all those characters who try to outsee the sun and are punished for it by blindness. Venn is Vye closed, stopped by that earthy final double "n." Clym: closed in in itself, blinded, as a blinded eye. Clym reverses Yeobright, as Eustacia is a kind of antithetical mirror image of Yeobright. "Eu" matches "yeo," but "stacia" is a dark counterpart of "bright," or sounds so to me, in spite of the presence in the "sta" of Eustacia's standing erect above the heath or the barrow.

All the proper names in *The Return of the Native* are words beginning in "Y," "V," or "W." Their initial letters or dominant vowels cluster at the end of the alphabet much more than does the statistical average of names in English. Missing only are "X" and "Z," those algebraic signs for the unknown. This is that unknown X, the unnameable and undiscoverable thing that all the names and places in the novel figuratively signify. They signify it as unattainable absence, as what the narrator calls "the abyss of undiscoverable things" (260). X and Z may be virtually there in topographical configurations. X stands for crossroads. Z stands for zigzag, like the course of a rapid river down its banks.

If the proper names of the novel may be hypothetically uncoded in this way, they also form a single system with the place names written out on Hardy's map of 1878. Or it might be better to say that the place names are incorporated into the covert system of proper names. This happens not only, for example, in the way the "eg" in "Egdon" forms a series with parts of some of the proper names (EG > eu > yeo > Vye [eye] > egg > [sun]). Moreover, each place name labels some topos in the itinerary traced out by the characters as those itineraries match the diurnal and annual journey of the sun. About the Quiet Woman Inn and its sign I have written earlier. Mistover Knap, where Captain Vye and Eustacia live, combines the notions of being veiled in mist with the notion of protruding above the mist (a "knap" is a hill) in a way that is made explicit in a chapter in which the hills slowly appear out of the low-lying integument of morning mist (120). Blooms-End, the Yeobright's house, is another way of saying "the return of the native." The bloom ends, the flower goes back into the ground from which it came and to which it is native. On Hardy's map of 1878, Rainbarrow is called Blackbarrow. Either name has a clear meaning. Each names a locus of darkness and depth, the darkness and depth of death, but also the place of a wild eve. Blackbarrow or Rainbarrow is the antithesis of the sun that the sun nevertheless manifests. The rain of Rainbarrow connects the tumulus with its moldering remains to the fierce rainstorm the night Eustacia and Wildeve drown in Shadwater Weir, the last crucial place in Hardy's map. This the place where Eustacia and Wildeve go to die. Their deaths fulfill the cycle of rising and falling and fulfill also the prophecy of Eustacia's dream. A "shad" is not only a kind of fish but also (though "chiefly U.S." [O.E.D.]) a flowering tree that grows especially well in moist soil by a stream. A weir is a wooden dam made of wood. It holds back the water in a stream to form a pool but also makes the stream flow with tumultuous force when there is a storm and it rises to break through the blockage.

~

The deaths of Eustacia and Wildeve form the climax of the novel, even though they are followed by the falsifying happy ending of Thomasin and Diggory's marriage in the sixth book. That book is entitled, significantly: "Aftercourses." In the drowning of Eustacia and Wildeve the movement of the characters back and forth on the heath is replaced by the rapid coursing of a river renamed and displaced by Hardy from its real topographical location in Dorset. It runs in snakelike curves down the righthand margin of Hardy's map.

Eustacia's itinerary along the paths she follows, like that of the other characters, is motivated, always, by desire. This desire is blocked as the stream is blocked. The blockage makes it flow all the more dangerously, as, in Kant's theory of the sublime, a *Hemmung* is necessary to the sudden flowing forth, *Ergießung*, of emotion in what Kant calls a "negative pleasure." Eustacia, of all Hardy's characters, is the one he most endowed with sublime feelings. He also attempted to make her, like the "colossal" heath itself, a source of sublime aesthetic experience for the reader. She fulfills her course in her plunge into the water, to be joined by Wildeve in a love embrace that is also death. Their drowning combines at last the two states that have always remained separate in their lovemaking on Rainbarrow above the dead warrior: love and death. Their love-death embrace is also a chain of three links, since Clym too plunges into the pool to save Eustacia. This breaks the ideal couple and makes it, as love always is in Hardy, an open triangle. In such a nontriangular triangle, one person is fascinated by another person who is fascinated by another person in a discordant row that can never be closed in a neat figure of appeased desire. A third always intervenes between any two. First Clym Yeobright is rescued from the pool. Wildeve comes next. He is not embracing Eustacia but his arms tightly embrace Clym's legs, figuring the relation between the two men who have vied for Eustacia's love. Eustacia remains alone in the pool, drawn to her death by the phantom lover who can never be encountered in life. Her corpse is brought out by Diggory Venn. It is as though she were being led back up from the underground cavern into which she has been attracted by the mailed warrior, drawn from beneath.

The juxtaposition of Rainbarrow and Shadwater Weir as figures of one another has been prepared for by the description of Eustacia's journey across the heath through the rainstorm on her way to her drowning. As she makes her way through the night, leaving the bank by the pond next to her house, miniature versions of the barrow and the weir, she goes first to Rainbarrow and then to the Weir. Susan Nonesuch at that moment is melting over the fire the wax image of Eustacia stuck with pins. This symbolic loss of her figure has already been anticipated by the description of her journey: "Skirting the pool [by her house] she followed the path toward Rainbarrow, occasionally stumbling over twisted furze-roots, tufts or rushes, or oozing lumps of fleshy fungi, which at this season lay scattered about the heath like the rotten liver and lungs of some colossal animal" (370). The shapeless lumps of fungi are like the melted wax of Susan Nonesuch's image. It is as though the guts of that great creature, the personified heath, were visible on this rainy night. When Eustacia reaches the summit of Rainbarrow, she is in a state of "isolation from all of humanity except the mouldered remains inside the tumulus" (371). Her weeping matches the sound of the rain dripping. If she has been proudest and most erect of all the characters, above them all as a pole or spike on Rainbarrow, even her cycle of rising and setting is about to be completed at last. The faceless warrior lover of her dream seems to be pulling her down in a sinking embrace that anticipates her drowning. This embrace makes death a reenactment of an event that has already occurred on Rainbarrow: "she sighed bitterly and ceased to stand erect, gradually crouching down under the umbrella as if she were drawn into the Barrow by a hand from beneath" (371).

~

When Eustacia and Wildeve have drowned and been buried, joining the dead warrior in his tumulus, and when Thomasin and Diggory have married,[12] only the rising and setting of the sun are left, that and "the imperturbable countenance of the heath, which, having defied the cataclysmal onsets of centuries, reduced to insignificance by its seamed and antique features the wildest turmoil of a single man" (342). What those seamed and antique features are, the reader knows. They are the heath's topographical characteristics, which allow it to be seen as a face. These include superficial marks—lines of roads, paths, and fences—marks made by man on the landscape, seams that are connecting filaments and also rifts. The characters have, in their comings and goings, ever so slightly altered those features and made them legible in a different way. They now tell a different story. This makes it possible to draw a new map, different from any real one, with different place names and a different configuration. The map Hardy drew for the edition of 1878, in its difference from the official topographical map, records those features. The text of the novel might be defined as a reading of the new map. A critical essay on the novel, this one, for example, is a reading of a reading. Of course the events of the novel never really happened. If the reader is aware of this, he or she will think of the novel as a paradigmatic representation of the way dwelling in a place, living and dying there, changes it.

~

The interpretation of fiction by way of landscape descriptions has turned out to be surprisingly productive. But the figure of figure and ground has turned out to be inappropriate. The relationship between landscape and story is rather that of figure to figure. The characters and their stories are figures, but the landscape in which they act out these stories is a figure, too. Moreover, the investigation of the spatial design of the action leads ultimately to the necessary hypothesis of the atopical or of the placeless. The true ground, the "it," is everywhere and nowhere. It can be located on no map. It remains hidden in any tracing out of the lines of the story, covered over rather than revealed by their comings and goings. Those lines are traces of its non-presence, the not having taken place, found a visible place for itself, of that "it." It must be somewhere but one cannot find where. It is always elsewhere from where anyone is. This placeless place, imaged in the crypt hiding the dead-alive warrior, always disfigured, faceless, or imaged as the non-place where the sun goes when it sets, both motivates the landscape mappings and at the same time ruins them. All fail to locate the most important item in the topographical system. On the temporal axis of the novel, the lovemaking of Wildeve and Eustacia on the heath precedes the novel as its presupposition but is not described directly. It remains a blank place in the narrative, just as does the true ending, in which Diggory disappears from the heath. Both the essential presupposition of the action—the un-spoken event that has occurred before the action begins—and the final version of the motif of vanishing that was to close it exist only as faint traces left in the text. The first is hinted only in Eustacia's statement to Wildeve after her marriage to Clym: "We have been hot lovers in our time, but it won't do now" (304). The second exists only in the belated footnote about the unwritten, "most consistent" conclusion, in which Diggory was to disappear from the heath.

The investigation of topography in *The Return of the Native* reveals the intimate connection between prosopopoeia and cata-chresis. Where nothing but figure is possible, that figure is always catachresis. The double crisscross personifications of *The Return of the Native*—the personification of the heath as a colossal being, and the representation of the heath by the characters—are catachreses. They are a system of figures for the placeless place where the sun goes when it has set. The sun, however, is not "it," but another figure for the it in its vanishing. This "it," Hardy's novel implies, seems not to be only an effect of language. Language, or any system of signs, such as the place names and proper names in *The Return of the Native* or the configuration of conventional representations on Hardy's sketch map, seems to be an effect of the "it," simultaneously shaped and undone by its force. Or rather, whether the it is an effect of language or whether language is effected, affected, infected by the "it" can never be decided, since the results would be the same in either case.

It is impossible to decide between the two positions because what would be presented in either case would be the same, without differentiating features. It is impossible to find a standpoint outside the two positions from which they might be compared and a decision made. Nevertheless, one would like to know which it is. Later chapters will return to this problem. Topology, topography, the mathematics of knots—all these are superficial. They are the investigation of configurations on a surface that may be twisted or waved, but that has no depth. It is never more than one- or two-dimensional. There is no space in such configurations, if one means by space a three-dimensional plenum. This means that it is in principle impossible to move behind the configurations to something that lies behind them. There is no attainable behind or within. Only the knots and surfaces exist, along with the possibility of tracing and retracing the intricate lines they make. These lines and surfaces seem to be twisted and turned by some force outside themselves, but no way leads from them to anything outside them. Wherever one goes, whatever way one takes, one remains on the surface or on the line. No lines or paths lead out of that place to *the* place. The "it" therefore stays placeless, atopical, without location on any map. It is without ascertainable face, figure, or feature. Any attempts to give it a face only deface it, as a critical essay defaces a literary work, writes all over it, perhaps in the way vandals deface a public monument by giving it a new face.

To put this in terms of a figure drawn from *The Return of the Native*, it is impossible to tell whether the Maypole outside

Thomasin's window springs up overnight as another phallic growth of the heath, then calls forth the wreaths of flowers and the men and women dancing in a ring around it, or whether the narcissistic "self-adoration" (401) of its celebrants calls up the Maypole, as a kind of phantasmal erection in their midst. In the second case, the Maypole would be a virtual presence created by the play of reflections from self-worshiper to self-worshiper, dancing in their labyrinthine knots. This might be seen as parallel to the way language creates meaning, signs the signified, by the differential interplay of phonemes. The uncertainty as to which possibility is the true one is evidence that language cannot function as a seamless garment, a protective hull consistent in its texture and determinable in its meaning. Language does not protect from the undecidable question about the "it" because it has incorporated within it what it would keep out. The nature and location of the "it" remain unanswerable questions within any integument of words.

In the case of *The Return of the Native*, this placeless "within" is within the landscape and within the persons. It is within each character as the lack which he or she tries to fill. It is within the other person whom each tries to appropriate in order to fill the lack, but who never fills it because he or she is only one more incarnation of the lack within the landscape that the narrator and characters personify. It is unavailable in the landscape, too, since the landscape is only another figure for the missing "it," as the sun is, or as is the barrow with the hidden body. The structure in question is a constantly moving ring or crisscross of substitutions, a relay of displacements with the original place nowhere to be found. Whatever element or place the reader focuses on is only a figure for something else missing, but that something else, when the reader turns to it, is only another trope in its turn.

~

What is the upshot of my implicit attempt to read Hardy in the light of Heidegger, to use Heidegger as the ground of a topographical reading of literature? The result is more the discovery of dissonances, ineradicable differences, than the well-grounded demonstration of a uniform critical method. Heidegger and Hardy are more different from one another than the same. Each is sui generis, singular, like a proper name. As with a proper name, however, this singularity is comprised by its inextricable entanglement in the contexts that give it meaning by being its differential others. Nevertheless, reading Heidegger tells you primarily about Heidegger, not about Hardy or any other author. My readings have shown once more, if there had still been any doubt about it, that each work must be read on its own terms, without much expectation of getting help in this from works by other authors. This does not mean that similar questions may not be posed to different works, in this case questions about the topographical assumptions each makes. It would be a mistake, however, to expect the answers to be in consonance. The dissonant answers modify and deflect the questions, as will be evident in the diverse angles of entry in the following chapters. The questions, in the end, must be guided by what is problematic in the work in question.

The essential differences between Hardy and Heidegger can be briefly stated. Heidegger is beguiled by the dream of a harmonious and unified culture, a culture rooted in one particular place. Hardy knows, and shows in his novels, that such an apparent unity, even in rural cultures, is riven by divisions and disharmonies. For Hardy the human predicament, even in a relatively stable and unified local society, is, ultimately, to be alone. Nor can the topographical assumptions of the two authors be made to chime, in spite of some beguiling congruences in the terrain mapped by each. No reconciliation can be made between Heidegger's portentous but ultimately cheerful, though somewhat hectically cheerful, "fouring of the four" and Hardy's dark drama of the appearance and disappearance of solar surrogates. Heidegger is confident that proper building and dwelling can bring Being into presence, perform an act of "aletheia" or uncovering, while for Hardy anything present, visible, out in the sunlight, is only another sign for a permanent absence. Heidegger's Dasein is universal and more or less undifferentiated, whereas Hardy stresses the way differences in gender and temperament determine different fates for people, even though their topographical contexts are the same. Thomasin is as different from Eustacia as Diggory and Clym are different from Wildeve, and Hardy does not forget the difference sexual difference makes. Hardy's landscape is strongly sexualized, even eroticized, which can hardly be said of Heidegger's. Moreover, Hardy was too close to farmwork and handwork himself to sentimentalize it as the proper way to dwell, as Heidegger does when he celebrates Black Forest peasant life. Death defines Dasein, for Heidegger, but in a quite different way from the way death is the endpoint for Hardy's most aspiring and Promethean characters. The assumptions about language and other signs, as these determine topography and toponymy, are quite different, and necessarily so, in each case. Heidegger must refuse symbolism and every other form of trope in order to assert that the bridge "presences" and brings the landscape around it into being. By contrast, things and people that the sun shines on in *The Return of the Native* are inadequate signs, catachreses for an always absent and unattainable "it."

Taking this example of incommensurability as a possible law, the chapters that follow explore a range of textual territories in which topography is an issue. In each case I have tried to respect what is most idiomatic, most special, about the work in question.

§ 2 Face to Face:
Faces, Places, and
Ethics in Plato

And if you had to face the further question,
What do you yourself hope to become by your association with Protagoras?
He blushed at this—there was already a streak of
daylight to betray him—and replied, If this is like
the other cases, I must say "to become a Sophist."
But wouldn't a man like you be ashamed, said I,
to face your fellow countrymen as a Sophist?
If I am to speak my real mind, I certainly
should.[1]

What is the role of prosopopoeia in ethical thinking and doing?
Why do both thinking about ethics and the act of ethical choice
always involve some act of personification?[2] "Prosopopoeia": the
word means the ascription of a voice or a face to the absent, the
inanimate, or the dead. The word comes from the Greek words for
face or mask (*prosopon*) and make (*poeien*). My hypothesis is that
what is problematic about prosopopoeia is intimately connected to
what is problematic about ethical responsibility. This includes the
form of ethical responsibility that may be generated by acts of
reading. What follows here is meant to explore just how and why
this is so. How these questions of ethical responsibility are related
to topographical delineations the chapter will show.

A way into this topic is Plato's *Protagoras*. I take it for my
purposes not only as a philosophical treatise but as for what it also
is, a narrative. It is a story about virtue that is meant to teach virtue. In its intimate substance this story involves the question of
prosopopoeia.[3]

The central action of this dialogue is the verbal contest between
Socrates and Protagoras over the question of whether virtue can be

taught. It is a contest in which the two apparently change places. Socrates, so it seems, comes to hold the position that Protagoras originally defended, and vice versa. Their confrontation, however, is staged within a complex narrative framing in which the end of the story turns back on its beginning and in which there are stories within stories. The outside is the opening frame in which Socrates comes late to an appointment at an unnamed friend's house. He then narrates to the friend the encounter with Protagoras that has delayed him. It was not, as you suppose, a tryst with the handsome Alcibiades, he says, but a fascination with something far more beautiful, the wisdom of the great Sophist Protagoras.

The whole of the *Protagoras*, then, after the proem, is told by Socrates to his "friend," just as Conrad's Marlow tells the stories of *Heart of Darkness* and *Lord Jim* to *his* auditors. In all three cases the storytelling is motivated. It is meant to do something, to perform a function, like all good storytelling, like Scheherezade's, to give one notorious example: "Just let me tell you one more story." Her storytelling is apotropaic. It is a way of holding off death, as, after all, Socrates' storytelling is too: "Just let me tell you one more story." Socrates, it might be said, was given the hemlock because he was not a good enough storyteller, or perhaps because he was too good at it. In the case of the *Protagoras*, which takes places when the young Socrates is just learning his craft, his narration of his discussion with Protagoras is framed by his recounting of an initial episode in which the young Hippocrates knocks on Socrates' door before dawn to tell him the great Sophist Protagoras is in town.

Within the verbal agon between the young Socrates and the old Protagoras, there is another story, told by Protagoras, retold by Socrates, then retold by Plato, who has probably made the whole thing up anyway. This is the first myth in Plato's work. It is the myth recounting the unequal distribution of gifts to all the creatures, including man, by Epimetheus and Prometheus. Protagoras, in response to Socrates' challenge to explain why he believes virtue can be taught, gives his first answer in the form of this myth. "Now shall I," he asks, "as an old man speaking to his juniors, put my explanation in the form of a story, or give it as a reasoned argument? . . . I think it will be pleasanter to tell you a story" (320c). Socrates' narration of his encounter with Protagoras ends at the moment when Socrates reports himself as having said, "Indeed I ought long ago to have kept the appointment I mentioned" (362a). That takes the reader full circle back to the beginning, when Socrates has presumably just knocked at his friend's door and has been received inside the house.

The several narrations are nested within one another, in a relation of inside and outside that is made overt in the dialogue by all the attention to knocking on doors and entering the enclosure of a house or courtyard. At the beginning Socrates has just entered the house of his friend. He tells how Hippocrates knocked on his door and woke him before dawn, and how they then later had difficulty persuading the eunuch who guarded the door of Callias's house to let them in so they could meet Protagoras. Three times the image of the threshold appears. The threshold is the border dividing inside from out, across which conversations and negotiations can nevertheless be carried on. Socrates knocks on his friend's door, just as Hippocrates has knocked on his, and the eunuch guards Callias's door, at first forbidding Socrates access to Protagoras.

The complex narrative structure of the *Protagoras* is carried by an urban topography of streets, houses, doors, porches, courtyards. This topography creates a complex mental scene for the reader. This scene is as important for the meaning of the dialogue as are the locations of the heath, houses, river, paths, and roads to the meaning of *The Return of the Native*.

Two kinds of interior spaces are implicitly opposed in the dialogue, though the opposition is canceled as much as it is affirmed. One is private space, the interior of Socrates' house or that of his friend. The other is the public space where Protagoras teaches virtue to a large crowd. Socrates' conversations with his friend and with Hippocrates are carried on, at least at first in each case, across the liminal border of the doorway. In the reader's imagination of the scenes, Socrates remains indefinitely poised, neither wholly out on the public street nor wholly within one or the other private domicile. Socrates' disputation with Protagoras is carried on in the public space of a large gathering for what might be called a peripatetic seminar. It is held, however, in the portico of Callias's house, again a space that is neither quite a private economy nor quite a public one.

Nor is this ambiguity as to public and private irrelevant to the dialogue. The question of whether virtue can be taught is both a public and a private matter. On the one hand, it is a public matter insofar as it is the state's responsibility to make sure its citizens are well educated and taught virtue. On the other hand, as all the attention to father-son relations in the dialogue indicates, the teaching of virtue is a family responsibility. The ambiguous mixing of public and private spaces in the mapping of Socrates' movements presents Athenian culture as one in which civic duty and family duty overlap. To be in a domestic interior is also still to be in public. One's private duty as a father is also at the same time a public duty. Socrates was condemned for leading the youth of Athens astray, that is, for a flagrant breach of both a civic responsibility and a quasi-paternal one.

As is usual in narrative structures like that of the *Protagoras*, inside and outside reverse in the moment when the text returns to its beginning. What has seemed progressive penetration deeper and deeper within, in a series of successive entries, leads back finally to an entry into the outside enclosure again. To put this another way, the *Protagoras* is an example, or almost on the verge of being an example, of an embedded or invaginated narrative that contains itself and so has entered into an infinitely repeated loop. If Socrates were to continue his narration just beyond the point where he stops, he would be telling in the first person what we as readers have encountered at the very beginning in the form of objective dialogue, the conversation between Socrates and his friend that frames and initiates Socrates' narration of his encounter with Protagoras. Had he continued, Socrates would have been led to enclose within his narration another version of that narration, and so on, ad infinitum. The paradigmatic example of this is the moment when Scheherezade begins telling her own story, which will contain again all the stories she has told, including the one she has just begun.[4]

Another way to put this is to say that in this dialogue the relation of generation reverses, in a metalepsis. One story is fathered by what it has seemed to father. This figure is, of course, central in the text itself, with all its overt attention to the relation between the generations. And, one might add, to the relation between brothers: the two sons of Pericles; Epimetheus and Prometheus; and so on. This generational complexity contaminates the clear figure of the father-son relation with the more ambiguous side-by-side relation of one brother to his *frère ennemi*. In the end, it may be, the relation between stories, for Plato here, is much more like the relation between two brothers than like the relation between father and son. It seems, at least at first, that the latter figure is the dominant one. One story fathers another or is fathered by it. One story leads to another as its commentary or explanation, in a proliferation that seems hard to stop once it has begun.

～

The whole text of the *Protagoras*, after the first few lines of dialogue between Socrates and his friend, is that particular form of speech act called an excuse. Socrates must excuse himself for being late for his appointment with his friend. In order to do so he tells a story explaining why he is late, as all of us no doubt tend to do, but one story leads to another in his narration, without any of them ever quite working as a successful excuse. This no doubt often happens when anyone tries to use a story as an excuse.

Socrates' narration to his friend is a striking example of the way a story may be used to tell the truth about virtue, to teach virtue, and to perform a virtuous act, all at the same time. It is also a striking example of what may be precarious about this multiple use of storytelling. It seems that the truth about whether virtue can be taught, the teaching of virtue, and a certain kind of virtuous act (for example, freeing oneself from guilt) can best be accomplished not just by a story but by a complex process of storytelling that we are more likely to associate with Conrad, Faulkner, or Borges than with Plato. As for the Marlow of *Heart of Darkness* and the Quentin of Faulkner's *Absalom, Absalom!*, so for Socrates here storytelling is a form of exculpation. It is a form, however, in which one story generates another and that another, as if the excuse could never quite get itself performed for certain. This seems to have something to do with the metaleptic reversal I have mentioned. One story fathers another in a never-ending but unsuccessful search for the foundational story that will have paternal authority over all the others and give the excuser grounds for his excuse. If that were to happen, the relation of fathering would reverse in an encounter with the father of all the stories.

This generational relation of story to story or of text to text is made explicit in a central episode of the confrontation between Socrates and Protagoras. This is their discussion of a poem by Simonides about the question of how to become virtuous and how to remain virtuous after you have become so. The verbal agon between Socrates and Protagoras becomes a little contest in extempore literary interpretation. The poem by Simonides, however, is the interpretation of a famous apothegm by Pittacus, and the saying of Pittacus is the interpretation in turn of a passage in Hesiod's *Works and Days*. Each text has fathered the next. The whole sequence fathers the interpretations by Protagoras and Socrates, though the sequence followed by Plato's text goes, of course, in the opposite direction.

What is problematic about the relation of father and son is, in fact, in various ways signaled or marked in the text of the dialogue. Protagoras says to the group assembled to hear his contest with Socrates, "Indeed I am getting on in life now—so far as age goes I might be the father of any one of you" (317c). Plato has Socrates identify those present to hear Protagoras and Socrates dispute not only by their names but also by the names of their fathers. No doubt it was customary in the Athens of Plato's time to identify a man by giving his father's name as well as his own name, but the litany of fathers' names exceeds its function of providing verisimilitude. It calls attention to the father-son relation. If it is a father's responsibility to teach his sons virtue, as Socrates says, then teaching virtue, the dialogue's topic, involves the father-son relation. We are told that Pericles has not done all that well in fulfilling this responsibility toward his two sons: "they simply browse around on their own like sacred cattle, on the chance of picking up virtue automatically" (320a). A symmetry exists between the father-son relation and the relation between one poem and its begetting precursor or between one story and the story it generates. These relations are presented by Plato as far from simple or straightforward.

For Plato the teaching or learning of virtue seems to require being figured in the relation of father and son and in its symmetrical analogues. This means that both narration and personification are fundamental to the doctrine of the dialogue. They are not just a pleasant way to present a doctrine that could have been expressed just as well in the form of abstract exposition. The central topic of the dialogue is the question of whether virtue can be taught. The goal of the dialogue is presumably to teach the truth about this, therefore to teach virtue, since virtue and knowledge are, for Plato, at least so it seems, intimately connected. This means, assuming Plato knows what he is doing (probably a wise assumption), that the dialogue presupposes both that teaching virtue and teaching the truth about virtue depend on storytelling and on the prosopopoeia that is necessary to any story.

Edith Hamilton and Huntington Cairns are therefore surely in error when, in the preface to the *Protagoras* in their edition of *The Collected Dialogues*, they say: "The reader who is interested only in Plato's philosophy would do well to pass over the first part of the *Protagoras*, the first three-quarters of it, in fact, up to the discussion about pleasure and pain when Socrates begins to speak in earnest" (*CD*, 308). They say this on the assumption that all that part of the dialogue is there only for the purpose of "giving a picture of Greek life" (ibid.). To assert this is at once to take Plato too seriously and not to take him seriously enough. It does not take him seriously enough in assuming that Plato did not know what he was doing and that the first three-quarters of the dialogue have no serious function in it. It takes him too seriously in assuming that Socrates speaks unequivocally for Plato, and that one already knows when

"Socrates begins to speak in earnest," namely, when he asserts what one already knows is Plato's serious position, namely "the familiar Platonic doctrine . . . that no man does evil voluntarily" (ibid.). If one assumes that Plato did know what he was doing, then one must assume that all the complexities and subtleties of the narration, as well as the use of personification, are necessary to say what Plato is trying to say. This means that "the reader who is [seriously] interested only in Plato's philosophy" must pay attention to every subtlety and nuance in the mode of presentation if he or she is to have any hope of understanding what Plato is saying. If this is so, then the *Protagoras* is a splendid example of the way the teaching about virtue and the teaching of virtue depend on storytelling and on storytelling's essential prerequisite, personification.

～

The problematic of prosopopoeia arises at three crucial moments in the *Protagoras*. The dialogue not only uses prosopopoeia but is *about* prosopopoeia. I have quoted as my epigraph the passage in which the question of saving face and facing one's family and friends comes up as the new day dawns and makes it possible for Socrates to see Hippocrates' blushes, the red of the dawn and the red of his face reflecting one another. Prosopopoeia is also central in Socrates' challenge to Protagoras's claim that virtue can be taught. After Protagoras's "long and magnificent display of eloquence" (328d) in his opening speech, Socrates sets the terms of his debate with the Sophist by way of a question about the validity of using a prosopopoeia to speak of virtue:

> Now then, Protagoras, there is just one small question left, your answer to which will give me all I want. . . . Is virtue a single whole, and are justice and self-control and holiness parts of it, or are these latter all names for one and the same thing? That is what I still want to know.
> Well, that is easy to answer, said he. Virtue is one, and the qualities you ask about are parts of it.
> Do you mean, said I, as the parts of a face are parts—mouth, nose, eyes, and ears—or like the parts of a piece of gold, which do not differ from one another or from the whole except in size?

In the first way, I should say—that is, they are in the relation of the parts of a face to the whole.

. . .

Has each also its own function? In a face, the eye is not like the ear nor has it the same function. Nor do the other parts resemble one another in function any more than in other respects. Is this how the parts of virtue differ, both in themselves and in their function? It must be so, I suppose, if the parallel holds good.

Yes it is so, Socrates. (329b–30b)

The importance of this figure for Socrates' argumentation against Protagoras is shown when he returns to it much later as he is about to make his final assault on the Sophist. What he says against Protagoras depends on Protagoras's initial choice between two possible ways of figuring virtue. The second formulation of this differs significantly from the first. To quote it will make clearer what is at stake in the choice between the two ways of figuring virtue:

Wisdom, temperance, courage, justice, and holiness are five terms. Do they stand for a single reality, or has each term a particular entity underlying it, a reality with its own separate function, each different from the other? Your answer was that they are not names for the same thing, but that each of these terms applies to its own separate reality, and that all these things are parts of virtue, not like the parts of a lump of gold all homogeneous with each other and with the whole of which they are parts, but like the parts of a face, resembling neither the whole nor each other and each having a separate function. (349b–c)

What are the implications of Protagoras's ready assent to the figure of the face? Even the wary Protagoras, who knows by this time that Socrates is a formidable antagonist and that he may be getting himself in all sorts of unforeseen trouble when he assents to what seems an innocent question, does not appear to know what is at stake in his choice. Socrates' questions have to do with names and with reality, with the relation between names and reality. The names "wisdom," "temperance," and so on each stand for an underlying reality, the genuine thing, wisdom, temperance, and so on, just as the words "eyes," "ears," "nose," and "mouth" stand for visible and identifiable entities. This means that wisdom, temperance, and so on are teachable. They have a circumscribed content that might be made, for example, the topic of a course of university lectures, just as it is possible to teach someone to paint or to ride a horse. A recurrent strategy of Socrates' attack on Protagoras is to argue that the teaching of virtue, unlike the teaching of painting or playing the flute, does not have an identifiable content, so that the claim of the Sophists to be able to teach virtue is a fraud. Virtue cannot be taught. (See 318a–20b.)

Another way to put this is to say that the word "virtue" is apparently different from the words "wisdom," "temperance," and the names of the other virtues. "Virtue" does not stand for an identifiable entity, out in the sunlight, as plain as the nose on your face, as manifest as an act of courage, something you can talk about and teach others about. Virtue has to be expressed indirectly, in a conglomerate figure made up of dissimilar signs, each with a separate function. The meaning of the whole figure is differential. It is generated by a surface relation laterally among the parts, not by a vertical relation between the whole sign or "term" and the "particular entity underlying it." Another way to say this is to assert that virtue can only be expressed in a composite allegorical or hieroglyphical emblem, just as a face, with its embodied expression and meaning, is made up of all the features of that face in a certain arrangement in which the whole exceeds the sum of its parts.

Virtue in fact, so it seems, has to be expressed in the figure fundamental to any allegory: prosopopoeia. Where is the face, with its particular expression? Well, it is not in the nose, nor in the eyes, nor in the mouth, nor in the ears, nor in the furrows on brow, cheek, or chin, nor in all these taken sequentially, but in the collection taken together as a single configuration. Where is virtue? Well, it is not courage or temperance or wisdom, but is represented by the whole lot of them together. Plato's figure of virtue's face is in the strict sense a prosopopoeia. It is the ascription of a face to the absent and inanimate. Virtue is not really a person with a face. The absence and unattainability of virtue as such, the difficulty of bringing it out in the open where it can be named, identified, and taught, is the main presupposition of the *Protagoras*, the main point Socrates keeps approaching from one direction or another.

This personification of virtue, whatever we may assume Plato "wished to say," contradicts concepts that are usually assumed to be "Platonic." We all assume that Plato held a notion of language something like his notion of mimesis. A word refers to an entity and that entity is in turn grounded in a higher reality, the "idea" of the thing. The figure of the face of virtue endangers that schema. Ludwig Wittgenstein, in a series of brilliant sections in *The Blue and Brown Books*, argues against our normal, one might say our "Platonic," assumption that we understand the expression on a face by comparing it to a state of mind that expression expresses. This example of the face is one of Wittgenstein's main analogies for our assumption that the meaning of a word is its reference to something extralinguistic. No, says Wittgenstein, the expression is *in* the face, just as the meaning of a word is *in* the word. Neither the face nor the word refers to anything outside itself. "We are, as it were," says Wittgenstein, "under an optical delusion which by some sort of reflection makes us think that there are two objects when there is only one. The delusion is assisted by our using the verb 'to have,' saying 'The face *has* a particular expression.' Things look different when, instead of this, we say, 'This *is* a peculiar face.' What a thing *is*, we mean, is bound up with it; what it has can be separated from it. . . . It is, when I let the face make an impression on me, as though there existed a double of its expression, as though the double was the prototype of the expression and as though seeing the expression of the face was finding the prototype to which it corresponded—as though in our mind there had been a mould and the picture we see had fallen into that mould, fitting it. But it is rather that we let the picture sink into our mind and make a mould there."[5]

Plato's figure of the face of virtue contains in itself, whatever Plato may have "intended," the possibility of being taken in the "Wittgensteinian" way as well as in the "Platonic" way that Wittgenstein so persuasively contests. In fact it is the other image, the one Protagoras rejects, apparently with Socrates' approval, that would appear to be more compatible with Platonism as it is traditionally conceived. The image of the lump of gold, every part of which is like all the others and like the whole, since it is all one homogeneous substance, is a perfect figure for a synecdochic or "symbolic" system of participation, based on resemblance. Such a system would not be a linguistic or semiotic structure at all. The part would be like the whole, not in the sense of standing for it as a sign stands for what is absent, but in the sense of actually being part of a whole that is everywhere the same with itself, as a lump of gold is all gold, through and through. If I show you a piece of a lump of gold and can persuade you that it is a fair sample of the whole, you have direct knowledge of the whole through the part, whereas the features of a face, as Socrates says, neither resemble one another nor resemble the whole. The whole face is an allegorical prosopopoeia of virtue, not something "really like" virtue, any more than the word "red" is really like the color red. The relation is truly semiotic. It is based on conventional "standing for." It is based, moreover, on dissimilarity rather than on resemblance. Such a prosopopoeia has the extravagantly fictive quality of any allegorical personification, the sort of thing that has given allegory a bad name since the eighteenth century, in examples like "Innoculation, Heavenly Maid, descend." But to say "Virtue, Stern Warrior, Descend" is no less fatuous or absurd.

The choice of gold rather than of some other homogeneous substance is far from innocent. Gold is the ultimate value, which measures all other values and for which all other values may be substituted. Gold is implicitly here, and more explicitly elsewhere in Plato, one symbol par excellence, along with the sun and the father, of the One, the Idea of Ideas, that is, of Virtue itself, of which all particular virtues—temperance, courage, wisdom, and the rest—are parts. The image of the face of virtue, by contrast, is semiotic through and through. Like all such figurative systems it contains two simultaneous contradictory possibilities. On the one hand, the personification of virtue may indicate that virtue exists as a transcendent, non-linguistic entity, but one so absent, so unavailable to the senses and even to direct thinking, that it can only be expressed, with manifest inadequacy, in an allegorical story depending on that most artificial of tropes, prosopopoeia. On the other hand, such a figurative system suggests the possibility that there is no virtue in the sense of an independently existing ontological entity, the highest good. Virtue is a function generated by the interaction of particular virtues, as the expression of a face does not lie in its reference to a prototype but in the surface interaction among the various features that make it up, so that they form a unified configuration.

In concluding, as he notoriously does in this dialogue and elsewhere, that no one does evil willingly and that virtue is therefore a matter of knowledge, Socrates is not really saying that virtue can be taught, but that it is a matter of innate knowledge. It is a matter of anamnesia. The appropriateness of the prosopopoeia is that it carries this meaning as one of its implications. Just as we cannot avoid imposing a face on that mountain, because ordinary language tells us to do it, so virtue is an immanent habit. Virtue is manifested by a story but not taught by it, at least not in the sense that the story works as a mediation between the listener and some abstract principle of virtue or source of virtuous commands. Being virtuous and reading a story are like playing a game, to borrow Wittgenstein's figure. In fact both being virtuous and reading a story are language games. You do not learn to read a story or learn how to be virtuous by being taught abstract rules for either, but by a kind of leap within the culture in which certain behavior is virtuous or within the complex assumptions that make it possible to read the story.

Just this distinction is the pivot of Socrates' refutation of Protagoras's misreading of Simonides' attack on Pittacus in his poem about virtue. Simonides, says Socrates, does not say that it is hard to *be* virtuous but that it is hard to *become* virtuous. He attacks Pittacus for saying it is hard to *be* virtuous. Being virtuous is like playing a game. Once you have got the hang of it, it is relatively easy. The difficulty is to get the hang of it. As in the case of a game, so in the case of becoming virtuous or learning how to read a story, one probably learns best by imitation, by watching someone who is an expert do it. The best and most successful teaching in the humanities is probably of this kind. Learning to be virtuous and learning to read a story both depend, I have been arguing, on the figure of prosopopoeia and on learning to be adept in manipulating this figure, no easy task. Stories function to teach virtue not because they mediate some abstract message, but because they are the best practical training in using and reading prosopopoeia, though perhaps also in coaching us to take it for granted and to forget that it is a figure.

~

I conclude this chapter by returning to the *Protagoras* for two extraordinary examples of prosopopoeia in it not so far identified.

The first occurs early in the dialogue, when Socrates describes to his friend what he saw when he and the young Hippocrates entered the house of Callias and saw the great crowd of men young and old gathered there to listen to the great Protagoras, as he paced back and forth in the portico discoursing, followed by a long line of respectful auditors. Two of those present are immobile, since they are of special age and dignity, almost as important as Protagoras himself. It is in relation to them that the oblique prosopopoeia occurs. The passage has memorable charm and power. It is a marvelous image of a culture in which "cooperative research in the humanities" takes place, so it seems, in a way so natural and so habitual as not even to need to be formally institutionalized. Of course, humanistic learning in Plato's Athens is constrained by all sorts of implacable limitations, for example, the total exclusion of women, slaves, servants, eunuchs. Though the latter three are mentioned in the dialogue, women have vanished from this culture. Each man, as I noted earlier, is identified as his father's son, as though women were not even needed for generation:

> When we were inside, we came upon Protagoras walking in the portico, and walking with him in a long line were, on one side Callias, son of Hipponicus; his stepbrother Paralus, the son of Pericles; and Charmides, son of Glaucon; and on the other side Pericles' other son, Xanthippus; Philippides, son of Philomelus; and Antimoerus of

Mende, the most eminent of Protagoras' pupils, who is studying professionally, to become a Sophist. Those who followed behind listening to their conversation seemed to be for the most part foreigners— Protagoras draws them from every city that he passes through, charming them with his voice like Orpheus, and they follow spellbound— but there were some Athenians in the band as well. As I looked at the party I was delighted to notice what special care they took never to get in front or to be in Protagoras' way. When he and those with him turned round, the listeners divided this way and that in perfect order, and executing a circular movement took their places each time in the rear. It was beautiful.

"After that I recognized," as Homer says, Hippias of Elis, sitting on a seat of honor in the opposite portico. . . .

"And there too spied I Tantalus"—for Prodicus of Ceos was also in town. (314e–15a)

The two quotations from Homer come of course from book 11 of the *Odyssey*, the description of Ulysses' visit to the underworld. At first this might seem no more than a graceful way Socrates takes (in Plato's imaginary reconstruction of his encounter with Protagoras or, it may be, in Plato's imaginative creation of an encounter with Protagoras that never actually took place) to elevate somewhat whimsically and ironically the scene he is describing. It also shows he knows his poetry, an important point later in the encounter with Protagoras. But nothing in Plato is likely to be quite so casual. The more one thinks of the implications of these two odd references to Homer, the more extraordinary their implications become. One might say that the passage in Homer is the allegorical prosopopoeia of prosopopoeia. This is so in the sense that Homer's language here ascribes a face and a voice to the dead in the literal sense of speaking for the dead in the underworld. The famous scene calls attention by way of an extravagant example to what goes on in prosopopoeia. Ulysses pours blood in the fosse so the dead can approach, drink, and speak. This figures the poet's power to bring back the dead and endow them with faces and voices within his language. This, it might be argued, is the fundamental poetic power. It is certainly the power that makes narrative possible. Storytelling, oral or written, depends on the power to create persons out of modulated sounds in air or black marks on the page. The poetic topos of the hero's visit to the underworld, one might say, is the original myth on which all lesser prosopopoeias depend or of which they are miniature imitations. All prosopopoeias are visits to the underworld. They depend, in a shadowy way, on the assumption that the absent, the inanimate, and the dead are waiting somewhere to be brought back to life by the words of the poet or orator. The artificiality and conventionality of the topos, its regular appearance in epics, for example, in the *Aeneid* as well as in the *Odyssey*, suggest that its function is to call attention to prosopopoeia as a fundamental poetic power. This is the power to speak for the dead, who have no voice of their own. Without prosopopoeia no poetry, no narrative, no literature. Ulysses' visit to the underworld is a personification of that power.

Plato's brilliant placing of Socrates' narrative of his encounter with Protagoras under the aegis of Ulysses' visit to the underworld, as a repetition of that visit, has, however, a quite different function for Socrates from the one it has for Plato himself.

Socrates speaks of still-living men whom he has just left. In a sense the moment of his visit to Callias is indeed already dead, together with all those who took part. As soon as something has happened, it falls instantly into an irrecoverable past. From this point of view something that happened two minutes ago is already as dead, as "historical," as something that happened centuries or millennia ago. There are no degrees of distance from the past. Socrates telling his story to his friend was already as far from the events as we are. Nevertheless, Socrates' speaking of Hippias, Prodicus, and the rest as though they were already dead and must be brought to life again in his discourse is a kind of supreme insolence. It strikes those still-living wise old men dead. Though they still live he describes them as if they were already dead. This is a somewhat impudent way of saying that he is about to displace them, make them part of the outmoded past. Prodicus is presented as a master of exact use of language. To speak of him as Tantalus ("And there too spied I Tantalus") is ironically to represent such literal exactitude in language use as the tantalizing offer of a feast of knowledge that is always taken away at the last moment. It is taken away in the flatness of Prodicus's failure to understand wordplay, figurative language, and irony, on which Socrates' mastery so conspicuously depends. Prodicus's method is dead. It strikes language dead. He is himself virtually dead, though he lives and breathes. For Socrates to put his narrative under the aegis of Ulysses' visit to the underworld is simultaneously to bring Prodicus and the others to life by prosopopoeia and to strike them dead by calling attention to the artifice in storytelling.

If the reader thinks, by contrast, of Plato himself, the author of the dialogue, the effect of the allusion to Homer has a different function. When Plato wrote the dialogue, Protagoras, Hippias, Prodicus, and all the rest, including Socrates himself, were really dead. All these people were ghosts. Plato's writing, also our reading, are like Ulysses' journey to the underworld. Without Plato's life-giving power, the power of the written not the spoken word, they would remain dead, Socrates included. Who can doubt that this is literally the case? Which of us would have been likely to have heard of Protagoras, Hippias, Prodicus, or even the great Socrates himself if Plato had not written his dialogues? Plato's insertion of the two apparently casual allusions to Homer calls attention to his own poetic and narrative power. He can raise the dead, all those long-gone Sophists and their followers with whom Socrates disputed. He can revive them, invoke them, and keep them in life, as long as there is one copy of "Plato" left and someone to read it. But there is a price to pay for this act of resurrection. The dead are raised as dead.

The ambiguity of Plato's narrative is suggested indirectly in another earlier passage. Socrates describes Protagoras as "charming them [his followers] with his voice like Orpheus, and they follow spellbound" (315a). Orpheus, notoriously, exerted this vocal power over the dead. Socrates' own power as a pied piper leading the youth of Athens astray, as Orpheus in the underworld swayed the dead with his music, earned him the hemlock and made him become a shade like the others, to be resurrected by Plato in his dialogues. Plato here is covertly admitting the kinship between Socrates' guilty act and his own repetition of that guilt in writing the dialogues. If one regards Platonic philosophy as a mystification, Plato can be said to have charmed and led astray down through the centuries with his "dear gorgeous nonsense" far more youths than Socrates.

The function of the ostentatious prosopopoeias in the *Protagoras* is to call attention to the use of that artifice in the dialogue. Personification is the basic trope on which the dialogue depends for its existence. The whole of the *Protagoras* is one extended, multiple prosopopoeia, not least in invoking the dead Socrates himself, giving him a face and a voice once more. These acts of resurrection form a chain of acts performed "first" by Socrates only a few minutes after the events have occurred, then by Plato years later, then by us today as readers centuries later. But in all three cases, in a different way in each case, the dead are raised as ghosts, as dead, as purely fictive or verbal entities, as shades or shadows, as shadows of shades. One thinks of an analogous act of ambiguous resurrection, Yeats's "The Delphic Oracle upon Plotinus," where Plato himself is spoken back into existence, as Plato spoke Socrates back, but spoken as an insubstantial ghost in the Elysian fields:

> Scattered on the level grass
> Or winding through the grove
> Plato there and Minos pass,
> There stately Pythagoras
> And all the choir of love.[6]

For Plato, as for Yeats, such shades are able to keep in existence only because, so to speak, they have drunk the blood of language spoken by the living. They exist only so long as we go on giving them our blood in individual acts of reading and in individual acts of prosopopoeia, ascribing a face, a voice, and a personality to those inanimate black marks on the page. The moment no one, anywhere, is reading Plato, all the figures in his dialogues will die again. Reading is one major form of the responsibility the living have to the dead.

~

The final overt prosopopoeia in the *Protagoras* returns the reader to the question of the use of narrative to teach the truth about virtue and to teach virtue. This extraordinary passage comes just before the end of the dialogue:

> I assure you, said [Socrates], that in asking all these questions I have nothing else in view but my desire to learn the truth about virtue and what it is in itself. I know that if we could be clear about that, it would throw the fullest light on the question over which you and I have spun such a coil of argument, I maintaining that virtue was not teachable and you that it was. It seems to me that the present outcome of our talk is pointing at us, like a human adversary, the finger of accusation and scorn. If it had a voice it would say, "What an absurd pair you are, Socrates and Protagoras. One of you, having said at the beginning that virtue is not teachable, now is bent upon contradicting himself by trying to demonstrate that everything is knowledge—justice, temperance, and courage alike—which is the best way to prove that virtue *is* teachable. If virtue were something other than knowledge, as Protagoras tried to prove, obviously it could not be taught. But if it turns out to be, as a single whole, knowledge—which is what you are urging, Socrates—then it will be most surprising if it cannot be taught. Protagoras on the other hand, who at the beginning supposed it to be teachable, now on the contrary seems to be bent on showing that it is almost anything rather than knowledge, and this would make it least likely to be teachable." (360e–61c)

"If it had a voice," but of course the "present outcome of our talk" only has the voice that is ascribed to it by Socrates. He here shows himself a master of prosopopoeia. The function of this final appearance of personification just here is subtle and not all that easy to pin down. Like the questions of what virtue is and whether it can be taught, it is elusive. At the farthest reaches of their interchange, at the present end of their "coil of argument," Socrates and Protagoras have reached an impasse, an "aporia." This aporia takes the particular form of a chiasmus. Beginning with similar assumptions about virtue (that it is like a face and not like a lump of gold), but opposite opinions about whether virtue can be taught, Socrates and Protagoras have crossed one another at some point in their discussion. Each now appears to hold the opinion formerly held by the other. This is a particularly unpleasant form of madness, if one means by sanity the ability to control one's argument and remain logically consistent, everywhere and through time one with oneself, as a coherent self ought to be. It is as though the "coil of argument" had a life of its own and were able to depersonalize those caught up in it, forcing them in spite of themselves to reach positions they thought they were contesting. It appears as if "Socrates" and "Protagoras" are not so much real people as the personification of certain procedures of argumentation. These procedures, moreover, lead those caught up in them to the blankness and logical absurdity of an impasse in the argument beyond which it is not clear that it is possible to progress.

What about Plato himself? Is he not in full control of the dialogue he has so cunningly constructed, with an irony that outdoes and masters Socrates' own? Who, after all, speaks or orchestrates the dialogue, labeling the opening speeches as made by "Friend" or by "Socrates"? The answer is surely that Plato himself is the ultimate authorizing authority. He exerts that authority through an extravagant use of prosopopoeia, that is, in a way that depersonalizes him, renders him without personal authority. It is impossible to quote any sentence of the dialogue and say, "Plato says this," since everything is spoken by some invented character, with how much or how little irony on Plato's part it is always impossible to say. Plato has effaced himself, made himself faceless. He has vanished into the personae of the dialogue. Not only can we not say, "Plato says," we cannot even say, "He [Socrates or Protagoras] says," since the trope of prosopopoeia is dismantled within the text itself. It is shown to be the fictive ascription of personality to an impersonal power of language. We can only say, "Language speaks." In the *Protagoras*, however, language speaks in a way that deprives it of the commanding authority of logical coherence. This incoherence, along with the impossibility of knowing whether anything said by anyone in the dialogue is affirmed by Plato himself, is the particular way in which the *Protagoras* is "unreadable." The reversal of the positions of Socrates and Protagoras that leads the dialogue to end in what Socrates calls "utter confusion" indicates that language itself cannot be trusted to lead to clarity, even by the most extravagant procedures of linguistic hygiene, such as Prodicus advises. Language leads rather to a tantalizing lack of clarity and conclusiveness. The chiasmus of Socrates and Protagoras indicates that if you just go on talking you will perhaps ultimately change places with your adversary.

The *Protagoras* shows personification to be necessary to teaching about virtue and to teaching virtue. At the same time the use of that trope is shown to deprive the teaching of whatever authority it might have if it were the unequivocal affirmation of some wise man who knows what virtue is and can speak coherently and persuasively about it.

After all this talk we do not yet know what virtue is and whether it can be taught. We have not confronted virtue face to face. The situation, however, is even worse. As though by another kind of reversal, the depersonalizing of Socrates and Protagoras, making them into artificial tropes for an impersonal possibility of argument, has led to the personification not of virtue itself (*that* has slipped away altogether) but of "the present outcome of our talk." As for Wallace Stevens in so many of his late poems, the human face remains at the farthest reach of the imagination, blocking the attempt to reach "not ideas about the thing but the thing itself" (as he titles one poem), so here for Plato the final end of the coil of argument is the confrontation of a laughing, scornful face, not the face of virtue but the face of the aporia itself, the present outcome of the talk. This face blocks further progress in the attempt to reach and face virtue. The fundamental means of the argument, prosopopoeia, becomes in the end the barrier forbidding further progress beyond what is now presented as no more than a trope, a rhetorical artifice. "*If* it had a voice, it would say," but of course it does not have a voice.

The *Protagoras* ends, not with a face-to-face confrontation with virtue, but with a confrontation with the trope that has both made the dialogue possible, with all its brilliant narrative complexity, and led in the end only to a confrontation with itself, not to a clarification of the topic it was meant to identify and teach. This self-confrontation is mimed by the invaginated structure of the narration, as it turns back on itself or inside itself, like the finger of a glove reversed within itself, making the inside outside, the outside in. The topographical structure of the dialogue mirrors its tropological structure. This gives a striking example of the intimate connection between personification and topography. There are always figures in any landscape, but this is especially true for a crowded urban scene like that of the *Protagoras*. The intricate spaces of the *Protagoras* are generated by the public and private relations among the characters. Those in turn personify the themes of the dialogue, not least important of which is personification itself.

∼

Socrates' response to the dead end they have reached is to say he would like to start all over again, to see if he cannot untangle the confusion and reach the truth about virtue and its teachability: "For my part, Protagoras, when I see the subject in such utter confusion I feel the liveliest desire to clear it up. I should like to follow up our present talk with a determined attack on virtue itself and its essential nature. Then we could return to the question whether or not it can be taught" (361c). Plato presents Socrates as doing just that, for example in the *Meno*, which follows the *Protagoras* in the usual ordering of Plato's dialogues, though, alas, the *Meno* too leads once more to uncertainty about what virtue is in itself and how men get it: "But we shall not understand the truth of the matter until, before asking how men get virtue, we try to discover what virtue is in and by itself" (*Meno*, 100b).

No doubt we should follow Socrates' lead and keep searching, as I shall do in the chapters that follow this one. I claim, however, to have shown, with Plato's help, not just that narrative examples are necessary to the teaching of virtue, but that analysis of the trope of prosopopoeia is fundamental to an understanding of how stories might perform both an epistemological and an ethical function, teach what virtue is, and at the same time make an ethical demand on their readers that leads those readers to act, decide, and judge according to virtue. I have also shown, in a different way from the demonstration in my reading of *The Return of the Native*, the intimate relation between personification and topography. The next chapter continues this investigation. It focuses on a story by Kleist in which legal and ethical responsibility are dramatized in terms of borders and frontiers.

§ 3 Laying Down the Law in Literature: Kleist

die Wahrscheinlichkeit nicht immer auf
Seiten der Wahrheit ist
—Heinrich von Kleist

The establishing of territorial borders legitimates a jurisdiction. Within that jurisdiction a certain legal code applies. To cross a frontier of that country is to go outside that particular law. Legislation may therefore be thought of as topographical work, work not entirely unlike the naming of places. Heinrich von Kleist's "Michael Kohlhaas" turns in part on a conflict of jurisdictions brought about by border crossings.

The story also raises questions about the legislative power of the story itself. Can a work of literature lay down the law and transform a certain topographical domain? What would it mean, for literature and for the law, to say yes to that proposition? Shelley in the "Defense of Poetry" said that "poets are the unacknowledged legislators of the world." Can we take that seriously, or is it just hyperbolic poetic license? To ask this another way, is a work of literature ever a speech act that inaugurates a new law? If a work of literature may sometimes posit law, does this happen when the work is written or only later on when it is read? If the latter, does the work have to be read justly to be efficacious or does it work if it is just read? What kind of law would a poem or a novel make statutory? If a work of literature lays down the law, does it do so only in its own original language, or does its legislative power continue in translation? Is it the whole work that legislates, or just some particular, perhaps detachable, part of it? This is like asking whether the whole marriage ceremony is necessary to marry the couple, or whether certain words in it would work performatively alone: "I pronounce you man and wife." The first quarter of the story by Kleist I shall discuss was first published in a periodical in 1808, two years before the whole story appeared in the first volume of Kleist's collected stories. Was that fragment, from the point of view of legislative power, like a marriage ceremony broken off after only part of it has been performed? To ask these subsidiary questions is to see how unlikely or even absurd it is to suppose that a work of literature might in any practical or literal sense legislate. Inaugural originality a work of literature may conceivably have, but not, it would seem, the universality of law, the demand made by a law on all people within its jurisdiction to obey it or suffer the consequences.

That works of literature reflect the law and may even, in part at least, be determined by the legal conditions in a given country at a given time cannot be doubted. Brilliant recent studies have been published in this area. An example is Brook Thomas's *Cross-examinations of Law and Literature: Cooper, Hawthorne, Stowe, and Melville*.[1] This book explores the legal contexts of nineteenth-century American literature. The number of such studies is constantly growing. Nor can it be doubted that recent theoretical developments in law, especially so-called "critical legal studies," have been decisively influenced by literary theory. This relation is by no means straightforward. Some work in critical legal studies has conflated "reader response" criticism with so-called "deconstruction" to produce a new, productive amalgam not quite faithful to either progenitor. There is no reason to be dismayed by this. It is an example of the transformative torsion that occurs when theories are transferred from one discipline to another, or from one language or country to another. My concluding chapter discusses in more detail what is at stake here. In any case, no one can doubt that recent literary theory has been appropriated by legal theory.

Moreover, there are a number of ways in which law and literature, along with their respective, elaborately institutionalized disciplines, overlap. Literary theory attempts to derive general laws from particular cases or to apply general law to the reading of particular cases. "Real" law depends in manifold ways on assumptions about what makes a plausible narrative and about the proper legal procedures for moving from a particular story to legislation or to a court decision that is quasi-legislative. As scholars of the law well know, there are disquieting implications for the law in recent work suggesting some fundamental unreadability in narratives generally. The just application of the law, for example, in criminal cases, depends on getting a story straight about what happened, just as major Supreme Court decisions, as we know, depend on the presupposition that it is just to move from the contingent details of a specific case, *Roe v. Wade*, at bottom a particular story about particular people, to a judgment of constitutionality that decisively affects the lives of millions of people. The appeal to precedent in law means, most often, the appeal to an agreed-upon narrative of particular cases, often agreed upon only after lengthy litigation. Both law and literature depend on resolving (or tacitly avoiding) the vexed question of the validity of example, or, in traditional rhetorical terms, the validity of synecdoche, part standing for whole. This issue is not absent from the present essay. How could I be justified in drawing general conclusions about whether literature lays down the law on the basis of a single, perhaps eccentric, example? The institutions of both law and literature are determined by complex assumptions, often "unwritten laws," about what makes a good argument or a proper narrative. It is instructive for someone from within one discipline to move momentarily within the unfamiliar, sometimes even seemingly absurd, conventions of the other.

Nor can it be doubted, finally, that some works of literature contain thematic reflections about law or dramatizations of legal topics that add something important to our understanding of law. Examples are Shakespeare's *The Merchant of Venice* and *Measure for Measure*, or, as I shall try to demonstrate here, the stories of Heinrich von Kleist.

My question is a different one. A precondition for asking it is accepting all three of the relations of law and literature I have named: the reflection by literature of law; the influence of literary theory on legal theory, and vice versa; and the presentation within literature of insights into the law that do more than reflect the legal situation of the time. I ask rather whether a work of literature can in any sense be conceived to be law-making. Can literature inaugurate or establish law? Can literature not only preserve the law or break it, but posit a new law? I shall investigate this question, in its relation to the other three connections of law and literature, through a reading of Kleist's "Michael Kohlhaas."

⁓

All Kleist's stories, not to speak of his plays and many of his anecdotes and short works, contain thematic elements involving the law, often disturbing and paradoxical elements. The question of doing or not doing justice was a fundamental topic for Kleist. He was fascinated by the way various kinds of law impinge on individual human experience: divine law, civil or human law, moral law, physical law (for example the "law" of causality), and aesthetic law (for example the millennial assumptions, going back at least to Aristotle, about what makes a shapely narrative, and therefore about the relation of narrative to truth). Legal studies and literary studies, as I have said, share a need to set up rules for interpreting narrative in order, for example, to establish guilt or innocence in criminal cases by getting a story straight or to decide, for example, whether *Macbeth* is a tragedy in the same sense that *Oedipus the King* is a tragedy.

Readings of Kleist's strange and unsettling stories have played an important part in recent demonstrations of how difficult it is to manage narratives. Kleist's stories are unsettling in part because they show people decisively affected (often by being haled before the law), when entirely erroneous but plausible stories are told about them. The empirical data, which everyone agrees on, can be put together this way or that way. There is a disastrous tendency for the data to be put together wrong, through malice, by accident, or just by application of normal assumptions about probability, *Wahrscheinlichkeit.*

Part of what is unsettling is the way the reader is engaged in the same activity of "reading" that is shown in the story to be so difficult and so likely to lead to catastrophe when it is done wrong. When we read one of Kleist's stories, we are reading a story about the disastrous legal consequences of storytelling and story reading.

Kleist was also fascinated by the possibility of conflicts among various jurisdictions, the conflict, for example, between divine and human law, or between the laws of physical causality and the requirements of plausible concatenation imposed traditionally on storytelling, or between the incongruent jurisdictions of adjacent or superimposed domains, as in the conflicts between Saxony law, Brandenburg law, the law of the Holy Roman Empire, and Protestant or Catholic church law, in "Michael Kohlhaas." Kohlhaas is subject to all these laws, and if one does not condemn him, another will. The question of topography comes up overtly in Kleist's expression of this.

Kleist's concern for the law can be exemplified in any of his stories. "The Marquise of O——" turns on the question of a rapist's obligations to his victim (and, uneasily, vice versa). The next to the last act of violence in the sequence of violent acts that makes up "The Foundling" is precipitated by a decree from the government giving the protagonist's property to his wicked foster son. The strange last episode of "The Foundling," in which the protagonist is ultimately hanged without absolution by papal decree, is determined by a law in the papal states "forbidding a criminal to be executed without his first receiving absolution."[2] In hanging Piachi without absolution, the pope breaks a knot in the law by breaking the law, in order to preserve the legal system. In "The Earthquake in Chile" a great earthquake briefly suspends, in an idyllic interlude, the implacable operation of social, civil, moral, and ecclesiastical law. All these laws return with a vengeance in the final scene, instigated by a Judgment Day sermon in the cathedral following the earthquake. In "The Duel" a pure woman is accused, on the basis of apparently irrefutable circumstantial evidence, of fornication. God, so it seems at first, confirms her guilt in a "holy trial by combat" (E318; G261), though the story ends with a characteristically Kleistian ironic twist. The story involves law of various sorts throughout. In one way or another, most of Kleist's works, like the ones I have mentioned, explicitly involve the law.

~

No story by Kleist, however, is more dominated by legal questions than "Michael Kohlhaas." It is Kleist's earliest written and by far longest story, the first to display his characteristic narrative innovations. The subtitle is "Aus einer alten Chronik" ("From an Old Chronicle") (E85; G9).[3] Many of the chief events of the story, including the unlikely sounding interview of the eponymous hero with Martin Luther, are based on actual chronicles.[4] The events in question occurred around 1540 in Saxony and Brandenburg. Kleist could with some justice claim that he has not invented or inaugurated anything. He is just telling it like it was, obediently following his historical sources, submissive to their law.

One episode, the anecdote of an unlikely prophecy's fulfillment, comes from another source, a work of fiction. The crucial intervention of an old gypsy fortune-teller appears to be Kleist's invention. Kleist apparently made up other events and episodes, as well as most of the circumstantial details of conversation and behavior, along with many, but not all, of the proper names. Even the hero's name is changed from Kohlhasen to Kohlhaas, and from Hans to Michael, the latter presumably to suggest associations with the destroying Archangel Michael. Kohlhaas is twice in the story called a *Würgengel* ("avenging angel") (E134; G54).

Uniquely Kleist's own, in addition, are the brutal violence, the laconic abruptness with which episode follows episode. Kleistian motifs also include the decisive role of unlikely happenstance and, most of all, the telling of the story with the distinctive Kleistian rapidity of staccato tempo and rhythm. This abruptness is imaged in the stories themselves by frequent references to lightning bolts or by episodes in several of the stories in which someone's brains are dashed out. This new rhythm, it could be argued, is what Kleist most invented. It is something new and unheard of, something other than any other narrative mode before or since. It is as distinctive, say, as the style of a sonata by Domenico Scarlatti, therefore inimitable. One could not imagine someone else writing a "Kleist story." The imposture would be immediately evident.

As is characteristic of fictions claiming to justify themselves with the prior authority of history, Kleist's assertion that he is only following sources is a cover for a high degree of inventive originality. The *aus* in the subtitle must be taken to mean not only "from" but "out of" in the sense of "going far away from," as Kohlhaas goes out of Brandenburg into Saxony in the opening episode of the story. The story, as I shall show, has much to do with crossing borders from one jurisdiction to another. Kleist in "Michael Kohlhaas" also continually crosses from history to fiction without saying so. Without signaling the transgression in any way, he moves repeatedly from the safely grounded and lawful realm of history into another realm under the jurisdiction of a law the story itself establishes.

The distinction, however, between inaugural fictions and recapitulation of historical events will not hold. A fiction is worthless, from the point of view of laying down the law, if it does not somehow take hold. The work must get itself institutionalized, "legalized," sanctioned in some community of readers. "Rewriting history," even in the sense of getting historical events into a form accepted by the community as "right at last," may have decisive performative power in that community. An example today is the role in the women's movement of rewriting history to include more of women's roles in making history, including literary history.

Nevertheless, the reader concerned with the potential law-making power of literature is made uneasy by a story like "Michael Kohlhaas." It is impossible to tell from any markers within the story itself where history stops and fiction begins, even though the subtitle implicitly claims that it is all history, since it is taken "from an old chronicle." This claim is repeated within the story, for example in one notation about the Elector of Saxony: "Where he actually went, and whether in fact he arrived in Dessau, we shall not attempt to say, as the chronicles which we have compared oddly contradict and cancel one another on this point" (E179;

G99). This makes it sound as if Kleist has scrupulously followed his sources. He has refrained even from choosing between them when they contradict one another. This is an ironically fictitious claim, though it is a claim that has been made often enough in fictions masquerading as history. Kleist's story would be very different if it contained only things for which he has historical authority.

~

Even without that anxiety, the story is disturbing enough. The horse dealer Michael Kohlhaas was "one of the most upright and at the same time one of the most terrible men of his day [*einer der rechtschaffensten zugleich und entsetzlichsten Menschen seiner Zeit*]" (E87; G9). At first he was in every way admirable: quiet, law-abiding, an excellent husband and father, hard-working, "the very model of a good citizen" (E87; G9). "But," as the narrator says, "his sense of justice [*Rechtgefühl*] turned him into a brigand and a murderer" (E87; G9). That sense of justice, the reader is told a little later, "was as delicate as a gold balance" (E93; G14). The image of the delicate balance is not casual, since the story turns on Kohlhaas's demand for equity and recompense. He wants back exactly what he has lost. He has a refined sense of equivalences and is a connoisseur of differences. Or rather, he will not accept equivalences at all. For him only the same is the equal of the same. He is a strict literalist in his sense of justice. He does not want recompense for what has been done to his horses, for example, money or other horses. He wants the same horses returned to him in just the condition in which he left them.

Kleist's word *Rechtgefühl* ("sense of justice"), used twice, is more than a little ominous. It does not name a willingness to obey external law but a scrupulous inner measuring scale by which Kohlhaas evaluates on his own the justice or injustice of what someone does. He tries people's actions "before the bar [*Schranke*] of his own conscience" (E93; G14). The Protestant Reformation of Kohlhaas's day was promulgated through an appeal to the priest-hood of all believers and to the independence of each person's spiritual witness and power to read the Bible. Luther's most revolu-tionary act, it could be said, was to translate the Bible into German.

Kohlhaas's sense of justice may, in a given case, measure things differently from the way lawyers, judges, courts, and other legal authorities measure them. He lives under a double jurisdiction, one external, one internal. The latter is the call on him of something other than any external law, just as "Michael Kohlhaas," the story, makes its call on its readers from a place and according to a law that may not easily be assimilated into any previous law.

The story tells of just such a conflict between the two jurisdictions. When Kohlhaas is crossing the border from Brandenburg to Saxony one day with a string of horses he means to sell in Leipzig, he is illegally detained at a castle on the border for lack of an imaginary pass. Two black horses from his string are kept behind, ostensibly as gage, when he is allowed to proceed. Kleist stresses the contingency and irresponsibility of this injustice. It is not a concerted plan by the castellan, steward, and Junker of the castle. It just "happens." When Kohlhaas returns several weeks later with legal proof that the pass is not necessary, he finds that his once plump and glossy blacks are skinny and dull, scarcely able to stand on their feet. They have been worked nearly to death in the fields. The groom he has left behind to care for the horses has been robbed, beaten, and driven from the castle. The rest of the story describes the extraordinary escalation of Kohlhaas's attempts to get just recompense for the damage done to him.

This means return of the stolen possessions of the groom, payment of the groom's medical expenses, and, most of all, the return of his horses just as they were. He demands that they be fattened by the lord of the castle, the Junker Wenzel von Tronka. "Those are not my horses, your worship!" he cries to the Junker. "Those are not the horses which were worth thirty gold gulden! I want my well-fed and healthy horses back!" (E94; G15).

Justice is not done to him by the courts of either Saxony or Brandenburg, in part because influential people in both capitals are related by blood or marriage to the Junker von Tronka. Family loyalty is stronger than the law and subverts it. The authorities at Dresden and Brandenburg dismiss his suit. They tell him to fetch his horses from Tronka Castle and forget about the whole incident.

Finally, his wife is mortally injured by an over-zealous bodyguard when she tries to press the suit on his behalf in a personal appeal to the Elector of Saxony in Berlin. After burying his wife, Kohlhaas takes the law into his own hands. During his interview with Luther later on he justifies what he has done by saying, "I call that man an outcast [*verstoßen*] . . . who is denied the protection of the laws! . . . whoever denies me it thrusts me out among the beasts of the wilderness [*den Wilden der Einöde*]; he is the one—how can you deny it?—who puts into my hand the club that I defend myself with" (E125; G45). Kohlhaas here claims that he has been put back into a state of nature. He is therefore justified in initiating a new social contract.

Kohlhaas draws up "a decree [*einen Rechtsschluß*]" that, "by virtue of the authority [*Macht*] inborn in him," demands that the Junker fatten the blacks with his own hands in Kohlhaas's stables (E111; G31). When this is not done, he gathers followers, burns Tronka Castle, kills the steward and castellan and their families, but not the Junker, who escapes. He then sets himself up with an increasing band of armed men as an independent force seeking the Junker to wreak vengeance on him. He scourges the countryside. He sets fire to Wittenberg and then Leipzig, punishing them for harboring the Junker. He and his men are seemingly invincible. All attempts to capture him fail. Only the intercession of Martin Luther, in a strange interview based on historical fact, but going beyond historical documentation in its circumstantial detail, persuades Kohlhaas to lay down his arms, accept amnesty from the Elector of Saxony, and seek justice again through the court at Dresden. In the end justice is done to him, the Junker is given a prison sentence, the black horses are returned to Kohlhaas as fat as ever, along with full compensation for the damages to him and his groom. But Kohlhaas is a moment later beheaded by judgment of the Emperor of the Holy Roman Empire in Vienna. The latter considers himself not bound by the amnesty. The legal authorities support him in this. Kohlhaas's crime is "breach [*Verletzung*] of the peace of the Empire" (E174; G94).

As is so often the case in Kleist's stories and plays, the verdict repeats the crime.[5] If it is unjust for Kohlhaas to have "made a business of a bushel of oats" (E127; G47), as the proverb he cites has it, if it is wrong to burn down the castle, kill all those people, pillage the countryside, set fire to two cities, over an affair of two black horses, it also seems unjust to execute him for what is legally defined as no more than a breach of the Emperor's peace. Neither punishment fits the crime. Both are incommensurate. It would not take a delicate gold balance to see that something is amiss in both cases with the scales of justice.

Kleist's way of telling the story stresses the mortal irony of the double ending. The day of Kohlhaas's execution, the day when he "was to make atonement to the world for his all-too-rash attempt to take its justice into his own hands [*sich selbst in ihr Recht verschaffen zu wollen*]" (E179–80; G100), is also, as the Elector of Brandenburg tells him as he is led to the scaffold, "the day on which justice is done you" (E181; G101). "Look here," he says, "I am giving you back everything that was taken from you by force at Tronka Castle, which I as your sovereign was duty bound [*schuldig war*] to restore to you: the two blacks, the neckerchief, gold gulden, laundry—everything down to the money for the doctor's bills for your man Herse" (E181; G101). With one hand the law makes him full recompense. With the other it deprives him of his life. The story makes clear that he would never have gotten justice in the affair of the blacks if he had not taken justice into his own hands and so earned himself the headsman's axe. The scales of justice do not balance. From the point of view of the law, justice has been done. The law has been maintained and fairly administered. The authorities can sleep with good consciences. From Kohlhaas's point of view, he has lost everything, at the very moment he has regained everything he has lost.

~

How can we read this story justly, do it justice? One curious fact about "Michael Kohlhaas" is already evident. Even more than is the case with most works of fiction, in order to talk about it, "read" it, analyze it, evaluate it, it seems necessary to tell the story again. Much of the "criticism" of Kleist's stories more or less limits itself to that, for example the introductory essays by Thomas Mann and Martin Greenberg to the English translation cited here. If "Michael Kohlhaas" is inaugural, original, inventive, perhaps culpably so, if it lays down its own new Kleistian laws of storytelling, in defiance of traditional laws of the relation of narrative to history or of probability to truth, the story's effect on its reader seems to be a compulsion to tell the story over again. We must repeat the crime, if crime it is, in the effort to account for the story, to do it justice, to assimilate it into what is already known about literature and into conventional ways of rationalizing literature, just as, *in* the story, the highest authorities seem compelled to do again in a new form what Kohlhaas has done. They do this in an effort to heal the breach of the peace he has caused, to reassert their jurisdiction and justify their authority.

This compulsion to retell suggests an answer to the question posed earlier about how a work of literature might not only be original, invent something unheard of before, but also proliferate itself as a universal law. The story tends to disseminate itself and to compel its readers to do again what it does, just as Kohlhaas's demand for justice turns into widespread injustice, if that is the right word for it. This injustice expands not only in what he is led to do, but also in what he leads others to do. This is an ironic and exceedingly disquieting version of Kant's formulation of the categorical imperative: "I should never act in any other way than in such a manner *that I could also will that my maxim should be a universal law*" [Kant's italics].[6]

How does it happen in the story (as opposed to *with* the story) that Kohlhaas's initial demand for justice in the matter of his two horses escalates to a universal juridical, political, and moral level? The series of "decrees" Kohlhaas issues shows how a worldwide new law is implicit in Kohlhaas's stubbornly maintained demand for justice from the courts on the basis of his own private and exceedingly delicate *Rechtgefühl.* The German word for "decree," *Rechtsschluß,* sounds stronger to an English speaker than its English equivalent. It suggests establishing a right or laying down a right.

For Kohlhaas, one *Rechtsschluß* leads rapidly to more and then quickly to the revolutionary establishment of a new order of law. Speaking first in the name "of the authority inborn in him," Kohlhaas claims in the "Kohlhaas Manifesto" [*Mandat*] that he is "waging righteous war" on the Junker Wenzel von Tronka. He demands support from all citizens of Saxony "on pain of death and the certain destruction by fire of everything they [call] their own" (E114; G34). In a seemingly inevitable crescendo, this becomes in his second manifesto a definition of himself as "a free gentleman of the Empire and the world, owing allegiance to none but God." On this basis he invites "all good Christians" to join him (E116; G36). He issues yet another manifesto when he sets fire to Leipzig. In this he describes himself as "as viceroy [*Statthalter*] of the Archangel Michael, come to punish with fire and sword, for the wickedness into which the whole world was sunk, all those who should take the side of the Junker in this quarrel" (E121; G41). Kohlhaas's final manifesto, issued from the captured castle of Lützen, where he has established his command, "summon[s] the people to join with him to build a better order of things." It is signed from "the Seat of Our Provisional World Government [*Weltregierung*]" (E121; G41). Now when he goes forth "a large archangelic sword [is] borne before him on a red leather cushion ornamented with gold tassels, while twelve men with burning torches [follow] after" (E123; G43–44). This is appropriate for someone who, like his namesake the Archangel Michael, wields fire and sword as his chief instruments of destruction.

The reader will see the mad logic of this rapid expansion from the particular and parochial to the universal. Though Kohlhaas's quarrel is only over a pair of horses, as soon as he appeals from the judicial system of Saxony to his own private sense of justice, he has in effect renounced his citizenship and challenged the legitimacy of the courts. He has implicitly declared himself the leader of a revolutionary new world government, with its own new code of laws along with the other appurtenances of a state: legislators, courts, universities, and the rest. Though the appeal from the public courts to the bar of his own breast is not apparently violent, it implicitly possesses the violence of all inaugural positing of new law and the legitimation of a new state. Kohlhaas's appeal to his innate sense of justice in the affair of the two horses implies the setting up not of just a single new law or provisional court but of a new world order. The initial limited demand contains its own implicit universalization. It contains also within itself the possibility of all the violent acts Kohlhaas and his men commit. The appeal to a justice that is private and at the same time universal, a law above the law, is intrinsically violent, even when that appeal is performed in the most nonviolent way, for example, by passive disobedience or by peaceful assembly.

Kohlhaas's proclamation of a new world order takes the usual form of such proclamations, whether they are successful or not. Though his decrees and manifestos would create, performatively, the new people and the new law in the name of which they speak, his declarations speak as if that law and the people brought together under it already exist and are merely described in his proclamation. Declarations of independence do not take responsibility for what they do. They speak in the name of a preexisting people and preexisting rights, a people and rights that they create by performative fiat.[7] "We hold these truths to be self-evident," but they were not self-evident before our founding fathers enunciated them, in a speech act that was not just a statement of preexisting fact.

Kohlhaas's new declaration of the rights of man, however, is an infelicitous performative. The context and circumstances are not right. His proclamation is not ratified by a new contract and a new constitution. That this might happen is what the authorities in Saxony fear and what leads them to treat him with such violence. Some similar fear, it may be, motivated the authorities who put down so ruthlessly the pro-democracy movement in the People's Republic of China. It began as a few students hanging posters and meeting to make speeches, but soon a million citizens were rallying and there were posters everywhere.

~

At the moment of Kohlhaas's greatest military success, Luther intervenes to persuade Kohlhaas "to return within the confines of the social order [*in den Damm der menschlichen Ordnung*]" (E122; G42). In a notice posted all over the Electorate and then in an interview, he accuses Kohlhaas of being "filled with injustice [*Ungerechtigkeit*] from head to foot," and of being "a rebel and no soldier of the just God" for daring to take justice into his own hands (E122, 123; G42, 43). Kohlhaas's reply, as I have said, is that he has been "denied the protection of the laws," and therefore has been cast out of the state community in which he lives, and so is justified in setting up his own state (E125; G45). But Kohlhaas does not really mean that he has been returned to a state of nature, outside all laws. He means that the courts of Saxony and Brandenburg do not mediate the law for him, the law that he carries in his own breast. He is therefore justified in setting up a new law and a new social order in which justice in the name of the law will be done to him. Luther replies that no one has denied him the protection of the laws, that he should forgive his enemies, take back the horses, thin and worn as they are, and fatten them himself. No one but God has the right to declare the Elector unjust for denying his suit. In the end Kohlhaas agrees to disband his army, accept amnesty, and press his suit again before the courts of Saxony with Luther's sponsorship. Nevertheless, he stubbornly refuses to budge on the main point. "Let judgement [*die Erkenntnis*] be pronounced as is my due," he says, "and let the Junker fatten my pair of blacks" (E127; G47).

This interview with Luther is profoundly ironic. Only a few years earlier the same Martin Luther had nailed his theses to the church door in Wittenberg and had uttered his "Ich kann nicht anders" ("I cannot do otherwise"). Luther has behaved just as Kohlhaas is behaving. He has defied all civil and ecclesiastical authorities. He has appealed beyond them to a higher justice. On the ground of that justice, he has established on his own something even more important than a new state: a new church. Luther's revolution has been a success. In two decades his church has been institutionalized and accepted by certain states as legitimate. Luther himself wields great political as well as spiritual power. Nevertheless, he sternly refuses to Kohlhaas the right to act as he himself has acted, though, curiously enough, in his message to the Elector of Saxony he more or less accepts the argument by Kohlhaas that he has refused to countenance in his interview with Kohlhaas. "As a matter of fact," the narrator reports him as writing,[8] "the wrong done Kohlhaas had in a certain sense placed him outside the social union [*außer der Staatsverbindung*]; and, in short, so as to put an end to the matter, he should be regarded rather as a foreign power that had attacked the country (and since he was not a Saxon subject, he really might be regarded as such) than as a rebel in revolt against the throne" (E129; G49).

The complicated jurisdictional situation of the time is not entirely different from the situation in the United States today. In the United States, too, a crime that crosses state borders may be subject to the laws in one or the other of the states or to Federal law. In the United States too it may take much litigation to decide in which court a defendant should be tried. Kohlhaas seeks justice from Saxony and then from Brandenburg. He is ultimately condemned by a high court of the Empire, on the technicality that the amnesty granted by Saxony does not bind the Emperor's court.

But to define Kohlhaas as a "foreign power" is to put him in a sense outside any of these laws. Or rather, it is to subject him either to the laws governing warfare between states or to the conventions of the delicate diplomatic negotiations between states that keep the peace, often by endless inconclusive discussions. Such discussions, strictly speaking, are outside the laws of any state. They are in a sense unlawful, since they are subject only to international law or to the unwritten laws of diplomacy. They are governed by the laws of neither state that engages in the diplomatic negotiations. What is concluded by diplomacy must be ratified separately in each state in order to become effective. Walter Benjamin compares the conventions of diplomacy to the unwritten laws that govern discussions within families. For him both these realms are outside the "violence" [*Gewalt*] that characterizes state power and law.[9]

Though Luther is willing to argue that Kohlhaas is in a sense a foreign power, he is unwilling to let him define himself as the justified emissary of God's vengeance. He refuses to hear Kohlhaas's confession and administer him the Sacrament unless he will forgive his enemies and give up taking private vengeance. Nevertheless, the possibility that Kohlhaas really is the viceroy of the Archangel Michael, sent by God to punish a wicked people who have a corrupt judicial system, hovers as a faint possibility over the story, just as Kleist plays ironically with similar possibilities of divine intervention in his other stories. Kohlhaas compares his unwillingness to forgive to Christ's: "even the Lord did not forgive all his enemies" (E128; G48). As the narrator says of the sack of Tronka Castle: "In such a fashion [*Also*] does the angel of judgment descend from heaven" (E112; G32). A lot hangs on how the reader takes the *also* or "in such a fashion" in this last sentence, as it also does when Kant says, "I should act in such a fashion [*also*] that the maxim drawn from what I do could be made a universal law for all mankind."

What is the difference between Luther and Kohlhaas? Is it no more than the difference between a successful and an unsuccessful revolution, one that gets itself institutionalized, legitimized, and one that ends, like most revolutionary attempts, with the execution or imprisonment of the insurrectionist? Kohlhaas's revolution may be justified but unsuccessful. On the other hand, if Kohlhaas is not an emissary from God, he is making an entirely unjustified trouble about a small matter. He has made a business of a bushel of oats. He should submit himself to the law of the country he lives in or does business in and take whatever judgment the court hands down.

How would we decide about that fine line between a Luther and a Kohlhaas? Should we let history decide? Suppose the South had won the Civil War in the United States? Would that retroactively make the South's cause more just? Somehow it does not make sense to let the contingencies of history decide matters of justice. On the other hand, if Kohlhaas *is* a second Archangel Michael, a viceroy of God sent to punish those who do not administer the law rightly, then what he does is not revolutionary, original, or originary at all. He is a keeper of the law, a preserver of it, neither a breaker of the old law, nor a present-day Moses, Lycurgus, or Christ, who institutes a new law, fulfilling and canceling the old. He does not set up a law unheard-of before, the basis of a novel world order, original and inaugurative, without precedent. The same thing can be said of Luther. He claimed not to be founding a new religion but to be reforming a corrupt Christendom by returning to an old, traditional, and entirely authorized Christianity. The fact that Lutheranism has been so thoroughly institutionalized and merged into state power by the time Luther has his interview with Kohlhaas indicates, one could argue, how little truly initiatory the Protestant Reformation was. Luther is by 1540 an instrument of the established civil order, at least as he is presented by Kleist, but also as he is presented in standard historical accounts.

Here is the paradox inherent in the idea of the laying down of a new law, whether as a political act described in a work of literature or as a law-positing act performed by the work of literature itself. In order to work it has to appeal to precedent. It cannot authorize itself. It has to claim merely to describe and reinforce preexisting rights and laws. In order to work it must also be institutionalized after the fact, legitimated by the elaborate machinery of society, inscribed in statutes and rules, with some kind of police for their enforcement and an agreed-upon and publicized code of sanctions. In order to be socially effective, a work of literature must be canonized, surrounded by a complex context of editions, reviews, commentary, pedagogical traditions, and so on. But as soon as either Kohlhaas the man or "Michael Kohlhaas" the story is authorized from the past and institutionalized for the future, it is no longer novel, unheard-of, original, heterogeneous to what already has been legislated. It does not lay down a new law. It confirms an old one. The story of Kohlhaas as told by Kleist admirably exemplifies this contradiction.

～

So far I have been talking primarily about events or themes described in the story. What about the working of the story itself, as a historical event, a text written by Heinrich von Kleist at a certain time and place and published under certain circumstances, then later on published and republished, translated, commented on, until finally it fell under my eyes as reader? I have said that the paradox inherent in the idea of laying down a new law applies not only to the political acts described in a work of literature, for example Kohlhaas's insurrection and execution, but also to the law-positing act performed by the work, for example, by this story. How can that claim be defined, understood, and justified?

In order to do so I turn to a crucial episode in "Michael Kohlhaas" not so far discussed, the episode of the gypsy fortune-teller. This episode is an allegory of the working of the story. It shows that the story is not descriptive, constative, but performative. Or rather it shows that the story performs by describing or telling, since, strictly speaking, within the terms of traditional speech act theory, there is nothing performative about Kleist's story. "Michael Kohlhaas" does little more than narrate, in a dry, terse, economical, chroniclelike style, events that are said to have occurred in history. Its intention appears not to be performative at all, but purely epistemological, to get the facts right, to tell it like it was. Such judgment as the narrator passes on Kohlhaas is profoundly ironic. It expresses rather the collective judgment of the time or of our time than the evaluation to which the story itself leads the reader: "And now the fateful Monday after Palm Sunday arrived, on which Kohlhaas was to make atonement to the world for his all-too-rash attempt to take its justice into his own hands" (E179–80; G100).

The story of the improbable fulfillment of the gypsy woman's prediction about a roebuck is borrowed and modified by Kleist from an almost forgotten novel, Friedrich Maximilian Klinger's *Der Kettenträger* (Amsterdam, 1796), read by Kleist in March 1801 (see G898–99). The main part of the gypsy woman's story, however, seems to have been Kleist's addition to history. It is a fabulous element that intervenes decisively into the life story of the historical Kohlhaas as Kleist tells it. Several motifs characteristic of Kleist's storytelling come together in this episode: the ironic hint of signs indicating God's inscrutable judgment; the working of exceedingly improbable coincidence in human life; the performative function in human history of messages, letters, notes, papers, decrees, manifestos, court judgments—writing of all kinds. For Kleist, such writings do not simply describe, communicate, or inform. They make something happen. An example is the way Kohlhaas's failure to get justice from the courts is mediated by documents. The law's delay, the interminable "process" that keeps postponing Kohlhaas's suit, throwing it out of court, telling him to give it up, works by way of papers and documents, never by direct face-to-face confrontation. Kohlhaas cannot obtain such confrontation until it is too late and he has put himself outside the law by taking the law into his own hands.

The first of these motifs, the possibly supernatural sign, appears early in the story when "a huge lightning bolt" and "a sudden fierce downpour of rain" (E115; G35) stop Kohlhaas just as he is about to burn down the cloister where von Tronka's aunt is abbess and has been harboring von Tronka. Are we to take this seriously as a manifestation of God's judgment on Kohlhaas? Is it the sign of the abrupt intervention of eternity into time? The text does not allow the reader to decide certainly either way. There is the lightning bolt. You can read it any way you like.

The second motif, coincidence or improbable happenstance, pervades the whole episode of the gypsy woman. Kohlhaas encounters her by sheer accident, though the encounter is decisive for his fate. He just happens to be in the market town of Jüterbock when the gypsy woman is telling the fortunes of the Electors of Saxony and Brandenburg, who just happen to have met there to transact some business. She predicts good fortune for the Elector of Brandenburg, but bad fortune for the Elector of Saxony. She refuses to tell the latter what that bad fortune will be, but writes down on a little piece of paper "the name of the last ruler [of his house], the year in which he shall lose his throne, and the name of the man who shall seize it for himself by force of arms" (E172; G92). For some mysterious reason, never explained, she gives the paper to Kohlhaas, who has joined the curious crowd around the fortune-teller. She tells him it is an amulet that will save his life. Kohlhaas does not read the paper until the last moment of his life. The narrator says somewhat obscurely that he refrains "for various reasons" (E166; G86). The paper unread has in a way more power. Once Kohlhaas knows what it says, then he will have the power, and with it the responsibility too, to tell it or not to tell it, as his conscience directs. As long as he has not read it, he can use his ability to read it or not read it as an additional weapon.

That what she has predicted for both Electors will infallibly come to pass is guaranteed when "the pledge for the truth of everything she said" (E172; G93) is improbably fulfilled. The roebuck does come to meet them in the marketplace, just as she said it would, even though the Elector of Brandenburg has the deer slaughtered for the table to prevent the fulfillment of the prediction. A huge butcher's dog takes the carcass from the kitchen and drops it at their feet. As the Elector of Saxony says, in a sentence that recalls the earlier lightning bolt: "The lightning that plummets from a winter's sky is no more devastating than this sight was to me" (E173; G93).

Later on, it just happens, by an exceedingly unlikely coincidence, that the Elector of Saxony encounters Kohlhaas as the latter is being taken in chains to be tried before the High Court at Berlin. Until then he has not known the identity of the man to whom the gypsy woman gave the paper, nor has he been able to find him. The Elector suffers a stroke when Kohlhaas explains to him how he got the paper he keeps in a lead capsule around his neck. The Elector becomes obsessed by his awareness that Kohlhaas has the paper that will tell him his future. Tormented by a desire to know what that future is, he tries every available expedient to get the paper from him. He promises Kohlhaas freedom and full pardon, tries to get his execution postponed, all to no avail.

Most improbably of all, the Elector's Chamberlain just happens to choose the actual gypsy woman (who just happens to look marvelously like Kohlhaas's dead wife and to have the same name) when he takes an old woman from the streets at random to impersonate the real fortune-teller and persuade Kohlhaas to release the paper. Apropos of this event the narrator utters the words I have taken as an epigraph for this paper: "probability is not always on the side of truth" (E175–76; G96). Kleist justifies this event by a solemn appeal to history, but the event in question, we know, is fictitious: "something had happened here which we must perforce record but which those who may wish to question are perfectly free to do" (E176; G96). "I cannot help it," Kleist in effect says; "this is the way it happened." This is like Luther's "Ich kann nicht anders." But this is *not* the way it happened. The apparent appeal from Aristotelian laws of probability in mimesis to the higher authority of what actually happened in history is rather an appeal from Aristotelian poetics to a new Kleistian poetics based on improbable but veracious contingency.

The gypsy woman betrays her charge from the Chamberlain and tells Kohlhaas to keep the paper. On the day of his execution she sends a message warning him that the Elector intends to dig up his body after he is executed in order to get the paper. Kohlhaas retaliates, just before he is beheaded, by looking the Elector in the eye, unsealing the paper, reading it through, and then swallowing it. The Elector promptly falls down unconscious in a fit. The story ends with the report that the Elector of Saxony returns to Dresden "shattered in body and soul," while Kohlhaas's children are made knights, and his descendants flourish. He is universally respected by the people for his respect for a law that is above all positive, institutionalized laws. To that law he alone has access, through his *Rechtgefühl*.[10] As for the fulfillment of the gypsy woman's prophecy, "what happened subsequently," says the narrator in his laconic way, "must be sought in history" [*in der Geschichte nachlesen muß* (literally, "must be read after in history")] (E183; G103).[11] The gypsy woman's political and personal prophecy echoes the oracle of Apollo that tells Laius his son will kill him. It echoes also the witches' prophecy in *Macbeth*. To hear such predictions, in literature if not in life, is to know that, however improbable they are, they will inevitably come to pass, down to the last detail.

～

What is the reader to make of this episode? Why did Kleist not tell the reader what was the fulfillment of the prophecy? Why did he add just this fiction to his historical sources? The added episode of the gypsy fortune-teller is a fiction smuggled into history that radically changes the meaning of that history. It is an admirable allegory of the relation to history of both Michael Kohlhaas and "Michael Kohlhaas," both the man and the story. The addition signals the transformation of history into literature, that is, into a collocation of words that has its own power, at the later date when it is written, published, and read, to intervene performatively into history. By "literature" here I mean any retelling, since even the driest after-the-fact chronicle will have "literary" or rhetorical elements that make it effect something in its own time and later on, whenever it is read.

Kohlhaas's setting up of a new world government in order to get justice over an affair of two horses is like Kleist's writing of this strange story. Each is an abrupt interruption of the course of history, political history in the one case, literary history in the other, and, by way of literary history, in however small a way, political, ethical, and social history. Kohlhaas would initiate a new state law. The story would initiate new laws of narrative probability and truth, and implicitly, by way of that, new codes for everything in society that depends on narrative, for example, the pleading of cases before the law.

"Michael Kohlhaas" is without recognized power or authority. It is not a sacred text, nor even a work as central to the established canon of Western literature as are, say, works by Goethe and Schiller. "Michael Kohlhaas" is no more than one relatively obscure item in the swarm of works written during the period of German Romanticism. Nevertheless, "Michael Kohlhaas" is a work that works. It performs.

The story tells the reader the likely outcome of such a performative fiat. Kohlhaas's revolutionary gesture is quashed. He is executed. The preexisting law closes around him. He leaves scarcely a ripple on the surface of European history. He is better known through Kleist's fictitious story about him than through any conspicuous effect he has on the course of history. The episode of the fortune-telling paper, however, informs the reader that Kohlhaas is the bearer of history. He carries the future within himself and will have a decisive effect on it. But that future remains unknown until it happens. Only Kohlhaas reads the paper. He carries its secrets to the grave. The separation of his head, which knows the secret future, from his body, which incarnates the script on which the future is written, expresses with savage irony the separation between doing and knowing. The future Kohlhaas carries in himself remains unreadable, impossible to codify or to institutionalize. What will happen will happen. On the fated day the last member of the Elector's family will be deposed, his throne seized by force of arms. Kohlhaas, like the avenging Archangel Michael, will have helped bring this about by deflecting the course history would otherwise have taken.

In the same way, Kleist's story also posits a new law, but this law is also unreadable in the sense that it resists theory. The effect of reading the story cannot be rationally predicted. The story cannot be satisfactorily assimilated into the institution of literary study or study of the social effects of literature. Insofar as the story is explained, rationalized, theorized, accommodated into the general enterprise of accounting for literature, its own inaugural, heterogeneous law is obliterated, forgotten. That law, nevertheless, goes on working more or less secretly every time the story is read, just as Kohlhaas's revolutionary law-making power vanishes when he is executed and yet goes on working from "beyond the grave" in the fulfillment of the gypsy woman's prophecy, in the example of an exigent sense of justice he has left behind, and even in the flourishing of his progeny.

"Michael Kohlhaas" does what it tells. It establishes the law of the absence, unavailability, or failure of the law. In it an affront to the law is repaired by a repetition of an affront to justice. The same thing may be said of the performative effect of the story itself. Insofar as it fails to account for the events it tells—in the sense of making them reasonable, telling them justly, "justifying" them, making them square, as when we speak of a "justified margin"—it is a performative that does not perform. Or what it does is to bring to light the failure of narrative to serve as the handmaiden of the law by making the grounds of just law perspicuous. The story enunciates the law that forbids direct access to the law in the name of which all particular laws are promulgated and justified.

Like Michael Kohlhaas, literature lays down the law. That new law is socially and historically effective, but always in unforeseen, unpredictable ways. Such effects occur whenever "Michael Kohlhaas" is arraigned before the bar of justice each reader carries in his or her own breast. The story's effects are always unreadable in the story. In order to find out the performative effect of literature in history, we must read that effect afterwards in history itself.

The legislative power of a literary work cannot be read in the work itself. Nevertheless, it commands and institutes. It brings something "other" into history, even in essays, like this one, that attempt to explain the work rationally. The law-making power of the work carries over even into commentary that tries to explain it. Though it is impossible to tell whether the story speaks with the authority of the law above all laws or whether it just happens, as a natural fact, it makes law and enforces it, like a Kleistian lightning bolt.

§ 4 Sam Weller's Valentine: Dickens

On the thirteenth of February, 1831, the day before the great trial of *Bardell v. Pickwick*, Sam Weller strolls through "a variety of bye streets and courts" (536)[1] in East London. He makes his leisurely way from the George and Vulture Hotel, George Yard, Lombard Street, toward the Blue Boar in Leadenhall Market to meet his father. Dickens's exact naming of streets and hotels is characteristic of his topographical circumstantiality. He assumes his readers will have a detailed map of London in their minds and will be able to follow Sam's progress. Sam is streetwise. Dickens assumes his readers will be streetwise, too. *Pickwick Papers* as a whole depends on the reader's detailed foreknowledge not only of London's streets and buildings but also of southern England's roads, towns, and cities. It is a good example of the way many novels assume a shared topographical inner space in the community of their readers. Many meanings are elliptically conveyed just through toponymy. If you do not know what sort of place the Blue Boar in Leadenhall Market is, and how it is different from the George and Vulture in Lombard Street, an important dimension of sociological and personal meaning in this chapter will be lost on you. The complex array of class and gender distinctions—manners, customs, laws, ways of eating and living—are in *Pickwick Papers* embedded in a topography dominated by human constructive activity. Dickens's characters are surrounded and circumscribed by roads, buildings, bridges, not to speak of public and private interiors—all that men and women have built to incarnate their ways of living. These are already in place as a presupposition of the action.

As Sam saunters toward the Blue Boar in Leadenhall Market, he pauses "before a small stationer's and print-seller's window" (ibid.). Thereupon he smites his right leg "with great vehemence" and exclaims "with energy": "If it hadn't been for this, I should ha' forgot all about it, till it was too late!" Dickens describes what Sam sees in the stationer's window as follows:

> The particular picture on which Sam Weller's eyes were fixed, as he said this, was a highly coloured representation of a couple of human hearts skewered together with an arrow, cooking before a cheerful fire, while a male and female cannibal in modern attire: the gentleman being clad in a blue coat and white trousers, and the lady in a deep red pelisse with a parasol of the same: were approaching the meal with hungry eyes, up a serpentine gravel path leading thereunto. A decidedly indelicate young gentleman, in a pair of wings and nothing else, was depicted as superintending the cooking; a representation of the spire of the church in Langham Place, London, appeared in the distance; and the whole formed a "valentine," of which, as a written inscription in the window testified, there was a large assortment within, which the shopkeeper pledged himself to dispose of, to his countrymen generally, at the reduced rate of one and sixpence each. (536–37)

What can be said about this admirably circumstantial description? The passage raises a cascade of questions. Was a valentine, then or now, protected by patent or by copyright? Are valentines printed and published or are they manufactured and sold? Is a valentine a speech act, a performative use of language? If so, exactly what kind of performative is it? Can a picture be a performative? If so, what would make a picture performative as opposed to merely constative, that is, a picture of something, say, the spire of Nash's All Souls' Church, built in 1822–24 in Langham Place at the top of Regent Street? That church is pictured in Dickens's valentine. All Souls' was built just a few years before the action of *Pickwick Papers,* so it would have been a spanking new church in 1831. Is the act of publication, for example, the publication of *Pickwick Papers* by Chapman and Hall, a speech act? If so, of what sort? Why does Dickens have Sam Weller sign the handmade valentine he writes to Mary the housemaid with Pickwick's name: "Your love-sick / Pickwick"? Can a valentine be a legitimate marriage proposal? To put this another way, can a valentine be a marriage promise that might lead to a breach of promise suit if the promise is not kept? What kind of performative is a promise to marry? Does one interpret a breach of promise as another form of speech act? If a promise is a performative, does it take another performative to break that promise? Is it possible that "Chops and Tomata sauce" and "Don't trouble yourself about the warming-pan" (562–63) really do constitute a marriage promise on Pickwick's part? How could one be sure they do not? Or, to put this another way, can one make a promise without intending to do so, for example, by sending a valentine signed with someone else's name or by sending a valentine as a friendly courtesy or on a whim, taking the "privilege of the day"? Or are valentines exempt from being taken seriously, just as a man cannot be arrested for debt if he walks out of his house on Sunday, whereas on any other day of the week he would be fair game for the bailiff? Could one commit oneself by chance to a lifetime marriage partner, without intending to do so, and yet by a contract that is no less binding for being unintentional? Is commitment to a marriage partner ever anything but aleatory, a matter of chance or the drawing of lots? Does intention, to put this another way, have anything to do with the efficacy of a performative utterance? Might thinking it does be no more than another version of the "intentional fallacy," in this case the fallacious assumption not that intention controls meaning, but that it controls what speech acts do?

What, finally, is the meaning of Sam's father's objection to poetry in the scene in which he "delivers some Critical Sentiments respecting Literary Composition," as the chapter title puts it? Tony Weller comments on the style of Sam's valentine letter, putting in question anything that even "werges on the poetical" (542). Phiz's

Fig. 3. "The Valentine," by Phiz (Hablot K. Browne). Etching for chapter 33 of *Pickwick Papers* (1837). Reproduced from a copy owned by Robert W. Newsom, with his kind permission.

illustration shows this scene (fig. 3). Is Tony Weller against poetry because it is performatively efficacious and therefore might get Sam entangled into marriage? Or is it just the opposite? Is his objection to poetry that it makes the language it contaminates performatively ineffective, an infelicitous speech act? J. L. Austin, in *How to Do Things with Words*, firmly excluded poetry from the realm of efficacious speech acts. For a speech act to be effective, he sternly asserted, "I must not be joking, for example, nor writing a poem."[2] Is *Pickwick Papers* as a whole in poetry or in prose? Is this novel, consequently, whatever the answer to that question may be, a felicitous performative, a way of doing something with words? What difference would a "yes" to that question make to our reading of *Pickwick Papers*?

A swarm of such questions rises in the mind of a contemplative reader confronting the episode of Sam Weller's valentine. Now to try to answer them.

～

Valentines have always been associated with what stands on the border between the accidental and the deliberate in courtship and marriage. St. Valentine was beheaded, according to his legend, on February 14, 270 A.D., for aiding Christian martyrs persecuted under Claudius II. His final offense was to use the occasion of his interrogation by the Emperor to try to convert Claudius rather than to save his own life by agreeing to abjure Christianity. Part of St. Valentine's legend asserts that he became friends with the blind daughter of his jailer, cured her blindness, and wrote her a letter on the eve of his execution. He signed the letter "From your Valentine," thereby sending the first valentine. All subsequent valentines, it might be said, are, like Sam's valentine to Mary, signed with another's name, since they are sent in the name of St. Valentine. Sam Weller's valentine says, "Except of me Mary my dear as your valentine" (542).

Valentine's Day appears to be a Christianization of the Roman Lupercalia, a fertility festival celebrated in February, and of a Roman festival celebrated on February 14 in honor of Juno. In the latter, young men drew by lot the names of the young women who would be their partners for the day. A millennium and a half later, this custom of drawing by lot the name of a potential marriage partner was still carried on in England, then introduced into America, where it is reflected in the rhetoric of eighteenth-century handmade valentines. One verse, for example, given by Ruth Webb Lee in her history of valentines, reads: "Our lots we cast and, thus I drew, / Kind fortune says it must be you."[3] On the other hand, some valentine verses make the choice deliberate: "I choose you from among the rest / The reason was I loved you best" (Lee,

16). Another example combines these two sentiments in sequence: "Lots was cast and one i drew . . . kind fortune is it must be you . . . I choose you out amongst the rest . . . It was becaus I love you best" (Lee, 19). The verses are clearly as formulaic as our "Roses are red; violets are blue." A version of the latter already appears in these early valentines: "The rose is red the violet blue / Lilies are fair and so are you" (Lee, 16). Bathsheba, in Thomas Hardy's *Far from the Madding Crowd*, writes at her servant Liddy's suggestion another version of these verses: "The rose is red, / The violet blue, / Carnation's sweet, / And so are you."[4] Though already in the eighteenth century there were "Valentine Writers," small books of verses to be copied in the making of handmade valentines, the basic verses were undoubtedly part of an oral tradition circulating among young people, just as such rhymes still do today. Some of these early valentines are explicitly marriage proposals: "My only wish is to make you happy and to be united with you in marriage" (this translated from a Pennsylvania Dutch valentine in German, dated about 1814, Lee, 22). The tradition of using a valentine as a proposal of marriage, serious or feigned, is registered in Bathsheba's disastrous valentine to Farmer Boldwood, in *Far from the Madding Crowd*, with its randomly chosen seal: "Marry Me."

The history of valentines may be briefly told. The earliest valentines remaining, from the late Middle Ages and Renaissance, were letters. Eighteenth- and early-nineteenth-century valentines in England and America were still handmade, but often incorporated elaborate cutout or pinprick lace designs, colored pictures, and handwritten verses. Commercial valentines began to be made in the early nineteenth century, first from hand-colored copperplate engravings. Then, about the time Dickens was writing *Pickwick Papers*, the method of manufacture shifted from engravings to hand-colored lithographs (fig. 4). Both Robert and George Cruikshank produced valentines in the period just prior to the publication of *Pickwick Papers*. The time between 1840 and 1860 was the high point of elaborate lace-paper valentines, embossed and perforated, manufactured by such stationers as Mansell, Kershaw, and Dobbs in England and in America through home factory assembly-line production by, among others, an enterprising young woman in Worcester, Massachusetts, named Esther Howland, active in the mid-nineteenth century (figs. 5, 6, 7). Of so-called comic valentines, a whole genre in themselves, little needs to be said here, except that the valentine Sam sees in the stationer's window is not a comic valentine. They were crudely satirical and usually did not employ the standard valentine iconography. The story thereafter is of a gradual cheapening until we reach the mass-produced valentines of today, though Kate Greenaway produced in the 1870's and 1880's some admirable valentine cards. Esther Howland's craftsperson girls making each valentine by hand were replaced in the late nineteenth century in Worcester by George C. Whitney & Company. Whitney bought her and other smaller companies out and set up a large valentine factory with "the best possible machinery . . . for embossing and making paper lace . . . giant double-cylinder presses together with all the other necessary appurtenances" (Lee, 71–72).

Several of the valentines in my illustrations bear some resemblance to the one Sam Weller sees in the stationer's window. Ruth Webb Lee reproduces, though not in color, a lithographed valentine made of paper watermarked "J. Whatman, Turkey Mill, 1842" in which, as she tells us, "the gentleman in the scene wears a dark blue coat and his prospective bride is quite dashing in a red coat lavishly trimmed with ermine" (Lee, 135). Those colors seem to have been conventional. Frank Staff reproduces a handmade valentine of 1803 with a stipple engraving in which the lover's coat is blue, the girl's skirt red.[5] The Whatman valentine also has a church in the distance, as in the valentine Dickens describes. I have not found one with the motif of the skewered and cooking hearts. The cooking hearts may be Dickens's satirical invention, though two hearts skewered by an arrow and naked cupids were of course essential parts of the traditional iconography of valentines, as was the idea that on Valentine's Day Cupid set lovers' hearts afire with desire. Dickens's valentine is a reification of this traditional trope. The church in the background was also part of the conventional iconography of valentines. It represented the goal of matrimony,

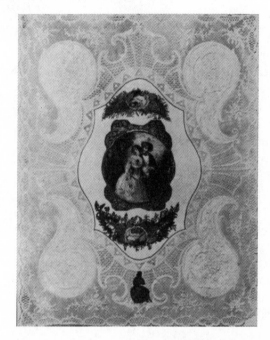

Fig. 4. English valentine, ca. 1825–35. (From William Morton Janse, *The History of Valentines* [Chatham, Mass.: William M. Janse, 1950], 14.)

Fig. 5. Valentine, by T. H. Burke of 12 Bull Head Court, Newgate, ca. 1840. (From Ruth Webb Lee, *A History of Valentines* [New York: Studio Publications, Inc., in cooperation with T. Y. Crowell, 1952], 176.)

Fig. 6. Valentine, by Joseph Mansell, Fancy Stationer, of 35 Red Lion Square, London, with his famous perforated and gilded lace border, ca. 1850. (From Lee, *A History of Valentines,* following 105.) Dickens's *All the Year Round* for February 20, 1864, has an article entitled "Cupid's Manufactory" describing in great detail Mansell's factory and the procedures used in making lace for valentines.

Fig. 7. Quarto size valentine, by Dobbs, Bailey & Co., 8 New Bridge Street, London, ca. 1850. This fancy-paper manufacturer and stationer had opened business in 1803, but was still going strong in the mid-Victorian period. (From Frank Staff, *The Valentine & Its Origins* [New York: Frederick A. Praeger, 1969), 76. Reprinted with permission of Greenwood Publishing Group, Inc., Westport, CT. © 1969, in England, by Frank Staff. World rights granted by the Lutterworth Press, Cambridge.

Fig. 8. Valentine, inspired by Halley's Comet in 1835. Originally a copperplate engraving, but later reprints are lithographs. Warshaw Collection of Business Americana, Archives Center, NMAH, Smithsonian Institution. Reproduced by permission.

the telos of valentine courtship. Figure 8 is the valentine nearest to the one Dickens describes I have found.

~

Answers to some of my initial questions about valentines may be approached by way of a more exact description of them. An enormous number and variety of valentines were produced, particularly as the industrial revolution proceeded. The making and selling of valentines became a big business. Valentines in England in 1863 cost anything from a penny to seven shillings sixpence, though it was possible to pay up to twenty-five pounds for a single valentine (Staff, 138–39). American prices for valentines in 1874 went from five cents to three dollars, a lot of cash in those days (Staff, 140).

Some hack writers appear to have eked out a living producing valentine verses. An advertisement in the *Boston Transcript* of February 9, 1847, for English valentines (cited by Ruth Webb Lee) gives some idea of their variety:

ENGLISH VALENTINES. PER 'HIBERNIA.'

A. S. Jordan, No. 2 Milk Street, respectfully informs his friends that he has just received by the above steamer, the greatest assortment of Valentines to be found in Cupid's regions, among which may be found the following kinds: Comic, Sentimental, Lovesick, Acrostic, Funny, Burlesque, Curious, Characteristic, Humorous, Beautiful, Heart-struck, Witty, Arabesque, Courting, Serio-Comical, Bewitching, Poetical, Heart-rending, Love-encouraging, Trifling, Caricature, Heart-piercing, Serio-tragical, Laughable, Silly, Spiteful, Original, Enlivening, Heart-aching, Despairing, Raving-mad, Heart-killing, High-flown, Lampooning, Romantic, Look-out, Proposal, Espousal, Matrimonial, Hen-Pecking, Suicidal, and many other varieties. Wholesale buyers would do well to call before purchasing elsewhere, as the selection has been made by one of the first London houses engaged in that particular business. (Lee, 90)

This is an odd list, though the word "Lovesick," used in Sam Weller's valentine, appears in it. The list is almost as miscellaneous as the contents of Mrs. Jellyby's closet in *Bleak House*. One wonders if all these different kinds were kept in separate, labeled bins. Little, if any, order appears in the sequence, though if I only knew what a "Look-out Valentine" might be, I would claim to see a sad story in the final sequence that goes from Romantic to Look-out to Proposal to Espousal to Matrimonial to Hen-Pecking to Suicidal. That's not much of an advertisement! A clear warning message is given by the sequence: "Don't send or receive a Romantic Valentine! It will lead you step by step through matrimony to suicide." Farmer Boldwood, in *Far from the Madding Crowd*, finds out something like this to his sorrow. It is just what Tony Weller fears for Sam, and just what his own henpecked state forewarns. *Pickwick Papers*, like all great comic masterpieces, derives its greatest comic force from the way it displaces the tragic themes of human mortality and unassuageable desire. I shall return to this. The "Wellerisms" in *Pickwick* are a case in point, as I shall show.

Most, though not all, valentines were multimedia productions. They combined words, pictures, and a purely decorative graphic aspect, such as the elaborate borders of lace and embossing popular in the mid-nineteenth century. Some valentines were mechanical contrivances that pulled out, opened up, stood up, or could be moved in one way or another. What is the meaning of the convention of the lace border to a valentine, a border around a central picture or verse often on a lower layer of superimposed sheets? Are these lace borders a covert allusion to the lace bordering feminine apparel and therefore a promise of *jouissance* when the top layer is lifted or when the looker penetrates to the picture or poem behind?

Valentines, in any case, began as a form of handmade folk art with elaborate conventions. This folk art was gradually replaced by what Walter Benjamin in the title of a celebrated essay calls "mechanical reproducibility" (*technischen Reproduzierbarkeit*). Even in the age of reproducibility, however, handmade valentines consisting only of words or with hand-drawn pictures, still rather like the earliest surviving ones from the late Middle Ages and Renaissance, continued to be written and sent. An example is Sam Weller's valentine. Sam does not buy the cannibal valentine in the stationer's window. He laboriously writes his own valentine to Mary.

Like other multimedia productions then and now, commercially produced valentines were and are something of a challenge to the laws of copyright and patent. Dickens took a deep interest in copyright law. He mounted a vigorous campaign to get the United States to recognize international copyright and to stop pirating his books. The original edition of *Pickwick Papers* (1837) was dedicated to "Mr Serjeant Talfourd, M.P.," that is, to Dickens's friend Sir Thomas Noon Talfourd (1795–1854). Talfourd had in May 1837 introduced in Parliament his Copyright Bill. The bill finally became law in 1842. This law increased the copyright period to forty-two years or seven years after the author's death, whichever was longer. Dickens's dedication speaks with feeling of Talfourd's great service to literature.

Like computer hardware and software today, a valentine could be protected partly by patent, partly by copyright. Just as a new process for making computer hardware can be patented, while software programs are protected by copyright and their titles are registered as trademarks, such as the Apple logo , so the verses on a valentine could be protected by copyright, while the sometimes elaborate procedures used to manufacture them, for example, to make so-called "mechanical valentines," could be protected by patent. Ruth Webb Lee mentions certain valentines produced in New York in the mid-nineteenth century as being identifiable by the embossing along the fold in the center: "Lang's Pat. process. Berlin & Jones, Mfrs. N.Y."

Historians of valentines sometimes speak of them as "manufactured," but most often their makers are called "publishers." Valentines belong to the history of Victorian publishing and yet do not quite fit within it. They were both published and manufactured. They were able therefore to be protected both by copyright and by patent. Valentines show that copyright law, even at its inception in its modern form, was mined with pitfalls and inconsistencies. That law had to be used to protect forms of language that do not easily fit within the ideology of single, identifiable authorship and property ownership. It is easy to see how copyright laws are jeopardized today when the concept of the "author" has been put in question and when there has been a return to various forms of collaborative or anonymous composition, for example, interactive computer texts or collaborative work by disempowered minorities. But already in the nineteenth century copyright laws were not quite appropriate for forms of popular art like valentines.

Copyright does not, of course, prohibit the making of copies. It prohibits the making of copies without suitable payment to the owner of the copyright. What can be copyrighted is by definition capable of being copied, word for word. If it could not be copied there would be no need to copyright it. An idea may not be copyrighted, only a specific form of words or a typographical layout. Copyright protects a possible exact iteration. This would seem to exclude what can be protected by copyright from the realm of performatives, since a performative is a unique, one time only, unrepeatable, doing of things with words. I am married only once to this particular person on this particular occasion, even though I may be remarried on a later performative occasion. A ship is christened once and for all, even though it may be rechristened. But as Jacques Derrida has argued, however unique a speech act occasion may be, it is performed by an assemblage of words, which draw their efficacy from their iterability.[6] Examples include the words of the Christian marriage ceremony: "I pronounce you man and wife"; or the traditional words naming a ship, "I christen thee the *Queen Mary*"; or the words of a promise, for example, a mortgage contract, a promise to marry, or an invitation to marry, like Bathsheba's "Marry me." Another example is a valentine: "Roses are red; violets are blue," and so on. The peculiarity of all these sorts of performatives is that they must be both unique and repeatable. In order to have meaning at all, words must be iterable and at least implicitly already an iteration. There is no first and only time for words. Even the first time is already implicitly a repetition. On the other hand, a performative enters a situation at one particular time and place to change those once and for all. It uses a repetition to do the unique. This means that a combination of words and pictures capable of being used performatively, for example, a valentine, might be protected by copyright. Derrida, in *Limited Inc*, associates performatives with the question of copyright in his ridicule of Searle's attempt to control dissemination and assert his ownership of his essay by stamping "Copyright © 1977 by John R. Searle" on the first page, above the title.[7]

I have included valentines along with the words of the marriage and christening ceremonies among examples of performatives. It is easy to see how they fit. As the examples given from the texts of early American handmade valentines show, even a handmade valentine written on a particular occasion by one person who intended to send it to another specified person characteristically employed formulaic phrases for a unique purpose. Even Sam Weller's valentine, an idiosyncratic document if ever there was one, contains echoes of traditional valentine formulas: "the first and only time I see you, your likeness was took on my hart"; "Except of me Mary my dear as your valentine" (542). Commercial valentines are even more evidently the product of an iteration. A given one may be produced in thousands of copies. Each one is made up of an arrangement of standardized parts: pictures, verses, and decorative borders. Nothing could be more anonymous and impersonal than a commercial valentine. Like a blank check or a standardized will, a commercial valentine has performative force only when the blanks are filled in, the valentine signed and addressed to a particular person in a particular place: "To Mary, Housemaid, at Mr Nupkin's Mayor's, Ipswich, Suffolk." Then, as with Bathsheba's valentine or Sam's, it may have performative force and make something happen. Examples are the unintentional devastation of Farmer Boldwood's life that follows from Bathsheba's whim, or the implicit commitment that, in the wake of Sam's valentine, leads in the end to happy marriage.

～

Why then, if a valentine, like a check, is only validated, activated, charged with performative efficacy when it is signed, does Sam sign his valentine with Pickwick's name and why does he do so in a rhyming verse? The signature verse is given at the end of a discussion with his father about the stylistic proprieties of valentine signatures. To sign with a fictitious name is something like writing poetry, a topic to which I shall return:

> "Ain't you a goin' to sign it?" [asks Sam's father.]
> "That's the difficulty," said Sam; "I don't know what *to* sign it."
> "Sign it, Veller," said the oldest surviving proprietor of that name.
> "Won't do," said Sam; "never sign a walentine with your own name."
> "Sign it 'Pickwick,' then," said Mr Weller; "it's a werry good name, and a easy one to spell."
> "The wery thing," said Sam, "I *could* end with a werse; what do you think?"
> "I don't like it, Sam," rejoined Mr Weller. . . .
> But Sam was not to be dissuaded from the poetical idea that had occurred to him, so he signed the letter,
>
> "Your love-sick
Pickwick." (543)

No doubt the joke lies partly in the analogy drawn between Samuel Weller and Samuel Pickwick. Pickwick's trial for breach of promise is about to commence the next day. He can ironically be taken as a model for ardent lovers. Pickwick is about to be convicted of breach of promise on the basis of some words ("Chops and Tomata sauce") that Mrs. Bardell's lawyers convince the jury are a marriage proposal. Perhaps this is because tomatoes were once thought to be an aphrodisiac. For a man to say "Chops and Tomata sauce" to a woman is an implicit proposition. At least that is what the infamous Dodson and Fogg persuade the jury to believe. Sam's valentine constitutes another fictitious proposal of marriage by Pickwick and may get him involved in another breach of promise suit.

From the perspective of Sam's own intentions, what is the meaning of the principle he enunciates? "Never sign a walentine with your own name." That may be for two contradictory reasons. When Sam tells his father that he has written a valentine, Mr. Weller, who is unhappily married to a "perwerse, and unpleasant"

(538) religious fanatic, says it'll be a trial "to see you married, Sammy—to see you a dilluded wictim, and thinkin' in your innocence that it's all wery capital." To which Sam disingenuously replies, "Nonsense . . . . I ain't a goin' to get married, don't you fret yourself about that" (539). If he signs his valentine with a fictitious name, it will be no more efficacious than if I were to sign a check with someone else's name. Only the one who owns the name can use it to do something with words. Signing a valentine with someone else's name is a way to send the valentine and yet protect oneself from the consequences of doing so. Signing Pickwick's name turns the valentine into a forgery and so into an infelicitous speech act.

On the other hand, Sam's principle ("Never sign a valentine with your own name") sounds as if it might be meant to apply to serious as well as to unserious valentines. Many a forgery has functioned as an efficacious performative. It may be that the act of making a declaration of love.so changes the person who makes it that he becomes another person, in this case a great lover like Pickwick, though Casanova, Romeo, or Don Giovanni might have done as well. In order to make the valentine work, Sam has to borrow the name of someone who has prowess in lovemaking, just as, it may be, he has to write it in a style that "werges on the poetical," in spite of his father's warnings (542).

The borrowing on Valentine's Day of a Roman custom of drawing lots for a mate, as well as the similar motif in eighteenth-century American valentines I have cited, shows the contradictory mixture of free choice and accident or fate in the valentine tradition. This might be seen as a ritual institutionalization of the actual circumstances in which most marriages in our tradition are made. For us both the woman and the man are presumed to be free to choose, though of course all sorts of social constraints "circumscribe" that choice, to borrow a word from Sam Weller's valentine.[8] Most marriage "choices" probably happen largely by accident. A young woman happens to fall in a man's way or a young man in a woman's way, one thing leads to another, and before they know it they are married.

A comic example of that is the way Tony Weller married his second wife. He was going to Doctor's Commons to pick up his inheritance of four hundred pounds from his deceased first wife when he was nabbed by a lawyer's tout. As Sam says, such people "puts things into old gen'lm'n's heads as they never dreamed of" (199). The next thing Tony Weller knew, he was filling out a marriage license and putting in Susan Clarke's name, though he had had until that moment no intention of marrying her: "She'll have me, if I ask, I des-say—I never said nothing to her, but she'll have me, I know" (200).

The selection of a mate, even though it may always happen in some such way, is so decisive a moment in an individual's life that one would like to put the blame somewhere else. One would like to make the alliance seem grounded and justified, not the result either of a random encounter or of a free and ungrounded choice. The traditions of Valentine's Day help us to do that by combining, against logic, fate and free will. The alogic, however, is hidden because "that's the way you do it on Valentine's Day."

A valentine reveals an obscure fate. On the one hand, "Our lots we cast and, thus I drew, / Kind fortune says it must be you." On the other, Valentine's Day gives the lover license to express his free choice. It allows him to use a traditional formula to express his own particular love: "I choose you from among the rest / The reason was I loved you best." As Sam Weller puts this: "So I take the privilidge of the day, Mary, my dear . . . to tell you that the first and only time I see you, your likeness was took on my hart" (542). Sam takes advantage of the day to let Mary know that his accidental encounter with her was fateful for his life, just as his writing of the valentine was the result of an accidental seeing of the valentine in the stationer's window. That reminded him tomorrow was St. Valentine's Day: "If it hadn't been for this, I should ha' forgot all about it" (536).

The figure Sam uses to describe how Mary's image was inscribed in his heart repeats the combination of fate and free will. "Your likeness," says Sam, "was took on my hart in much quicker time and brighter colours than ever a likeness was took by the profeel machine (which p'raps you may have heerd on Mary my dear) altho it *does* finish a portrait and put the frame and glass on complete, with a hook at the end to hang it up by, and all in two minutes and a quarter" (542). As Tony Weller says, "I am afeered that werges on the poetical, Sammy" (542). The profile machine was a mechanical ancestor of photography. One end of an armature followed the contours of someone's face, while a pencil attached to the other traced those contours on paper. How could Sam help falling in love with Mary? Her features were duplicated exactly on his heart, in an automatic, machinelike process over which his will had no control, though of course the sitter for a profile must be willing to sit still while the machine does its work. With modern photography even that complicity in one's dispossession is no longer necessary. The photograph is taken in the blink of an eye, in a "snapshot" that is as violent as a gunshot.

~

Bathsheba's valentine to Boldwood, in *Far from the Madding Crowd*, repeats in more somber colors this mixture of choice, accident, and the appeal to a justifying fate in order to displace responsibility. The chapter of Bathsheba's valentine is entitled "Sortes Sanctorum—the Valentine." Among the traditions of Valentine's Day was the notion that the first person you happened to see on that day would be the one you would marry. Bathsheba uses another traditional way to identify a future marriage partner. This is the custom of divination by Sacred Scripture. "Sortes sanctorum" meant putting a big house key on a Bible open at Ruth I:16, tying the Bible shut, suspending it by the protruding ends of the key, repeating the verse from Ruth, fixing one's mind on the potential mate, and waiting to see if the Bible moved: "And Ruth said, Entreat me not to leave thee, or to return from following after thee: for whither thou goest, I will go: and where thou lodgest, I will lodge: thy people shall be my people, and thy God my God." Bathsheba thinks of Boldwood: "The verse was repeated; the book turned around; Bathsheba blushed guiltily" (77). This prophecy seems to justify the whim of sending to Boldwood the valentine that was bought for a child, "little Teddy Coggan." Bathsheba's valentine is "a gorgeously illuminated and embossed design in post-octavo, which had been bought on the previous market-day at the chief stationer's in Casterbridge" (75). As for the seal, the "pert injunction" (80) "Marry Me" was affixed by accident, though Bathsheba ratifies the accident by sending the valentine: "Here's one [seal] with a motto—I remember it is some funny one, but can't read it. We'll try this, and if it doesn't do we'll have another" (79).

Like Dickens, though in a way that is characteristic of himself, Hardy makes a scrupulously exact notation of the way such an event transgresses the borders separating accident, choice, and fate. The event arises from an inextricable mixture of the three that defies decisive interpretation or the allocation of responsibility: "So very idly and unreflectingly was this deed done. Of love as a spectacle Bathsheba had a fair knowledge; but of love subjectively she knew nothing" (79). Poor Farmer Boldwood takes the idle valentine seriously and is gradually driven by unassuaged desire for Bathsheba to madness, to the murder of Sergeant Troy, and to his own indefinite imprisonment for homicide while insane.

This combination of the fortuitous and determined in valentines would seem inconsistent with the freely chosen enactment of an institutionalized ritual presumed in the standard analysis of performative speech acts. All performatives presuppose the freely willing and choosing "I," self-consistent through time. Speech act theory belongs to the post-Cartesian era of the assumption that subjectivity is an a priori given. The ego is the one thing that cannot be put in question. It survives all skeptical suspension of belief. The paradigmatic examples of performative utterances always involve the self-conscious subject uttering a form of words that makes something happen: "I promise"; "I pronounce you man and wife"; "I christen thee the *Abraham Lincoln*." Nevertheless, as Jacques Derrida and Paul de Man have in different ways persuasively demonstrated, performatives always exceed the intentions of their performers. They do not depend on intention for their efficacy. A performative always makes something happen, but it by no means always makes happen what the one who utters it intends or expects. The words work on their own, mechanically, impersonally, independently of any conscious, willing subjectivity, just as grammar does. A performative exceeds the firm and clear opposition between willed and accidental. It is the product of a machinelike power in the semantic and grammatical aspects of language that cannot be entirely controlled by intention or cognition.[9] Bathsheba did not mean to do Farmer Boldwood any harm. That did not keep much harm from befalling him as a result of that accidentally chosen "Marry Me." The phrase "marry me" is a special kind of performative, something like a bet, an excuse, or a promise, though not quite the same as any of these. To say "marry me" puts the one to whom it is said in a new situation, the situation of having either to accept or refuse the challenge. That Bathsheba does not intend the words to be taken seriously does not prevent them from working. As Hardy puts this, somewhat ponderously, apropos of Boldwood and Bathsheba, "It is foreign to a mystified condition of mind to realize of the mystifier that the processes of approving a course suggested by circumstance, and of striking out a course from inner impulse, would look the same in the result. The vast difference between starting a train of events, and directing into a particular groove a series already started, is rarely apparent to the person confounded by the issue" (80).

In the case of Pickwick's promise to marry Mrs. Bardell, the unwitting perpetrator of the performative, not its object, is confounded by the issue. Pickwick did not mean to propose to Mrs. Bardell when he wrote "Chops and Tomata sauce." The note gets him in deep trouble anyway, as does the fact that his remarks to Mrs. Bardell about his intention to hire Sam Weller were taken by her as a proposal of marriage. Sam goes to some lengths to keep his valentine from being something he must take responsibility for having written. He assures his father that "I ain't a goin' to get married." Nevertheless, the valentine leads to his marriage anyhow. Far from disqualifying valentines from being performative speech acts, the way they mix inadvertence with machinelike effectiveness matches similar features in all performatives. This helps confirm my hypothesis that valentines are indeed a species of performative.

∼

If so, what does this have to do with Tony Weller's abhorrence of poetry? Is Sam's valentine poetical or not? Would its being poetical

inhibit it from having performative efficacy? I have referred to
Austin's claim that in order for a performative to work, its utterer
must not, for example, be writing poetry. Tony Weller's objection
to poetry, so it seems, is not too different from Austin's. Both share
with Dickens himself a pleasant but dangerous gift for irony. A
little irony may even have crept across to contaminate my own
discourse. Who knows? It may in principle be impossible to know.
Irony is dangerous because, as de Man says, it is "the systematic
undoing . . . of understanding."[10] Sam's dialogue with his father, in
any case, is an admirably witty exchange of ironies. Each tries to
outdo the other in a kind of pingpong game of stroke and return,
with Dickens as ironic referee or referee of ironies supervising the
game.

Tony Weller approves of Sam's plainspeaking literalism in his
valentine: "you *are* a nice gal and nothin' but it" (541). For Sam, in
this sentence at least, a thing or person is what it is and nothing but
what it is. If so, metaphorical comparisons and displacements are
unveracious. The unique is not like anything else. As he says later
in his valentine: "there ain't nobody like you" (542). Poetry, according to Wellerian poetics, is against nature. Nobody who is not a
fraud talks poetry. An example of poetry is a poetic request for
money by a low public official such as a beadle, or, alternatively,
someone writing advertising copy for bootblacking or a quack
medicine. "Poetry's unnat'ral," says Tony Weller to his son; "no
man ever talked poetry 'cept a beadle on boxin' day, or Warren's
blackin', or Rowland's oil, or some o' them low fellows; never you
let your self down to talk poetry, my boy" (540). We know from
Oliver Twist what Dickens thought of beadles. On Boxing Day, the
day after Christmas, beadles went around to their parishioners
chanting a poem asking for a tip. Warren's Blacking Factory was, of
course, where Dickens worked as a child during the traumatic six
months he makes so much of in the autobiographical fragment
written at the time he was composing *David Copperfield*. Dickens's
job at Warren's was to tie on the bottles the papers that bore the
advertising. He had a good chance to see Warren's poetry close up.
Such poetry was a precocious example of the work of art in the age

of mechanical reproducibility. For Dickens as for Benjamin, poetry now is deprived of all aura and therefore meretricious. Nothing grounds its extravagant figurative transfers.

As Tony Weller's next assertion makes clear, poetry is a species of lie generated by metaphor: "Wot's the good o' callin' a young 'ooman a Wenus or a angel, Sammy?" he asks. "You might jist as well call her a griffin, or a unicorn, or a king's arms at once, which is werry well known to be a col-lection o' fabulous animals" (540–42). "Angel," it might be remembered, is just what Mr. Tupman calls Miss Wardle when he woos her (171). Poetry calls one thing by the name of another, transferring the properties of one thing to something else that does not really have them. An example is calling a young woman a Venus or an angel. Since such comparisons are not grounded in any empirical similarity, there is no way to control them or to distinguish proper from improper ones. Start calling a young woman a Venus or an angel, and you might as well call her more or less anything: a griffin, a king's arms, or whatever. Since these are fabulous animals, such a comparison would add the lie of their fictionality to the lie of the ungrounded comparison, making such poetry a double lie. The examples that come to Tony Weller's mind are all characteristic names of pubs, as are "Venus" and "Angel." In Tony Weller's fertile mind, calling a young woman by any of these names would be grotesquely unflattering, like comparing her to a public house.

Such lies, moreover, are the fathers of evil, as Tony's final pronouncement makes clear. If, according to Samuel Johnson, a man who would pun would pick a pocket, for Tony Weller a man who writes poetry is bound to be a criminal. He is certain to be a criminal of a particularly vicious kind. Tony's example is the Camberwell coachman who turned against his own profession and became a highwayman: "I never know'd a respectable coachman as wrote poetry, 'cept one, as made an affectin' copy o' werses the night before he wos hung for a highway robbery; and *he* wos only a Cambervell man, so even that's no rule" (543). Camberwell is across the Thames, almost another country. Who knows what those lawless people will do, perhaps even rob themselves? For a coachman to rob coaches is a species of self-robbery. In a similar way, the man who writes poetry or speaks poetry is defrauding his own language of power to work, to do something, to get you from here to there with something valuable you want transferred. On the other hand, to be a respectable coachman who does not write poetry is to work honestly to take people and things from one place to another. This is just what a happy performative does, for example, in the transfer of real estate or other property from one owner to another in a will or a deed.

If the logic of Tony Weller's poetic theory is carried to its implicit conclusion, the opposition is seen to be not so much between poetry and prose as between lying poetry and another use of language that hardly has a name. It might be called "truth-telling poetry." Such poetry is exemplified throughout *Pickwick Papers*. It is brought especially into the open in this scene. Truth-telling poetry might be defined as an exploitation of the figurative possibilities of language that calls attention to its own operation. Such reflexivity functions to demystify lying figures that may do much harm, such as calling a young woman a Venus or a Griffin. Sam's comparison of the impression Mary made on him to the profile machine certainly "werges on the poetical," by Tony Weller's definition. This metaphorical comparison, however, is grotesque and original enough, its hyperbole is so insisted on, that it works as a cleansing satire on the merely conventional comparisons Sam's father disdains.

～

The best way to understand the truth-telling poetry of Sam's valentine, of the entire episode, and of *Pickwick Papers* as a whole is through an interpretation of one of Dickens's great inventions. Or, rather, it was more probably a borrowing from the vigor of everyday working-class speech. I mean the "Wellerisms" that pervade the novel like a continuously renewed and endlessly variable joke. Two punctuate this episode, one uttered by Tony Weller, the other in Sam's valentine itself. When Tony fears that his son will be married, he says "it'll be a wery agonizin' trial to me at my time of life, but I'm pretty tough, that's vun consolation as the wery old turkey remarked wen the farmer said he wos afeerd he should be obliged to kill him for the London market" (539). In his valentine, Sam writes, in a sequence already quoted in part: "So I take the privilidge of the day, Mary, my dear—as the gen'lm'n in difficulties did, ven he valked out of a Sunday" (542).

What can be said of such locutions? They are certainly poetical by Tony Weller's definition, since they compare one thing to another. But their poetry depends on the comic incongruity of the comparison. No one thinks that a man writing a valentine is like a man who will be arrested if he leaves his house except on Sunday, when the whole city becomes a kind of church sanctuary. The dissimilarity is a big part of the joke. On the other hand the two situations *are* alike in one way. The same form of words can be used appropriately at the right moment in both situations, two grotesquely unlike contexts. There are at least two different circumstances in which it would be appropriate to say either "I take the privilege of the day," or "I'm pretty tough." The joke and the explosion of laughter arises from seeing this strange similarity in dissimilarity. We recognize the peculiar fact that the meaning of a given group of words is not intrinsic to the words. Meaning arises from the way a given context determines one sense out of a virtually limitless number of possible different ones.[11] Seeing this liberates one momentarily from the coercive constraints of the context one is really in. We glimpse the performative role forms of language can have when those forms are inserted arbitrarily in a given context. In effecting that liberation, the Wellerism is itself a miniature performative. The Wellerism gives the one who uses it or hears it a brief power over language, a sense of language's power, and a momentary escape from its coercions. The understanding the Wellerism gives by no means, however, prevents anyone from being the victim of unintentional performatives, as *Pickwick Papers* abundantly demonstrates. Cognition and power here are incompatible. A performative, like a Wellerism, is a form of language that works, but it works differently in different contexts. Any form of words can function as a performative if the context is right.

The Wellerisms show that it is impossible not to speak or write poetry. No form of words means just what it says. Even the most literal and referential set of words ("Chops and Tomata sauce," for example) can have a different meaning in a different context and a performative effect there. This means that whatever I say has a disquieting kind of poetry about it. It is likely to exceed my intentions and knowledge by having a quite different meaning and effect if it is taken within a different context from the one intended. You write a note saying "Don't trouble yourself about the warming-pan," meaning just what you say, and you find yourself involved in a breach of promise suit.

The central event of *Pickwick Papers*, the suit and the trial of *Bardell v. Pickwick*, is generated by an inadvertent Wellerism. The difference between an inadvertent and a deliberate Wellerism is that the former makes its perpetrator potentially the victim of false ideological forms and bad institutions like the law, whereas the latter liberates by bringing the mechanisms of language for a moment into the light. A deliberate Wellerism uses poetry against poetry, so to speak. It does this by showing how poetry works as a ubiquitous ideological power for harm within society. Poetry, like Jingle's masterly manipulation of Bouvard and Pecuchet–like clichés, tells lies and does things with them.

More can be said of the Wellerisms, however. They tend, like the two in this episode, to bring together a benign context, one involving a life-affirming situation like courtship, the other involving crime, the ruinous power of institutions, and the ever-present possibility of death. This is just what *Pickwick Papers* as a whole does, for example, in the interpolated tales or in the central episode that brings Pickwick into Fleet Prison, as against the generally prevailing comedy, most often comedy arising from a perennial source: relations between the sexes. The Wellerisms, like the whole novel, assert that two apparently unrelated aspects of life are in some way alike or are inextricably involved with one another: the life drive, generated by sexual desire, and the certainty of death.

Like all great comedy, *Pickwick Papers* in the end must be defined as tragicomedy. This mixture is constantly reaffirmed by the poetico-prosaical Wellerisms. A man in love really is in some way like a man who is in danger of being imprisoned for debt. For a father to say "I'm pretty tough" when his son is in danger of marrying really is like the situation of the old turkey who may be killed and who takes pleasure in the fact that he is so tough no one will enjoy eating him. The marriage of a son is the beginning of the end for a father's patriarchal authority, though fathers, like the tough old turkey, have ways of keeping some command even beyond the grave. Marriage, to turn to Sam's Wellerism in his valentine, does have a way of putting both men and women in debt in more than one sense, needing to take the privilege of the day to get a little freedom. Marriage "circumscribes" anyone, man or woman, with a complex web of institutional and social constraints.

∼

I asked initially whether *Pickwick Papers* as a whole may be performative. The question may now be answered in the affirmative. *Pickwick Papers* is a high-spirited reflection of early Victorian class and gender relations. It represents a wide range of English institutions and forms of behavior, along with the languages employed by them—languages scientific, historical, journalistic, political, legal, and so forth, even including the language of hunting and cricket. The novel also employs most of the narrative, dramatic, and even poetic conventions available to Dickens. But *Pickwick Papers* also brings into the open these elements' absurdity and their potential for causing harm. It thereby puts in question the repertoire of features making up English ideology at the moment of Victoria's accession to the throne.

This comic demystification is effected by hyperbole, by irony, and by other forms of displacement that call attention to language by wresting it from its usual contexts. In this way, like all powerful critiques of ideology, *Pickwick Papers* did not merely reflect Victorian society, its institutions, and its narrative conventions. It changed them, in however small a way. Like cultural creations generally, *Pickwick Papers* is not fully explicable by what preceded it. Its biographical, historical, and social contexts do not fully explain it. As the successive monthly numbers appeared, the novel rapidly became immensely popular and widely read, particularly after Sam Weller entered the scene. Just as Sam changes Pickwick's life, so *Pickwick Papers* entered the culture of its readers to change them in all sorts of complex though not easily specifiable or verifiable ways. No one can doubt, however, that the novel had an effect on Victorian society, as did Dickens's subsequent novels.

Pickwick Papers uses poetry, as Tony Weller defines it, to criticize, demystify, and momentarily suspend the baneful efficacy of the ideological "poetry" with which its readers were surrounded, the obfuscations of the law, or the low blandishments of advertisements for products like Warren's Blacking. At the same time, the novel recognizes the necessity of poetry. Poetry is shown to be ubiquitous in everyday life. The novel shows this by being written in a species of poetry itself. At the beginning of the valentine episode, the imaginary Sam Weller is shown walking through real East London streets. In a similar way *Pickwick Papers* throughout works its magic by presenting, as one might say, altering Marianne Moore's formula, real gardens with imaginary toads in them.

Like all performative utterances, *Pickwick Papers* exceeded Dickens's intentions. It was radically improvisatory. Dickens had no idea where the story would go when he began writing it. Moreover, neither he nor anyone else could have predicted its popularity or the effects it would have. The most he could do was to utter another kind of blind performative. This is the promise he made binding himself to go on writing the novel. Dickens did this not only in his contract with Chapman and Hall, but also in the original "Advertisement" in *The Athenaeum* for March 26, 1836, and in the "Announcement" at the conclusion of Part 10 in December, 1836. In the "Advertisement" Dickens says, "it is presumed the series will be completed in about twenty numbers" (900). In the "Announcement" Dickens promises to "keep perpetually going on beginning again, regularly, until the end of the fair" (903). In saying this, as he confesses, Dickens uses someone else's words to make a promise. He says again "what the late eminent Mr. John Richardson, of Horsemonger Lane Southwark, and the Yellow Caravan with the Brass Knocker, always said on behalf of himself and company, at the close of every performance" (902). Dickens uses someone else's words to make a promise, just as Sam Weller signs his valentine with Pickwick's name, and just as I have borrowed Dickens's words for purposes of my own. In all three cases the language or the signature of another is used to get something done with words. No doubt the result in my case too will not quite be what I intended.

§5 Temporal Topographies: Tennyson's Tears

Allegory signifies precisely the non-being of that
which it represents.
                                        —Walter Benjamin

We ordinarily distinguish sharply between criticism and poetry.
Some poets, we say (Coleridge, Arnold, and T. S. Eliot, for example), were also great critics, but other poets (Shakespeare, Byron,
Browning, or Thomas Hardy) were not critics at all or not critics of
distinction. Tennyson would usually be put in the latter category.
For one thing, he is supposed to have had no aptitude for reflection
or for theoretical generalization. W. H. Auden said of Tennyson:
"He had the finest ear, perhaps, of any English poet; he was also undoubtedly the stupidest."[1] Tennyson left no body of criticism. Such
observations by Tennyson about poetry as exist—for example, in
the *Memoir* by the poet's son, Hallam Tennyson—are, as Gerhard
Joseph shows,[2] a version of Victorian commonplaces about the
superiority of symbol over allegory. Though he sometimes speaks
of using a "sort of allegory" in the weak and conventional sense of a
rationally concocted "*this* for *that*" Tennyson favors latitude of
subjective interpretation. He refuses to pin down definitively the
meanings of his poems. He speaks of an "allegory in the distance"
or of a "parabolic drift" in the *Idylls of the King*,[3] but he always
refused to fix that "drift" with exact interpretations. Tennyson is
committed to the idea that poetry should be socially useful. Perhaps letting his readers make what they like of it is part of that
program.

In any case, no one in his right mind would claim that Tennyson is an important critic in the sense that Arnold, Pater, Eliot, and even Gerard Manley Hopkins are important critics. Nevertheless, I shall show that one significant dimension of Tennyson's poems is the way they represent what might be called "poetic thinking" about the nature and powers of poetry. And I shall show that what Tennyson's poems obliquely say about poetry is far more interesting than the relatively conventional views about poetry he expressed outside his poetry, or even inside the poetry when he makes overt assertions. If Tennyson was stupid, his poems are far from stupid about the nature of what they themselves are and what they do. As theoretical reflection about poetry they are deep, profound, as I shall show through the example of "Tears, Idle Tears." Here is the poem:

> Tears, idle tears, I know not what they mean,
> Tears from the depth of some divine despair
> Rise in the heart, and gather to the eyes,
> In looking on the happy Autumn-fields,
> And thinking of the days that are no more.
>
> Fresh as the first beam glittering on a sail,
> That brings our friends up from the underworld,
> Sad as the last which reddens over one
> That sinks with all we love below the verge;
> So sad, so fresh, the days that are no more.
>
> Ah, sad and strange as in dark summer dawns
> The earliest pipe of half-awakened birds
> To dying ears, when unto dying eyes
> The casement slowly grows a glimmering square;
> So sad, so strange, the days that are no more.
>
> Dear as remembered kisses after death,
> And sweet as those by hopeless fancy feigned
> On lips that are for others; deep as love,
> Deep as first love, and wild with all regret;
> O Death in Life, the days that are no more.[4]

Much has been written about this powerful and moving poem. I shall not try to recapitulate that commentary here, but shall try to read the poem afresh. Though "Tears, Idle Tears" has its own integrity, is usually read outside its context, and was probably written without *The Princess* in mind, nevertheless the poem is inserted at a dramatic moment in *The Princess*. The singing of it by one of Princess Ida's "maids" helps precipitate the catastrophe of the poem: the revelation that Princess Ida's female college has been invaded by three men disguised as women. "Tears, Idle Tears" is therefore placed against a background of questions about gender roles and women's liberation. Like Henry James's *The Bostonians*, *The Princess* ends with the triumph of traditional marriage: "Accomplish thou my manhood and thyself; / Lay thy sweet hand in mine and trust in me," says the hero (ll. 344–45). This is something a lot of men have said to women before and since. The ending of *The Princess* occurs according to a male wish fulfillment that neither the great Victorian poet nor the great modern novelist seems to have been able to resist. Both, nevertheless, allow the women in their narratives the opportunity for a full and even hyperbolic expression of their sense of wrong. The happy marriages at the end are accompanied in *The Bostonians* by an anticipation that the heroine has by no means been thoroughly tamed and in *The Princess* by many promises from the Prince that he will assist the Princess in her work for women's liberation.

If "Tears, Idle Tears" is, in part at least, oriented around an axis of height and depth, its immediate context reinforces that orientation, with its iteration of the word "down." The Princess and her company have just come down from a geological expedition when the song is sung:

> we
> Down from the lean and wrinkled precipices,
> By every coppice-feathered chasm and cleft,
> Dropt through the ambrosial gloom to where below
> No bigger than a glow-worm shone the tent
> Lamplit from the inner. (IV, 3–8)

After the song is sung, the Princess reproaches the maiden for singing a song "hatched in silken-folded idleness" (IV, 48–49) on the theme of "the mouldered lodges of the Past." Her reproach invokes the irresistible downward flow of time toward its utopian future: "Let old bygones be, / While down the streams that float us each and all to the issue," and so on (IV, 52–53).

The Princess has, in a conversation with the disguised Prince before the song is sung, elegantly expressed the traditional metaphysical view of time:

> For was, and is, and will be, are but is;
> And all creation is one act at once,
> The birth of light; but we that are not all,
> As parts, can see but parts, now this, now that,
> And live, perforce, from thought to thought, and make
> One act a phantom of succession: thus
> Our weakness somehow shapes the shadow, Time. (III, 307–13)

For the Princess, who, according to the poem, is wrong about just about everything, time is what it has been in the Western tradition since Plato and St. Augustine. For her, time is a series of presents—past present, present present, and future present. These presents are gathered into one by being all copresent from all time to the *nunc stans* of God. The Princess is right to be affronted by "Tears, Idle Tears," when a little later it is sung, since among other things it expresses a radically different view of time from the traditional one she so glibly expresses. It is impossible to know whether or not Tennyson knew this. His poem, however, speaks for him. It speaks poetically for a view of time as generated by difference, non-presence, distance, unattainability, and loss that can never be made up by a recovered presence in the bosom of God. God, in fact, suffers from a "divine despair" at not being able to recuperate and encompass all the times and places of his creation. By "speaking poetically" I mean speaking through image and rhetorical structure rather than through conceptual formulation.

Other songs from *The Princess* also move from high to low, most notably "Come down, O maid, from yonder mountain height / . . . For Love is of the valley, come thou down / And find him" (VII, 184–85). This adjacent poem suggests that the up/down axis of

"Tears" has something to do with the issue of gender in the main narrative. It has also to do with the opposition between idle nostalgia for the past and work to fulfill the promise of the future. Associating time with a movement down from heights also prepares for the use of spatial images to express human temporality in "Tears." The up/down axis, however, has a different meaning in the poem, since there up is this present life and moment, while down is death.

As Heidegger observes in *Being and Time,* the terminology available in Western languages for expressing time is remarkably impoverished. Since we lack adequate temporal language, we Westerners always express time (and falsify it) in some spatial image or other, for example, in the movement of the hands of a clock. In fact, however, space is the opening out of time, an opening out that is generated rather than merely registered by language. If there is no proper language for time, then time can only be expressed figuratively, that is, by one or another species of catachresis, through the importation of an improper word where there is no proper one.

The project of "Tears, Idle Tears" is to find a way with topographical images to express Tennyson's peculiar apprehension of human time, especially his sense of the past. Tennyson must, that is, try to turn time into language or make time of words. This is both a poetic and a theoretical project. For Tennyson one of the major uses of poetry is to express the human sense of time. This is an example of what I mean when I say Tennyson's critical and theoretical thinking about poetry takes place in his poems, not in prose about poetry.

Temporal distance is associated with spatial distance in the first stanza of "Tears," when the theme of the poem is announced. "Looking on the happy Autumn-fields, / And thinking of the days that are no more" makes the speaker of the poem cry, but the tears are idle and without ascertainable meaning. Though the poem is sung by one of the Princess's maidens, no doubt it expresses Tennyson's own obsession with what he called the "passion of the past." Twice in comments about the poem he asserted that it was written at a particular "mouldered lodge" of the past, Tintern Abbey: "This song came to me on the yellowing autumn-tide at Tintern Abbey, full for me of its bygone memories. It is the sense of the abiding in the transient" (Ricks, 784). Tennyson does not mention Words-worth, but "Tears, Idle Tears" has the same theme as Wordsworth's poem and might almost be called Tennyson's "Tintern Abbey." Among the "bygone memories"[5] was surely this one of Words-worth's many poems about memory, as well as memory of the history that is inscribed materially in the ruined abbey. Tennyson insisted, however, that the tears of the poem were not generated by "real woe, as some people might suppose; it was rather the yearning that young people occasionally experience for that which seems to have passed away from them for ever" (H. Tennyson, II, 73). This is an important clue. The poem, Tennyson is saying, with however much or little denegation, does not express sorrow about separa-tion from any real person, for example, his separation by death from his friend Arthur Henry Hallam, who is buried not far from the ruins of Tintern Abbey and who is, of course, the subject of Tennyson's great elegy, *In Memoriam* (1850). All the images in the poem about separation from friends and the woe of unfulfilled desire are just that, images, prosopopoeias for something that is imageless and has nothing to do with persons. They are images, that is, for human temporality.

The pattern of repeated adjectives woven and interwoven as the grammatical armature of the poem names no specific sorrow or loss. The adjectives name, rather, the quality that "the days that are no more" have just because they are no more: "fresh"; "sad"; "so sad, so fresh"; "sad and strange"; "so sad, so strange"; "dear"; "sweet"; "deep"; "wild." Even a child who has had no actual loss to weep, says Tennyson, experiences this sense of loss as an intrinsic and apparently causeless feature of consciousness. To mourn this loss is the human condition. The problem for poetry is to find words to express what is outside specific experiences, even prior to them, something that has nothing to do with intersubjective rela-tions. It is something, moreover, that seems even prior to language, at least the language of direct reference.

One mode of figurative expression exploited in this poem is to personify that primordial sense of loss by embodying it in something that *can* be put in words, that is, in a series of situations embodying loss or separation: friends returning by boat but not yet here; friends leaving by boat and disappearing over the horizon; a dying person waking at dawn; the memory of kisses given a dead loved one when he or she was alive; the unassuageable desire to kiss "lips that are for others"; the desire of first love, a desire so deep that somehow it cannot be distinguished from regret for something lost. These personifications are explicitly labeled similes by the "as" that follows each adjective: "fresh as"; "sad as," and so on. These images are systematically genderless. Just as it is impossible to know whether we should think of the speaker of the poem as male or female, since it was an autobiographical poem put by the male poet in the mouth of a female character in a narrative poem, so it is even impossible to tell whether the pain of unassuaged love in the poem is heterosexual or homosexual. Tennyson speaks in *In Memoriam* about Hallam in language not unlike that used in "Tears."

The other figurative strategy for expressing the inexpressible in the poem is the use of spatial images for time. If the up/down axis in the surrounding context in *The Princess* is appropriated in "Tears" to express the presence here and now of something that is so deep it belongs to another world, horizontal spatial figures serve a similar purpose. Tennyson's comments to James Knowles are helpful here: "It is in a way like St Paul's 'groanings which cannot be uttered.' . . . It is what I have always felt even from a boy, and what as a boy I called the 'passion of the past.' And it is so always with me now; it is the distance that charms me in the landscape, the picture and the past, and not the immediate to-day in which I move."[6] It was not Hallam's death that generated Tennyson's feeling of loss. Rather, the death gave Tennyson an occasion to personify a loss he already felt. This loss finds its most immediate embodiment in landscape distances. Distance in the landscape is the immediate correlative of distance in time and so may be used for what has no language, the "groanings that cannot be uttered" caused by a sense of temporal loss or fugaciousness, what Tennyson elsewhere called "a gulf that ever shuts and gapes." The tears that rise to the speaker's or singer's eyes in this poem happen when he or she is "looking on the happy Autumn-fields, / And thinking of the days that are no more." The one makes him or her think of the other.

I have spoken of such figures as catachreses for a temporality that has no literal names. But the primary figure in the poem is, of course, the tears. What can be said of them? Tears are an extraordinary phenomenon. They are not articulate speech. They are mute, but no one can doubt that they are signs. They say even more than words do. Oozing involuntarily from the intimacy of the body as it is moved by thoughts and feelings, they betray that intimacy, speak for it, whether the one who cries wishes to or not. They break down the chaste division between inside and outside. They turn the body inside out. As bodily fluids that are at the same time unmistakably signs, they blur the division between spirit and body. Tears are profoundly embarrassing or shocking because they are the involuntary making material of what, we think, ought to be secret and immaterial. Much has been written recently about "the materiality of the sign." Tears are a paradigmatic example of such a sign. The tears in "Tears, Idle Tears" are particularly indiscreet and troubling just because they have no sufficient cause. Looking on the happy Autumn-fields, and thinking of the days that are no more hardly seems something to cry about. But tears rise to the singer's eyes.

If the tears have no sufficient cause, their meaning is also unknown. "I know not what they mean," says the singer. If the tears are signs, they are signs in an unknown language. They have come as messengers from beyond this world, from "the depths of some divine despair," but what message it is they have brought all this way is unreadable. As Leo Spitzer long ago argued, "divine despair," if it means anything, must mean what it says: the despair of some god. The phrase sounds like an oxymoron, since gods are not ordinarily thought of as ever needing to despair. These tears begin, it appears, in the weeping of some unhappy god. They rise from the depths of some divine despair. Then, after a mysterious transition from one world to another, they become the tears of the singer of the poem.

What might this God or *Sondergott* have to weep about? It may be his or her failure to dwell immanently within this world. The singer's sense of loss is also a despairing sense of loss for the god who must remain transcendence without immanence and cannot, as I have said, encompass the times and spaces of his or her creation. (The gender of the god who divinely despairs is not specified.) The god of this poem is a divinity who cannot save his or her creation or redeem it from guilt and death. Far from being the way to a resurrection in the other world, death now leads nowhere and cannot be dialectically recuperated. The dead are gone forever, or they return as ghosts to haunt this world as embodied memories, for example, the personified figures of loss and unassuageable desire that inhabit the final three-quarters of "Tears, Idle Tears."

The world of Tennyson's "Tears, Idle Tears" is like the world of the baroque mourning plays Walter Benjamin, in *The Origin of German Tragic Drama*, defines as a realm of nature (*physis*) bereft of any divine presence. Tennyson's poem, like those mourning plays, is a work of mourning not for any particular death, but for the loss of any redeeming relation to transcendence. Tennyson's tears of mourning are brought back up like Eurydice from the underworld, but their function as communicating messengers is lost along the way. They connect this world with the other one, but in the mode of non-connection. The message the tears bring is lost in the transition from the depths of some divine despair to the singer's heart to her or his eyes. They are now unreadable signs in an unknown language.

I have said the tears are paradigmatic examples of the materiality and therefore unreadability of the sign. They are this in part because they bring to the surface the aspect of language or of any other sign that is mute, obscure, opaque, if not meaningless, at least without any ascertainable meaning. The tears seem somehow related to the days that are no more, but more as meaningless signs generated by thinking about the past than as signs for them that put the one who uses those signs in possession of what they signify. The tears signify the non-being of what they represent. They are like a word repeated so often that it loses its meaning and becomes pure, meaningless sound. Tennyson used to say his own name over and over until it lost meaning. He then seemed to expand and become identified with the universe in a kind of waking trance. Try it: "Alfred, Alfred, Alfred, Alfred, Alfred." What could be a more useless and idle thing to do?

The tears are "idle" presumably because they are generated in a moment of idleness, whether "silken-folded" or not. In this moment the speaker or singer has turned away from the future-oriented work that normally occupies human beings just to look on the happy Autumn-fields, and think of the days that are no more. This is an activity that is idle in the sense of accomplishing nothing, as the tears, so it seems, accomplish nothing. Nothing can be done to alter the non-being of the past. Or can it? The tears appear to be "idle" because they do not work. They do not do anything. The days that are no more are no more. No words can bring them back. If the tears are cognitively empty ("I know not what they mean"), they also appear to be performatively void. They are signs that fit the category of what is called an infelicitous speech act.

On the other hand, by a paradox that is at the center of what this poem says about poetry, the poem about the tears, the naming of the tears in poetry, *is* performatively efficacious. The poem is inaugural, a new start. The song brings tears to the eyes of the maid who sings it: "She ended with such passion that the tear / She sang of, shook and fell, an erring pearl / Lost in her bosom" (IV, 41–43). "The tear she sang of": surely that is an odd statement! These tears are generated by the song or they are the very ones the song names, though it is not autumn and the maid has presumably not suffered the various losses or unsatisfied desires that are named in the poem. Nevertheless, "the tears come to her eyes," as we say. Sing this poem and you will cry. But you will cry tears not for your own loss but for a generalized loss, loss in general, a loss that is, for Tennyson, the essential feature of the human sense of time past. To sing about these tears is to bring them up from the depths and to confront them again as signs whose meaning is unknown. If the tears rise up, they then fall. They fall in a way that is ominously suggestive of a moral as well as physical loss, a loss that has some shadow of sexual guilt about it. The tear is "an erring pearl / Lost in her bosom," erring presumably because it ought to have stayed in place on its string.

Another odd fact about these tears, or about tears in general, is that they obscure clear vision of what generated them. We speak of how someone's eyes are "misted with tears." The weeper in this poem can no longer clearly see the happy Autumn-fields that brought on the tears through their association with the past. Tennyson himself was extremely nearsighted. He had to hold a book close to his eyes in order to read it. The happy Autumn-fields always presumably looked misty to him, as if he were crying, even when there were no tears in his eyes. When what is seen is seen obscured by tears, its deeper meaning is at the same time revealed, in this poem by the crescendo of sideways displacements into one simile or another. Tears are apocalyptic. They unveil and veil at the same time.[7]

Tears are ruined symbols, symbols that do not communicate what they stand for. If this is so, a more proper name for the tears would be "allegorical sign," defining "allegorical sign" as a symbol turned inside out. I follow here not Tennyson's commonplace definition of allegory as "*This* for *That*" but the tradition of allegory that goes from Friedrich Schlegel through Ruskin and Pater to Proust, Benjamin, and de Man. To the latter tradition Tennyson's poetic practice and its implicit theory in "Tears, Idle Tears" belong, whatever he may have said elsewhere, in casual comments about allegory. A symbol, according to the canonical definition by Coleridge cited by Gerhard Joseph for its presumed application to Tennyson, combines the individual and the general in a material image. A symbol, says Coleridge, "always partakes of the Reality which it renders intelligible; and while it enunciates the whole, abides itself as a living part in that Unity, of which it is the representative."[8] An allegorical sign, on the contrary, does not participate synecdochically, as part for a whole, in what it signifies. Nor can it be said to be of the same nature as what it symbolizes. Nor can it be defined as a making present, bringing near, or making intelligible of what is named.

Tennyson's idle tears are a paradigmatic example of an allegorical sign as opposed to a symbol. Such a sign is defined in terms of temporal distance, not spatial contiguity; by its unlikeness to what it stands for, not its similarity to the symbolized; by its opacity and lack of discernible meaning, not by its transparency. An allegorical sign is characterized by its failure to put the one who contemplates it in present possession of what it stands for. It has performative force, not a constative function. The tears work as signs through a strange efficacy of putting weeper, singer, and listener or witness in touch at a distance with what they cannot name as perspicuous meaning. This failure of the tears to express what they mean makes them function admirably as allegorical signs for temporality, the strange non-being of the days that are no more.

Another peculiarity of "Tears, Idle Tears" will reinforce my claim that the tears are allegorical signs in the Benjaminian or de Manian sense rather than transparent symbols sharing in what they name and transporting what they name to the beholder. The Coleridgean theory of the symbol is always associated with oxymoron and with the dialectical reconciliation of opposites: the general in the par-ticular, the spiritual in the material, the far in the near, and so on. The symbol is the place where thesis and antithesis, death and life, past and present, this world and the other, transcendent one, come together and are synthesized in a higher unity.

It seems at first that Tennyson's poem fits neatly into this para-digm. "Happy Autumn-fields" is an oxymoron if there ever was one. It prepares for the seemingly "oxymoronic" juxtapositions in the image structure and chain of adjectives used in the poem to define the days that are no more as, so it seems, a combination of presence and absence. The days that are no more are fresh as the first beam glittering on a sail that brings our friends up from the underworld and at the same time sad as the last which reddens over one that sinks with all we love below the verge. They are like dawning to the eyes and ears of someone who is about to die, someone with "dying ears" and "dying eyes" who hears and sees, but with an awareness of imminent absolute loss, just as the "glimmering square" of the window at dawn is neither visible nor invisible but both at once.

The problem with this reading of the poem is that the pattern of dialectical opposition reconciled in an oxymoron breaks down as the poem progresses. It is replaced by a cascade of adjectives and similes all describing the same absence and loss. If "fresh" and "sad," in the first stanza, seem opposites, the sort of opposites that might be dialectically synthesized in the symbol, "sad" and "strange" in stanza two are not so much opposites as differential versions of the same alienation of the days that are no more. It is as if the days that are no more were a sad and strange ghost in grave clothes come back to haunt the singer as an apparition walking those happy Autumn-fields. The words of the poem successfully raise that ghost. In the last stanza the adjectives multiply in a crescendo of shaded variations trying to evoke a single elusive entity (or non-entity), not in an alternation among opposites. The days that are no more are "dear," "sweet," "deep," and "wild with all regret." What began as a dialectical opposition potentially capable of being synthesized breaks down as the emotion of the poem intensifies in the confrontation with something that resists dialectical synthesis and therefore cannot be symbolized in the Coleridgean way.

A final peculiarity of the similes chosen to define the days that are no more will confirm that the past, for Tennyson, can be named only in allegorical sign, not in symbol. Though each of the similes is affirmed to be another approach to naming what the days that are no more are like, they are not by any means all images of the past. Quite the contrary. The days that are no more are as fresh as the first beam that brings our friends up from the underworld. This may refer to a past separation, but it is oriented toward the reunion that will take place in the immediate future. If the days are sad as the last beam which reddens over a sail that sinks with all we love below the verge, that simile seems oriented toward a future separation. It is not an image of something past at all. The dying person who awakens at dawn to hear the half-awakened birds and see the window slowly grow a glimmering square is oriented toward his imminent future death. He or she is not thinking of the past. "Remembered kisses after death" belong to the past all right, but the second kind of kisses mentioned, those "by hopeless fancy feigned on lips that are for others," are longed-for future kisses that will not happen. "First love" is surely a longing for union with the beloved in the future, though Tennyson adds, characteristically, that "first love" is also "wild with all regret." It is as if in the moment of first love the lover already foresees the future loss of the beloved and the wild regret that loss will cause. To be deeply in love is to suffer a wild regret for something that has not yet happened, in a curious form of future anterior.

The strangest thing about the past, for Tennyson in this poem, is that the days that are no more seem to be located in the future as much as in the past. There is a coming and going or metaleptic reversal of past and future that might be defined by saying that in this poem we go forward in time to come back to the past or by saying that in this poem we remember the future. But this is precisely the characteristic of time that is best expressed by the allegorical sign in its emphasis on perpetual reversal and on a continual broken repetition rather than by the *nunc stans* of the symbol. The singer of "Tears, Idle Tears" mocks and contradicts the concept of time so confidently expressed by the Princess a little earlier in the poem and replaces it with an allegorical time of perpetual loss and absence.

Tennyson's final name for this perpetual loss and absence is "Death in Life." The phrase is a prosopopoeia, the culmination of the chain of images personifying the days that are no more as like one or another person or interpersonal situation. But like all prosopopoeias, this one is as much an invocation as a name. It can be read either as an exclamatory definition, a constative assertion— " 'O Death in Life,' that is what the past is"—or as a performative apostrophe, a trope of address to the absent, the inanimate, or the dead, that is, the days that are no more. Like Christ's "Lazarus, come forth," Tennyson's speaker implores the days that are no more to come forth and manifest themselves in the form of an allegorical personification: "O Death in Life." Like Wordsworth's "Ye knew him well, ye cliffs and islands of Winander," Tennyson's vocative address to "Death in Life" presupposes that this personage might appear or answer back. But the poem ends abruptly with this line. No evidence is given that the days that are no more appear in answer to the speaker's call. "O Death in Life" is a failed prosopopoeia, the ruin of the trope of personification that has been a chief rhetorical tool in the poem for naming by one catachresis or another something that has no proper name, or for performatively invoking it. Insofar as the days that are no more are accurately described as death in life they could not manifest themselves except as an absence, as a ghost.

"Death in Life": the phrase reverses Coleridge's "Life-in-Death" in "The Rime of the Ancient Mariner," one of the grisly figures that dices for the soul of the mariner. What is the difference between Life in Death and Death in Life? Even though Coleridge may have thought that his "Life in Death" was an allegorical rather than symbolic figure, his distaste for allegory and failure to understand it seem to have caused his allegorical figure to be rather a defective version of symbol. Indeed that is how he defines allegory in *The Statesman's Manual.* The difference between "Life in Death" and "Death in Life" is precisely the difference between Coleridgean symbol, in which Tennyson may have thought he believed, and allegory, the ruin, the "broken grange," the idle figure without ascertainable meaning, that his poetry consistently produced. Coleridge's "Life in Death" names the carrying over, as in symbol, of life, this present life here, into death, thereby giving us, as symbol does, possession now of the transcendent realm beyond life. Tennyson's "Death in Life" names the undermining of all presence and possession in this life by a principle of loss. The poet names that principle of loss, appropriately enough, "Death." This death is not a future end but a dimension of separation, loss, or difference that permeates life from childhood to old age, from birth to "death" in the usual sense. As Dylan Thomas said, "After the first death there is no other." The "first death" occurs the moment we are born. Human life thereafter is undermined by this constant presence of death.

I claim to have fulfilled the promise made at the beginning of this chapter. I have shown that if Tennyson's abstract thinking was conventional and traditional, his poetic thinking went against that conventional thinking. "Tears, Idle Tears," as one example of that, expresses a profound apprehension of temporality as well as a profound sense of the way the poetic devices of topographical equivalent, allegorical sign, prosopopoeia, and catachresis can be used performatively to call forth that apprehension of temporality.

§ 6 Naming, Doing, Placing: Hopkins

> I did say yes
> O at lightning and lashed rod;
> Thou heardst me truer than tongue confess
> Thy terror, O Christ, O God.[1]

Gerard Manley Hopkins is one of the great English landscape poets, not only in his poems but also in his journal. These describe with loving care (and a brilliant gift for metaphorical toponymy) the land and weather of England and Wales. This chapter, however, will investigate another dimension of Hopkins's work, one that has been important throughout this book: the role of speech acts in legislating meaning, including topographical meaning. The naming of places is one of the most important performatives.

I pose a cascade of questions to initiate this investigation. Are the lines in my epigraph, quoted from "The Wreck of the Deutschland," a speech act? Do they do rather than merely say? Or are they no more at most than the report or "mention" of a past speech act, the naming of it, the naming, moreover, of a speech act that was not spoken, but uttered inwardly by a silent speech that was "truer than tongue"? Is saying yes in this way a performative act of language in the strict sense? If not, what is it? More generally, is there a performative dimension to Hopkins's poems, for example, the late sonnets? Did Hopkins have a theory of speech acts, explicit or implicit? Finally, is my posing of these questions itself a speech act? Can I speak of speech acts without performing a speech act myself?

A frequent temporal structure of Hopkins's poems is that of repeating a past locution, apparently a speech act, which is remembered and renewed, perhaps performed again, in the present. In "The Wreck of the Deutschland" this structure is triple: the tall nun's saying yes to the appearance of Christ at the moment of her death in the wreck repeats the poet's own past saying yes "O at lightning and lashed rod." That is then repeated again in the writing of the poem and in the moment when Christ appears to the poet's "fancy." The poet now speaks in the present tense, and the invoked Son of God appears:

> . . . Fancy, come faster—
> Strike you the sight of it? look at it loom there,
> Thing that she . . . There then! the Master,
> *Ipse*, the only one, Christ, King, Head. (ll. 218–21)

A speech act is a form of words that does not name something but makes something happen. As J. L. Austin observed, the usual grammatical form of a performative is a sentence in the first-person present indicative: "I promise"; "I bet"; "I do"; "I order"; "I apologize"; "I accept"; "I shall."[2] Yet it is possible that a piece of language lacking these distinguishing marks of the performative might nevertheless function as a performative. If so, it might take a sharp eye to spot some performatives.

Moreover, though the neat distinctions theorists of speech acts make have their heuristic value and their apparent conceptual necessity, they always break down when a rigorous inspection of examples is made. "Mention" of a word or phrase may always be slightly contaminated by some dimension of "use." A constative, referential, or descriptive phrase may always have an obscure performative side, and vice versa. To say "I did say yes" not only describes a past speech act; it is also implicitly a new saying yes in the present. This is accomplished by the emphatic "did." To say "I did say yes" is a way of saying "Yes, I said yes."[3]

It is not only necessary to discriminate carefully among various kinds of performatives, to show that a promise does not work in quite the same way as an excuse, nor an oath in the same way as a bet. It is also necessary to distinguish performatives from closely adjacent forms of language that may or may not possess what is necessary for an efficacious performative. Such forms of language would include apostrophes, imperatives, injunctions, questions, commands, invocations, prayers, blessings, interjections like the "O" in Hopkins's "I did say yes / O at lightning and lashed rod," optatives, like the exceedingly strange past optative at the opening of "Henry Purcell," in which another ejaculatory "O" also appears: "Have fair fallen, O fair, fair have fallen, so dear / To me, so arch-especial a spirit as heaves in Henry Purcell" (ll. 1–2). This means "Let Purcell have fared well after his death." In a letter to Bridges Hopkins explained that "*Have* is the sing. imperative (or optative if you like) of the past, a thing possible and actual both in logic and grammar, but naturally a rare one," and he paraphrased the line to mean, "I hope Purcell is not damned for being a Protestant, because I love his genius" (*L*, 174, 170). It is difficult to be certain that such speech acts have nothing of the performative about them, though they appear different. To Glendower's boast, "I can call spirits from the vasty deep," Hotspur responds: "Why, so can I, or so can any man; / But will they come when you do call for them?" (*Henry IV*, Part One, 3.1.53–55), whereas the bride's and bridegroom's iterated "I do," spoken in appropriate circumstances, does really always work to get the couple married. A prayer simply asks the deity to do something. It by no means ensures that God will do what he is prayed to do. An apostrophe merely addresses someone or something, with an explicit or implicit personification, as does in a slightly different way an invocation. Questions hardly seem to be performative. They simply interrogate.

Nevertheless, each of these forms of language may have a performative aspect. The spirits may actually come from the vasty deep. Who knows beforehand? Is any question "simply interrogative"? To ask a question demands an answer. Even the refusal to answer is an answer. A question establishes a field of discourse that defines the status of what is said or written thereafter. In that sense a question is a form of words that makes something happen. A prayer or other form of direct address to God might be seen as constraining God, at least in the minimal sense of putting him in the position of having to say yes or no to the prayer. Hopkins shows he

well knew this in the slight tinge of cheeky insolence of the "sir" in
the second line of "Thou art indeed just, Lord, if I contend": "But,
sir, so what I plead is just." To address God as "Sir" is to speak to
him as a schoolboy speaks to a teacher or as a man on trial and
serving as his own lawyer speaks to a judge. The prosopopoeia that
is an inextricable part of an apostrophe may be seen as a way of
using words to make something happen, namely to give a face, a
voice, and a name to entities that do not have these.[4] Even to
address God as "Thou," as in the first two lines of "The Wreck of
the Deutschland" ("Thou mastering me / God! giver of breath and
bread"), is to assume that God might answer back. It is to invite or
even demand an answer. The "Thou" mingles apostrophe with
prosopopoeia, the trope of address. All of these forms of speech act
are clearly distinct from one another and from true performatives.
At the same time there are tantalizing crossovers and overlappings
that make it impossible to hold rigidly to the distinctions in any
given case. Even so, one thing is sure: not one of these language
forms simply names something, even though each may have a
constative function along with its speech act function.

My hypothetical starting place has been the assumption that
Hopkins's poems might well have a performative dimension, but
before trying to see in detail if that is really the case, two further
problems must be identified. It should be remembered, first, that
Austin explicitly excludes poetry from the realm of efficacious
speech acts. Poetry, for him, like some other frivolous uses of
language, cannot ever be a "serious" way of doing things with
words. "A performative utterance," says Austin, "will, for example,
be *in a peculiar way* hollow or void if said by an actor on the stage,
or if introduced in a poem, or spoken in soliloquy."[5] It may have
been some fear that, compared, for example, with the priest's
transubstantiation of bread and wine in the Mass, or the priest's
work for the salvation of others and himself, poetry could not be
other than frivolous that made Hopkins so anxious about his poetic
vocation. He saw it possibly in conflict with his vocation as a priest.
If "to admire the stars is in itself indifferent" (*S*, 166), then a poetry
that does no more than describe beautiful things in nature, how-

ever powerfully, is also indifferent, "etiolated," as Austin would say. So Hopkins feared, as he said in a letter to Bridges, that the writing of poetry would "interfere with [his] state and vocation" (*L*, 24). In a letter to Dixon he expresses unequivocally his conviction that the writing of poetry is a waste of time: "The question for me is not whether I am willing . . . to make a sacrifice of hopes of fame . . . , but whether I am not to undergo a severe judgment from God for the lothness I have shewn in making it, for the reserves I may have in my heart made, for the backward glances I have given with my hand upon the plough, for the waste of time the very compositions you admire may have caused and their preoccupation of the mind which belonged to more sacred or more binding duties, for the disquiet and the thoughts of vainglory they have given rise to" (*C*, 88).

On the other hand, Hopkins may have been anxious about his great gifts and clear calling as a poet for just the opposite reason, namely a fear that his poetry might really be performatively efficacious. Far from being trivially descriptive, his poetry might work, might make something happen. If that were the case, his poetry might be a species of dangerous, secular magic. It might be irregular, inassimilable to the performative rituals authorized for him as a priest. His poetry might perhaps even be sacrilegious or blasphemous. In a letter to Bridges of 1879, Hopkins said: "Feeling, love in particular, is the great moving power and spring of verse and the only person that I am in love with seldom, especially now, stirs my heart sensibly and when he does I cannot always 'make capital' of it, it would be a sacrilege to do so" (*L*, 66). Christ, it is safe to assume, is the only person Hopkins is in love with. "Sacrilege" is defined in *The American Heritage Dictionary* as "the misuse, theft, desecration, or profanation of anything consecrated to a deity or regarded as a sacred." The word combines the roots *sacer*, "sacred," with *legere*, "to gather, pluck, steal." *Legere* in Latin also means "to read," and the Indo-European root *leg-* means "to collect, with derivatives meaning 'to speak.'" The Greek word for word, *logos*, has the same root. An unattested Germanic word *lekjaz* would have meant "enchanter, one who speaks magic words." The particular sacrilege involved in using religious feelings as material for poetry is not just any stealing of sacred things. It is a misreading or mis-speaking, a misappropriation of the Word for profane uses, as an enchanter or magician misappropriates spiritual powers, constraining them to his own ends.

Another way to identify this counter-fear on Hopkins's part—not the fear that poetry may be a trivial and inefficacious speech act, but the fear that it may be only too efficacious—is to remember that for Hopkins each man can do little toward his own salvation. Only God's grace freely given can save fallen man with his inherent, inveterate turn or twist away from God and toward damnation.

Hopkins's theory of grace is complex and subtle. It is expressed in a series of not quite analogous analogies or vigorous figures. But all these metaphors are ways of defining grace as the action by God that "shifts" a man from one "pitch" or "arbitrium" (in the sense of radical disposition of the will) to another more in "correspondence" with God (*S*, 148, 151). This "shift" changes the very selfhood of a person and lifts it "through the gulf and void between pitch and pitch of being" (*S*, 156). "Pitch" means here at least three things at once: "musical pitch," "thrown," as in "pitched past pitch of grief," and "angle of the self away from or toward the absolute vertical of its possibility of being Christlike," as in "pitch of a roof."

The work on the human being's side in making grace efficacious is so slight, so small, so nearly equivalent to passive acquiescence, as scarcely to seem able to be defined as "performative" in the strict sense. A person's acceptance of God's grace would seem to be quite unlike a poetry seen as vigorously performative. Hopkins's figure for the acceptance of grace is "saying yes." Is this a true performative? It would seem not. When I say, "Yes, the sun is shining," my statement seems purely descriptive, constative. It affirms that I name the way things are. To say that does not change things one whit. Almost all of the work of grace, changing man from less to more Christlike, comes from God's side. Hopkins's images for this stress the violence of what God does to man through grace. It is like being twisted or wrung, or like being beaten into a new shape on an anvil, or like being defeated in a wrestling match, or like being threshed, the grain violently separated from the chaff, or like being

eaten or becoming what one eats, or, most violent and even shocking image of all, though still a perfectly traditional one, like a sexual
act in which the soul, self, or "brain" "conceives" Christ, is filled
with Christ, and so becomes Christlike:

> For so conceivèd, so to conceive thee is done;
>> But here was heart-throe, birth of a brain,
> Word, that heard and kept thee and uttered thee óutríght.
>> ("The Wreck of the Deutschland," ll. 238–40)

> it is Christ in his member on the one side, his member in
> Christ on the other. It is as if a man said: That is Christ playing at me
> and me playing at Christ, only that it is no play but truth; That is
> Christ *being me* and me being Christ. (*S*, 154)

Hopkins so stresses the quasi-physical violence involved in God's
action of grace that it would seem inappropriate to think of it as in
any way a performative speech act. In this God's action of grace is
like the original creative "fiat," His "Let there be light." As Hopkins says, God's grace completes the original work of creation.
Grace, in Hopkins's definition, is "any action, activity, on God's
part by which, in creating or after creating, he carries the creature
to or towards the end of its being, which is its selfsacrifice to God
and its salvation" (*S*, 154).

God's *fiat lux* might seem to be the very type or archetype of a
proper performative, a way of doing things with words: "And God
said, Let there be light: and there was light" (Genesis 1:4). But this
by no means fits the definition of an efficacious performative as
defined by Austin and other speech act theorists. For one thing, it is
the report of a putative speech act, not the speech act itself: "And
God said: Let there be light." The Bible tells us what Moses says
God said. Though all performatives, it can be argued, are citations,
for example, when the words of the marriage ceremony are repeated in each new marriage, nevertheless no one in his right mind
would claim that Moses' repetition of God's words repeats the act
of creation and makes light anew.

The problem of translation, or what might be called "babelization," also arises here. In what language did God say, "Let there be light"? In Hebrew, Latin, English, or what? Even Moses' "original" Hebrew may be the displaced report and translation of a *fiat* spoken in an unknown and forever unknowable tongue. Moreover, as Augustine long ago recognized in book 11 of the *Confessions*, there is great difficulty in thinking how God's speech, which must have the all-at-once quality of eternity, a time out of time to which all times are copresent, can get transposed into human time, where words must follow one another in temporal sequence and where meaning depends on rhythmic phonemic differentiations within time. Augustine's example is not only the *fiat lux*, but also God's "This is my beloved son" in the New Testament.[6] Of both examples of God's speech, Augustine affirms that "what was spoken was not spoken successively, one thing concluded that the next might be spoken, but all things together and eternally" (220). The first creative act of all, moreover, is not said in the Bible to require words at all: "In the beginning God created the heaven and the earth" (Genesis 1:1).

Most of all, however, God's *fiat lux* does not fit the definition of a performative because in it knowledge and power, the power of the word, are in perfect congruence, whereas a performative as defined by Austin, Derrida,[7] de Man, and others is a form of language in which knowledge and act are asymmetrical, never in perfect harmony. God is omniscient and omnipotent. In him knowledge and power go hand in hand. God's perfect foreknowledge, combined with his limitless power, meant that he knew exactly what was going to happen when he said, "Let there be light." A true performative, on the other hand, is a contingent act in the human and social world that makes something happen all right, though it can never be known for sure beforehand exactly what that something will be. There is always an element of contingency in a true performative. God's "fiat lux" is entirely autonomous and solitary. It does not depend on anything or anyone else for its efficacy, whereas the efficacy of a performative speech act in the Austinian sense depends on the presence of a whole set of social conventions, agreements, contracts, laws, constitutions. It depends on the ratification and approval of other people in the right circumstances. A true performative, in addition, is always an iteration, even though the act it performs is unique, for this time only. The efficacy of a marriage ceremony depends on the fact that the participants repeat just the right words in just the right circumstances, words that have been used innumerable times before. Moreover, a true performative, somewhat paradoxically, always in one way or another demands outward material embodiment for its efficacy, even though it is a way of doing things with words rather than with tools or with weapons. Nevertheless, a performative uttered silently to myself, a promise or an oath, would not be efficacious. I cannot commit myself to a mortgage by silently promising myself to make the payments. I must take pen in hand and write my signature on a document, or I must utter aloud the right words before appropriate witnesses, modulating air so as to leave a trace or mark on the material world. A true performative is always an intersubjective, social, and material phenomenon, whereas God can create light before creating man, nor is there mention of any other creature, earthly or divine, as necessary to the ratification of his act. God himself approves of his own act of creation: "And God saw the light that it was good" (Genesis 1:4). Nor is God's *fiat lux* the iteration of a form of words ratified by convention and used many times before. It is radically inaugural, said for the first and only time, once and for all. It is not without significance that God's *fiat* produces light, since light is the precondition for human knowing and seeing. It is also therefore the precondition for human performatives, in which knowledge and power are asymmetrical.

Nor can it be said that, since God creates the world by means of Christ the Word, this means that the intersubjective and material conditions for an efficacious performative are present. Hopkins's doctrine of the Trinity is a complex matter, as Hopkins specialists well know. It involves the notion of a going forth of Christ from God in aeonian or angelic time as well as in the actual Incarnation, when Christ was conceived and then born into the created world. But for Hopkins there is never any doubt that God is three in one and that Christ has been part of God's triune being from all time.

From all time he was, and Christ with him, just as the whole creation could be destroyed and the Trinity would still be, three in one. The Incarnation, as a moment of the materialization of God, is a historical event occurring long after the creation and is not presupposed by the latter. To say (as of course *Genesis* does not) that God created the world by means of Christ the Word by no means makes the *fiat lux* into a performative. To say that would be like accepting as a successful performative a marriage in which one person was bride or bridegroom, officiating priest or other authority, and witnesses, all three at once. Nor does God's creating word need to be inscribed, materialized, and made public in the way a true human performative must. God, so to speak, speaks to himself, since there is no one else to hear him. Augustine speaks of God's "Eternal Word in silence" (219) and denies that God's *fiat lux* was sounded at all. To be efficacious, God's creating words do not need materialization in the way human performatives do, since they do not need to be witnessed, as, for example, a signature on a promissory note must be. It is a sign of the difficulty of understanding just what is at stake in Austin's theory of performatives that God's "Let there be light" is so often mistakenly cited as an example of a performative. The essential conditions of what Austin calls a "happy performative" are not at all fulfilled by God's *fiat lux*.

If God's acts of creation and grace are not performatives, neither, it would seem, to return to man, is man's tiny action of accepting, saying yes, to what has been done to him. Hopkins agrees that, yes, "there must be something which shall be truly the creature's in the work of corresponding with grace: this is the *arbitrium*, the verdict on God's side, the saying Yes, the 'doing-agree'" (*S*, 154). He stresses, however, the minimal strength, autonomy, or originating power involved in this saying yes. It is a response to a demand, a "correspondence," a verdict in the sense of a speech making a choice between alternatives (e.g., between "guilty" and "innocent"), an aspiration in answer to an inspiration, a tiny sigh breathing out in response to God's all-powerful creative breath coming in. Though only "the aspiration in answer to his inspiration" (*S*, 158) can complete the work of sacrifice and change the "Jackself" into

Christ, this is described as the "least sigh of desire" (*S*, 155), as a "bare acknowledgment," a "counterstress which God alone can feel" (*S*, 158), for "even the sigh or aspiration itself is in answer to an inspiration of God's spirit" (*S*, 156). This least sigh is man's "correspondence with grace and seconding of God's designs" (*S*, 197), but it is practically nothing in itself. It is like one of those fictitious entities in infinitesimal calculus: "And by this infinitesimal act the creature does what in it lies to bridge the gulf fixed between its present actual and worser pitch of will and its future better one" (*S*, 155).

If God's acts in creating and in proffering grace are not performatives, neither, then, are man's "least sighs" of correspondence to God's grace. They do not independently make anything happen. Man's yes-sayings are heard only by God. They do not have the public quality requisite for a true performative. They may be spoken inwardly and so lack that additional essential requisite: embodiment, materialization, registration as a permanent mark in the world. Hopkins's saying yes to God's lightning and lashed rod was spoken "truer than tongue," that is, unvoiced, silent, spoken inwardly.

Hopkins's poems, on the other hand, do contain a genuine performative component, as Hopkins, I am hypothesizing, feared they might and as he had reason to fear, given his anxious and exclusive focus on his own salvation and that of those in his care. How may that performative component be characterized?

Here two further discriminations are necessary. First, all Hopkins's poems contain a strong constative, naming, descriptive component. The nature poems describe nature, the topographical poems describe topography, though "describe" or "name" is a weak word, as any reader of Hopkins knows, for the dynamic mimesis of the inscapes of nature as they are inhabited and vitalized by Christ. But even late nature poems like "Spelt from Sibyl's Leaves" and "That Nature is a Heraclitean Fire and of the comfort of the Resurrection" are, it could be argued, primarily descriptive, referential, mimetic. They tell the reader the way things are. In the so-called "terrible sonnets" Hopkins names his desperate inner state.

These too are constative poems. Whatever there may be of the speech event or speech act in Hopkins's poems, more particularly speech acts truly performative, will be intertwined with a strong constative component, sometimes naming an imagined present ("Cloud-puffball, torn tufts, tossed pillows ǀ flaunt forth, then chevy on an air- / built thoroughfare" ["That Nature is a Heraclitean Fire . . . ," ll. 1–2]), sometimes a past scene ("I caught this morning morning's minion" ["The Windhover," l. 1]).

A second requisite discrimination must be made. In searching Hopkins's poems for their possible performative dimensions, it is necessary to identify carefully their addressees. A surprisingly wide variety of these exists. In many poems the addressee shifts, sometimes repeatedly, during the poem. Some of Hopkins's poems are addressed boldly and directly to God: "Thou mastering me / God!" ("The Wreck of the Deutschland," ll. 1–2); "Thou art indeed just, Lord," l. 1. Some are addressed to fictive, capitalized, personified entities, "Earth," "Peace," or "Despair": "Earth, sweet Earth, sweet landscape" ("Ribblesdale," l. 1); "When will you ever, Peace, wild wooddove, shy wings shut, / Your round me roaming end, and under be my boughs?" ("Peace," ll. 1–2); "No, I'll not, carrion comfort, Despair, not feast on thee" ("[Carrion Comfort]," l. 1). Sometimes Hopkins addresses a particular person, Margaret in "Spring and Fall": "Márgarét, áre you gríeving" (l. 1), or Robert Bridges in "To R. B." Sometimes Hopkins appears to be speaking primarily to himself, so that the reader overhears the poet's secret meditations, as in the "terrible sonnets": "O what black hoürs we have spent / This night! what sights you, heart, saw; ways you went!" ("I wake and feel the fell of dark, not day," ll. 2–3). Many of the poems, finally, seem to be addressed primarily to the reader, as though they were speeches or sermons delivered in public. Such poems would include many of the nature poems, for example "As kingfishers catch fire," as well as more explicitly religious poems like "To what serves Mortal Beauty." But, of course, all of Hopkins's poems are in a sense addressed to the general reader, once they are written down and made public. This may explain why he was so loath to let his poems be published. To publish a poem addressed to God or to his own secret interior self, his "heart," would be like publishing his private correspondence, even if that correspondence were, as Hopkins says in one of the more moving phrases in the sonnets of desolation, "cries countless, cries like dead letters sent / To dearest him that lives alas! away" ("I wake and feel the fell of dark, not day," ll. 7–8).

What forms of language pervasive in the poems are candidates for the identification of a performative dimension there? In asking this we must remember that a performative by no means needs to take the form of a first-person present indicative locution. Candidates would include imperatives, pleadings, interjections, prosopopoetic apostrophes, and, most of all perhaps, all the poetic devices of alliteration, assonance, rhyme, the cunning sequences of words Hopkins called "vowelling on and vowelling off," strongly marked and echoing sprung rhythm, and so on, that go in Hopkins's poetry to make words into things. These things then have power to do other things in their turn, by a performative transformation that makes them embodied or materialized breathings, sighs, cries, yes-sayings.

Hopkins's poems are punctuated by a multitude of "O's," "Oh's," and "Ah's." These are sometimes just ejaculatory interjections, the inarticulate cry that precedes, it may be, and is presupposed by, all articulate language: "I did say yes / O at lightning and lashed rod" ("The Wreck of the Deutschland," ll. 9–10); "Oh, / We lash with the best or worst/Word last!" (ll. 58–59); "Ah, touched in your bower of bone, / Are you!" (ll. 137–38); "O unteachably after evil, but uttering truth" (l. 141); "Ah! there was a heart right!" (l. 225); "Finger of a tender of, O of a feathery delicacy" (l. 246); "Our King back, Oh, upon English souls!" (l. 276). All those are in "The Wreck of the Deutschland" alone, but there are dozens more in the later poems.

Here are a few: "Oh, morning, at the brown brink eastward, springs—" ("God's Grandeur," l. 12); "O look at all the fire-folk sitting in the air!" ("The Starlight Night," l. 2); "Complete thy creature dear O where it fails" ("In the Valley of the Elwy," l. 13); "O half hurls earth for him" ("Hurrahing in Harvest," l. 14); "O if

we but knew what we do" ("Binsey Poplars," l. 9); "O fair, fair have
fallen"; "Let him oh! with his air of angels then lift me, lay me!"
("Henry Purcell," ll. 1, 9); "O surely, reaving Peace, my Lord should
leave in lieu / Some good!" ("Peace," ll. 7–8); "O is he dead then?";
"Ah well, God rest him . . ." ("Felix Randal," ll. 1, 8); "O let them be
left, wildness and wet" ("Inversnaid," l. 15); "Ah, the hier / To his
own selfbent so bound" ("Ribblesdale," ll. 11–12); "But ah, but O
thou terrible" ("[Carrion Comfort]," l. 5; there are two more "O's"
in this poem alone); "O the mind, mind has mountains" ("No
worst, there is none," l. 9); "Oh what black hoürs we have spent"
("I wake and feel the fell of dark, not day," l. 2); "O pity and indig ¹
nation" ("That Nature is a Heraclitean Fire and of the comfort of
the Resurrection," l. 13); "Oh, the sots and thralls of lust / Do in
spare hours more thrive than I that spend, / Sir, life upon thy cause"
("Thou art indeed just, Lord," ll. 7–9). Often the sentences containing "O" or "Ah" end with an apostrophe, the unvoiced mark of
punctuation that indicates an exclamation or ejaculation.

Sometimes, however, the "O" is the signal of the prosopopoeia
of apostrophic address, often also signaled by the mark of punctuation called an apostrophe. The distinction, in some cases, between
interjection and apostrophe proper is not easy to maintain, for
example, in "O Deutschland, double a desperate name! / O world
wide of its good!" ("The Wreck of the Deutschland," ll. 155–56),
where the "O" may be read as simply exclamatory or as an apostrophic address to the ship and the country. The apostrophic "O" is
often associated with the crucial moment so characteristic of Hopkins's poems when description gives way to an imperative, an
optative, a prayer or blessing, in any case, to a form of locution that
is in one way or another no longer constative but has turned the
poem into a speech event.

First a few apostrophic "O's," all addressed to Christ or God,
then some examples of direct address without the "O," moments
that are in one way or another a calling of spirits from the vasty
deep, and finally some examples of the ubiquitous imperative or
optative moment in Hopkins's poetry: "O Christ, O God"; "O
Father"; "O Christ, Christ, come quickly" ("The Wreck of the

Deutschland," ll. 12, 83, 191); "O maid's child" ("Spring," l. 14); "O my chevalier!" ("The Windhover," l. 11); "Mine, O thou lord of life, send my roots rain" ("Thou art indeed just, Lord," l. 14). Now some apostrophes without the "O": "Thou mastering me / God!"; "thou Orion of light"; "Jesu, heart's light" ("The Wreck of the Deutschland," ll. 1–2, 165, 233); "When will you ever, Peace" ("Peace," l. 1); "Márgarét, áre you gríeving" ("Spring and Fall," l. 1); "Earth, sweet Earth" ("Ribblesdale," l. 1); "Not, I'll not, carrion comfort, Despair, not feast on thee"; "That night, that year / Of now done darkness I wretch lay wrestling with (my God!) my God" ("[Carrion Comfort]," ll. 1, 14–15; in the second citation the second "my God" is simply constative, while the first is a violent apostrophe); "Thou art indeed just, Lord." As for imperative or optative moments in Hopkins, they are ubiquitous: "Let him easter in us" ("The Wreck of the Deutschland," l. 277); "Look at the stars!" ("The Starlight Night," l. 1); "Have, get, before it cloy / Before it cloud, Christ, lord, and sour with sinning / Innocent mind and Mayday in girl and boy" ("Spring," ll. 11–13); "here / Buckle!" ("The Windhover," ll. 9–10); "Have fair fallen" ("Henry Purcell," l. 1); "Let them be left, / O let them be left, wildness and wet" ("Inversnaid," ll. 14–15); "Lét life, wáned, ah lét life wind" ("Spelt from Sibyl's Leaves," l. 10); "Here! creep, / Wretch, under a comfort serves in a whirlwind" ("No worst, there is none," ll. 12–13); "My own heart let me more have pity on"; "Mine, O thou lord of life, send my roots rain" ("Thou art indeed just, Lord," l. 14). All of these speech act features of Hopkins's poetry are present in this last example, the apostrophic "O," the prosopopoetic direct address, the constative assertion that turns into an imperative with a performative tinge, as "mine" is read first as an adverbial adjective modifying "roots" ("Whose roots?" "Mine!") and then as an imperative meaning "please dig down to my roots so the lifegiving rain can reach them."

The samples I have given of bits and pieces of Hopkins's verse also give sufficient examples of the devices of alliteration, assonance, vowel sequences, and strongly marked rhythm I have identified as giving substance to his poetry, but the best example of "vowelling on and vowelling off" I know in Hopkins's poetry will make it more manifest. In the first two lines of "Spelt from Sibyl's Leaves," the initial "û" of "earnest" is turned by degrees, as word follows word, into the "oo" of "stupendous" and then back finally to the "û" again of "hearse," followed by the final "i" of "night," in which all these distinctions among sound vanish, just as the play of "t's," "v's," and "w's" vanishes, too. The lines mime what they describe or do what they say:

> Earnest, earthless, equal, attuneable, ׀ vaulty, voluminous, . . . stupendous
> Evening strains to be tíme's vást, ׀ womb-of-all, home-of-all, hearse-of-all night.

Finally there is "yes." If Hopkins's verse from one end to the other is a massive "doing agree" or saying yes, then a "yes, I affirm this, I do say it" is implicit everywhere, unvoiced except in the inarticulate cry or sigh that everything Hopkins utters rises from but never wholly frees itself from, present still in all those "O's" and "Ah's" I have cited. "But indeed," says Hopkins, "I have often felt when I have been in this mood and felt the depth of an instress or how fast the inscape holds a thing that nothing is so pregnant and straightforward to the truth as simple *yes* and *is*" (*J*, 127, and see *J*, 129). It is by no means necessary actually to say "Yes" in order to say yes. But the actual word "yes" or "yea" appears at several crucial places in Hopkins's poetry, as the surfacing of an implicit "yea-saying" present everywhere. I began by citing "I did say yes / O at lightning and lashed rod" from "The Wreck of the Deutschland." That "yes" is echoed in "Yes I cán tell such a key, I dó know such a place" in "The Leaden Echo and the Golden Echo" (l. 7). The "yes" is iterated as "yea" in the last line of "To what serves Mortal Beauty": "Yea, wish that though, wish all, ׀ God's better beauty, grace" (l. 14). "Yes" appears once more by itself as the emphatic first word of "(The Soldier)," initiating the poem and underlining the whole poem with an implicit, "I do say this": "Yes. Whý do we áll, seeing of a soldier, bless him?"

If Jacques Derrida is right to say that "yes" is the transcendental condition of all performative language,[8] Hopkins's poetry, as a massive and continuously materialized saying yes, has a pervasive performative dimension that goes counter to his desire to submit his poetry to a religious world in which man's proper speech, his least sigh of aspiration, the infinitesimal mite of breathing "yes," should be as disembodied, as little public and dependent on social conventions, as little truly performative, as God's inspiration through grace or His initial *fiat lux*, to which man's saying yes is a response.

"Yes" is always double, paradoxical, self-contradictory, for example, in the "Yes" at the very beginning of "(The Soldier)." "Yes" is always a response, an answer presupposing previous language or other signs. You always say yes to something someone or something, some "other," has previously said. At the same time, "yes" is radically inaugural, initiatory. It is presupposed in all performatives. It perhaps necessarily leads to a performative dimension in the language that follows, for example, in the poems Hopkins wrote that came after his saying "yes" to God. That saying yes is always anterior but at the same time continuous. It is murmured as an implicit undertone or "underthought" in all Hopkins's poems. If all language, whether constative or performative, presupposes an initial "yes," that yes in turn always presupposes some preexisting language, word, Word, or marks, some "other," to which the "yes" says yes. The yes, however, always goes beyond acquiescence to become a performative act of its own. "Doing agree" is not the same thing as simply agreeing, just as saying "I did say yes" is not the same thing as saying "I said yes." Yes as "doing agreeing" turns the yes of passive acquiescence into the yes that is a speech act. Hopkins's poems are that "doing agree."

"Yes" is (in Hopkins's phrase from "The Wreck of the Deutschland" for the words and the tears that "break" from him in recreating in imagination the death of the nuns) "a madrigal start" (l. 142). It is both a rhythm in response to a previous rhythm, as in a madrigal, canon, or round, and at the same time a "start," an abrupt beginning. Hopkins's "sprung rhythm" is double in just the same way. On the one hand, it is a radical innovation in English metrical practice. On the other hand, it is, as Hopkins argued, an appropriation of rhythmic features already present in common language and in popular verse forms like nursery rhymes. Moreover, that "new rhythm" whose "echo" had long haunted Hopkins's ear and which he first "realised on paper" in "The Wreck" (*C*, 14) was a response to the deep rhythm of the creation. It was a kind of breathing in and out present, for example, in the "sway of the sea" ("The Wreck of the Deutschland," l. 3). Hopkins's sprung rhythm is a "madrigal start" in the sense of being an aspiration in response to that inspiration, but it goes beyond what inspires it. It initiates performatively something new of its own.

The performative dimension of Hopkins's poems, now that they are published and available where all who wish may read them, goes beyond and exceeds any inward, private, and disembodied saying yes into a public realm where they are indeed a way of doing things with words. They materialize the "O" or "Ah" or "Yes" that permeates them. This makes them the emergence of articulate meaning out of inarticulate cry. But that meaning still remains in one of its dimensions pre-performative inarticulate cry, as in the line from "(Carrion Comfort)," "But ah, but O thou terrible, why wouldst thou rude on me / Thy wring-world right foot rock?" (ll. 5–6), where the "ah" and "O," the "ow" and "ou" in "thou," "thou," and "rude," the obtrusive "w's" and "r's," and all the other devices of materializing non-semantic echo, as well as the performative prosopopoeia in the address to God as a triumphant wrestler, work against constative meaning to keep the words at the level of sound, sigh, cry, and thereby to make them words that do, that work.

The word "sigh" not only names a certain kind of aspiration or suspiration, to utter that word is to do what it names. One of the ways to sigh is to say "Sigh" or "Sss-iii-gh," drawing out the initial sibilant, prolonging the "i" and then cutting off the expiration of breath with the "gh" at the end, before all breath has been expelled. Hopkins's poems throughout turn names into acts by stressing in manifold ways the pure sounds of speech as opposed to their meaning and stressing also the way words do what they say, according to one of Hopkins's definitions of poetry. "Poetry," he said, "is speech framed for contemplation of the mind by the way of hearing or speech framed to be heard for its own sake and interest even over and above its interest of meaning. Some matter and meaning is essential to it but only as an element necessary to support and employ the shape which is contemplated for its own sake. . . . Poetry is in fact speech only employed to carry the inscape of speech for the inscape's sake—and therefore the inscape must be dwelt on" (*J*, 289). The inscape of speech is a pattern of echoing sounds, and therefore "verse is . . . inscape of spoken sound, not spoken words, or speech employed to carry the inscape of spoken sound" (*J*, 289).

I affirm that, yes, speech employed in this way is necessarily and radically performative.[9] Far from being that almost disembodied, infinitesimal sigh Hopkins wanted man's work toward his salvation to be, Hopkins's poems are initiatory, autonomous, even anomalous. They bring something new into the world, something that *does*, that is a way of doing things with words. This way is neither wholly controlled beforehand by social conventions nor by the expectations and assumptions of its auditors. In that sense Hopkins's poems are not lawful. They make their own laws. What a poem by Hopkins does was not predictable, just as Hopkins's formal innovations, for example, his use of the curtal sonnet and what might be called the exploded sonnet, build on the conventional rules of poetry but go beyond them in unexpected ways.

§ 7 Nietzsche in Basel: Changing Places in 'Thus Spoke Zarathustra'

> Nietzsche in Basel studied the deep pool
> Of these discolorations, mastering
> The moving and moving of their forms
> In the much-mottled motion of blank time.
>
> —Wallace Stevens, "Description without Place"

> Truth content is only to be grasped through immersion in the most intimate details of subject matter.
>
> —Benjamin, *The Origin of German Tragic Drama*

This chapter might have been called "Places, Turns, and Mappings," that is to say, "Topoi, Tropes, and Topographies." The starting place for my journey from one place to another is a series of questions. Is the topographical armature of *Also Sprach Zarathustra* (*Thus Spoke Zarathustra*)—all that toponymy of mountains, seas, deep sky, paths, roads, bridges, and so on—adventitious to the work's meaning or essential to it? Could the same thing have been said without the topographical paraphernalia, for example, in a straightforward conceptual exposition? If not, why not? What is the connection, if any, between Nietzsche's early writings on rhetoric and *Zarathustra*?

By "early writings on rhetoric" I mean primarily the lectures on rhetoric, "Darstellung der Antiken Rhetorik" ("Description of Ancient Rhetoric") of 1872–73, a course delivered in the winter semester at the University of Basel to two students, and the incomplete essay of summer 1873, "Über Wahrheit und Lüge im Außermoralischen Sinne" ("On Truth and Lies in an Extramoral Sense").[1] In these early works Nietzsche, as Wallace Stevens puts it, "studied the deep pool / Of these discolorations, . . . In the much-mottled motion of blank time," that is, he studied the colors of rhetoric as they (and our understanding of them) have evolved through Western history.

Why did Nietzsche have only two students and those from the institutes of Germanistic and Jurisprudence? Because in the aftermath of the controversy over *The Birth of Tragedy* all the students in classical philology were boycotting his course.[2] Nietzsche had been appointed an ordinarius professor of classics at Basel in 1869, at the extraordinarily young age of twenty-four. He resigned his post in 1879, ostensibly for reasons of ill health. Thereafter he published the series of great works for which he is known. Though Nietzsche is a master of German style, though his works are an admirable exploitation of the resources of the German language, they hardly conform to normal standards of correctness. Even *The Birth of Tragedy*, published in 1872, while Nietzsche was, of course, still a professor and prior to the lectures on rhetoric, is more a parody of an academic treatise than a solemn fulfillment of its requirements.

Why did Nietzsche write the way he did? The early works on rhetoric may suggest an answer to that question. They may also hint at a deeper reason why Nietzsche left the university. How could he fulfill the terms of his contract to teach and write in a certain way and at the same time say what he wanted to say, or what he found himself saying? On the one hand, the lectures on ancient rhetoric follow the norms of an academic course. On the other hand, when they are read carefully, with the attention to minute detail for which Benjamin calls, they turn out to be strangely complex and heterogeneous.

These early works are inhabited by a contradiction. As scholars have shown, Nietzsche borrowed freely from books by Friedrich Blass, Gustav Gerber, and Richard Volkmann for his account of ancient rhetoric. The contradiction is present in these sources. On the one hand, the lectures on rhetoric present a traditional and derivative typology of tropes. Even the examples he uses often come from those sources. Except for an occasional qualification, nothing, for example, could be more conventional than Nietzsche's account of "Der Tropische Ausdruck" ("The Tropical Expression") in the seventh lecture and of "Die Rhetorischen Figuren" ("The Rhetorical Figures") in the eighth lecture. His descriptions of tropes ("metaphor, synecdoche, metonymy, antonomasia, onomatopoeia, catachresis, metalepsis, epithet, allegory, irony, periphrasis, hyperbaton, anastrophe, parenthesis, and hyperbole" [55]) depend on the traditional distinction between the literal use of a word and its transferred uses: "Tropes deal with transferences [*Übertragungen*]: words are used instead of other words: the figurative is used instead of the literal [*an Stelle des Eigentlichen das Uneigentliche*]." (A more literal translation of the last phrase would be: "in place of the proper the improper.") (64, 65.)

Such formulations depend on an unambiguous concept of literal or proper language. They presuppose that literal meanings are prior to figurative meanings: "Die eigentlichen Bedeutungen erscheinen so als die älteren, schmucklosen." ("The proper meanings, therefore, seem to be the older, plainer ones.") (52, 53.) First there is the literal word that calls a ship's prow a prow. Such words are authorized, made proper, by their direct relation to the thing they name. There, before our eyes, is the front of the boat. We properly or with propriety call that the prow. The truth value of such language is a truth of correspondence or *adaequatio*. The complex Aristotelian epistemology connecting the seeing and naming of a thing with access to its essential form lies behind and supports the notion of proper language.[3] With the literal or proper name firmly in place, the tropical expression is then brought in, or carried over, from its own literal meaning to substitute for that proper name. Now the transferred literal term is used figuratively in place of the literal expression. The improper displaces the proper. We say, "The ship plows the waves." Tropes, it can be seen, are a matter of transference or changing places. The figurative word takes the place of the literal word, the improper the place of the proper. Tropes are usurping placeholders.

Along with this traditional theory of tropes is present even in Nietzsche's early works a quite different concept of figurative language. This too comes from Nietzsche's sources, especially Gustav Gerber's *Die Sprache als Kunst* (*Language as Art*).[4] Gerber, in turn, served as a conduit to Nietzsche for the theories of language in German Romanticism, that is, in Friedrich Schegel, Novalis, Jean Paul Richter, and others. But Nietzsche would already have known these authors through his training in Greek, Latin, and German literature as well as idealist philosophy at Schulpforta and the Universities of Bonn and Leipzig.[5] The co-presence and mutual interference of two ideas about tropes constitute the originality and interest of Nietzsche's early writings on rhetoric. According to the alternative theory, interwoven inextricably with the other, all words are aboriginally metaphorical transferences. No proper language exists. The "proper" is already "improper." "Truth" is therefore not grounded in access through the senses to the essence of the thing. Truth is rather a conventionally agreed-upon set of lies. Truth is lie not in the sense that it can be measured as false against some attainable correct naming. Truth is lie in the sense that it claims a false grounding in things as they are, when in fact it is constitutive, not constative. Here is the crucial paragraph in "On Truth and Lies in an Extramoral Sense":

> What is truth? a mobile army of metaphors, metonyms, anthropo-morphisms, in short, a sum of human relations which were poetically and rhetorically heightened [*gesteigert*], transferred [*übertragen*], and adorned, and after long use seem solid, canonical, and binding to a nation. Truths are illusions about which it has been forgotten that they *are* illusions, worn-out metaphors without sensory impact [*sinnlich kraftlos*], coins which have lost their image [*Bild*] and now can be used only as metal, and no longer as coins. (E250; G182)

This passage has been frequently interpreted, explicitly or implicitly.[6] Nevertheless, it needs to be read carefully again here, in the context of the particular questions I am raising now. One obvious feature of the paragraph is the way Nietzsche uses figures to talk about a truth that exists only as a fabric of figures. This already contradicts Nietzsche's apparent goal: to give clear conceptual knowledge of what truth is. Along with being told that truths are illusions, we are told that truth is a mobile army and that truth is a worn coin. Each figure Nietzsche uses has its own implications. To call truth a "mobile army" (*bewegliches Heer*) is to ascribe to that swarm of figures a martial function. Those metaphors, metonymies, and anthropomorphisms are engaged in a *Blitzkrieg*. A *Blitzkrieg* against what? Presumably against the knowledge that these illusions *are* illusions. This army of tropes has force. It is a force that irresistibly brings about a forgetting. Ultimately a whole nation, *ein Volk*, using that language is bewitched by the figures into forgetting that the figures are figures, the illusions illusions. As Nietzsche puts this in "On Truth and Lies," the human situation is to be "clinging to a tiger's back in dreams" (E247; G174). The image of the army and the image of the tiger join a long series of violent figures in the essay. These figures suggest that the human condition is one of extreme danger. We forget the figures are figures and take them as truth-telling concepts, solid, canonical, and binding. To make this aboriginal error of taking a figure literally is not a benign or noble illusion. Rather, it is like living in danger of being eaten by a tiger we do not even know is there because we are sound asleep on its back.

The concluding metaphor saying truths are coins that have lost their image seems clear enough until you begin to think about it. Then it can be seen to be an example of what it talks about. It is a figure whose conceptual value is too easy to take at face value, as we use a coin without bothering about what it is made of. Figurative language is to the illusory literal or conceptual language derived from it as a coin stamped with the image that makes it a coin worth so much in a given currency is to the same coin when its image has been worn away to invisibility and the coin has become a mere piece of metal. I conflate literal and conceptual language because Nietzsche does so, for example, in his account of the way the word "leaf" falsely subsumes all the variety of leaves, no two of which are alike, under the general concept of "leaf." Truth (in the sense of the conventional, illusory truth a "folk" accepts) is like a coin that no longer has its image.

A little reflection will show that something is wrong with this figure. The functioning of the figure depends on the traditional Aristotelian definition of a figure as a substitution for a literal word.

But Nietzsche is putting just that hierarchy into question. When the image is worn from the coin, the bare metal beneath is revealed. This is supposed to correspond to the figure when it is taken literally as a concept or a literal term. But the bare metal is rather the underlying, meaningless matter, substratum of the image. The image gives the metal meaning, makes it a coin. A bare piece of metal is hardly an appropriate image for the columbarium of concepts Nietzsche describes later in the essay as a figure for a fully established canonical language. The image makes the metal something that passes current as a value among the folk of a particular nation, just as it is the figure taken literally that is solid, canonical, and binding. The crisscross of substitutions put in play by the figure does not correspond to the concept. The figure rather obscures or reverses the putative concept. The image on the coin is more like the concept that gives the coin value, while the underlying metal is more like the sensible figure that sustains it. Nietzsche seems to have got his lines crossed in making the crisscross of displacements.

Far from untangling or reversing the play of substitutions that has made us take illusion as truth, far from putting real truth in place of the illusory truth of figure, as Nietzsche's formulations promise to do, his figure of the coin worn bare reasserts the illusion it would demystify. This occurs another way in what happens to the figure of force in the passage. If the mobile army of tropes has military force, the kind of force brute physical nature has, the return of the coin to bare metal, that is, to brute physical nature, deprives the coin of sensible force and renders it *kraftlos*, powerless. The two attributions of force are not congruent or logically coherent. Nietzsche's attempt to use figure to demystify the power of figures has reasserted that power in a way that gives only an illusory clarity. Rather than substituting a tropical expression for a literal one, an improper expression for a clear and distinct proper one, Nietzsche has substituted one trope for another and has remained always within the same domain of tropical language. The figure of the coin substitutes for the initial conceptual formulation about the way truth is a mobile army of metaphors, metonymies, and anthropomorphisms. The figure "illustrates" the concept in a sensible figure, making it easier to understand, while remaining subservient to it. But the original conceptual formulation was already a figure, the figure of an army. The new figure of the coin displaces the initial figure of the army. The operation of Nietzsche's language gives an example of what he is claiming to talk about in clear conceptual language, but that fact prevents his language from being conceptual, clear, or literal. It does not and cannot give the knowledge it promises, since no metalanguage exists to take us outside the illusions of ordinary language, its taking of figurative language as literal, the improper as proper. This should come as no surprise, since by Nietzsche's own account no proper language exists for which the army of figures he presents is the displacement.[7]

∼

Zarathustra reverses in a different way the traditional submission of figurative to literal language, as I shall show. Is this erasure of the traditional relation between literal and figurative language anticipated at all in the lectures on classical rhetoric, given just a few months before "On Truth and Lies" was written? The evidence given so far would suggest that it is not. This would lead to a plausible scenario, even though the publication in 1872 of *The Birth of Tragedy* shows that "On Truth and Lies" did not spring from nowhere. Nevertheless, it might be argued that Nietzsche presented to his students during the school year a conventional and derivative account of ancient rhetoric. Then in the summer of 1873 he developed his own rhetorical theory, something that anticipates or contains in germ the ideas about morality, language, and rhetoric of the "mature Nietzsche," the Nietzsche of *The Genealogy of Morals* or of the so-called *Will to Power*. A little more reading in the lectures on rhetoric shows that this teleological scenario is false. The ideas about tropes, language, and rhetoric in "On Truth and Lies" are already fully sketched out in the third lecture of "Description of Ancient Rhetoric," "Verhältniss des Rhetorischen zur Sprache" ("The Relation of the Rhetorical to Language"). This lecture systematically undoes the presuppositions about language, rhetoric, and tropes that are the basis of ancient rhetoric. Formulations almost identical to those in "On Truth and Lie" already occur. The latter might be defined as an expansion of the third lecture in the course. That third lecture was taken chiefly from Gerber, often word for word, as the concordance prepared by Anthonie Meijers and Martin Stingelin shows.[8]

That third lecture develops a series of interrelated propositions. All language is figurative from the beginning. It is tropological because it is based on a sequence of displacements from a forever-unknowable reality. Therefore the distinction between literal and figurative language is false. No literal language exists. This means that the distinction between rhetoric as knowledge of tropes and rhetoric as knowledge of various persuasive techniques is also false, as is the distinction between rhetoric and ordinary language. Classical rhetoric employed tropes as one way to aid persuasion, as Nietzsche shows in detail in his account of the various forms of rhetoric: forensic, epideictic, deliberative. For Nietzsche, on the other hand, following Gerber, rhetoric as persuasion and rhetoric as tropes are the same, since all language is tropological and the tropes persuade. All language is persuasive rather than truth-telling. All language is primordially rhetorical. The means of this persuasion is the figurative displacement of all language. The latter is not a possible persuasive force in language freely manipulated by an orator to achieve a certain goal. It is an irresistible persuasive power built into a given language from the beginning. This force persuades the users of that language to take a pack of lies as the truth.

"But, with respect to their meaning [*Bedeutung*]," says Nietzsche, "all words are tropes in themselves, and from the beginning" (E23; G22). A little later: "What is usually called language is actually all figuration" (E25; G24). It follows from this that "the tropes are not just occasionally added to words but constitute their most proper nature. It makes no sense to speak of a 'proper meaning' [*eigentlichen Bedeutung*] which is carried over to something else only in special cases" (E25; G24).

It follows, "in turn," or by a further displacement, from this rejection of literal meaning that no separation can be made between "natural" language and rhetorical language. All language is already rhetorical through and through. It "desires" not to give true knowledge of the essence of things but to persuade its users to accept a set of illusions as true. Nietzsche's personification of language here as a being with desires not only uses one of the primary tropes, prosopopoeia, he identifies, it also displaces the orator's conscious desire to persuade (for example, the lawyer trying to persuade the court of his guilty client's innocence) to the unconscious workings of the language:

> There is obviously no unrhetorical "naturalness" of language to which one could appeal; language itself is the result of purely rhetorical arts. The power to discover and to make operative that which works and impresses [*was wirkt und Eindruck macht*], with respect to each thing, a power which Aristotle calls rhetoric, is, at the same time, the essence of language [*das Wesen der Sprache*]; the latter is based just as little as rhetoric is upon that which is true, upon the *essence* of things [*auf das* Wesen *der Dinge*]. Language does not desire to instruct, but to convey to [*übertragen*] others a subjective impulse and its acceptance. (E21; G20)

Nietzsche's theory of language, in particular his rejection of the traditional distinction between literal and figurative words, follows naturally and inevitably from his presuppositions about the human epistemological situation. This is an important point in my argument. Aristotle defines figurative language as a double displacement of literal language. The literal word is displaced by a figurative one, which has itself been displaced from its literal meaning. We say "The ship plows the waves." This account of figure, as I have said, is inextricably tied to the assumption that we have direct access, through our senses, to the true essence of things. Literal names record and take possession of the truth of things as they are. For Nietzsche, on the other hand, again following his sources, human beings are forever cut off from the truth about things by the mediated nature of their access to things through the senses and by way of the body. It follows from this situation, again as something inextricably tied to it, that all language is tropological displacement, figurative names for an unknown and forever unknowable *X ignotum*. The prow of that ship is *not* there before our eyes. We "see" only a nerve excitation, so "prow" is already a figure. To say "the ship plows the waves" substitutes one figure for another, not a figurative word for a literal one. This is argued first in the third lecture of "Description of Ancient Rhetoric" and then in a similar way in "On Truth and Lies." In both cases the claim is that so-called literal language is already the result of a whole series of figurative displacements:

> Man, who forms language [*der sprachbildende Mensch*], does not perceive things or events, but *impulses* [Reize]: he does not communicate sensations, but merely copies [*Abbildungen*] of sensations. The sensation, evoked through a nerve impulse, does not take in the thing itself: this sensation is presented externally through an image [*ein Bild*]. But the question of how an act of the soul can be presented through a sound image must be asked. If completely accurate representation [*Wiedergabe*] is to take place, should the material in which it is to be represented, above all, not be the same as that in which the soul works? However, since it is something alien—the sound—how then can something come forth more accurately as an *image* [Bild]? It is not the things that pass over into consciousness, but the manner in which we stand toward them, the *pithanon* [power of persuasion, plausibility; also a thing producing illusion]. The full essence of things [*die volle Wesen der Dinge*] will never be grasped. (E23; G22)

This short passage is a systematic dismantling of Aristotelian epistemology and its replacement by the claim that every human being is enclosed not only in the prison house of language but, outside that prison, by another, the prison of false nerve impulses that give us no direct access to the "essence of things." A given word naming some putative thing is the result not just of one, but of a whole series of displacements that can metaphorically all be called metaphors. The thing produces a nerve impulse. The nerve impulse produces a sensation, a mental image. The sensation is then expressed in a sound, the spoken word. This is another metaphorical displacement, since the spoken word is by no means of the same substance as the sensation-image but merely stands for it. It is in this sense that for Nietzsche "all words are tropes, in themselves, and from the beginning." They are tropes for that forever unavailable "mysterious X." It follows from this that what are ordinarily thought of as primary tropes, metaphor and metonymy, are no more than secondary displacements of the primary displacements producing language in the first place. This is what Nietzsche means when he says, "The second form of the *tropus* is the metaphor" (E23; G22). In fact metaphor "proper" would be the fourth degree of metaphorical displacement: from the nerve excitation to the sensation to the image of that sensation in a spoken word to the displacement of that word to a new use. Nietzsche says just this in a passage in "On Truth and Lies" that corresponds closely to the account of the origin of language in the third lecture:

> The 'thing-in-itself' [*das "Ding an sich"*] (which would be pure, disinterested truth) is also absolutely incomprehensible to the creator of language [*Sprachbildner*] and not worth seeking. He designates only the relations of things to men, and to express these relations he uses the boldest metaphors. First, he translates a nerve stimulus into an image! [*Ein Nervenreiz, zuerst übertragen in ein Bild!*] That is the first metaphor. Then, the image must be reshaped into a sound! The second metaphor. And each time there is a complete overleaping [*Überspringen*] of spheres—from one sphere to the center of a completely different, new one. . . . When we speak of trees, colors, snow, and flowers, we believe we know something about the things themselves, although what we have are just metaphors of things, which do not correspond at all to the original entities. . . . The mysterious *X* of the thing [*das rätselhafte X des Dings*] appears first as a nerve stimulus, then as an image, and finally as a sound. (E249; G178)

Nietzsche's assertion that all language is originally metaphorical must be distinguished from similar assertions by Rousseau and Condillac in the eighteenth century. Each has a different historical placement, a different location within the history of ideas. Rousseau and Condillac, each in a different way, hold to an empirical, or Lockean, epistemology. For Rousseau, for example, it is not some unhappy enclosure in a world of nerve excitations that leads his exemplary maker of the first metaphors to call a man a giant. It is a misinterpretation born of fear. Nietzsche's explanation of why all language is tropological, on the other hand, is rooted in nineteenth-century physiology and psychology. If you have a different conception of nerves, brain, body, senses, and consciousness, you will have a different notion of the origin of language and of the relation of language to reality. Nietzsche's ideas about nerve stimuli, sensations, the separation of what he calls "spheres," and our inability to confront the essence of things directly are essential to his theory of language, tropes, and rhetoric, not adventitious components of it. The same thing can be said of Aristotle. His ideas about *energeia*, *enargeia*, essence, being, form, and so on, are the presupposed background of the *Poetics* and the *Rhetoric*.

What then are we to make of the passages I cited earlier from the lectures on rhetoric in which Nietzsche appears to reaffirm the traditional formulation that makes figurative language a displacement of an original literal language? These passages must be a species of indirect discourse or *erlerbte Rede*. Nietzsche is repeating as a good pedagogue should what the authors he is telling his students about said and believed. Another way to put this is to say that the lectures on ancient rhetoric are, with the exception of the third lecture and a few touches here and there revealing what Nietzsche really thought, ironical through and through. They are the ironically solemn repetition of a colossal, centuries-long mistake, a mistake based on a false idea of language and epistemology that dominated both Greek and Roman ideas about rhetoric. Only rarely does Nietzsche allow his own opinions to break through the ironic deadpan miming of what Aristotle, Quintilian, and the rest had to say. An example is his comment on Quintilian's distinction between popular tropes and rhetorical tropes: "Thus, the popular tropes originated from embarrassment and stupidity [*Verlegenheit und Dummheit*], the rhetorical tropes from art and delight [*Kunst and Wohlgefallen*]." "This," says Nietzsche firmly, "is an entirely false contrast [*ganz falscher Gegensatz*]" (E53; G52), as indeed it would be if he is right in refusing to distinguish between ordinary language and rhetorical language. A moment earlier Nietzsche had quoted Jean Paul Richter as being right where the ancients were wrong when he said in the *Vorschule der Aesthetik* (*Elementary Course in Aesthetics*) that "each language is a dictionary of faded metaphors [*ein Wörterbuch erblasster Metaphern*]" (E53; G52). Though Nietzsche's early writings on rhetoric are an event, a decisive moment in the history of rhetoric, the ideas in them are by no means absolutely new. They have an immediate history in German Romanticism and a much longer history going back to a countertradition within Greek and Roman rhetoric.

~

Does this account of Nietzsche's early writings on rhetoric help in reading *Thus Spoke Zarathustra*? Anyone who has tried to come to terms with *Zarathustra* will know what the problems are. *Zarathustra* is generally considered to be one of Nietzsche's most important works, perhaps even the most important of all. It is the centerpiece, included in its entirety, of Walter Kaufmann's widely used *Viking Portable Nietzsche*. Nevertheless, it can hardly be said to be the center of attention in recent important studies of Nietzsche.[9] Nietzsche called it "A Book for All and None." This may mean that it is, as Kaufmann says, "by far Nietzsche's most popular book" (ZE103), while at the same time never actually being read. What would it mean to read *Thus Spoke Zarathustra*?

Zarathustra is quite unlike any other work by Nietzsche. Here Nietzsche's main "ideas"—the death of God, the eternal return, the overman, the revaluation of all values, the great noon—are "presented" (if that is the right way to put it) not discursively, conceptually, and aphoristically, in the first person, as in most of Nietzsche's work, but in dramatized, narrative form. *Zarathustra* has a protagonist, an elaborate setting, and a rudimentary story involving various personages and animals, as well as journeys across a landscape of solitary mountains, inhabited plains, seashore, and sea. Moreover, the style of *Zarathustra* is, to say the least, heightened, portentous, melodramatic. Zarathustra preaches in a loud voice. Here the Dionysiac is practiced, not just described. The irony and light touch that Nietzsche prized in Mozart or Stendhal and that leavens even his own *Ecce Homo* seems for the most part absent here. Finally, if the large-scale structure of *Zarathustra* is narrative rather than aphoristic or argumentative, the local grain or texture of the style is not just pervasively figurative. That would be too little to say. Much of the time Nietzsche presents figures without the clear and distinct concepts they appear to be in aid of presenting. The reader is given the figurative without the literal, as if what Zarathustra has to say can only be said in figure. These local figures are often, though by no means always, drawn from the large-scale topographical setting of the narrative. One example is the last sentence of the sixth section of "On Old and New Tablets," from the Third Part: "Those who are going under [*die Unterge-henden*] I love with my whole love: for they cross over [*gehn hinüber*]."[10] What in the world does that mean? The sentence uses "figuratively" the geographical terminology of the "literal" setting. How can this mode of expression be justified as a way of presenting what everyone agrees are Nietzsche's central concepts, the eternal return, the death of God, the overman, the great noon, and so on? Is the mode of presentation necessary, the only way Nietzsche could say what he had to say, or are these stylistic features a way of dressing up in dramatic and ornately figurative form what could just as well have been said in a straightforward logical, argumentative, conceptual way?

In order to answer these questions, it will be necessary to exemplify in a little more detail what the problems are in trying to read *Thus Spoke Zarathustra*. The third part of *Zarathustra* begins with a section called "The Wanderer." The first three parts of *Zarathustra* were initially published separately, so one might imagine someone who had picked up part three in a bookstore and was sitting down in all innocence to begin to read. The first sentences are straightforward scene setting. They might have appeared in a novel: "It was about midnight when Zarathustra started across the ridge of the island so that he might reach the other coast by early morning; for there he wanted to embark. There he would find a good roadstead where foreign ships too liked to anchor, and they often took along people who wanted to cross the sea from the blessed isles" (ZE264; ZG403). So far so good. The reader feels perfectly at home, except for the place name "the blessed isles," which sounds a little odd. A few sentences later, however, when the reader enters into Zarathustra's meditations as he climbs the mountain to reach the harbor on the other side of the island, she enters another world of discourse:

"And one further thing I know: I stand before my final peak [*meinem letzten Gipfel*] now and before that which has been saved up for me the longest. Alas, now I must face my hardest path! Alas, I have begun my loneliest walk! But whoever is of my kind cannot escape such an hour—the hour which says to him:

"Only now are you going your way to greatness! Peak and abyss—they are now joined together. [*Gipfel und Abgrund—das ist jetzt in eins beschlossen!*]"

. . .

"And if you now lack all ladders, then you must know how to climb on your own head [*so mußt du verstehen, noch auf deinen eigenen Kopf zu steigen*]: how else would you want to climb upward? On your own head and away over your own heart!"

. . .

"But you, O Zarathustra, wanted to see the ground and background of all things [*wolltest aller Dinge Grund schaun und Hintergrund*]; hence you must climb over yourself [*so mußt du schon über dich selber steigen*]—upward, up until even your stars are *under* you!"

. . .

Alas, destiny and sea! To you I must now go *down*! [*Ach, Schicksal und See! Zu euch muß ich nun* hinab*steigen!*] Before my highest mountain I stand and before my longest wandering; to that end I must first go down deeper than ever I descended—deeper into pain than ever I descended, down into its blackest flood. . . .

Whence come the highest mountains? I once asked. Then I learned that they came out of the sea. The evidence is written in their rocks and in the walls of their peaks. It is out of the deepest depth that the highest must come to its height. [*Aus dem Tiefsten muß das Höchste zu seiner Höhe kommen.*] (ZE264–66; ZG403–5)

Something strange has happened to the language here. The topographical elements of the setting—mountains, night sky, and sea—have become the vehicles for expressing something else, but that something else is not expressed in conceptual terms. Rather, it is expressed exclusively in terms drawn from the landscape: "Alas, destiny and sea! To you I must now go *down*! . . . It is out of the deepest depth that the highest must come to its height." Nor is this strange mode of expression intermittent in *Thus Spoke Zarathustra*. It is the pervasive and almost universal level of discourse. Reading *Zarathustra* right depends on getting right what it means to use language in this way. "The Wanderer," for example, is followed by "On the Vision and the Riddle" ["Vom Gesicht und Rätsel"], one of the most important sections in the whole of *Zarathustra*. Here the eternal return is most powerfully affirmed. But it is affirmed not in conceptual terms but precisely in "vision and riddle," in the form of a story Zarathustra tells to those on shipboard as they sail away from the Blessed Isles. It is the story of a vision, or rather of a vision within a vision, both of which are told in the same circumstantial, topographical terms that are used in the first sentence of part three, cited above. First Zarathustra tells the sailors the story of how he climbed a wild mountain path with a dwarf on his back, the "spirit of gravity," and then expounded to the dwarf the meaning of a gateway they reach in their climb: "From this gateway, Moment [*Augenblick*], a long, eternal lane leads *backward*; behind us lies an eternity. Must not whatever *can* walk have walked on this lane before? Must not whatever *can* happen have happened, have been done, have passed by before? . . .—must not all of us have been there before? And return and walk in that other lane, out there, before us, in this long dreadful lane—must we not eternally return?" (ZE270; ZG408–9).

Then within that vision, as Zarathustra tells it to the sailors, another vision displaces the first, a parable of the first parable, the vision of the shepherd with the snake in his mouth and throat who is transfigured when he finds the courage to bite off the head of the snake: "No longer shepherd, no longer human—one changed, radiant, *laughing*!" (ZE272; ZG410). A moment before, Zarathustra gives four names for the story he tells. It was a vision, a riddle, a foreseeing, and a parable: "You who are glad of riddles! Guess me this riddle that I saw then, interpret me the vision [*das Gesicht*] of the loneliest. For it was a vision and a foreseeing [*ein Vorhersehn*]. What did I see then in a parable [*im Gleichnisse*]?" (ZE271–72; ZG410.)

The stylistic texture of all of *Zarathustra* remains more or less like this, even when what is presented is not explicitly vision and riddle. Almost any passage would serve as example. I cite one more passage from much later in part three, from the second section of "On Old and New Tablets":

> My wise longing [*Sehnsucht*] cried and laughed thus out of me—born in the mountains, verily, a wild wisdom—my great broad-winged longing [*meine große flügelbrausende Sehnsucht*]! And often it swept me away and up and far, in the middle of my laughter; and I flew, quivering, an arrow, through sun-drunken delight, away into distant futures which no dream had yet seen, into hotter souths than artists ever dreamed of, where gods in their dances are ashamed of all clothes—to speak in parables and to limp and stammer like poets; and verily, I am ashamed that I must still be a poet [*daß ich nämlich in Gleichnisse rede, und gleich Dichtern hinke und stammle: und wahrlich, ich schäme mich, daß ich noch Dichter sein muß!*—]. (ZE309; ZG444)

These passages contain a terminological clue that will make it possible to name the mode of discourse of *Zarathustra* and so have a hypothetical way to read it all. Zarathustra says he has been speaking in parables. What does this mean? The word "parable" is the only rhetorical term that appears repeatedly in *Zarathustra*. It is used here and there to name what sort of thing the book itself is. The word "parable" does not appear in the early lectures on rhetoric. It was not part of the ancient taxonomy of tropes. The trope of "allegory" is, however, defined, as is "riddle." The definition of allegory is cited from Quintilian: "Allegoria (inversio) . . . aliud verbis, aliud sensu ostendit" ("Allegory [inversion] . . . presents one thing in words and another in meaning)" (63). The riddle (*das Rätsel*), is "a very obscure allegory" (*eine ganz dunkle Allegorie*). It is, says Quintilian, "not permitted in a speech" (*ist in der Rede unstatthaft*) (62, 63). Though the term "fable" (*Fabel*) does not appear in the lectures, it does appear just at the beginning of "On Truth and Lies" as the proper term to define the initial story of the clever but ephemeral animals that appeared on a star in a remote corner of the universe and "invented knowledge [*das Erkennen erfanden*]" (E246; G170). What is the difference between an allegory, a fable, and a parable? Why does Nietzsche in *Zarathustra* define what he is doing as parable rather than as allegory?

One answer is clear enough. In a multitude of ways *Thus Spoke Zarathustra* is modeled on the gospels. It tells the story of a wandering preacher who teaches a new doctrine, often by way of parables. One section of part three is called "Upon the Mount of Olives." Another is called "On Old and New Tablets." Many passages are more or less explicitly reversals of what Jesus taught, as when Zarathustra, "the godless," says, "Do love your neighbor as yourself, but first be such as *love themselves*—loving with a great love, loving with a great contempt" (ZE284; ZG421).

The publication of part four of *Zarathustra* was held up after the onset of Nietzsche's insanity by the fear that it would be confiscated for blasphemy. That did not happen, perhaps because no one read it. In any case, "parable" is a key word in the gospels (*Gleichnis* in Luther's translation): "And he spake many things to them in parables" (Matthew 13:3). Nietzsche's (or Zarathustra's) use of the term "parable" is part of the parodic reversal of the gospels in *Zarathustra*. What, then, is a parable, and how do Zarathustra's parables differ from Christ's?[11]

A parable is a little, realistic story that has a hidden meaning. It means something other than what it says. The figurative meaning, according to the etymology of "parable," is "thrown beside" the literal meaning. As the German word *Gleichnis* implies, the figurative meaning is presented in a "likeness" or "image." *Gleichnis* means "image, simile, metaphor, figure of speech; allegory, parable" (*Cassell's German Dictionary*). Parable differs from allegory not only in the biblical resonance of the former and the more classical resonance of the latter (in spite of the fact that both are derived from Greek words), but in the fact that a parable is a short, realistic story embedded in another argument or narrative, whereas a long text may be allegorical from one end to the other. This is true whether we are thinking of Dante's definition of Christian allegory or of Paul de Man's contention that all texts are allegories of their own unreadability.[12]

The difference between Christ's parables and Zarathustra's is easy to state. Christ's parables all have to do with the kingdom of heaven and how to get there. As many commentators have noted, the biblical parables have to do with their own working. An effective parable is a performative use of language. When it works, when it is presented to those who have eyes to see and ears to hear and understand, the parable is a way to get from here to there. A parable is a way to cross over to the kingdom of heaven. Moreover, though the parables of Jesus were probably originally presented as enigmatic little stories—riddles without a "solution," the corresponding spiritual truths—as the parables exist now in the gospels the literal meaning is explicitly given. Jesus' explication of the parable of the sower is a good example: "But he that received seed into the good ground is he that heareth the word, and understandeth it; which also beareth fruit, and bringeth forth, some an hundredfold, some sixty, some thirty" (Matthew 13:23). The parables of Jesus are told by the Word, the Logos, since Christ is the Word. Their meaning is governed by the Word. This Word can be stated conceptually as well as in parabolic form. The Word is the ground and guarantee of all words, whether conceptual or parabolic. It may be reached by those who hear the word and understand it. For them words are transparent windows opening to the Word.

Why then does Jesus speak to the people in parables? Jesus gives the answer to the disciples, who ask just that question: "Because it is given to you to know the mysteries of the kingdom of heaven, but to them it is not given. For whosoever hath, to him shall be given, and he shall have more abundance: but whosoever hath not, from him shall be taken away even that he hath. Therefore speak I to them in parables: because they seeing see not; and hearing they hear not, neither do they understand" (Matthew 13:11–13). The paradox of Jesus' parables is that they are addressed to ears that will not understand them. If you can understand them you do not need them. If you need them you will not understand them.

The parables of Zarathustra are radically different from the parables of Jesus. They are different because Nietzsche's theory of language and his conception of the human epistemological situation are radically different from the New Testament one. The phrases at the end of the passage quoted above from "On Old and New Tablets" tell the reader what that theory of language and that situation are: "—to speak in parables and to limp and stammer like poets; and verily, I am ashamed that I must still be a poet!" (ZE309; ZG444). As Freud says by way of the citation from al-Hariri at the end of *Beyond the Pleasure Principle,* "What we cannot reach flying, we must reach limping [*erhinken*]. . . . The Book says, it is no sin to limp. [*Die Schrift sagt, es ist keine Sünde zu hinken.*]"[13] In what comes just before the identification of speaking in parables, on the one hand, and limping and stammering like poets, on the other, Zarathustra has described a flight of his "wise longing" into a visionary future "where gods in their dances are ashamed of all clothes." The gods need no clothes and are ashamed of them. Zarathustra, though he is ashamed of it, must clothe what he says in the covering of parabolic language. To do this is to limp rather than to dance and to stammer rather than to speak clearly. To stammer is to speak a language that cannot be understood because the material or bodily dimension of language—sounds and the effort of tongue, lips, palate, and throat—gets in the way of comprehensible meaning. Instead of perspicuous speech, repetitive and almost incomprehensible sounds are produced. Of Zarathustra's language and the language of *Thus Spoke Zarathustra* it can be said, to borrow phrases from *The Birth of Tragedy,* that it is "almost undecided as to whether it will communicate or conceal, as if stammering in a foreign tongue."[14] Or, rather, Zarathustra has no choice but to stammer. He must, willynilly, cover what he says in the garments of parable because no naked language exists for what he is trying to say. Here is another reversal of biblical precedent. When Adam and Eve ate the apple of knowledge they saw that they were naked, were ashamed of it, and covered their nakedness with fig leaves. Zarathustra, reversing this, is ashamed that he cannot go naked. Even, or perhaps especially, his vision of those "hotter souths than artists ever dreamed of, where gods in their dances are ashamed of all clothes" must be expressed in the shameful garments of parable. The passage is an example of what it talks about. Rather than defining parable it gives more parabolic or figurative definitions of it: limping, stammering like poets, wearing clothes when you ought to dance naked.

Unlike Jesus' parable of the sower, where the answer to the riddle is clearly given in literal language, the distinction between figurative and literal language clearly marked, Zarathustra's language attempts to lift itself, so to speak, by its own bootstraps, or to climb on its own head. It is parable about parable rather than parabolic expression of some available literal language. It must be this because for Zarathustra, as for Nietzsche in the early lectures on rhetoric and in "On Truth and Lies," no literal language exists. The ideas about language of the early writings on rhetoric are still the underlying presuppositions of *Thus Spoke Zarathustra*. Zarathustra (or *Zarathustra*) speaks in parables from one end of the book to the other, but it is a curious kind of parabolic language, which cannot be translated into its conceptual or literal meaning.

The traditional rhetorical name for this kind of language is "catachresis." Catachresis is the bringing in of a term from another realm to cover or clothe a gap in language. Nietzsche's example in "Description of Ancient Rhetoric" is the use of *lapidare* to describe the throwing of clods or potsherds: "while *lapidare* has the obvious meaning of 'to stone,' there is no special word to describe the throwing of clods or potsherds. Hence abuse or *katachresis* of words becomes necessary" (51). When Nietzsche says, "Those who are going under I love with my whole love: for they cross over," he means just that and only that. It is an error to think that the proper reading of this sentence would translate it into some conceptual language for which it is the parabolic expression. *Zarathustra* is throughout parables without proper meaning.

I have spoken of such language as an impossible self-suspension whereby Nietzsche's parabolic language sustains itself on itself rather than by its decipherable reference to the ideas it presents parabolically. A parabolic figure for this appears repeatedly in

Zarathustra: the reversible image of a vehicle that becomes itself carried by what it carries. Zarathustra carries the dwarf, spirit of gravity, up the mountain, but his own lightness and laughter rise above that heaviness and, so to speak, ride on it. When Zarathustra climbs the mountain at the beginning of the third part, he says, "You must know how to climb on your own head." Zarathustra's most important definition of parable, in "The Return Home," depends on just this reversal of rider and mount, of tenor and vehicle, to use familiar twentieth-century terms for the literal meaning and its metaphorical expression. The terms are appropriate, since metaphor means, etymologically, "carried to another place," "transferred." But in Nietzsche's figures carrier becomes carried and vice versa. As Zarathustra's "*home*, solitude" says to him in "The Return Home": "Here [meaning here in your home solitude] all things come caressingly to your discourse [*Rede*] and flatter you, for they want to ride on your back. On every parable you ride to every truth. [*Auf jedem Gleichnis reitest du hier zu jeder Wahrheit.*]" (ZE295; ZG432). When Zarathustra is at home, all things are easily turned into language. Things are carried by words. In being turned into words they become parable. Parables are the vehicles of things, by the series of displacements Nietzsche describes in the early rhetorical writings, each displacement further from the unknowable thing in itself: from nerve excitation to subjective image to word-sound. The passage, in its personification of things as caressing, fawning animals that want to be carried on Zarathustra's back, is an example of what it names. In this figure the unknown and unknowable things are turned into parabolic images, as in the fable of the man who ended by carrying his own donkey. Then the relation of rider and beast of burden reverses again. The things turned into parabolic words become the beast of burden on which Zarathustra rides: "On every parable you ride to every truth." What those "truths" are we know. They are the mobile army of metaphors, metonymies, and anthropomorphisms that constitute the parables. They are truths that cannot be extricated from the figures used to express them, for example, the topographical notations that form the narrative armature of *Thus*

Spoke Zarathustra. Zarathustra remains constrained to speak in parables and to limp and stammer like poets even when he is naming as accurately as possible the nature of those parables.

Nietzsche in *Thus Spoke Zarathustra* remains true to the theory of language he proposed in his early writings. But to say he remains true to his early theory of language is not enough. Those ideas about language cannot be detached from the epistemological presuppositions that underlie them. A theory of rhetoric, for example, Aristotle's, Quintilian's, or Nietzsche's, can never be detached from the epistemological and ontological presuppositions that underlie it. Aristotle's theory of tropes cannot be separated from his confidence in our ability to know the essence of things through our senses. Nietzsche moves without transition from language about our imprisonment in "nerve excitations" to language about the linguistic displacements of metaphor. To accept a theory of tropes is implicitly also to accept its epistemological or even physiological ground. In the case of *Thus Spoke Zarathustra*, the topographical language does not name the scenic background within which a dramatic action or a conceptual argument unfolds. That language remains in the foreground as a primary vehicle of meaning. It says something that can be said in no other way.

§ 8 Ideology and Topography: Faulkner

Does any feature of Faulkner's *Absalom, Absalom!* escape from ideology or is every bit of it, from one end to the other, ideological through and through? How would one recognize the right answer to that question or verify it? What difference would it make if we gave a yes or a no answer to the question? Would we like the novel better or worse if some aspect of it could be shown to be not ideological?

In order to begin to answer these questions, a definition of ideology is necessary. "Ideology" is an odd word. In the English language, it has a complex and to some degree contradictory history, though not a long one. The earliest example in the *O.E.D.* is from 1796. The *O.E.D.* defines ideology either as meaning "The science of ideas; that department of psychology which deals with the origin and nature of ideas," especially as "applied to the system of the French philosopher Condillac, according to which all ideas are derived from sensations," or as meaning, by 1813, "ideal or abstract speculation; in a depreciatory sense, unpractical or visionary theorizing or speculation." The word originally came into English as a borrowing from the French word *idéologie. Idéologues* was the name given to Condillac, Destutt de Tracy, and other empiricists who, following Locke, believed in the material or sensationalist origin of ideas. The contradiction inherent in the word today is already present in the earliest uses. On the one hand, ideology is the science of ideas, a mode of clear and distinct knowledge. On the other hand, ideology is visionary error, a lack of clear and distinct knowledge. In one case, the origin of ideas in sensation is known. In the other case, ideas are freed from their material origin and taken in error as an independently valid realm.

The word "ideology" is used in many conflicting ways today. The word is a battleground fought over by warring ideologies. But in all its uses it bears the marks of its appropriation by Marx and Marxism. It also still retains some version of the contradiction inherent in the word from the start. In the People's Republic of China or in the now defunct Soviet Union "ideology" is (or was) a set of beliefs and practices consciously promulgated by the state. In the United States or Western Europe, by contrast, the word tends to suggest something bad, a set of prejudices and valuations, for example, racial or gender prejudice, taken so much for granted that the victims of ideology are not aware that their prejudices are imaginary, not real. But the latter definition is already present in Marx. In *The German Ideology* Marx sees the Germans as living in a dream world cut off from the material determinants of their lives. As Louis Althusser puts this in his influential essay "Ideology and Ideological State Apparatuses (Notes Towards an Investigation)": "Ideology, then, is for Marx an imaginary assemblage [*bricolage*], a pure dream, empty and vain, constituted by the 'day's residues' from the only full and positive reality, that of the concrete history of concrete material individuals materially producing their existence."[1]

Whether or not Althusser is being entirely fair to Marx here is a complex question. It would require a detailed analysis of *The German Ideology* and other works to answer this question. It can also easily be seen that the words "concrete" and "material" in Althusser's formulations are problematic, to say the least. What Marx says in *The German Ideology* about language can be shown to anticipate what Althusser regards as his own way of going beyond Marx. Althusser conceives his crucial modification of Marx to be seeing ideologies as historical and as materially embodied in everyday practices and in what Althusser calls, in his quaint Marxist language, "ideological state apparatuses" such as church, school, and mass media. Such apparatuses are opposed to "repressive state apparatuses" like the police. Ideological state apparatuses determine the way we see and evaluate people and things around us. Ideology distorts and screens from our knowledge the real material conditions of our lives. Far from being a pure dream, as for Marx in Althusser's view of him, ideologies for Althusser have a solid reality in radios, television sets, newspapers, school buildings, textbooks, and even in works of high culture like Faulkner's *Absalom, Absalom!*. On the one hand, says Althusser, "Ideology is a 'representation' of the imaginary relationship of individuals to their real conditions of existence" (162). The word "relationship" is important here. Ideology is not a self-enclosed dream world. It is a way of representing the relation between the individual and his or her material existence. On the other hand, for Althusser "an ideology always exists in an apparatus, and its practice, or practices. This existence is material" (166). For Althusser this materially embodied ideology interpellates individuals as subjects. Subjectivity, consciousness, is not a natural given but is called into being by various ideological state apparatuses such as family, school, the media: "all ideology has the function (which defines it) of 'constituting' concrete individuals as subjects" (171). Applying this to *Absalom, Absalom!* one would say that Sutpen, Henry, Charles, Judith, Miss Rosa, and the rest of the novel's characters are not born what they are. They come to be what they are as the result of the impingement on them of various ideological forces. These call them into being as what they are. Whether Faulkner's own presentation agrees with that formulation remains to be seen.

One form of the material existence taken by ideologies is language or, more concretely, some specific text or other, for example, the text of *Absalom, Absalom!*. It is this form of material existence that Paul de Man stresses in the definition of ideology he gives in "The Resistance to Theory." De Man's definition of ideology is close to Althusser's or Marx's, unexpectedly close given their radically different intellectual heritages. For all three ideology is an erroneous relation between consciousness and material reality. For de Man this mistake goes by way of a linguistic confusion. De Man's definition of ideology is one of the few places where he appeals directly to Marx, specifically to a way of reading *The German Ideology*, as a means of defending literary theory from critics on the left who accuse it of neglecting social and historical reality:

> It would be unfortunate, for example, to confuse the materiality of the signifier with the materiality of what it signifies. This may seem obvious enough on the level of sight and sound, but it is less so with regard to the more general phenomenality of space, time or especially of the self; no one in his right mind will try to grow grapes by the luminosity of the word "day," but it is very difficult not to conceive the pattern of one's past and future existence as in accordance with temporal and spatial schemes that belong to fictional narratives and not to the world. This does not mean that fictional narratives are not part of the world and of reality; their impact upon the world may well be all too strong for comfort. What we call ideology is precisely the confusion of linguistic with natural reality, of reference with phenomenalism. It follows that, more than any other mode of inquiry, including economics, the linguistics of literariness is a powerful and indispensable tool in the unmasking of ideological aberrations, as well as a determining factor in accounting for their occurrence. Those who reproach literary theory for being oblivious to social and historical (that is to say ideological) reality are merely stating their fear at having their own ideological mystifications exposed by the tool they are trying to discredit. They are, in short, very poor readers of Marx's *German Ideology*.[2]

For Marx, Althusser, and de Man, though in a different way for each, ideology is falsehood, error, aberration. It is not entirely clear, however, whether the notion of falsehood and error in question for any of the three is the reciprocal of any notion of attainable truth. It may be that, according to de Man's concept of ideology, Althusser's, or Marx's, we can at best replace one ideology with another. We cannot help confusing linguistic with material realities in one way or another, so we can only replace one error with a different error. We cannot help living our lives according to unconscious assumptions that are replaced, when they are brought into the clear light of consciousness, by new unconscious assumptions that just as successfully hide the real material conditions of our lives. For Marx and Althusser even a radical change for the better in the material conditions of production, distribution, and exchange might still leave us subject to the interpellations of ideology that bring the subject into existence. De Man sees study of "the linguistics of literariness," by which he means "rhetorical reading," the study of figurative language in texts, as a powerful tool for unmasking ideological aberrations. Elsewhere, however, for example, at the end of the same essay, he sees even this as leading only to the replacement of illusion by illusion. Behind each mask there is only another mask, not the face of reality. Theory itself, says de Man, is the resistance to theory, that is to say, resistance to the clear seeing and correct reading that would unmask ideological aberrations: "To the extent that they are theory, that is to say teachable, generalizable and highly responsive to systematization, rhetorical readings, like the other kinds, still avoid and resist the reading they advocate. Nothing can overcome the resistance to theory since theory *is* itself this resistance" (19). Is there any possible escape from these sad scenarios of our domination by ideology? Or, to ask the question more concretely, does Faulkner's *Absalom, Absalom!* have any aspect that might be said to escape from ideology? Does reading *Absalom, Absalom!* free us from ideology or only imbed us more inextricably within it?

It is far easier to identify the features of *Absalom, Absalom!* that *are* ideological than to find anything in it that escapes ideology. Nor is it all that easy to defend a claim that by dramatizing the suffering caused by Southern ideology Faulkner unmasks that ideology. Too many of the ideological aberrations are asserted by the primary narrator as opposed to the various characters who narrate. Moreover, the image of unmasking presupposes a true face behind. The unmasking of ideology should be a revelation of the truth as well as a showing that aberrations are aberrations. Exactly what true face beyond ideological masking does Faulkner reveal?

No careful reader can doubt that *Absalom, Absalom!* is a magnificent dramatization of the various assumptions about race, gender, and class that make up what might be called "Southern ideology." As is characteristic of Faulkner, this dramatization is made by way of a story that is told with what might be called, in a scarcely excessive oxymoron, hallucinatory realism. Faulkner excels at presenting human consciousness as suspended in amazed outrage at its own situation, poised immobile and at the same time in terrific motion. Emblems of this are Lucas Burch (Brown) in *Light in August* hanging momentarily in the air as he leaps into the boxcar to run once more from Lena Grove ("he sees a man materialise apparently out of the air, in the act of running"),[3] or Miss Rosa, in *Absalom, Absalom!*, sitting bolt upright in her chair with her feet not quite touching the floor imposing with implacable intensity her obsessions about the Civil War and about the Sutpen story on Quentin Compson.

Like all great novelists, Faulkner embodies a larger historical and social context in a family narrative that might be said to represent it allegorically. I say "allegorically" because the analogies between the one and the other are by no means transparent or literal. An effort of interpretation is required to read one as the expression of the other. In this case the parallels between the Civil War as experienced by the South and the Sutpen story are complex and not altogether straightforward. Retrospective contemplation of the two in their intertwining generates the amazement and outrage in the various characters. Rosa's telling is a voice inhabited by Sutpen's ghost "by outraged recapitulation evoked,"[4] just as, much later, Sutpen's own telling of his life story to Quentin's grandfather is described as "patient amazed recapitulation" (263). This amazement and outrage might be expressed as two related questions. The first: Why did the South lose the war? or, as Shreve poses his question to Quentin at the end of the novel, "Why do you hate the South?" (378). The second: Why did the Sutpen family story have to come out the way it did? or, as Thomas Sutpen puts it to Mr. Compson, "You see, I had a design in my mind. Whether it was a good or a bad design is beside the point; the question is, Where did

I make the mistake in it, what did I do or misdo in it, whom or what injure by it to the extent which this would indicate. I had a design" (263).

If the characters of *Absalom, Absalom!* spend their lives going over and over the events of their personal and historical pasts trying to understand them and so free themselves from those pasts, Faulkner's way of telling the story (or the primary narrator's way) matches the recapitulative obsessions of the characters. The "time shifts" that repeatedly violate chronological time are related to the brooding recapitulation that characterizes all the narrators, including the primary one. To Faulkner's way of storytelling in *Absalom, Absalom!* applies perfectly the splendid description by Henry James of Conrad's method of narration in *Chance.* James described Conrad's narrative as "the prolonged hovering flight of consciousness over the outstretched ground of the case supposed." No doubt Faulkner learned much from Conrad in this regard. It is as though all the events of *Absalom, Absalom!*, covering more than a century in time, were going on occurring over and over all at once somewhere in a kind of simultaneous spatial array, so that the primary narrator and each of the narrating characters—Miss Rosa, Mr. Compson, Sutpen, Quentin, and Shreve—can move back and forth across time as though it were a landscape. The narrators anticipate events, withhold facts from the reader, for example, the fact that Charles Bon has African-American blood. They put the story together in the way that will have the most powerful performative effect on the reader.

The compulsion to patient amazed recapitulation that characterizes human consciousness for Faulkner may be defined as subjection to a set of ideological assumptions not seen to be ideological. These assumptions are taken as natural. They are a confusion of linguistic with material or phenomenal reality. Though it may not be easy to decide what Faulkner thinks or what the novel thinks, it is clear that the characters think, mistakenly, that they have been victimized by some malign fate or perhaps by some meaningless mischance or trivial mistake. Their erroneous assumptions about race, gender, and class have prevented them from understanding the real material conditions of their lives and have brought on their suffering.

Worst of all, these ideological errors are shown in a series of eloquent formulations to be passed from generation to generation, from person to person, by that most ineradicable of human habits: storytelling. We think that if we can just go over the story once more, in outraged recapitulation, explaining it carefully to another person, putting all the ingredients carefully and clearly together, we shall succeed in understanding why it happened as it did and so free ourselves from it. But in retelling the story we succeed only in passing on to others the ideological mistakes that we have not been able to understand and are perhaps in principle doomed never to be able to understand. Quentin broods over the way a story that involves his part of the country and his fellow townspeople but only tangentially his own family nevertheless is determining not only his own life but even the lives of those he knows, for example Shreve, his roommate at Harvard. Such people are entirely out-siders to the Sutpen story and come from a different part of the world. For them the story should be no more than a story, but just hearing infects the hearer with its obsessions: "*am I going to have to hear it all again* he thought *I am going to have to hear it all over again I am already hearing it all over again I am listening to it all over again I shall have to never listen to anything but this again forever so apparently not only a man never outlives his father but not even his friends and acquaintances do*" (277). In another passage Quentin invents a splendid image to express this compulsion to a repetition that is like the biblical belief, alluded to obscurely in the title of the novel, that the sins of the fathers are visited on the sons, generation after generation. The biblical allusion in the title is a powerful reinforcement of the concept of repetition the novel dramatizes, since the story of Sutpen, Henry, Charles, and Judith repeats with many differences the story in 2 Samuel of David, Absalom, Am-non, and Tamar, though no character, not even the primary narra-tor, is shown to be aware of this. In Quentin's case, his incestuous desire for his sister Caddy, the central motif of *The Sound and the Fury*, repeats (proleptically, since *The Sound and the Fury* was published first, though its action is later), as if by an implacable fatality, the incest motif in *Absalom, Absalom!*, though not the motif of miscegenation. This kind of repetition seems to Quentin like the duplication in one pool of the perturbations in another:

> Maybe nothing ever happens once and is finished. Maybe happen is never once but like ripples maybe on water after the pebble sinks, the ripples moving on, spreading, the pool attached by a narrow umbilical water-cord to the next pool which the first pool feeds, has fed, did feed, let this second pool contain a different temperature of water, a different molecularity of having seen, felt, remembered, reflect in a different tone the infinite unchanging sky, it doesn't matter: that pebble's watery echo whose fall it did not even see moves across its surface too at the original ripple-space, to the old ineradicable rhythm. (261)

Whether or not this belief in an inescapable repetition is itself an ideological construct may be difficult to decide, though nothing more urgently needs deciding. As readers of the novel we are in the situation of Quentin listening to Miss Rosa or Quentin's grand-father listening to Sutpen or Shreve listening to Quentin. If the novel is right in what it says about the power of storytelling, then we as readers of *Absalom, Absalom!* can never be in the situation of detached indifferent readers simply learning about Faulkner or about the South or about narrative technique. To read the novel is to subject ourselves to the effects of a speech act. It is a performative rather than a constative event. Far from achieving a liberating understanding, we readers submit ourselves, willynilly, to the pattern of the story. We will be forced in one way or another to repeat that pattern again in our own lives. In order to learn enough of this disquieting fact to try to avoid it we must read the novel. By then it is too late. In seeking knowledge, for example, knowledge about Southern ideology, we have unwittingly and without wishing to do so subjected ourselves already to its perhaps irresistible power. Does the novel offer no possibility of an escape from this fate? That this is no light matter is indicated by the fact that Quentin's obsession with his Southern heritage perhaps contributed to his suicide in 1910, a short time after the "now" of Quentin's reconstruction with

Shreve of the story of Sutpen, Henry, Charles, and Judith. This is true, that is, if it is legitimate to link this novel to *The Sound and the Fury*, published several years earlier.

~

Just what are the ideological errors that cause all this grief and why do they have such power to cause suffering? I have mentioned the Three Fates of contemporary cultural studies: race, gender, and class. Ideological assumptions about all three are materially embodied in the characters of *Absalom, Absalom!*. Ideology is also embodied in the characters' way of life, in the concrete material conditions of their existence, in their houses, roads, institutions, in what they have done to the landscape. These assumptions determine what happens in *Absalom, Absalom!*. If these assumptions were not so inalterably in place the story could not have happened as it did. Sutpen is never shown for one instant suspecting that he may be living his life as the mystified victim of ideological delusions, nor is he shown for one instant suspecting that it might be possible to think otherwise about these things. He is convinced that he has just made some "mistake" that has defeated his project.

First, class ideology: Sutpen's "design" is generated spontaneously in response to the episode in his childhood that labeled (Althusser would say "interpellated") him poor white trash. The slave house servant in the big plantation who turns him away from the front door and orders him around to the back brings him into existence as a subject. From then on he belongs to the class of poor whites. This new sense of himself does not lead him to want to transform the class structure. *That* he never questions. It generates, rather, a fierce and unremitting desire to put himself in the place of the white plantation owner. He wants to treat those beneath him, black and white alike, as he has been treated. This desire motivates everything he does until the moment of his death. It even lies behind his final attempt to father a son on poor Milly Jones. His fanatical pursuit of his goal makes his story a hyperbolic Southern version of the American dream. Fitzgerald's Jay Gatsby is also a victim of that dream. It is the belief that though you may be born in a log cabin you can end up in the White House: "I had a design. To accomplish it I should require money, a house, a plantation, slaves, a family—incidentally of course, a wife. I set out to acquire these, asking no favor of any man" (263). No doubt Sutpen's refusal to recognize Charles Bon as his son is motivated primarily by racial prejudice. It also has an element of class prejudice. Just as he was fifty years before turned away by the slave servant from the plantation owner's door, so when he has become a slave-owning plantation owner himself he does to another, in this case his own son, what has been done to him. He treats Charles as he has been treated. In doing so he perpetuates, by what seems a fateful repetition, the class as well as racial prejudice that has been imposed on him. The "fate" in this case, however, is his inability to free himself from the ideology that has called him into existence as the subject he is. The connection is made explicit in Quentin's imagination of what must have happened when Henry brought his college friend Charles Bon home for Christmas and Sutpen recognized that it was his son by his first marriage to the daughter of the West Indian planter:

> he stood there at his own door, just as he had imagined, planned, designed, and sure enough and after fifty years the forlorn nameless and homeless lost child came to knock at it and no monkey-dressed nigger anywhere under the sun to come to the door and order the child away; and Father said that even then, even though he knew that Bon and Judith had never laid eyes on one another, he must have felt and heard the design—house, position, posterity and all—come down like it had been built out of smoke, making no sound, creating no rush of displaced air and not even leaving any debris. (267)

Second, gender ideology: If Sutpen's "design" is determined by class assumptions, his way of carrying it out is determined by assumptions about gender. Sutpen himself is the embodiment of certain presuppositions about male nature and power. The mythologized memory of Confederate bravery and suffering during the Civil War is the broader social concomitant of this. Sutpen's self-contained silence, his indomitable, stubborn bravery in carrying out his design against all odds, his prowess as a hunter, his naked battles with one or another of his slaves while his male neighbors look on as audience—all these make him a hyperbolic version of the stereotypical strong, silent American frontier male.

Absalom, Absalom! is also permeated by certain ideological presuppositions about the "nature" of women. These are not only expressed by characters like Mr. Compson, Quentin, or Shreve. They are also expressed by the primary narrator. Not just Sutpen but all Yoknapatawpha society shares some version of these presuppositions. The features of the Southern gender ideology about women make a complex and not entirely coherent whole. The lack of coherence makes this set of preconceptions all the more able to motivate actions that seem to be based on material reality, the supposed "nature" of women, but are in fact motivated, as de Man puts it, by a confusion of linguistic with phenomenal reality.

One element in this intertwined set of what might be called "ideologemes" sees women as unfathomably mysterious and strong. They are strong both in love and in hate. This is expressed succinctly in a thought Shreve imagines Charles Bon as having about his mother: "maybe he knew now that his mother didn't know and never would know what she wanted, and so he couldn't beat her (maybe he learned from the octoroon [his mistress before he meets Judith] that you can't beat women anyhow and that if you are wise or dislike trouble and uproar you dont even try to)" (310). Women have motivations that remain impossible for men to understand, that men should primarily respect and fear. Examples are Miss Rosa's implacable hatred of Sutpen, or Ellen Coldfield's incomprehensible dream world, or Judith's inscrutable faithfulness to Charles Bon and her stoic silence after his death, or Sutpen's Haitian wife's prolonged, implacable revenge, her willingness to sacrifice her son to get even with Sutpen for having repudiated her. These women are presented more or less from the outside, from the male perspective, for example, in what Quentin says to himself about Rosa Coldfield: "Beautiful lives women live—women do. In very breathing they draw meat and drink from some beautiful attenuation of unreality in which the shades and shapes of facts— of birth and bereavement, of suffering and bewilderment and despair—move with the substanceless decorum of lawn party charades, perfect in gesture and without significance or any ability to hurt" (211). Such women are incomprehensible to men, however hard men may try to understand them. Nevertheless, one thing is sure. Faulkner's women are presented as just as obsessed, just as mad as the men are, just as much caught up in the prolonged recapitulation of some decisive event of the past that has frozen them in the terrific immobility of a backward look. The past event that obsesses them is almost always some wrong done them by men: Sutpen's first wife's outrage at Sutpen's repudiation of her; Judith's mourning as a widowed virgin after the death of Charles Bon, slain by her other brother; Miss Rosa's decades-long obsession with the insult Sutpen dealt her.

Another Southern ideologeme sees women as valuable only so long as they remain absolutely pure, innocent, virginal, white as snow. This facet of Southern gender ideology may help to explain Faulkner's fascination with the theme of brother-sister incest. He is said to have suggested more than once to crews of script writers with whom he collaborated in Hollywood that when you get stuck with a script the solution is to introduce incest. Just as for the Egyptian Pharaohs or for the French nobleman John, Duke of Lorraine (to whom Henry Sutpen appeals in his mind as a justification for the marriage of his sister Judith and his half-brother Charles Bon), so for Henry in *Absalom, Absalom!* or for Quentin Compson in *The Sound and the Fury*, the only way to preserve a sister's purity is, paradoxically, to marry her yourself. In Henry's case, the strategy is to marry his sister vicariously by way of her marriage to the half-brother whom he loves with an abject homosexual adoration and identification. If he can join together Judith and Charles he can join himself to both of them in a hetero-homosexual triangle that is the only thing capable of satisfying his secret desires.

The complex of contradictory ideologemes about women includes, finally, the assumption that the real purpose of women is to bear children, to carry on the male line. In order to make certain this happens without any contamination, women must be kept altogether innocent and pure before marriage. Men are permitted to visit brothels, to father children on their slaves, or to keep mistresses without any stain on their honor or blemish on their right to marry pure women and father sons to carry on their names. The novel ascribes to Sutpen an ugly analogy to express this conviction that women are valuable only as a means of producing sons. When he insults Miss Rosa, who would eagerly have married him, by suggesting that they mate first and then marry if she produces a son, this is described by Miss Rosa as "the bald outrageous words [spoken] exactly as if he were consulting with Jones or with some other man about a bitch dog or a cow or a mare" (168). Later Sutpen is killed by Wash Jones because he repeats the same insult in what he says to Wash's granddaughter Milly just after she has borne Sutpen a daughter on the same day his mare has foaled to his black stallion: "Well, Milly; too bad you're not a mare too. Then I could give you a decent stall in the stable" (286).

Third ideological motif, race: Of the three motifs, class, gender, and race, race is without doubt the most important by far. Southern society was built on slavery and on the ideological assumptions about race that accompanied slavery: the radical differences between blacks and whites, the inferiority of African Americans to European Americans, the ineradicable contamination that even a drop of black blood causes in a white man or woman, the assumption that it is all right for a white man to father children on a black woman, though he has no responsibility to accept such children as his own, while the mating of a black man with a white woman is an abomination. The ugly word "nigger" echoes through *Absalom, Absalom!* as the invidious name that holds in a single sound all those ideological assumptions, as when Charles Bon at a climactic moment in the novel says to his half-brother Henry: "So it's the miscegenation, not the incest, which you cant bear. . . . I'm the nigger that's going to sleep with your sister. Unless you stop me, Henry" (356, 358).

All the decisive events of *Absalom, Absalom!* are the result of racial ideologemes. The civil war was fought, at least in part, to protect the institution of slavery and in the name of all the ideological assumptions that went with slavery. The fact that Sutpen is turned away from the plantation owner's door by an African American servant is an important part of his humiliation in the primal scene that calls him into being as what he is. He repudiates his first wife when he discovers she has African American blood. He refuses to accept his son by that marriage as his own for the same reason, though if he had given Charles Bon the least sign of recognition Charles would have been satisfied and his murder at Henry's hand would not have occurred. The building of Sutpen's Hundred depends on slavery and on the twenty "wild" African Americans Sutpen brings to help him build his plantation, just as the colonialism in Haiti where Sutpen meets his first wife is built on slavery. If the reader tries to imagine *Absalom, Absalom!* for a moment without those racial ideologemes (it is not easy to do so) the whole novel vanishes in smoke just as instantly as Sutpen's design vanished when he saw that the friend Henry was bringing home from college was his son by the first, "tainted" marriage. Everything that happens in *Absalom, Absalom!* depends on the ideology of racism and would be impossible without it.

Whatever Sutpen does, every move in his life is in response to the call on him of one or another of the set of assumptions making up Southern ideology. If he is the blind victim of that ideology, his mystifications cause him to inflict prolonged, unremitting suffering on all those around him: Eulalia Bon, Ellen Coldfield, Henry, Judith, Charles Bon, Clytie, Miss Rosa. They too share his ideological assumptions and are victims of them as much as he is.

～

Does the novel offer the reader no possible escape from being the momentary last in the line of those called to act somnambulistically according to the patterns of judgment Southern ideology determines?

It is by no means easy to answer that question. On the one hand, it could be argued that the hyperbolic presentation in *Absalom, Absalom!* of Southern ideology in all its complexity, along with the dramatization of the savage retribution of suffering brought on those who live their lives according to that ideology, make of the novel a critique of ideology, an exposure of its mystifications.[5] Shreve the Canadian is the reader's representative. He is the outsider who wants to understand the South and who, so the notes at the end tell the reader, lives on to become a practicing surgeon in Edmonton, Alberta. His survival is evidence that it is possible to know about Southern ideology and not be destroyed by it.

On the other hand, the novel shows Shreve joining with Quentin in the imaginary reconstruction of the events of the novel. Shreve becomes, like Quentin, identified with Henry and Charles as they ride together toward the moment when Henry will turn on his horse to shoot his brother, kill him "dead as a beef" (133). Moreover, as I have already shown, the novel constantly reinforces the notion that patterns of belief and action ineluctably perpetuate themselves from generation to generation in blind repetitions. These repetitions are like the way the characters in *Absalom, Absalom!* repeat the biblical story of David, Amnon, Tamar, and Absalom without being shown even to be aware of it. Since ideology is by definition unconscious, how could we be sure that reading *Absalom, Absalom!*, or perhaps not even reading it, just hearing about it, or just living in the same nation in which it could be written, might lead us unwittingly to repeat in our own lives something like Sutpen's unwillingness to recognize Charles Bon as his son or the blind submission of Ellen and Rosa Coldfield to Sutpen's commands (not really proposals) that they marry him, the one acceptance duplicating the first many years after?

On the one hand, the novel may give knowledge about ideology that might help liberate us from it. On the other hand, the novel may have an irresistible performative effect that goes against that knowledge. The epistemological and performative dimensions of the novel may go in different directions. It might be difficult if not impossible to decide which one would win out in a given case, for example in my rereading of *Absalom, Absalom!* in order to write this essay.

~

Without trying to mitigate either the difficulties or the urgencies of this need to decide, I turn back to the novel for a look at several elements not yet identified. These might tip the balance toward saying that *Absalom, Absalom!,* if it is read with vigilance, may not so much free the reader from ideology as put him or her in a new position where a decision about it may be made, must be made. The knowledge reading the novel provides is performative in the sense that it puts the reader in a new situation. Reading *Absalom, Absalom!* imposes on the reader a new responsibility and makes necessary a new decision. The novel itself gives the reader the terms in which this might be understood.

Reading the novel puts the reader in a situation different from that of any of the characters. We see the whole novel, hear the stories all the characters tell, and benefit in addition both from the narrator's commentary and from Faulkner's careful organization of the various blocks of narration so they have the effect created by these juxtapositions. Reading the novel is not just a passive act of absorption. It is an active intervention. Reading *Absalom, Absalom!* requires the reader to make energetic efforts. He or she must put two and two together, emphasizing this or that passage, filling in gaps. For the results of these acts of reading the reader must take responsibility. If the reader repeats the ideology the novel gives knowledge of, this is something for which the reader can be blamed, even though what happens in reading happens, willynilly.

Two passages in the novel articulate the way the activity that might be called "reading" in an extended sense is not an automatic passing on of a certain pattern but a violently neutral transition space, like the "terrific immobility" of consciousness as Faulkner defines it. What passes through that space, the space of decision, comes out different on the other side. For that difference the reader must be held liable.

My argument here shifts the focus from Althusser's opposition between seeing and knowing to a relation that is not simply oppositional between knowing and doing, or between seeing/ knowing and doing. By stressing the performative effect of reading or storytelling, I propose an alternative paradigm for the way a work of literature puts its reader in a different situation. In this new situation new decisions and new acceptances of responsibility must take place. Like all decisions and acceptances of responsibility, the ones demanded by reading can never be based on sufficient knowledge, that is, on knowledge fully justifying the decision or the taking of responsibility. Like all ethical acts they are performative leaps in the dark, what Faulkner calls, in a passage discussed below, "overpassing to love."

The first passage is the speech Judith makes when she gives Charles Bon's letter to Quentin's grandmother. This is the same letter that Quentin's father gives him to read, to make of what he will. She begins by saying that life is "like trying to, having to, move your arms and legs with strings only the same strings are hitched to all the other arms and legs and the others all trying and they dont know why either except that the strings are all in one another's way like five or six people all trying to make a rug on the same loom only each one wants to weave his own pattern into the rug" (127). Judith then goes on to assert that in any case the endpoint of each life is "a block of stone with scratches on it provided there was someone to remember to have the marble scratched and set up or had time to, and it rains on it and the sun shines on it and after a while they dont even remember the name and what the scratches were trying to tell, and it doesn't matter" (127). The conclusion she draws from this and the decision she makes for action is a strange non sequitur from the grim darkness of this view of human life. She says the thing to do is to pass something on that will make a mark or scratch not on dead stone but on a living person. This is obviously an image of our own activity as readers of the novel. We allow ourselves to be marked by the text. Judith, however, emphasizes not the legibility of the scratch but its materiality and the fact that it is inscribed not on a block of stone but on living mortal flesh, flesh that is living because it can die:

> And so maybe if you could go to someone, the stranger the better, and give them something—a scrap of paper—something, anything, it not to mean anything in itself and them not even to read it or keep it, not even bother to throw it away or destroy it, at least it would be something just because it would have happened, be remembered even

if only from passing from one hand to another, one mind to another, and it would be at least a scratch, something, something that might make a mark on something that *was* once for the reason that it can die someday, while the block of stone cant be *is* because it never can become *was* because it cant ever die or perish. (127–28)

Judith distinguishes between two kind of marks or scratches. The distinction is not, as might have been expected, between random, meaningless marks, on the one hand, and significant marks like letters, on the other. No, from the perspective of the distinction she is making, both kinds of marks work in the same way. The distinction is rather between marks of any kind made on stone and those made on flesh. Scratches made on stone, for example, the inscriptions on the Sutpen tombstones Quentin visits with his father in the cedar grove, are not happenings. They are not events because they are made on something that cannot die, that is outside time. Only living flesh, flesh that is mortal, is within time, has a history, and can remember. Therefore only a mark made on living flesh is an event in the present. Such a mark is an *is* because it can become *was*, whereas a tombstone has no *is* because it cannot become *was*. Just as Miss Rosa, as Quentin realizes, tells Quentin about Sutpen because "she wants it told" (10) to others so her anger, hatred, and shame will be perpetuated, so Judith takes Bon's letter to Quentin's grandmother not so she can read it but so it can just make an impression on her flesh and thereby be given a kind of immortality as it is passed on to Quentin's father, then to Quentin, and then to us as readers.

This concept of a memory that is material rather than legible escapes ideology. It recalls Marx's emphasis in *The German Ideology* on the way ideology is bodily, material, not the highest but the lowest. Ideology is, paradoxically, consciousness that is without consciousness. It is part of obscure organic life, not above it in some ideal realm.[6] Faulkner's notion of the materiality of memory is not only an explanation of the way ideological elements are passed from generation to generation, it also shows that in the moment of passing the recipient is liberated from being the blind repetition of a previous pattern. The person receiving the mark is given freedom and the responsibility to decide. This freedom is inserted in the interval between seeing the marks as mere scratches and seeing them as legible. The one who is marked has to decide how to read them and what to make of them.

~

Judith's notion of a memory that is primarily material, only secondarily articulated and readable, links this passage with the topographical motifs in the novel. Like Hardy or Trollope, Faulkner has a strongly topographical imagination. The events of his novels take place within an elaborately mapped mental or textual landscape in which characters are associated with places. The configuration of houses, roads, fields, rivers, swamps carries a considerable part of the meaning of the novel. Like Trollope and Hardy, Faulkner made an actual map of the landscape within which his novels take place. That map is reproduced at the end of the Vintage edition of *Absalom, Absalom!.* The legend identifies it as "Jefferson, Yoknapatawpha Co., Mississippi, William Faulkner, Sole Owner and Proprietor." On that map the reader can see the location of Sutpen's Hundred, of Miss Rosa Coldfield's house, of the "Church which Thomas Sutpen rode fast to," and of the "Fishing Camp where Wash Jones killed Sutpen." Even without the literal map the reader produces a mental map of the landscape as she or he reads. The landscape is like the tombstone in Judith's speech. It remains after the characters have died, marked with the signs of their living. These marks remain in an atemporal spatial array, in which Sutpen's building of Sutpen's Hundred, his marriage, and his death are simultaneous. The reader understands the novel in terms of the movements of the characters across it, the changes they make in it. Examples are that slow movement of Sutpen's family when he is a child back from the West Virginia cabin to the Tidewater plantation where he is refused entrance at the front door, or Faulkner's presentation of the later stages of the Civil War as the constant movement of retreat by the Confederate Army, or Sutpen's physical embodiment of his design in the making of Sutpen's Hundred:

Immobile, bearded and hand palm-lifted the horseman sat; behind
him the wild blacks and the captive architect huddled quietly, carrying
in bloodless paradox the shovels and picks and axes of peaceful conquest. Then in the long unamaze Quentin seemed to watch them
overrun suddenly the hundred square miles of tranquil and astonished
earth and drag house and formal gardens violently out of the soundless
Nothing and clap them down like cards upon a table beneath the up-
palm immobile and pontific, creating the Sutpen's Hundred, the *Be
Sutpen's Hundred* like the oldentime *Be Light.* (8–9)

For Faulkner, as for Althusser and for Marx, ideology is not
something abstract and dreamlike, the confusion of linguistic with
material reality. That confusion is, literally, embodied. It is marked
on the bodies of the human beings who are mystified by the
ideology. It is embodied in another way in all the material changes
men and women have made on the "tranquil and astonished
earth," turning that earth into a landscape, a topography. That
remade earth, a kind of remainder or *Dreck*, according to the
undialectical dialectic or dialectic of a movement in place Marx
and Engels sketch out, becomes the scene in which the evil done by
ideological aberrations can work itself out. Subjectivity, including
all the subject's ideological presumptions, is inseparable from his or
her body. Not just the minds but the bodies, too, of Sutpen, Rosa,
Judith, Clytie, and the rest are the incarnations of their "stubborn
and amazed outrage" (174).

Subjectivity, including its ideological presumptions, is also diffused into the landscape. It is not just projected there but incar-
nated there. Sutpen, in Rosa's sense of him when he returns to his
ruined plantation after the war, is:

absent only from the room, and that because he had to be elsewhere, a
part of him encompassing each ruined field and fallen fence and
crumbling wall of cabin or cotton house or crib; himself diffused and
in solution held by that electric furious immobile urgency and awareness of short time and the need for haste . . . not . . . anywhere near the
house at all but miles away and invisible somewhere among his
hundred square miles which they had not troubled to begin to take
away from him yet, perhaps not even at this point or at that point but

diffused (not attenuated to thinness but enlarged, magnified, encompassing as though in a prolonged and unbroken instant of tremendous effort embracing and holding intact that ten-mile square while he faced from the brink of disaster, invincible and unafraid, what he must have known would be the final defeat). (160, 162–63)

If the earth, like a stone, cannot have a history, cannot be *is* because it can never be *was*, nevertheless for Faulkner the earth turned into topography is essential to the making material of human history. This is analogous to the way Judith's love for Bon and his for her is carried from generation to generation by way of its material embodiment in the letter. The bare earth made topography, like Bon's letter to Judith, is an essential medium of communication between one person and another, one generation and another.

Faulkner articulates this in a passage explaining that the fact that Shreve too came from the Mississippi trough helps explain why he is able to understand as well as he does Quentin's heritage of family and regional history: "both born within the same year: the one in Alberta, the other in Mississippi; born half a continent apart yet joined, connected after a fashion in a sort of geographical transubstantiation by that Continental Trough, that River which runs not only through the physical land of which it is the geologic umbilical, not only runs through the spiritual lives of the beings within its scope, but is very Environment itself which laughs at degrees of latitude and temperature" (258). Faulkner's insight into the role of landscape in making ideology concrete is another non-ideological element in the novel, like Judith's distinction between marks on flesh and marks on stone.

~

This insight is reinforced in another crucial passage in the novel, the one describing the imaginative recreation of the lives of Sutpen, Henry, Judith, Bon, and Rosa in the collective recapitulation by Quentin and Shreve. When a mark making history is transferred from one topographical locale to another, it is made material in a new way and in a new situation. The role of material surroundings in making possible a new start, not just a passive repetition, is signaled in the novel's vivid emphasis on how the ice-cold Harvard dormitory room where Quentin and Shreve sit up long after midnight is so different from the wisteria and cigar-smoke scented porch where Quentin's father had passed the story on to him. The re-creation of the story by Quentin and Shreve is a free (and yet bound) response made to a demand for narration inherent in the facts as Quentin knows them. Quentin and Shreve go beyond the data, as has Faulkner in his writing of a great novel about the South. All three have created new stories with their own coherence and meaning. For this new coherence and meaning, as well as for the effects this may have on those who hear it, Quentin, Shreve, and Faulkner can be held liable. This is the case even though this new version of the story is a result of the marks made on them by the events and even though the effects on us as readers are irresistible, since what happens in reading happens as it happens.

This remaking and re-embodiment is defined by Faulkner, in a brilliant phrase, as an "overpassing to love." The love in question is first that of Judith, Henry, and Bon for one another. But the imaginative recreation of the past is also an overpassing to love. The love reached by "overpassing" is not just the love between Judith, Henry, and Bon, seen as something positive and a going beyond the situation that has been imposed on them by their father. It is also the love between Shreve and Quentin and their love for Judith, Henry, and Bon. These new loves repeat the old ones and are the result of a joint act of re-creation. In a similar way our relation as readers to the characters in the novel is also a kind of love. Love here is the name for a relation to history and to other people that may transform ideology and provide the glimpse of an escape from it:

> all that had gone before [had been] just so much that had to be overpassed and none else present to overpass it but them, as someone always has to rake the leaves up before you can have the bonfire. That was why it did not matter to either of them which one did the talking, since it was not the talking alone which did it, performed and accom-

plished the overpassing, but some happy marriage of speaking and hearing wherein each before the demand, the requirement, forgave condoned and forgot the faulting of the other—faultings both in the creating of this shade whom they discussed (rather, existed in) and in the hearing and sifting and discarding the false and conserving what seemed true, or fit the preconceived—in order to overpass to love, where there might be paradox and inconsistency but nothing fault nor false. (316)

Ideological presuppositions have a stubborn recalcitrance. They tend to form themselves again even when we think they have been abolished. Nevertheless, *Absalom, Absalom!* gives the reader a momentary free space in which he or she might go beyond ideology— if he or she chooses to do so. It does this not so much in its exposure of Southern ideology and its malign effects, as in its demonstration of how those malign effects are determined by the embodiment of the ideology in topography and in the bodies of those subject to it. Understanding here is a possible means of liberation. This will happen if the right action occurs in response to "the demand, the requirement," in this case if changes are effected in the material conditions that supported Southern ideology in the first place. This does not mean that knowledge guarantees right action. Knowledge never determines either decision or the effects that follow action. An incommensurability between knowledge and action remains the human condition. Nor does knowledge of the past give foreknowledge of what will happen in the future if we follow a certain course of action. But it does change our relation to the past. That change provides a new space within which decision and action are possible.

§ 9   Slipping Vaulting Crossing: Heidegger

"Heidegger misses everything but in an interesting
way."   —Jacques Derrida

I placed a jar in Tennessee
And round it was, upon a hill.
It made the slovenly wilderness
Surround that hill.

                —Wallace Stevens, "Anecdote of the Jar"

An alternative title for this chapter might have been: "Double-Crossing Heidegger." "Double-crossing" may be read either as a participle or as an adjective. The double-crossing may be done either by Heidegger or to him. The purport of the two titles will become clearer as the chapter progresses.

The chapter on Hardy in this book cites Heidegger as an authority on topography. Heidegger is taken more or less "straight" there. Nevertheless, his tenets on topography are tentatively challenged, at least at one point. A question is raised about the equivocation in one of Heidegger's phrases. He says a bridge "admits" or "installs" the topography that rises up around it. Which is it? It makes a lot of difference. I shall return to this here. Heidegger is certainly one of the great philosophers of human topography. He is also one of the most problematic. What he says is problematic in part because he penetrates so deeply into the questions involved in this region of human thought and action. A group of Heidegger's major essays focuses on this topic: "The Thing" ("Das Ding"), "Building Dwelling Thinking" ("Bauen Wohnen Denken"), "The Origin of the Work of Art" ("Der Ursprung des Kunstwerkes"). These essays contain some of the most provocative and challenging things ever said about topography. They give one to think. The question of space also has its place in *Being and Time*. What is said about space in *Being and Time* is presupposed, as I shall show, in what is said about topography in the later essays.[1]

We know now, however, that reading Heidegger, taking him seriously, taking him "straight," is not a politically innocent thing to do. We know now about Heidegger's active complicity in the programs of National Socialism. We know also that Heidegger's Nazism cannot be seen as a momentary aberration having nothing to do with his "serious philosophy." As Philippe Lacoue-Labarthe, Jacques Derrida, and others have shown, Heidegger's writings are pervaded by ideas that help explain why he was attracted to National Socialism. When I began reading Heidegger forty years ago, he was studied in the United States as one of a group of "existentialist" philosophers that included Kierkegaard, Sartre, and Camus. The members of this group were read, by many people at least, without much regard for the differing political commitments of each. Now we know better. We know that even the most abstract philosophical concepts cannot be detached from their political implications.

This precept is easy to state, however, but not always all that easy to demonstrate in a given case. The connection between philosophical or critical thinking and political commitment is often indirect, elusive, labyrinthine, not necessarily a matter of predictable, straightforward causality. Only a careful reading of a given text can work out for that text just what the political implications of its ideas may be. The proposition that all thinking is political is a problem, not a solution. Derrida has shown the political implications of Heidegger's use of the word *Geist*. Lacoue-Labarthe has shown the sinister implications of what he calls Heidegger's "national aestheticism." It may be, however, that Heidegger's ideas about topography are politically neutral. The only way to find out is to work carefully through Heidegger's own expression of those ideas. This chapter will read "Building Dwelling Thinking" to identify just what Heidegger's ideas about topography are and, by way of that, to identify just what political implications those ideas may have. It will be necessary to pay close attention to Heidegger's own language, that is, his German, since questions of language and of translatability are among the things at stake in "Building Dwelling Thinking."

What does it mean to "read" Heidegger? If the propriety and feasibility of translating Heidegger into English is in question here, so also we cannot take for granted that we know what is meant in a given case, for example, this one, by "reading," or even whether it is a task that can be accomplished, though of course we do read all the time. In any case it is clear that Heidegger must be read slowly, circumspectly, with nothing taken for granted, and much attention to detail. Reading is another form of translation, though, like translation "proper," reading, it may be, is translation of a text itself already a translation of an unknown and unknowable original. These disquietudes about reading, about translation, and about "original texts" are, however, just what Heidegger would refuse to accept. He would, it appears, want to claim that the language of his essay, like a bridge swinging or vaulting over a river, has an "originality" nothing precedes, an originality that does not substitute for anything prior or "represent" anything else. All that I have to say about "Building Dwelling Thinking" centers on this refusal. What I am going to say could be assembled under the label: "the refusal of the X in Heidegger" or "Heidegger's refusal of the crossing." These phrases name three different refusals: the refusal of chiasmus; the refusal of figurative substitutions; the refusal of the "unknown X."

～

"Building Dwelling Thinking" begins by invoking a certain *wir* ("we"), as I have done already in saying "Now we know." Who is this "we," the we who begins in Heidegger's essay by saying "In what follows we"?[2] A few lines later he says: "We attain to dwelling, so it seems, only by means of building." Are these two "we's" the same? If so, the "we," it appears, is simultaneously Heidegger himself, the authoritative professorial we, from whom "we" the readers or listeners are excluded, and also at the same time it is we the ignorant listeners who think we build in order to dwell. Heidegger in the second "we" mockingly and ironically identifies himself with us ignorant readers. At the same time he implies that he knows better. The implicit promise in the "we" is that we too will come to know better by the time we have finished the essay or that we already know better without knowing it and shall come to know we know it. Then we shall have reached the point where the speaker of the professorial "we" in the opening phrase of the essay already stands, that is, at the end of the essay. The "we" is at once at the beginning of the path to be followed and already at its end. We must already implicitly (or rather actually) be at the end if we are ever to get there. Heidegger's conclusions are for his readers recognitions rather than discoveries. They are something we knew already but have forgotten. We the readers will join "ourselves" at the end when we discover that we have always already been one with Martin Heidegger, without knowing it. We have all along been part of the we in the name of which he speaks in the beginning. We have only to listen to the silence of language, heed its call, and we shall be where he is.

This initial and at the same time ultimate "we" is caught in the "ecstacies" of temporality, as defined by Heidegger in *Being and Time*. For Heidegger time always stands outside of itself. Dasein moves forward into the future in order to come back to what it was in the past. The use of spatial figures here to express the paradoxes of the "we" is not accidental. Of time and space it can be said that each is another form of the other, though for Heidegger time takes precedence over space, as "we" shall see.

"Building Dwelling Thinking" has two parts: a first section to a considerable degree about language and a second section primarily about a bridge as an example of something man has built. What he says about language is problematic, to say the least. It is also, at least superficially, contradictory. Certainly it is counter-intuitive, by which I mean that it does not agree with what "we" normally think about language. "Building Dwelling Thinking," it could be said, though the essay itself does not exactly say so, has to do with the problematic relation between speaking and building. On the one hand, in the second part of the essay Heidegger says the bridge makes a site that makes a space with places, distances, and boundaries, just as Stevens's jar in Tennessee does. The bridge does this without any help from language. The bridge, as Heidegger firmly asserts, is not a sign, or at least it is not the sort of sign traditionally called a "symbol." It is not, that is, a representative or delegate by likeness of something else. On the other hand, in the first part of the essay Heidegger says only language, if we listen to its silence, can tell us this: "Language [*Die Sprache*] withdraws from man its simple and high speech [*Sprechen*]. But its primal call [*Zuspruch*] does not thereby become incapable of speech; it merely falls silent. Man, though, fails to heed [*achten*] this silence" (E148; G22; the translation misses the play from *Sprache* to *Sprechen* to *Zuspruch*).

What does that mean: "heed this silence?" How would we know there is a silence to listen to, or be ware of, if the words "build" and "dwell" have perfectly good everyday meanings now, covering over with anything but silence the primordial meanings Heidegger wants to recover? The silence is not noticeable unless you already know it is there. This is like the paradox, or better, the double bind, of the "we" that is both at the beginning and at the end of a journey of investigation. Or it is like the double bind of biblical parable. If you need the parable to find out how to cross over to the kingdom of heaven, you will not be able to understand it. If you can understand it, you will not need it because you already know what it has to teach you. This analogy is evidence of the profound influence on Heidegger's language of the rhetoric of biblical Christianity, in spite of the fact that Heidegger more than once insisted on the unbridgeable gulf that lies between philosophy and theology.[3] If Heidegger's philosophy has Christian motifs without Christ, it often also has what James Joyce, or rather Stephen Dedalus, in *A Portrait of the Artist as a Young Man*, calls "the true scholastic stink." Examples are Heidegger's analyses of the "fall" or of "the call of conscience" in *Being and Time*.

What is the place of language, for Heidegger, in topographical building or dwelling? Even though much of "Building Dwelling Thinking," as I have said, is about language, the title does not name language. Rather, it names "thinking" as a third activity along with building and dwelling. Presumably language has something to do with thinking, though that should not be taken for granted. We perhaps think with language or about language, so that language is the main tool in the "Workshop [*Werkstatt*] of thinking" (E161; G36). It is the tool we need for what Heidegger elsewhere calls "the craft of thinking" (*das Handwerk des Denkens*).[4] He does not, however, exactly say that, or he says it with much complexity of nuance.

An important paragraph in the essay, as I have said, firmly rejects the idea that the bridge is a symbol. The happenings in building and dwelling, it seems, must be material events, not signs of anything else. The bridge is not a symbol. It is a thing. There is nothing rhetorical about it. It is not an expression of any kind. Here is the way Heidegger puts this:

> To be sure, people think of the bridge as primarily and really *merely* a bridge; after that, and occasionally [*gelegentlich*], it might possibly express [*ausdrücken*] much else besides; and as such an expression [*Ausdruck*] it would then become a symbol, for instance a symbol of those things we mentioned before. But the bridge, if it is a true bridge, is never first of all a mere bridge and then afterward a symbol. And just as little is the bridge in the first place exclusively a symbol, in the sense that it expresses [*ausdrückt*] something that strictly speaking does not belong to it. If we take the bridge strictly as such, it never appears as an expression [*Ausdruck*]. The bridge is a thing [*ein Ding*] and *only that*. (E153; G27–28)

Authentic language, in an analogous way, must be for Heidegger literal. For profound reasons, he has a great distaste for metaphor, for the figurative dimension of language generally. His whole philosophical enterprise depends on assuming that language says what it says, just as a bridge is what it is. It would seem, then, that the bridge and the word "bridge" are, for Heidegger or by Heidegger, decisively separated.

But things are not quite that simple. Both the bridge and the word "bridge," according to Heidegger, "gather," whatever *that* means. This fact reveals their deep consonance. If they are separated, they are nevertheless in resonance, in *Stimmung*, as it is said in German. Do "things," that is, the particular kinds of things that have been constructed by man, such as bridges, do this gathering in a way that is analogous to the way language gathers? What is the relation between language and things? Is language a thing in the sense of being a gatherer? It may seem Heidegger thinks so. That might mean, for example, that Stevens's poem about the jar in Tennessee acts analogously to the way the jar itself acts. At the end of the essay Heidegger says thinking and building are the same, or at any rate parallel, two ways of doing the same thing, namely, gathering the fourfold one—earth, sky, gods, and men:

> But that thinking itself belongs to dwelling in the same sense as building, although in a different way, may perhaps be attested to by the course of thought here attempted.
>
> Building and thinking are, each in its own way, inescapable [*unumgänglich*, impossible to go beyond, uncrossable, like a bridge you cannot traverse] for dwelling. The two, however, are also insufficient for dwelling so long as each busies itself with its own affairs in separation instead of listening to one another. They are able to listen if both—building and thinking—belong to dwelling [*dem Wohnen gehören*], if they remain within their limits [*Grenzen*] and realize that the one as much as the other comes from the workshop of long experience and incessant practice. (E160–61; G35–36)

"Dwelling" (*Wohnen*) is the more universal word here. It names the broadest range of all the things people (Heidegger would say "men") do in living in a place. Thinking and building are different ways of dwelling, subordinate to it as to the more universal activity of Dasein's "being in the world."

But just how could building and thinking "listen to one another"? The prosopopoeia here seems an example of the figuration Heidegger wants to avoid at all costs. What justifies this figure? Thinking about the word "gathers" is surely different from the bridge gathering the landscape around it. Or is it? "Man" builds a bridge. "Man" writes a poem or a philosophical essay, such as "Building Dwelling Thinking." What, for Heidegger, is the relation between those two activities? An anti-Heideggerian like Paul de Man emphasizes the danger of confusing language and things, or at any rate language and things as they appear to us phenomenally. A passage in "The Resistance to Theory," quoted in chapter 8 above, speaks of the folly of growing grapes by the luminosity of the word "sun," though de Man goes on to say we commit versions of that folly all the time, for example, in assuming that our lives are ordered according to purely linguistic categories of continuity and wholeness. To commit this folly, to confuse phenomenal with linguistic reality, is, for de Man, the fundamental ideological error.[5] It *is* ideology. Could it be that Heidegger commits that error, in this case asserting that active thinking with the word "gather" will gather? If so, what larger ideological construct in Heidegger's thought would this error support?

An answer to this question may be approached by way of the relation between language and landscape in what Heidegger says. For Heidegger the landscape is already invested with bridges, buildings, roads, peasant farmhouses, forests with paths in them, some of them paths that lead nowhere (in German *Holzwege*, the title of one of Heidegger's major collections of essays). Heidegger's landscape is also always already mapped. It is inscribed with place names, even if they are generic rather than proper ones: words like "bridge," "stream," "banks," and so on. Or rather, Heidegger's landscape is already invested with the German words for these things: *Brücke, Strom, Ufer*. The landscape, for Heidegger, seems to be written over in the German language. It is not, however, as for Wallace Stevens, written on with unique and proper place names, names like "Tennessee," "Key West," "Haddam," "New Haven," or "Olney," however much Stevens may be aware that these place names inscribe a history of conquest. Heidegger's landscape is labeled, rather, with general names like *Brücke*. "Building Dwelling Thinking" does, it is true, name toward its end one particular bridge, the old bridge at Heidelberg, as an example of the way you can be somewhere distant by thinking about it. It is an odd moment. Something local and materially real enters into a discourse that remains at an austere level of abstraction. In any case, words like *Brücke* and *Ufer*, it may be, like universal terms for human activities such as *Bauen* and *Wohnen*, have "primal" meanings that still call out to us if we can listen to their silence, whatever *that* means.

To understand what that means we need to look more closely at the crucial early paragraph on language. Having said that "building is not merely a means and a way [*Mittel und Weg*] toward dwelling—to build is in itself already to dwell" (E146; G20), Heidegger asks a question that may already have sprung into the minds of his auditors: "Who tells us this? Who gives us a standard [*ein Maß*] at all by which we can take the measure [*durchmessen*] of the nature of dwelling and building?" (ibid.). The answer is that language tells us this, if we can heed its silence. We can understand building and dwelling, not by studying examples of houses, roads, bridges, and so on, in their history and locales, but only by listening to language. On the face of it this is an absurdity: "It is language that tells us about the nature of a thing provided that we respect [*achten*, again] language's own nature" (E146; G20). Here there is a slight mistranslation, as well as a missing again of some wordplay, in this case between *Zuspruch* and *Sprache*. Heidegger says: "Der Zuspruch [call, appeal; cf. this word in a passage cited earlier] über das Wesen einer Sache kommt zu uns aus der Sprache, vorausgesetzt, daß wir deren eigenes Wesen achten." A more literal translation would be: "The call about the nature of a thing comes to us from language, if it is posited [*vorausgesetzt*] that we respect its own being." Just how is it that language, if we respect its own nature [*Wesen*], will tell us the nature [*Wesen*] of a thing [*Sache*, also: "state of affairs," not, in this case, *Dinge*]? The answer is suggested in an odd sentence at the end of the paragraph. Language, says Heidegger, brings language out, "voices" it, brings it to speech (*zum Sprechen bringt*). Doing this is the highest thing we can do with language: "Among all the appeals [*Zusprüchen*] that we human beings, on our part, can help to be voiced [*zum Sprechen bringen können*), language [*die Sprache*] is the highest and everywhere the first" (E146; G20). The highest thing we can do with language is to answer the appeal to voice language, to make language effective again, to respond to the appeal of language by something we do with language.

Heidegger's essay grants sovereign authority to the language we are born into, the language of our ethnic group, for example, German for those whose mother tongue is German. He does not

allow that a given language might be a contingent historical creation, which could be otherwise and which is imposed on what it
names, perhaps in a sense creating its human reality and meaning
rather than revealing its "nature." It is possible to see already the
way a certain nationalist program could be underwritten by Heidegger's ideas about language. Nevertheless, it may be a condition
of sanity to believe that one's native language has a natural relation
to the way things are. Is it possible to live, from day to day, in a
community, with a continuous sense of the contingency of language? The recently passed law declaring English the official language of the State of California shows that something serious is at
stake, something not limited to the National Socialist program.

～

On the basis of his presuppositions or *Voraussetzungen* about
language, Heidegger goes about figuring out what building and
dwelling are. He does this not by going to experience, history, facts,
but by investigating the etymologies of words. This is not entirely
unlike Proust's assumption, ascribed to Marcel, that the secret
essence of a place is hidden in the name of the place. Heidegger's
Cratylism, however, is different from Marcel's. Marcel's Cratylism
always goes explicitly by way of figurative displacements. Quimperlé is empearled. Such figures assume the place is named in ways
that encode what it is like, even in the absurd and seemingly
accidental (but is it so?) materiality of the word. Heidegger, on the
other hand, by an odd and unaccountable slippage, moves from
language about how we must listen to the silent appeal of language
to claiming that the bridge as a thing or a site does what it does,
gathers, without any help from language. The same thing happens
with what Heidegger says about Van Gogh's shoes in "The Origin
of the Work of Art." He moves from the painting of the shoes as an
artwork to the shoes themselves as an artifact, something ready to
hand in the world. Heidegger's rejection of symbolism and of
figures is so total that in the end he must throw away all language,
throw away the very thing he began by claiming must be interro-
gated, listened to, responded to, *with* language, in order to find out
what building is. Here is a place where Heidegger misses every-

thing, but in an interesting way. He misses the necessary rhetoricity of all language, including his own. Other examples are what he says about crossing the last bridge as a figure for dying. All men are "always themselves on their way to the last bridge" ("immer schon unterwegs zur letzten Brücke") (E153; G27). The trope of life as a journey is present in this expression. Another example of an unrecognized figure is what Heidegger says about the tree of the dead (*Totenbaum*) as the peasant word for coffin. The matter is even more complicated just here. As Heidegger no doubt knew, or could have known if he went back to his etymological dictionary, *Baum*, tree, is probably from the same root as *Bauen*, so *Totenbaum* is the dwelling-place of the dead.[6] Heidegger also forgets or does not notice the tropological power of the prosopopoeia whereby he speaks of language as able to speak and as able to withdraw itself, as in a famous expression in another essay, the essay on Trakl called "Language": "Language speaks" ("Die Sprache spricht") (E190). Nothing could be more problematic than this ascription of a voice and an autonomous power of using it to language. All sorts of ideological presuppositions can be smuggled in on the basis of this claim that language masters us rather than being our tool: "Man acts as though *he* were the shaper and master of language [*Bildner und Meister der Sprache*], while in fact *language* remains the master [*die Herrin*] of man. ["Mistress" might be a better translation here, since *Sprache* is feminine in German.] Perhaps it is before all else man's subversion of *this* relation of dominance [*Herrschaftsverhältnisses*] that drives his nature into alienation [*Unheimische*: more properly, homelessness]" (E146; G20). The moral appeal of this is very strong. It makes us ashamed to think that we try to master language and makes us ready to listen, as to a sovereign leader, to what Heidegger says he hears in the silence of words.

I have said Heidegger ignores or veils the rhetoric of his own essay. What can be said about his rhetorical strategies? As in other essays, Heidegger begins by establishing a present-day context for his investigation or, as he calls it, "venture in thought." In this case the current context is the housing shortage in Germany in the years after the war. The essay was originally presented in 1951 at Darmstadt in a lecture series on "Mensch und Raum" ("Humans and Space"). Having established a current context, Heidegger then goes on in his characteristic late essays to express ironically what most people think about his topic. This includes both received opinion and the metaphysical tradition from Plato on (sometimes the modern tradition of subjectivist thought since Descartes). The traditional or everyday assumption in this case is the presupposition that building is a means toward the end of dwelling. Then he proceeds to show that this is all wrong. The obvious question is: "How do you know that, Professor Heidegger?" His answer is: "Because language tells me so, and language is the mistress of man." In the letter to a student at the end of "Das Ding" ("The Thing"), Heidegger gives a somewhat more complicated answer to this question. You must think, he says, you must learn the craft of thinking [*das Handwerk des Denkens*], in response to a call. This call, both essays affirm, is not simply from language. It speaks rather by way of the silence of language, not by way of the words themselves as they are ordinarily understood and used today.

Even before this opening move, Heidegger in an initial paragraph sets up the connection of thinking to dwelling and building he will argue for, against received opinion. He does this by way of the word "is" (*ist*). His inquiry is a fundamental one, he says, having to do with the essential being of things. He wants to think what building and dwelling are, that is, as he says, he wants to take building back into the domain of the "is": "rather it [this venture in thought (*dieser Denkversuch*)] traces building back into that domain to which everything that *is* [*was ist*] belongs" (E145; G19).

Heidegger's rhetoric turns on confusing the "is" of profound identity with the "is" of figurative equivalence. The trick is to utter sentences like "A bridge is a thing." Such sentences sound banal enough. They are ordinary language. Who would disagree with the proposition that a bridge is a thing? Then he goes about persuading you by a sideways displacement through a series of such sentences that what you have *really* said, without knowing it, when you utter this sentence, is that a bridge gathers the fourfold one of mortals, divinities, sky, and earth, or something else extremely unlikely that you did not know you had said. Language speaks through my speech, whether I know it or not. *Die Sprache spricht.*

The etymological paragraphs beginning "What, then, does *Bauen,* 'building,' *mean?*" ("Was heißt nun Bauen?") (E146; G20) imply without quite saying so that all this can only be thought in German. Only in German would *Ich bin* for "I am" be related to *Bauen,* though "been" and "be" in English have the same root. But they have no evident connection to the English word "building." The route Heidegger follows only exists in the German language. What does that mean? That building and dwelling are the same only in German? No, something more problematic, namely that thinking in German is universally valid, as when Fichte said anyone can philosophize—so long as they do it in the German language. Heidegger blithely draws universal, apodictic conclusions from the idiosyncrasies of a particular language or family of languages. He includes Greek, Latin, and sometimes, as in "The Thing," a word or two of English, but rarely French, Italian, or Spanish, much less Japanese, Chinese, or Hindi. Nothing is said about the problems of translation this raises. If you read "Building Dwelling Thinking" in translation, you are being told two contradictory things simultaneously: "listen to the appeal of language" and "you are out of it if you cannot listen to German, hear its *Zuspruch,* or maybe that of Greek."[7] Here is a place where as late as the 1950's Heidegger's nationalism discretely surfaces. The whole program of "national aestheticism," with its dangerous proximity to National Socialism, is implicit in these etymological reflections. Nor is it all that easy to dismiss this as dangerous nonsense. How are you going to think if you do not do it in some language or other? And what thinker, at least in the philosophical tradition, is going to be willing to admit that his or her thinking is good only for that language and has no validity when translated? Yet an important part of "Building Dwelling Thinking" is untranslatable. It depends on the material idiosyncrasies of the German language. This is obvious enough when German words are being discussed, but what about the rest of the essay? Could that be at least to some degree untranslatable too? Earlier I said "reading is translation—of something itself a translation of an unavailable text, a secret text." Such an idea depends on seeing translation as problematic.

~

Heidegger's etymological reflections lead him to the idea of oblivion or forgetting. This is another problematic concept. It is problematic in the sense that he ascribes to language as an autonomous activity what is the effect of his own rhetoric. He substitutes a personified language for his rhetorical activity. We have, he says, forgotten what *bauen* really means: "The real sense of *bauen*, namely dwelling, falls into oblivion [*Vergessenheit*]" (E148; G22). What does that mean? How did that forgetting happen? This is another way of asking: What, for Heidegger, is the relation between thinking and language? How is it that Heidegger can remember, that is, remove the veil of forgetting when all the rest of us have forgotten? By listening to language? But that is now a place of silence. By looking words up in an etymological dictionary? Nothing could be more problematic. Heidegger had taken that issue up overtly in "The Thing," presented as a lecture in 1950, the year before "Building Dwelling Thinking": "The suspicion arises that the understanding of the nature of thingness [*des Wesens des Dinges*] that we are trying to reach may be based on the accidents of an etymological game. The notion becomes established and is already current that, instead of giving thought to essential matters [*Wesensverhalte*], we are here merely using the dictionary" (E174; G46–47). Heidegger's response is flatly to deny this: "The opposite is true." But he does not really explain how or why this is the case, beyond asserting that "dictionaries have little to report about what words, spoken thoughtfully, say" (E175; G47). Having said this, he goes on serenely with the discussion of the basic meanings of Old High German *Thing* and *Dinc*, along with many related words, in the following pages of the essay.

These etymological speculations are grounded on the assumption that "language speaks," that words go on meaning what they mean even if no one understands them any longer. This presupposes the covert personification of language that is so important throughout the essay. It is as if language itself chose to hide itself, to keep itself secret, to cover itself with a veil. Language acts like a person, and a rather cruel and willful person, at that. This hiding is adduced as evidence of the sovereignty of the primal meanings Heidegger teases out of the history of the words he discusses. The fact that language withdraws these "real meanings" is evidence that they are primal. This seems thinking in a circle: "That language in a way retracts [*zurücknimmt*] the real meaning of the word *bauen*, which is dwelling, is evidence of the primal nature [*das Ursprüngliche*] of these meanings; for with the essential words of language, their true meaning easily falls into oblivion in favor of foreground meanings. . . . Language withdraws [*entzieht*] from man its simple and high speech" (E148; G22). If language speaks, it can, apparently, also choose not to speak. Does Heidegger really mean that, that language acts on its own in this way, as if it were a person or a god? This idea is, of course, a version of the personification of Being elsewhere in Heidegger's work. Being withdraws, leaving Nothing. Our predicament is a forgetfulness of Being that Being itself has brought about. Applying the same paradigm to language, as Heidegger does in this essay, makes it easier to see what is profoundly disquieting about these personifications. They are covert displacements of Biblical concepts about the way God can choose to turn his face away from his people, abandon them, become what Pascal called a *deus absconditus*. To say language does this, however, is not at all the same thing. It makes it easier for the reader to glimpse the rhetorical moves behind Heidegger's argument. It brings into the open another place where Heidegger misses everything, but in an interesting way.

What Heidegger misses in this case is the possibility Nietzsche recognized over and over, the possibility Jacques Derrida has been exploring tirelessly for many years, for example in "White Mythology." This is the possibility that language speaks through me, all right, *die Sprache spricht*, but what speaks is an ideology built into language, woven into its grammar and into the metaphorical force of its conceptual words. This ideology bears no necessary or ascertainable relation to "the truth of Being" or to any other truth. In fact, like any ideology, it is a confusion of linguistic with phenomenal reality.

Heidegger's claim that language has withdrawn itself is especially problematic if you set what he says in this essay about that enforced oblivion against the somewhat different argument a year earlier in "The Thing." In "Building Dwelling Thinking" he seems to be saying that once the primal meanings of words were known. Then language withdrew itself, and those meanings were forgotten. People once knew that building is dwelling, that to be is to dwell, because language told them so. Language named clearly "man's" sense that building is dwelling. But in "The Thing" he had said something rather different, namely, that the thingness of the thing has never come into the light out of its unconcealedness. I, Martin Heidegger, in the way I think, write, use words, by a careful process of incremental repetition, am teasing the thingness of the thing out of concealment, out of its secrecy, into the light. In "The Thing" Heidegger says, "In truth, however, the thing as thing remains proscribed, nil, and in that sense annihilated. This has happened and continues to happen so essentially that not only are things no longer admitted as things, but they have never yet at all been able to appear [*zu erscheinen*] to thinking as things" (E170–71; G43). Why is it that things have never yet been able to appear to thinking as things? The answer is that they have never yet come out into the open as things. It is not a matter of some limitation in man, but a reticence in things themselves: "Man can represent [*Vorstellen*], no matter how, only what has previously come to light of its own accord and has shown itself to him in the light it brought with it [*in seinem dabei mitgebrachten Licht*]" (E171; G43). Since the bridge is a thing, presumably its thingness, that is, its power to "thing," to gather, has also not yet appeared, or been able to appear. That would be implied in "The Thing," whereas in "Building Dwelling Thinking" Heidegger says that the primal meanings of the words that would have told us this have withdrawn into oblivion.

Various ways of dealing with this apparent contradiction present themselves. It could be said, for example, that in one essay he speaks of things themselves, in the other essay of the words for things. But "Building Dwelling Thinking" tells us that only through language do things come into the open, and then only if we can bring back from oblivion the aboriginal, *ursprüngliche*, meanings of basic words. It seems more as if Heidegger wants to have it both ways. He wants to say that he is recovering an original insight that has been lost, and at the same time he wants to claim that he has insights that have been granted to no thinker before him, not even to the Pre-Socratics at the beginning of philosophy, whose authority he so often invokes.

Heidegger's thought can be usefully set here against the important paragraphs in Marx's *German Ideology* about the rise of consciousness, language, and ideology.[8] These have already been discussed in a note to chapter 8. Heidegger and Marx in these passages are quite different in resonance but nevertheless similar in their basic patterns of thought. The peculiarity of what Marx says is that he describes a historical process of differentiation that is nevertheless not historical, since all the differentiation was always there already, from the beginning. Consciousness, for example, does not precede language, nor language consciousness: "The 'mind' is from the outset afflicted with the curse of being 'burdened' with matter, which here makes its appearance in the form of agitated layers of air, sounds, in short, of language. Language is as old as consciousness. [*Die Sprache ist so alt wie das Bewußtsein.*]" (E44; G357). Men and women are both continuous with the animal kingdom (through the difference of roles in sexual reproduction, the first division of labor), and at the same time far beyond the animal kingdom in their possession of or by ideology. This paradox is repeated over and over in different ways in what Marx says about "Primary Historical Relations, or the Basic Aspects of Social Activity" (E41; this title is not in the German edition). Though the paragraphs in Marx describe a world-historical temporal progression starting with the first separation of man from the other animals and going by stages to the present complexities of industrial capitalism, each moment in the progression only repeats in a somewhat different way differentiations that were there already.

There is no place where you can locate a decisive transition, a definitive break in history, a watershed, threshold, or border.

For Heidegger, in a somewhat analogous way, the coming to light of primal meanings, the oblivion of these, and their coming to light again is both historical and not historical. Language was always there already, speaking, and it still does, but a process occurred whereby the primal call and the primal meanings fell into oblivion, "withdrew" (as though language acted of its own volition). Now Martin Heidegger is bringing them back to memory by carefully listening to silence, though he does not want to take responsibility for this uncovering, since it depends on decisions language makes. At the same time he wants to say it is something that he alone has done. Only he, in these bad days at least, can listen to silence, so we had better listen to him.

∽

I have noted the way Heidegger's argument proceeds by sudden sideways slippages. A new motif not present before and not perspicuously inherent in what has been said is abruptly introduced. Often this slippage occurs by taking literally a figure implicit in one of the terms already used. This rhetorical sleight of hand is of course not overtly signaled. A good example is the displacement whereby he introduces the idea of mortality. Heidegger wants us to believe that man's mortality follows logically from the fact that to be human means to dwell. The implication is that language says it. Heidegger's own rhetorical agency is effaced. Here the slippage goes by way of a common word for human beings: "mortals" (*Sterblichen*). Heidegger gets a lot out of this term: "To be a human being means to be on the earth as a mortal. It means to dwell" (E147). The German original differs here. It is more elliptical, more cryptic: "Mensch sein heißt: als Sterblicher auf der Erde sein, heißt: wohnen" ("To be human means: to be on the earth as mortal, means: to dwell") (G21). Does the second *heißt* apply to the first or to the second phrase? Does the sentence signify that to be human means to dwell or that to be a mortal on the earth means to dwell, or does it mean both? To dwell is to be mortal! Where does the word "dwell" say that? It is certainly the case that human beings are mortal, but this does not seem, to me at least, to follow from the fact that to be human is to dwell and to build. Why could the immortal gods, if there were or are any, not also dwell? Could animals not dwell? What does dwelling have to do with dying or being mortal?[9] The words *Bauen* and *Wohnen*, even if Heidegger has heard their silence, do not seem to justify saying human beings alone are capable of dying, "capable of death *as* death" ("den Tod *als* Tod vermögen"): "Only human beings die [*Nur der Mensch stirbt*], and indeed continually" (E150; G24).

A similar paragraph in "The Thing" asserts that being capable of death fundamentally defines human beings, both as the basis of temporality and as the unique human connection to Being: "Only human beings die. The animal perishes [*verendet*]. . . . Death is the shrine of Nothing [*der Schrein des Nichts*], that is, of that which in every respect is never something that merely exists, but which nevertheless presences [*west*], even as the mystery of Being itself [*als das geheimnis des Seins selbst*]. As the shrine of Nothing death harbors within itself the presencing of Being [*das Wesende des Seins*]. As the shrine of Nothing death is the shelter of Being [*das gebirg des Seins*]. . . . Mortals [*Die Sterblichen*] are who they are, as mortals, present in the shelter of being" (E178–79; G51).[10]

This deplacement, whereby Heidegger gets from building to dwelling to death to the "presencing" of Being, is characteristic of "Building Dwelling Thinking" as a whole. A salient case is the introduction later on of the bridge as an example seemingly chosen at random. Heidegger constantly adds something in by a supplemental, sideways movement that does not logically follow from what has preceded. The alogic of this slippage is a version of the general alogic of supplementarity. Something new that does not quite fit is introduced as the ground of the thinking that preceded it.

What is the rationale of these displacements? Heidegger might answer that his argument presupposes a prior knowledge of his previous writings, from *Being and Time* on. *Being and Time*, notoriously, has much to say about the being toward death of Dasein. Each new essay, however, has an obligation, one might reply, to have a logic of its own, to make its connections explicit. The stark juxtapositions that vault across fissures and crevasses in Heidegger's thinking here may bring into the open discontinuities in his thought generally. Another way to put this is to say that the vaultings may indicate the way Heidegger's argument goes by way of many small performative positings (*Ersetzungen*) disguised as seamlessly connected insights dictated to him by words, as "language speaks." I shall return to this possibility.

As Heidegger develops his idea of the "fourfold one," he introduces not only earth and sky but also, by another unsupported slippage, the divinities. Though it is easy to see how the words *Wohnen* and *Bauen* might necessarily involve earth and sky, they contain no authority in themselves that I can see for bringing in the gods. But Heidegger hears the divinities in the words. One by one the elements of what might be called a rudimentary cosmological topography are laid down or deposited by Heidegger, like the foundation stones of a building. The idea that man dwells by building is followed by the idea that since man is mortal his whole life is a journey toward death. This leads to the idea that death is the Nothing that is the shelter of Being. Man makes his journey toward death on the earth, under the sky, and before the divinities. These separate motifs make a coherent and indissoluble unity, a fourfold one. This all-inclusive realm of man's dwelling sets up a paradigmatic scene for the bridge building in the second section of the essay. To say this realm is all-inclusive means it does not have any borders, though it does have horizons. Heidegger speaks of borders later on in the essay, but these frontiers do not seem to have any other viable culture beyond them. No other country, governed by some other laws or made up of different entities, exists over the border. Earth, sky, divinities, and mortals make up a universal imperium. All this is read out of the primal meanings of the words *Bauen* and *Wohnen*: "But 'on the earth' already means 'under the sky.' Both of these *also* mean 'remaining before the divinities' and include a 'belonging to men's being with one another.' By a *primal* oneness [*einer* ursprünglichen *Einheit*] the four—earth and sky, divinities and mortals—belong together in one" (E149; G23).

On the basis of this universal human topography and by way of some more wordplay or slippage, Heidegger introduces the idea that man's task is to spare and preserve: "Let us listen [*Hören wir*] once more to what language says to us. The Old Saxon *wuon*, the gothic *wunian*, like the old word *bauen*, means to remain, to stay in a place [*das Sich-Aufhalten*]. But the gothic *wunian* says more distinctly [*deutlicher*] how this remaining is experienced. *Wunian* means: to be at peace, to be brought to peace, to remain in peace. The word for peace, *Friede*, means the free, *das Frye*, and *fry* means: preserved from harm and danger, preserved from something, safeguarded. To free really means [*bedeutet eigentlich*] to spare" (E148–49; G23). Here is a particularly good example of the way Heidegger moves from one proposition to the next by way of the multiple meanings of words, that is, by a kind of rhetoric of the pun. He plays on the figurative ambiguity in the multiple meanings of words. He makes equivalences by taking the figures literally.

In this case the series of displacements gets him to the italicized proposition: "*The fundamental character of dwelling is this sparing and preserving*" ("Der Grundzug des Wohnens ist dieses Schonen") (E149; G23). That assertion in turn enables him to assert that if dwelling means saving and preserving, this really means setting the other three of the four free to be present: "To save really means to set something free into its own presencing [*etwas in sein eigenes Wesen freilassen*]" (E150; G24). *Wesen* is translated by Hofstadter, somewhat problematically, as presencing, though it is a participle of *sein*, to be. Dwelling is not an action for which the dwellers must take sole responsibility but an active/passive letting things be and waiting, for example, waiting for the absent gods to return: "Mortals dwell in that they await the divinities as divinities. . . . They wait for the intimations of their coming and do not mistake the signs [*Zeichen*] of their absence [*Fehls*]. They do not make their gods for themselves and do not worship idols. In the very depth of misfortune [*Im Unheil*] they wait for the weal that has been withdrawn [*des entzogenen Heils*] (E150; G25).

This idea of waiting for the return of the absent gods is of course taken from Judaism and Christianity. Jews await the Messiah. Christians await the second coming. Even after Christ came we still have to wait. The phrase "Let us listen once more to what language says," especially in Heidegger's German ("Hören wir noch einmal auf den Zupruch der Sprache") reinforces this Judeo-Christian resonance by echoing Biblical phrases like "Now hear the word of the Lord," or even like Jesus' "Who hath ears to hear, let him hear" (Matthew 13:9). Heidegger speaks as the prophet or even as the Messiah of a new dispensation reversing the withdrawal of the gods, of being, of language. Through him language, one might almost say "the Word," speaks.

On the basis of the idea that dwelling means sparing and preserving, Heidegger shifts suddenly to our responsibility to care for things: "Rather, dwelling itself is always a staying [*ein Aufenthalt*] with things" (E151; G25). The argument once more goes by the incremental addition of new factors that are unexpected in the sense that they are not obviously implicit in what has been said already. Heidegger is listening to the silence. This final move in the first section of the essay is crucial preparation for what he says about the bridge in the second section of the essay: "But things themselves secure [*bergen*] the fourfold *only when* they themselves *as* things are let be in their presencing [*in ihrem Wesen gelassen werden*]" (E151; G25–26). This idea of letting things be present allows Heidegger to pick up on the two modes of *Bauen* he identified earlier: building and cultivating. It is easy to see how cultivating is a kind of letting things be. It is not so easy to see how building a bridge is letting something be. This new sleight of hand is necessary to avoid thinking of bridge building as mere engineering or *Technik*. Much more is said about this in one of Heidegger's most difficult essays, "Die Frage nach der Technik" ("The Question Concerning Technology"), but "Building Dwelling Thinking" contains in miniature Heidegger's doctrine of technique or technology. *Technik*, he says, really still means what *techne* meant to the Greeks: "The Greeks conceive of *techne*, producing [*das hervorbringen*], in terms of letting appear [*Erscheinenlassen*]" (E159; G34). In order to avoid thinking of bridge building as an autonomous human activity, building a bridge must be seen as analogous to letting a thing be itself—to planting a potato and letting it be a potato. That allows Heidegger to conclude section one by saying that "*Dwelling*, insofar as it keeps or secures [*verwahrt*] the fourfold in things, is, as this keeping, *a building*" (E151; G26).

A crucial word here and throughout the essay is the little word "is" (*ist*). The deep structure or basic character (*Grundzug*, a key word in the essay, as I shall show) of his sentences is "A is B." Though in fact B is only a metaphorical transposition of A, the "is" in "A is B" asserts a literal identity between them. We know how Heidegger read Nietzsche, but is it worth speculating about how Nietzsche would have read Heidegger? Probably he would have read him as a hyperbolic example of the hypostatizing of grammatical accidents he condemns in the posthumously published notes. As Nietzsche recognizes, this error also lies behind anthropomorphisms, such as Heidegger's personification of language. Language does certain things. There must be a doer behind this doing. Hence language must be a quasi-person capable of deciding to withdraw or to come back from occultation.

Heidegger's trick is to affirm that analogies or figurative displacements are identities. He must forget, and lead us to forget, that they are figurative substitutions if he wants to claim he has purified his language of all rhetoric or figuration and can write as an absolute literalist. But the careful reader should always be wary when a writer says he or she is expunging all tropes. It is just then that the most powerful effects of figuration, powerful in part because obscured and unacknowledged, are likely to be doing their work. The covert speech act that declares a figure is a literal fact is perhaps the most powerful tool of ideology making.

~

The complex displacements of the essay's first part are preparation for the second section about the bridge and about the way the bridge creates a landscape around it. The sequence of positings in the first section is presupposed in the second section. It is not the bridge as such that makes the landscape, says Heidegger, but the bridge as a built thing let to be itself. The later details about the last bridge and the altar in the peasant house, in their turn, follow from ideas about the mortality of man, about death and the divinities, in the first section. Having answered the first question, "What is it to dwell?," he can now turn to the second, "In what way does building belong to dwelling?"

More specifically, he asks, "What is a built thing? A bridge may serve as an example for our reflections" (E152; G26). The careful reader should be wary when a philosopher or a literary critic says, "Take, for example, . . ." No example is innocent. Argumentation by way of examples depends on insinuating the validity of that most problematic of figures, synecdoche. Example asserts that the part is like the whole.[11] Heidegger's refusal to see the bridge as a symbol is an attempt to evade a linguistic problem he inadvertently reinserts by introducing the bridge "as an example."

The key word in the description of the way the bridge makes the region around it into a landscape, establishing zones, limits, and distinct elements, is "gather" (*versammeln*): "The bridge *gathers* the earth as landscape around the stream" ("Die Brücke *versammelt* die Erde als Landschaft um den Strom") (E152; G26). Heidegger says *versammeln*, not *sammeln*. The force of the *ver* here is as an intensive. The bridge performs a forceful gathering. The bridge for Heidegger has the same effect on what is around it as does Wallace Stevens's jar on the slovenly wilderness of Tennessee:

> The bridge swings over the stream "with ease and power." It does not just connect banks [*Ufer*] that are already there. The banks emerge as banks only as the bridge crosses the stream. The bridge designedly causes them to lie across from each other. [*Die Brücke läßt sie eigens gegeneinander über liegen.*] One side is set off against the other by the bridge. Nor do the banks stretch along the stream as indifferent border strips [*als gleichgültige Grenzstreifen*] of the dry land. With the banks, the bridge brings to the stream the one and the other expanse of the landscape lying behind them [*der rückwärtigen Uferlandschaft*]. It brings stream and bank and land into each other's neighborhood [*in die wechselseitige Nachbarschaft*]. (E152; G26)

"With ease and power" (*leicht und kräftig*) is a citation from Friedrich Hölderlin's "Heidelberg." Heidegger's essay can be read as an oblique commentary on Hölderlin's poem. A set of presuppositions underlies the topographical assertions in this passage.

The rest of the essay works these out. They include the reintroduction of the theme of the fourfold one by way of a new piece of wordplay on the word "Thing" (*Ding*), the projection on the basis of that of a paradigmatic life story that is enacted within the landscape brought into being by the bridge, and, on that basis again, a challenge to the traditional and commonsense concept of space, as well as an explicit rejection of the notion (present in different ways in Kant and Nietzsche) that an unknown and unknowable X underlies "things" as their unpresentable ground. Traditional notions of consciousness as a subject set over against its objects and of thinking as mental representation are also, and necessarily, rejected along the way.

The fourfold one is brought back into the discussion of the bridge by the introduction of yet another metaphorizing etymology. *Thing* meant in early Germanic languages a gathering or assembly, for example, the assembly of the elders of a tribe for collective deliberation. If a bridge is a thing, then it must do the same thing that the medieval thing as deliberative assembly did. Sure enough, just that is asserted: "The bridge is a thing [*ein Ding*]—and, indeed, it is such *as* the gathering [*Versammlung*] of the fourfold which we have described" (E153; G27). Just here Heidegger rejects the idea that the bridge is a symbol, or an expression of any kind. In doing this he sets aside implicitly all that he has said about listening to language to find out what dwelling and building a thing are. Heidegger wants to have his cake and eat it too. On the one hand, you can find out what kind of a thing a bridge is only by listening to language. On the other hand, the bridge is entirely free of language. If the bridge is a thing and nothing but a thing, then it does whatever it does without any help from language, and it not clear why we need language to see that. It would seem to be a matter of perception or apprehension, not of naming.

On the basis of this concept of the bridge as a thing that gathers not only the banks and landscape but also earth, sky, divinities, and mortals, Heidegger can take up a more general topographical idea, that of space as such. Along with space go the associated concepts of locations, sites, horizons, and boundaries. It is man's building, whether of a bridge, or a house, or a temple, that creates locations. Locations open space and make it into an organized field with boundaries:

A boundary [*die Grenze*] is not that at which something stops but, as the Greeks recognized, the boundary is that from which something *begins its presencing* [*von woher etwas* sein Wesen beginnt]. That is why the concept is that of *horismos*, that is, the horizon, the boundary. . . . That for which room is made [*Das Eingeräumte*] is always granted and hence is joined [*gestattet und so gefügt*], that is, gathered, by virtue of a location [*durch einen Ort*], that is, by such a thing as the bridge. *Accordingly, spaces receive their being from locations and not from "space."* [Demnach emfangen die Räume ihr Wesen aus Orten und nicht aus "dem" Raum.] (E154; G29)

Heidegger's topographical thinking, as is evident in this citation, cannot be detached from the complex of ideas about language, thinking, building, and dwelling that surrounds it in this essay and in Heidegger's writing as a whole. Once again his goal is to overturn our everyday, common ideas. In this case it is the assumption that that empty, Euclidean, scientific neutral space is there to begin with and then filled and outlined with various things man builds: houses, roads, walls, bridges, everything that makes empty space into a human territory that might be mapped. No, space is made by things, such as the bridge. The bridge "enspaces" (*einräumt*). Euclidean space is not original, already there. It is the reductive derivation from a space that has its ultimate origin not so much in the bridge as in man the builder and dweller who lets space be by building, who clears a place for space by making sites and locations that surround themselves with a landscape.[12]

In his discussion of space in this essay, Heidegger makes an implicit reference backward to *Being and Time*. There space is said to be generated by time. Paragraphs twenty-three and seventy are the crucial ones. In the latter Heidegger says "Dasein's specific spatiality must be grounded in temporality" ("Dann muß aber auch die spezifische Räumlichkeit des Daseins in der Zeitlichkeit gründen").[13] Time takes precedence over space. Why is this? The rest of paragraph seventy explains: "Dasein takes space in; this is to be understood literally [*im wörtlichen Verstande*]. Space is by no means just present-at-hand in a bit of volume which its body fills up. In existing it has already made room for its own leeway [*Spielraum*: literally, "play room," taking "play" in the sense it has when we say "There is play in this wheel"]. Dasein determines its own location in such a manner that it comes back [*zurückkommt*] from the space it has made room for to the 'place' which it has reserved" (E419; G368). This movement of going out and coming back is the basic movement of temporality. Dasein moves forward into the future in order to come back to the past. This is made explicit on the next page: "Because Dasein as temporality is ecstatico-horizonal in its Being it can take along with it a space for which it has made room [*einen eingeräumten Raum*], and it can do so factically and constantly" (E420; G369). The argument culminates in a portentously italicized sentence: "*Only on the basis [Grund] of its ecstatico-horizonal temporality is it possible for Dasein to break into space*" (E421; G369).

This account of space and human temporality in *Being and Time* is implicit in the account of enspacing in "Building Dwelling Thinking." Heidegger's thinking about space or enspacing has changed little, if at all, except in dropping the emphasis on "falling." In *Being and Time* Heidegger asserts that "Temporality is essentially falling [*wesenhaft verfallend*] and it loses itself in making present [*das Gegenwärtigen*]" (E421; G369). Nothing is said about falling in "Building Dwelling Thinking," unless the withdrawal of its primal meanings by language is a kind of fall.

The choice of a bridge as an example is crucial, since a bridge is a way to get from here to there through time. This is made explicit in what Heidegger says about crossing bridges. His examples of the uses of bridges are temporal. They implicitly contain a historical narrative tracing out the course of human life. Would Heidegger include graveyards among the works that organize space and make it a place—the barrow, for example, in the midst of Egdon Heath in *The Return of the Native,* or the country churchyard of which so much is made in Goethe's *Elective Affinities*? Every topography implies a narrative that unfolds through time. Heidegger's topography is no exception. An implicit story lies behind the humanized landscape Heidegger constructs around his imaginary bridge. This story surfaces at one point, in the paragraph about the Black Forest peasant house. This is a little story of birth, dwelling, cultivation, worshipping, and death. A good dwelling embodies the whole journey of "man" from birth to death. Heidegger's description of a two-hundred-year-old farmhouse in the Black Forest includes the room set aside "for the hallowed places [*geheiligten Plätze*] of childbed and the 'tree of the dead'—for that is what they call a coffin there: the *Totenbaum*—and in this way it designed for the different generations under one roof the character of their journey through time [*ihres ganges durch die Zeit*]" (E160; G35).[14] Already, death has unostentatiously appeared in the interpretation of the bridge as "the vaulting" (*das Überschwingende*) of men and women over a gulf or stream that takes them, as mortals, toward their final journey over the last bridge to death. In the midst of life, trying to get from here to there, mortals (*die Sterblichen*) are "always themselves on their way to the last bridge" ("immer schon Unterwegs zur letzten Brücke") (E153; G27). Building of all sorts, for Heidegger, makes earth and sky a domicile within which man can dwell, think, and, ultimately, die in proximity to the gods, as he makes his way through a space that is a dimension of time.

Another fundamentally temporal dimension organizes "Building Dwelling Thinking": the history of language. This contains the whole history of mankind (Heidegger says nothing about womankind), or at any rate of German-speaking mankind. This history is the story of the forgetting of what language says, or rather, of language's withdrawing and then its uncovering by Heidegger. The implication is that we do not really dwell now because we have forgotten, or technique has made us forget. We have even forgotten what technique is or used to be. It was another example of bringing things out and letting them be, according to Heidegger's understanding of the Greek word.

~

Just what further assumptions underlie the idea that the bridge "enspaces," that is, surrounds itself with an organized space making a landscape? A necessary presumption of these further positings, which has already been noted, is the rejection of symbolism. The bridge must act on its own, as an independent thing not in any way dependent on language. A further necessary presumption is the rejection of Kant's and Nietzsche's idea that the thing is "an unknown X [*ein unbekanntes X*] to which perceptible properties are attached" (E153; G28). This would make, Heidegger says, "everything *that already belongs to the gathering nature* [versammelnden Wesen] *of this thing*... appear as something that is afterward read into it [*als nachträglich hineingedeutete Zutat*]" (E153; G28). Kant's and Nietzsche's somewhat different notions that an unknown substratum lies behind each thing are replaced by Heidegger's idea of occultation, withdrawal, forgetting. The gathering may be a bringing into the open of something secret, hidden, but this is by no means to be understood according to the model of the *Ding an sich*, which eternally remains an unknown X.[15]

On the basis of this repudiation, Heidegger goes on to develop his idea of space as something for which the building makes a site. What the bridge does is to be a location that can make space for a site: "But only something *that is itself a location* [Ort] can make space for a site [*eine Stätte einräumen*]" (E154; G28). This space is defined by the fact that it is a particular gathering of the fourfold one of earth, sky, divinities, and mortals. To assert this Heidegger once more goes back to the "ancient meaning" of a word. "*Raum* (*Rum*) means a place cleared or freed for settlement and lodging" (E154; G28).

It will be necessary to follow Heidegger's argumentation a little more closely here in order to locate the hidden rhetoric that facilitates the argument. Once again, the procedure is a crisscross substitution. What seems to be the cause is shown to be derived, but, as throughout the essay, the way this depends on verbal reversals is covered over, crossed out. Heidegger argues first that building a bridge creates a location (*Ort*), which then can become a site (*Stätte*). The site organizes space around it from a horizon. Heidegger plays here on the etymology of the Greek word, which comes from a verb, *horizein* (to divide, separate), from *horos* (boundary, limit). A horizon implies the act of dividing or separating. This act is performed by the building that is put in an *Ort*, making it a *Stätte* that "ensites" and "enspaces." Each of those last two words is a neologism in English, so the argument Heidegger makes can only be made in German. Or it can only persuasively be made in German. In German you can much more easily than in English make a verb by adding a prefix to a noun, "ensites" from "site," "enspaces" from "space," both non-words in English, though "site" and "space" are perfectly good English verbs. A horizon, says Heidegger, is not a boundary or limit but the product of an act making a limit. It is that from which space begins, so nothing exists beyond it. The *Ort* that becomes a *Stätte* ensites and enspaces. It goes out to make the border from which a space is cleared, beyond which the same genius loci does not reign. About that beyond nothing can be said. It is not governed by the same logos, for example, the idioms of a given language. On this basis Heidegger can go on to say that we do not move through a neutral space, but are already anywhere within the space that is created by the act of making a given place into a site. Thinking of the old bridge at Heidelberg is being there, perhaps being there more than the people who thoughtlessly cross it every day.[16]

On the basis of the claim that spaces receive their being from locations and not from space, Heidegger goes on to ask: What is the relation between location and space? and What is the relation between man and space? The answer to the first involves a reversal of our usual idea that space is there to start with, able to be measured in a way that does not in any way depend on what is within the space. He contrasts the genuine space that is allowed (*eingelassen*) by the bridge to the space of pure extension that can have any of its distances measured mathematically. You could call the latter "the" space, he says, but "in this sense 'the' space, 'space,' contains no spaces and no places" (E155; G30).

A moment before Heidegger had said that in a space of pure indifferent extension, Euclidean space, the bridge could be re- placed by something else or by a mere marker: "In a space that is represented purely as *spatium*, the bridge now appears as a mere something [*ein bloßes Etwas*] at some position [*Stelle*], which can be occupied [*besetzt*] at any time by something else or replaced [*ersetz*] by a mere marker [*eine bloße Markierung*]" (E155; G30). This is an important sentence. The key words in it are *besetzt, ersetzt,* and *Markierung. Besetzt* and *ersetzt* are *setzen* words, that is, words that in one way or another suggest positing, placing. *Übersetzen* means "translate," that is, set across from one language to another. What Heidegger rejects, once more, is substitutability, one might say, figuration. He began by saying the bridge was just taken "as example," that is, the bridge is something that stands in for all the other possible examples. If it is just an example, there could presumably be other examples that would do as well, the peasant shoes or the temple in "The Origin of the Work of Art," for example. This rhetoric of exemplarity is now forgotten, and Heidegger wants to say the temple or bridge is irreplaceable. It is not a mere placeholder or marker, an X, a mere *Etwas,* or "something." This refusal is symmetrical with the refusal of symbolism. The bridge, however, was initially posited as a placeholder, a marker, a mere *Etwas,* an X, that is, it was posited as an example, one presumably out of many. Once again, Heidegger must ignore the rhetoric of his own essay.

Having posited the relation between locations and space, and having asserted that we live in a space provided for by locations, not just in wild nature or in empty space with no built things in it, no presiding spirit of the place, Heidegger goes on to identify the relation between man and space. Here he has to reject two other possibilities. One is that "man" is set over against space as subject to object, the other that space is an "inner experience." He says, categorically, that space "is neither an external object nor an inner experience" (E136; G31). In place of these possibilities he sets his model of a belonging together of man in the fourfold (earth, heaven, divinities, mortals) that has been "allowed for" by enspacing: "by the name 'man' I already name the stay within the fourfold among things" (E156; G31). Since all these things belong together in an inextricable, fourfold one, we are already everywhere in that space. Space has been generated by Dasein's building and therefore is an extension of it. Again Heidegger's underlying motive is rejection of substitution or trope, in this case, the idea that mental representations substitute for absent or distant things, the trope of mimesis. The German word for substitute, *Ersatz*, connects with *ersetzen* and *zusetzen*, already discussed: "We do not represent distant things merely in our mind—as the textbooks have it [*wie man lehrt*]—so that only mental representations of distant things run through our minds and heads as substitutes for the things [*so daß als Ersatz für die fernen Dinge in unserem Innern und im Kopf nur Vorstellungen von ihnen ablaufen*]" (E156; G31). Instead of that, thinking about the old bridge at Heidelberg gets us through the distance to that location: "If all of us now think, from where we are right here,[17] of the old bridge in Heidelberg, this thinking toward that location is not a mere experience inside the persons present here; rather it belongs to the nature of our thinking *of* that bridge that *in itself* thinking gets through, persists through, the distance to that location [*vielmehr gehört es zum Wesen unseres Denkens* an *die genannte Brücke, daß dieses Denken* in sich *die Ferne zu diesem Ort* durchsteht]. From this spot right here, we are there at the bridge—we are by no means at some representational content [*Vorstellungsinhalt*] in our consciousness" (E156–57; G31).

The rest of the paragraph asserts firmly that we pervade space, and are always already constantly near things and locations. When I move in space, for example, toward the door of the lecture hall, I can do that only because I am there already: "I already pervade [*durchstehend*] the room, and only thus can I go through [*durchgehen*] it" (E157; G32). The claim that we are at the old bridge in Heidelberg just by thinking of it is truly amazing if you think of it from the perspective of "our" commonsense assumptions. It is not only amazing but insidiously attractive. It satisfies in the form of omnipresence the infantile desire for omnipotence Freud ascribes to every baby. Only some counterintuitive concept such as the one Heidegger proposes can avoid seeing mental images as representations, symbols or tropes standing for objects that are external to the mind. Heidegger's refusal of figuration therefore has metaphysical and psychological as well as linguistic motivations. Or rather, the three motivations are aspects of the same insistence that everything unfolds from a Dasein that always already contains space and all things in it. About the political implications of this insistence I shall say more.

More than once Heidegger uses the word *Grundzug*, translated by Hofstadter as "basic character." One example comes several paragraphs from the end of the essay, where he says, "Dwelling, however, is *the basic character* [der Grundzug] of Being in keeping with which mortals exist" (E160; G35). *Grundzug* can be set against other words built on *Grund*: *Grund* itself in the sense of reason, base, logos, as in the title of Heidegger's *Der Satz vom Grund* (*The Principle of Reason*), *Grundriß*, or "groundplan," as used in "The Origin of the Work of Art," *Abgrund* or *Ungrund* for chasm, abyss. The other half of the word *Grundzug*, *Zug*, means "drawn" in several senses. It also combines with many other words. *Grundzug* is a crucial word in "Building Dwelling Thinking," one to which Heidegger does not call special attention, but one that is therefore all the more important. It hides a version of the unknown X in the guise of an apparently innocent word that appears to name something out in the open: "fundamental character." *Grundzug* is an equivocating word meaning "essential features" and "fundamental features" at the same time, that is, it names both the external features by which a thing is known to be what it is and its underlying, invisible but determining, characteristics. *Grundzug* in the latter sense underlies *Grundzug* in the former sense. *Zug* means features in the sense of something drawn out on the surface, like the features of a face, while *Grund* implies something hidden, the foundation of the rest. A *Grundzug* is hidden and out in the open at the same time. This word is Heidegger's covert way of smuggling back in the "unknown X" he had repudiated.

When Heidegger refuses the definition of the thing as an unknown X to which "perceptible properties are attached," and then chooses as an example a bridge that he initially defines as "crossing" the stream, he has both refused the X and introduced it in another way into his discourse. Though he speaks of the bridge as something that "lets the stream run its course" and that also lets mortals "come and go from shore to shore" (*daß sie von Land zu Land gehen und fahren*) (E152; G27), nevertheless he tends to speak as if the traffic on a bridge all goes one way. Heidegger's bridge is not a route for to and fro commerce, but a means by which the harvest wagon goes from the fields to the village or the means by which the lumber cart gets from the field path to the road. Heidegger does nothing conceptually in this essay with the other flow that crosses the bridge widdershins, namely, the flow of the stream. The stream is, of course, also a way of expressing temporality, for example, in Heraclitus's fragments, about which Heidegger elsewhere has much to say. The bridge is a means of transport for Heidegger in this essay. It gets him from one place to another in the trajectory he is following. The bridge works in this way because it is a metaphor or symbol that Heidegger is unwilling to admit is a metaphor or symbol. The examples he gives of what different bridges do are all examples of commerce or transactions of one kind or another. From the country various things are brought into town. The bridge is also a means of transport from castle to cathedral square, from temporal to spiritual power bases. But the paradigmatic passage is the one from this world to the other, from death to life. Whatever bridge we cross is oriented toward the crossing of the last bridge to death. Whatever Heidegger may say about going to and fro (*hin und her*) across the bridge, his bridge is ultimately a one-way crossing. It is not a means for the interchange of properties, such as those on which the hidden rhetoric of Heidegger's essay depends.

～

The final pages of the essay say the building of a bridge "admits and installs" the fourfold. This doublet, *zulassen* and *einrichten*, is of great importance as a clue for reading the essay. Heidegger's formulations posit forking alternatives between which a decision must be made and yet between which a decision cannot be made. His hesitation between the two terms, or his need to assert them both, is his version of the aporia of invention, the impossibility of knowing whether something invented is discovered or made. "The location [*Ort*]," says Heidegger, "*admits* the fourfold [lässt *das Geviert* zu] and it *installs* the fourfold [richtet *das Geviert* ein]. The two—making room in the sense of admitting [*Zulassen*] and in the sense of installing [*Einrichten*]—belong together" (E158; G33).

Admit or install? Which is it? There is no way to tell which precedes the other either in the activity of building that makes or allows a space for landscape or in the activity of writing a novel, a poem, or a philosophical essay—"Building Dwelling Thinking," for example, or *The Return of the Native*, or "The Idea of Order at Key West." Each such work depends on a landscape already there, admitting it into the work in a process of mimesis, or installing a new imaginary landscape, superimposing Wessex on Dorset, for example, as Thomas Hardy did when he wrote *The Return of the Native*, or creating a new poetic topography, as Wallace Stevens did when he wrote "The Idea of Order at Key West," or mapping a new philosophical landscape on the Black Forest and Heidelberg, as Heidegger does in this essay. Each activity, admitting and installing, presupposes the other as always already having been accomplished, in an unstillable oscillation of each between primary and secondary.

Heidegger defines technique as a "letting appear" (*Erscheinenlassen*) (E159; G34) and claims that thinking and dwelling belong to one another and to building. Building and thinking are analogous in being necessary for dwelling. "Building and thinking are, each in its own way, inescapable [*unumgänglich*] for dwelling" (E160–61; G36). The two must learn to listen to one another. What Heidegger does not see, must not see, is that both building and thinking go by way of the making or using of signs, and that sign using and making are always caught in the undecidable opposition between admitting and installing. If sign using and making are taken as a matter of installation, then once the installation is complete it appears that something already there has been admitted. If you say it is a matter of admitting you cannot know that or encounter that without first installing something, for example, composing an essay or building a bridge. Heidegger does not think by means of a recovery of the primal, literal meaning of certain words. He performs, rather, a mystified and mystifying thinking as though language were only grammar and logic and not also always rhetoric. Rhetoric must be taken here in the double sense of "permeated with figurative displacements" and "permeated also with persuasive speech acts." The latter are positings disguised as assertions of fact.

Another way to put that would be to say that Heidegger does not allow for the unauthorized performative power in language, his own language, for example. "Admit" and "install" can be read as different ways of saying the same thing. To admit is to allow the sky, earth, gods to enter into a space that has been cleared, according to that active/passive (it is both at once, and neither without the other) letting things be that Heidegger counsels. But to install is also active and passive at the same time. By building a bridge we install the earth, sky, gods, and men, in the sense of a specific culture and way of living. Heidegger means this installation not in the sense of an unauthorized, unsanctioned speech act but in the sense of letting language speak through us, letting space-making occur through our *Bauen*. In a similar way, it is always possible to see a purely human performative as allowing another power, say a divine power or a state power, to speak through language, as when the president of a university says, for instance: "By authority of the power vested in me by the State of California, I declare that you are doctors of philosophy." On the other hand, all performatives may be seen as unsanctioned, free, inaugural. What they do, for example, what Heidegger's essay does, has no precedent and no authority beyond the one that is created, installed, by just these words in just this order as Heidegger puts them together in this way.

Heidegger wants to put all the blame on language, which speaks through him. He wants, that is, to ignore or evade all the rhetorical devices his essay uses to install a whole architectural fabric of unauthorized equivalences by way of the "is" of metaphor taken as the "is" of ontological identity: building is dwelling is thinking is speaking. He wants also to evade his own agency and responsibility by surreptitiously projecting in covert prosopopoeia a personality and a sovereign autonomous power into language, as though language were an autocratic emperor who comes and goes when he likes.

Heidegger misses everything but in an interesting way. The reversal or crisscross whereby he blames language for what he does substitutes something that speaks through language for language itself. That is the "everything" he misses. When he says that building "installs" as well as "admits," he has the clue in his hand. That is the place where he brings momentarily into the open the chiasmus whereby he has projected a ground he in fact creates. The question raised by Heidegger's essay is parallel to Stevens's question in "The Idea of Order at Key West": "Whose spirit is this?" Heidegger is right to say it is not just the subjective spirit of the maker, just as Stevens is right to deny that when he says, "It was more than this." What Heidegger misses is the mechanism whereby signs of one sort or another open a new world that then infallibly seems to be grounded in some preceding spirit or genius. A new start both makes its own ground and seems to reveal a ground that was already there. Heidegger's error is not just a refusal to accept the groundlessness of creation through "building," including building through speech acts. It is also a refusal to accept responsibility for the inaugural power of language, for example, his own language in "Building Dwelling Thinking."

~

I began by asking whether or not Heidegger's topographical ideas are politically innocent. It is not immediately apparent what complicity there may be between Heidegger's concept of dwelling and his endorsement of the programs of National Socialism during the Nazi era. My reading of "Building Dwelling Thinking," however, has shown that this concept is tied in manifold ways to "national aestheticism" and even to National Socialism. Heidegger's conception of language universalizes German. If you can philosophize only in German or in ancient Greek, if the secrets of dwelling in the sense of the proper way to build, dwell, and think on earth are hidden in the now-withdrawn primal meanings of common German words, then a recovery of those primal meanings and building, dwelling, and thinking in their light would be not a local project but a universal one. This project would justify the imperial ambitions of the Reich. Using the covert personification in the claim that "language speaks" as a way of covering up the ungrounded performative claims of his own declarations, and as a way of occulting the figurative transfers on which the rhetoric of his essay depends, Heidegger ascribes a spurious transcendent validity to a local, nationalist ideology. This ideology, moreover, was used to justify the unspeakable atrocities of the Shoah. Those atrocities, finally, are a logical consequence of the specifically topographical ideas the essay posits on the basis of what Heidegger finds language saying. In spite of Heidegger's disclaimer when he says, "Our reference to the Black Forest farm in no way means that we should or could go back to building such houses; rather, it illustrates by a dwelling that *has been* [gewesenen] how *it* was able to build" (E160; G35), nevertheless the *Schwarzwaldhof* is presented as a paradigmatic example of proper dwelling. Just as Heidegger's celebration in "The Origin of the Work of Art" (written in 1935, that is, during the Nazi era) of the immemorial toil of the peasant woman he incorrectly assumes was the owner of the shoes painted by Van Gogh says nothing about the life most people in Germany were living at that time, as the Germans under Hitler prepared the great industrial might of the Wehrmacht, so "Building Dwelling Thinking," first presented in 1951, that is, six years after the end of World War II, says nothing about the fact that the housing shortage mentioned at the beginning and end of the essay was primarily urban and was a result of the bombing of German cities by the Allies.

Einfalt (oneness, or onefold) is a key term in "Building Dwelling Thinking," as in the repeated phrase "the oneness of the four" (*die Einfalt der Vier*). The imperialism of the Third Reich was publicly justified in part by the need of the German people for more *Lebensraum* (living space). The topographical ideas of "Building Dwelling Thinking" would authorize only the monolithic, onefold, culture of a people (*ein Volk*) sharing the same language, laws, and customs, and dwelling in one particular place. In that place their building has admitted or installed a single, unified landscape of hills, fields, and rivers, buildings, bridges, roads, and horizons. Beyond that horizon no other authentic culture may be conceived to exist. Such topographical assumptions would underwrite a unicultural nationalism. They could be used to justify the expulsion or extinction of all those who do not share that single language and culture. It is a little scandalous that Heidegger was imperturbably asserting these ideas six years after the end of the war and after the end of the thousand-year Reich's ambitions. It is also a little scandalous that the standard English translation of this essay and related ones under the title *Poetry, Language, Thought* says nothing about these political implications. On the other hand, ideas not too different from Heidegger's lie behind the disquieting return of a violent nationalism directed against immigrants in unified Germany today. Our own country is not entirely free from such dangerous nationalism, as in the law, already referred to, that declares English the official language of the state of California.

The lesson to be learned from reading Heidegger is not that we should not read him, but that we should read him, though with extreme care and wariness, as though we were entering on dangerous ground. We should read him as the most persuasive and intellectually exigent expression of an interlocking complex of ideological assumptions from which no one can these days with certainty claim to be entirely free. The conceptual study of ideology does not free one from ideology. The study of the way rhetoric, tropes, and the materiality of language generate ideological mystifications may possibly, however, have a good political effect. By good effect I mean conducing to a new form of democracy, a democracy of difference that puts the manifold (*Mannigfalt*) in place of the onefold (*Einfalt*). It would do that by trying to show "us" (another appeal to the solidarity of the "we") the political efficacy of the rhetorical, tropological, and material aspects of our own language. "Show" here does not name a revelation of anything that can ever be phenomenal. It would do that, rather, by giving us a glimpse of the way this efficacy is based on unauthorized performative effects of language and other signs. These effects would include those of unitary territorial delineation and sovereignty. For these effects those who utter the speech acts should and must take responsibility. We must not attempt to palm off the responsibility on language or on some transcendent, authorizing power that speaks through language. That is easy to say, but "we" should not minimize the difficulty of doing it.

§ 10 The Ethics of Topography: Stevens

It might seem perverse to look for ethical themes in Wallace Stevens's work, just as it might seem perverse to attack him for not writing poems about ethics. He is a poet in whose work the subject to object relation dominates, the domain of epistemology, not the intersubjective relation, the domain of ethics. No law that I know of, ethical or otherwise, demands that all poets write about ethics. Or maybe there is such a law, operating whether we know it or not? In any case, just as Frank Lentricchia could plausibly find a pervasive political dimension in Stevens's work,[1] so a concern with "How to Live. What to Do," as he puts it in the title of an early poem,[2] runs all through Stevens's poetry.[3]

"How to live. What to do": the formula defines the ethical relation as a resolute decision to live in a certain way and to do certain things. The ethical person knows how to live and what to do. Ethics traditionally grounds such decisions in a sense of strong obligation to some law. In response to the demand made on me by this law, I say, "I must live in such and such a way; I must do this or that." This living and doing, grounded in the law, define my relations to my fellows. The protagonist of "How to Live. What to Do" faces the moon, the rock, and the cold wind side by side with a "companion" (*CP*125). I live and do with others and toward others. I want this living and doing to be justified. I want it to be aligned with a command laid on me to live and do in just this way rather than any other.

The problem, as "How to Live. What to Do," along with a swarm of other poems by Stevens, makes clear, is that the traditional voices of the ethical law, mediated, for example, by one religion or another, no longer speak a clear message. In their place is only the inarticulate sound of a cold wind. This sound, it would seem, is hardly an intelligible voice laying a comprehensible command on me, even though it is a "heroic sound / Joyous and jubilant and sure" (ll. 19–20). Though Stevens says there was no "voice" speaking in this denuded scene, the adjectives just quoted covertly personify the wind. They make it speak through the sibilants of those initial "j's" and "s's." It is difficult, however, to tell how seriously to take the personification or what might follow if we do so. As I have elsewhere argued, a conspicuous feature of Stevens's poetry is the way the poet encounters at the limit of the farthest and most seemingly impersonal reaches of the poetry-making intellect a humanlike figure, face, or gesture.[4] This happens in the lines from "How to Live. What to Do" in question here:

> There was neither voice nor crested image,
> No chorister, nor priest. There was
> Only the great height of the rock
> And the two of them standing still to rest.
>
> There was the cold wind and the sound
> It made, away from the muck of the land
> That they had left, heroic sound
> Joyous and jubilant and sure. (ll. 13–20)

The ethical question, for Stevens, is whether this cold wind can be the ground of a new obligation. In the face of such a wind, one asks, "How to live? What to do?" One way to read the title is as a desperate posing of unanswered and unanswerable questions: In the face of such an inhuman jubilance, what am I going to do now? How am I going to live? The cold wind, joyous, jubilant, and sure though it is, seems to give me no directions or orders. It makes no claim on me. I incur no obligation in relation to it. By contrast, the cold wind in its indifference may lead the protagonist of this poem to a new kind of ethical obligation. The wind may impose on him and his companion a new kind of law. That is the question. Can there be a modernist or postmodernist ethics? This would be an ethics of those who have survived the devastating losses Stevens's poetry reports, for example, in "The Comedian as the Letter C": "Exit the mental moonlight, exit lex, / Rex and principium, exit the whole / Shebang" (IV, ll. 5–8). Can there be an ethics in the absence of any ascertainable "lex, rex, and principium"?

Even though it seems at first a little perverse, as I have said, to seek out ethical themes in Stevens, it might seem even more perverse to connect Stevens's ethical concerns with topography in his poems. Ethics has to do with the relations between people and with their submission to some ethical law. Ethics is the realm of performative uses of language. In this realm, we use language to make promises, sign contracts, engage ourselves in any of the manifold ways a person can be tied by social obligations. Topography, on the other hand, seems the realm of a purely constative language. Topography is primarily toponymy, the names, generic or proper, things have in a given region: "Instead there was this tufted rock." There is plenty of landscape in Stevens's poetry, but it seems primarily the vehicle of epistemological themes. The relation between "imagination" and "reality," not that between person and person, seems dominant in Stevens's poetry. That theme was certainly most salient in his comments on poetry, for example, in the essays in *The Necessary Angel.* Topographical elements are the vehicle of this theme.

What about topography in Stevens's work?

As any careful reader of Stevens knows, it is a mistake to try to reduce his work to universal concepts. His work is heterogeneous. He says now one thing and now another, apparently contradictory, thing. Nevertheless, it would seem that his poetry might be defined as pervasively "topographical" in the obsolete sense. Much of it is description of some place or other in Connecticut, Pennsylvania, Florida, the Caribbean, and many other places on the map. In these descriptions Stevens tends to stress the power of the imagination over reality. In "Anecdote of the Jar," the jar in Tennessee, a man-made object, surrogate for the human imagination, takes dominion everywhere. Sometimes, as in one important poem, the sovereignty of the imagination and its instrument, words, is so great that the human acts of living, remembering, and anticipating are firmly defined as "Description without Place." Description without place is *graphein* without *topos*, a strange kind of atopical topography. So all-powerful is description in its freedom from place and in its power over place that Stevens can say in this poem, "It is a world of words to the end of it, / In which nothing solid is its solid self" (VII, ll. 5–6). Other poems grant more recalcitrant and resistant solidity to the landscape. This interchange, in any case, seems to have little if anything to do with ethical obligation. It is the free and spontaneous exercise of a will to power over things as they are: "It was a queen that made it seem / By the illustrious nothing of her name. / Her green mind made the world around her green" (I, ll. 7–9). Here the proper name of the queen is the mediating link whereby the queen's green mind makes the whole world green.

Nevertheless, to return to "How to Live. What to Do," the ethical theme in that poem is carried by the topographical description that makes up most of the poem. The man and his companion have climbed away from "the muck of the land / That they had left" in order to confront the "tufted rock / Massively rising high and bare / Beyond all trees." There they encounter the cold wind. They have "left the flame-freaked sun / To seek a sun of fuller fire" and have seen instead the moon rising above the rock, "Impure upon a world unpurged." In a curious species of topographical allegory, the moral themes of this poem are carried by the coordinates whereby a scene, in this case not given a proper name, is outlined. A purely linguistic space is created. This space is oriented around the opposition between up and down, night and day, sun and moon, muck and rock, and so on. The poem is about "How to Live. What to Do." The title says so. But the poem itself is poetic topography, description without place. It names moon, rock, sun, clouds, and wind, as well as the two figures, the speaker and his companion, standing in that landscape. The ethical themes could not be expressed without the valences and tensions set up by the items in the landscape. The poem is an example of what might be meant by "the ethics of topography."

Are such poems by Stevens anything more than a factitious and calculated arrangement of topographical terms in order to say something "poetically," "allegorically," naming one thing and meaning another? Could the same meaning have been expressed with other allegorical paraphernalia? A lot hangs on the answers to these questions. How would one know that one had answered them right?

∼

To try to answer them I turn now to one of Stevens's greatest ethico-topographical poems, "The Idea of Order at Key West."[5] The poem is located just two pages after "How to Live. What to Do" in *The Collected Poems*. (Is that not, by the way, a strange kind of topographical reference, a naming of the place in the book where this poem takes place?) I must assume that the readers of this essay have its grave and somber cadences echoing in their minds. I must assume also that those readers find the poem as puzzling as I do. Its meaning is by no means perspicuous. Why, for example, is it called "The *Idea* of Order at Key West"? What is the force and meaning of the word "idea" here? "Idea" is one of the great, complex philosophical words in our tradition, but knowing that does not make it easier to decide just how Stevens is using the word. And what about "she" and "genius" in the first line of the poem: "She sang beyond the genius of the sea"? What in the world does that mean? Who is "she" anyway? Could "she" not be an embodiment or prosopopoeia of "the idea of order at Key West"? Such person-ifications are common in Stevens's poetry, for example, in "Notes Toward a Supreme Fiction" or "Chocorua to Its Neighbor." "She" is the first word of the poem, after the title: "The Idea of Order at Key West / She sang beyond the genius of the sea." "Idea" in Greek means the appearance of a thing as opposed to its reality, from *idein*, to see. The singing woman may be the idea of order at Key West in the sense of being the personification, in a visible form, of order. "She" may be the idea of order. But what would it mean to personify the idea of order as a woman singing as she strides the beach at Key West? The poem, for me at least, is full of questions like these about "idea," "she," and "genius." Only reading and re-reading, taking nothing for granted, can hope to answer them. I shall return to "idea" at the end of my reading.

Even a first reading, however, shows that the poem delineates a scene, a real one this time, "description with place." The poem gives that place its proper name: "Key West," like a name on a map. Like many so-called proper names, however, "Key West" hardly has the uniqueness of a name good for one place only. "Key" is a word for a small island or reef, and "west," of course, is just the name of a direction, though it presupposes the whole operation of topographical mapping. There could be as many Key Wests as there are keys that you can get to the east of, but you would need to have firmly in place the compass coordinates as a way of orienting places in relation to one another in order to use the word "west" as a place name. "Key," moreover, comes from the Spanish word "cayo," from the Taino word "cayo," "caya," small island. The Tainos were Indians of the Greater Antilles and the Bahamas, now extinct. Like many place names, "Key West" contains within itself in miniature the history of its human occupation, building, and naming, in this case from the Native American inhabitants to the Spanish conquerors to the English-speaking Americans who changed "cayo" to "key." Place names have a temporal as well as spatial dimension. They contain much encrypted history.

Key West is the last of the Florida keys. It is a small island in the Gulf of Mexico at the tail end of the line of little, nearly contiguous coral islands, now joined by a highway, that circle around toward the west from the southern tip of Florida. In that part of the United States, Key West is as far as you can go. There is plenty of open sea to confront from the beach there, "Theatrical distances, bronze shadows heaped / On high horizons, mountainous atmospheres / Of sky and sea." Stevens used to go to Florida annually for business and vacation. Except for his business trips to the annual cattle show in the Midwest, these trips to Florida were his primary relief from Hartford, Connecticut, and his job there as a Vice President of the Hartford Accident and Indemnity Company. Key West therefore has a special place within the internal topography of Stevens's work. Except for the trip by boat to the Yucatan, Havana, and South Carolina recorded in "The Comedian as the Letter C," Key West was as far as Stevens went. It was an outer edge, horizon, or boundary to his travels, a limit from which the more domestic landscapes of Pennsylvania and Connecticut were measured. When Stevens went to Key West in February 1934, Fulgencio Batista had a few months earlier led a successful military coup in Cuba. The battleship *Wyoming*, along with other ships of the U.S. Navy, were at anchor off Key West. Stevens wrote "The Idea of Order at Key West" after he returned home.[6]

As "The Idea of Order at Key West" continues, the elements of a topography emerge one by one, like the graphic representation of a fractal drawn bit by bit on a computer screen. Several protagonists inhabit this topography. A woman—perhaps, as I have said, a personification—walks on the beach at Key West facing the sea and singing. Out to sea, a great vista of waves, sky, and clouds extends all the way to the horizon. These scenic elements, plus someone walking at the border between land and sea and singing or chanting, appear elsewhere in Stevens's work. This rudimentary liminal scene also echoes similar places in the work of Whitman and Emerson, for example, Whitman's "Out of the Cradle Endlessly Rocking" and Emerson's "Seashore." The choice of mise-en-scène for "The Idea of Order at Key West" alludes to the American tradition of liminal poems. Whitman is named and identified with the sun in another seashore passage in Stevens, the admirable first stanza of "Like Decorations in a Nigger Cemetery":

> In the far South the sun of autumn is passing
> Like Walt Whitman walking along a ruddy shore.
> He is singing and chanting the things that are part of him,
> The worlds that were and will be, death and day.
> Nothing is final, he chants. No man shall see the end.
> His beard is of fire and his staff is a leaping flame.

In "The Idea of Order at Key West" Whitman as sun or the sun as Whitman is replaced by a female figure singing on the shore as night falls. But other protagonists are added here, the unidentified "we," of whom one member speaks the poem: "it was she and not the sea *we* heard" (my italics). The actual words of the poem are made up of the interpretative meditations of someone who beholds, apparently with at least one companion, a great twilight vista of the sea, the shore, and the singing woman and hears her song. Yet the "we" may be a poetic we, Stevens speaking for all of us, a collective "we" experiencing this topographical making.

Finally, there is the mysterious Ramon Fernandez, to whom the speaker toward the end of the poem poses an urgent question: "Ramon Fernandez, tell me, if you know." The poem is in the past tense until this moment when the speaker turns to address Ramon Fernandez in the present tense. The speaker is remembering from some unspecified place the scene by the shore, so the direct address to Fernandez by no means proves that he was one of the "we" for whom the poet speaks. He may or may not have been present. The poem may be addressed to him at a distance, as a kind of letter in blank verse. On the other hand, Fernandez may be there in the now of the poem, remembering with the poet their common experience. The poet turns to pose a question about it to him. It may be impossible to decide whether he is present or not. It depends somewhat on who Ramon Fernandez is. Stevens's answer when asked about that was more than a little evasive: "I used two every day names. As I might have expected, they turned out to be actual names."[7] "Ramon" and "Fernandez" are not quite everyday names, not even in Key West. They are certainly not names one would expect to be used by a poet from Reading, Pennsylvania, dwelling in Hartford, Connecticut. The names sound as if they must be motivated rather than random.

The only likely candidate is the Ramon Fernandez from Mexico who settled in Paris and became a member of the *Nouvelle revue française* group, which included Charles du Bos, Jean Paulhan, Jacques Rivière, André Gide, and others. Fernandez wrote several important books of criticism, including one on Proust, but most notably *Messages* (1926), translated into English in 1927.[8] Fernandez became a collaborator during World War II. Since Stevens kept up with French criticism and philosophy, he may well have read Fernandez, either in the *Nouvelle revue française*, or in the collected volume, or in the *Partisan Review*, or in translations by T. S. Eliot in the *Criterion*. Fernandez's essay "I Came Near Being a Fascist" appeared in translation in the *Partisan Review* in the same month Stevens's "The Idea of Order at Key West" appeared in *Alcestis*.[9] Fernandez, the author of an ambitious phenomenology of literature in a long essay in *Messages*, would certainly have been an appropriate person to ask the question Stevens puts to the "pale Ramon" of his poem, though the tone of the question suggests that Stevens does not think he will be able to answer it.

The Key West landscape of sea, shore, town, and harbor with fishing boats at anchor[10] is the carrier of a complex relay of inter-subjective relations projected on the topography in a spatiotem-poral array. Just what might be meant by "carrier" is a more difficult question. It is the central question of this chapter, the question of whether the topographical details are essential or accidental. Could a poem with the same meaning have been composed with the poet listening to the woman singing indoors, for example, in the ball-room of a hotel in Key West?

The woman on the shore sings in the face of the sea, but it is not yet clear that this locus matters. Most of the poem defines the relation between her song and the sea noises. The speaker and his unnamed and unidentified companions watch the woman and listen to her. The poem is a meditation on that, a response to the woman's response to the sea. Then, just as the "we" of the poem turned away from the seashore "toward the town," as night falls, so the speaker at some unspecified later time turns to Ramon Fer-nandez with a question: "tell me, if you know, / Why." The poem dramatizes a curious, one-sided interpersonal relation, sustained and dramatized by topographical and temporal distances. The male poet (if it is Stevens speaking) hears a woman singing, but she pays no attention to him. He reacts so strongly to her song as to be moved later to write a poem, a song about a song. The reader is not given the first song, but he is given the second: the poem he or she is reading.

This structure echoes, of course, another great poem in the Romantic tradition, Wordsworth's "The Highland Reaper." There the poet hears the highland girl singing in Gaelic as she reaps. He internalizes the song and produces a poem in response to her singing: "The music in my heart I bore / Long after it was heard no more." Wordsworth's poem passes the reaper's song and the poet's response on to us as readers, just as, in "The Idea of Order at Key West," the reader is given no citation whatever from the woman's song. The reader is given Stevens's poem instead, by a species of tropographical transfer. It is description without place, since we are not given the original song on which this poem is a commentary, just as Wordsworth did not understand the Gaelic song of the highland reaper and had to imagine what it might be about. More generally, one can say this is a situation in which the poet's experience and words are mediated by the experience and words of another. It is an extremely common situation in Wordsworth, not so common in Stevens.

A rudimentary seascape of shore, sea, sky, cloud, and horizon is outlined gradually in "The Idea of Order at Key West" in the course of meticulous meditations on the relation between the woman's song, on the one hand, and sea and sky, on the other. "The Comedian as the Letter C" or even "Description Without Place" make categorical, though contradictory, pronouncements about the relation of a person or a group to topographical surroundings. "The Comedian as the Letter C" opens by asserting that "man is the intelligence of his soil, / The sovereign ghost," but later reverses that to assert "his soil is man's intelligence. / That's better. That's worth crossing seas to find" (IV, ll. 1–2). "Description Without Place" seems unequivocally on the side of the human power over nature exercised through words: "the hard hidalgo / Lives in the mountainous character of his speech; / / And in that mountainous mirror Spain acquires / The knowledge of Spain and of the hidalgo's hat" (VII, ll. 7–10). But a little earlier in the poem Stevens had asserted that: "Description is revelation. It is not / The thing described, nor false facsimile" (VI, ll. 1–2). If saying this rejects any mimetic or referential theory of language, the word "revelation" suggests that description uncovers something rather than merely imposing fictions freely on what is described.

"The Idea of Order at Key West" attempts to adjudicate among these opposing views by a technique of iteration with a difference, negation, and gradual modification through a series of phrases in apposition. This procedure is familiar to readers of Stevens who, driven by a need to understand what "resists the intelligence almost successfully," as Stevens in the "Adagia" says all poetry should, pay careful attention to the syntactical and rhetorical devices in his poems. It is as though the poet, listening to the woman's song, tries first this formulation and then that one in a potentially interminable meditative attempt to "get it right." Stevens's poetry as a whole might be defined as the prolonged, ever-unsatisfied attempt to get it right. "The Idea of Order at Key West" is a luminous moment in that continuum.

The poem begins with a single enigmatic sentence: "She sang beyond the genius of the sea." The rest of the poem is an exfoliation of this sentence, an extended commentary on what it might mean. The line itself tells us that the sea has a "genius," just as, according to a long tradition, any place has its genius loci, its "spirit of the place."[11] The word "genius" comes from a root "gene-" or "gen-" meaning to give birth, beget. The word is akin to a wide range of words, including "kin," "kind," "gentle," "generate," "genre," "genesis," "genealogy," "ingenious," "ingenuous," "gender," "genital," "genitive," "gene," "progenitor," "naive," "native," and "nation." In Latin "genius" meant procreative divinity, inborn tutelary spirit, innate quality. A genius loci was the guardian deity of a particular locality, but also the distinctive atmosphere or particular character of a place,[12] as when the poet exhorts his sister, "move along these shades / In gentleness of heart; with gentle hand / Touch—for there is a spirit in the woods."[13]

The notion that the guardian deity of a particular locality is "procreative" is important. The spirit does not just hover around, nor has it been born of the place. The genius of the place preceded the place and generated it, speaks in it and through it. The idea of the genius loci goes back to a polytheistic time when the air and earth seemed swarming with many deities, not yet pervaded by one single, ubiquitous, immanent God. Each place had its own god, taking place in that place only, sovereign over just that region. A skeptical latecomer might even say that the idea of the genius loci is an inevitable concomitant of topographical delineation. Topography, either as the name for the inherent features of a landscape or as a term for the mapping of those features in words or images, always involves the notion of limits or borders. Topography, as the name implies, is the graphing of some specific region or place. It is easy to move from that and from the uniqueness of local place names to the feeling that each place is unique. It draws that uniqueness from being generated by and presided over by a divinity special to that place. This divinity draws borders and establishes different places within the whole: the sacred spring, the road to the mountaintop, the frontiers.

Stevens's originality in his use of "genius" is to suppose that the whole wide sea, at least the sea around Key West, is the locus of a single sovereign spirit, the genius of the sea. This might be called the sublime of topography or a sublime topography. The sublimation is achieved by taking away the borders, that is, by choosing a vista, like the seascape at Key West, that is sublime in being virtually limitless and thereby exceeding the human power of comprehending and ordering. The sea goes on out to vanishing horizons. Such a seascape is one of Kant's examples of the sublime in the third *Critique*. The open sea seen from the shore is something so great in size and in impersonal power that it exceeds comprehension and language. Kant emphasizes the impersonality of the sublime seascape. For the sea to seem sublime we must not, for example, he says, be thinking of the sea as a means of transporting goods from one place to another, or as a reservoir of edible fish. We must be seeing it as immeasurably exceeding man's power to know, to master, or to name.

Stevens's genius of the sea has dominion everywhere, as far as the eye can see, out to the "high horizons" later mentioned in the poem. It therefore takes some doing to sing "beyond the genius of the sea," to import a new spirit exceeding the spirit of this sublime place and holding dominion over it, taking place within it. Nevertheless, the singer in Stevens's poem is said to do that. What can this mean? How can she do it?

The conflict between the singer and the genius of the sea is worked out as a kind of a singing competition. This is another ancient topos. In such myths the human singer is usually bested by the divine one and comes to a bad end. An example is the faun Marsyas. Though he was not quite human, he was less than a god. He made the mistake of trying to compete with Apollo in a singing contest, was defeated, and then was flayed in punishment for his temerity. Stevens's singer fares better in the contest, though whether or not she wins an outright victory is another question. The genius of the sea, in Stevens's poem, manifests itself primarily through the sounds of the sea and the wind, "the grinding water and the gasping wind." These sounds are the sea's song. It is hardly an apollonian one. The sea's grinding and gasping is an ur-language. It is the progenitive origin of human language, therefore its base, the ground of our speech, the logos of its logos, to use the word "logos" in two of its many meanings. "Logos" means ground or base, as well as ratio, mind, word, voice, speech, and discourse. The word "logos" does not appear in Stevens's poem, but some of its English equivalents do: "idea," "genius," "mind," "voice," "spirit," "measure." "The Idea of Order at Key West" could even be said to be a commentary on the word "logos," an English commentary on an absent Greek word, though a related word, "idea," is, of course, salient in the title. But is the sound of water and sea truly the originary base of human language? How does one get from one to the other? What is the relation between the sea's song and the woman's song?

The fundamental difference between the two songs, stressed throughout the carefully modulated variations of the poet's meditations, is this: the woman's song is articulated in time and space. It is articulated in time because it is different from moment to moment, articulated in space because that difference is projected through space as modulated sounds. The sea's song, on the other hand, is inarticulate, undifferentiated. This is expressed first in an odd but powerful metaphor. "The water," Stevens asserts in line two, "never formed to mind or voice." This means, I take it, two things: first, that neither mind nor voice, those two versions of the human logos, could assimilate the sea and give it mental or linguistic shape, and second (though without priority of the one over the other), that the water never spontaneously generated its own independent mind or voice. The second possibility is stressed in the figure I have mentioned. The water is "Like a body wholly body, fluttering / Its empty sleeves." Just as Nietzsche in "On Truth and Lies in an Extramoral Sense" figures our predicament as being like a painter without hands, forced to translate what we see into the displacements of sound as a metaphor for sight,[14] so Stevens figures the sea's inability to express itself as its being like a body without arms, legs, or head, that is, without all the appendages we human beings use to make gestures, speak, and so communicate with others. No human being is wholly body, even though all human beings are embodied. The ability to point, beckon, or wave, as well as the ability to expel modulated air in speech, lightens and spiritualizes the human body, making it never wholly body. The sea, on the other hand, is like a multiple amputee fluttering the empty sleeves of a shirt with no arms to put in them. Like Beckett's *innomable*, the sea is so undifferentiated, so exceeds our comprehension, that it is unnameable. It exceeds names both proper and generic, even though we call it "the sea" or "the veritable ocean." Nevertheless, the "mimic motion" of the sea, mimic presumably in the sense that it mimics the movements of a mutilated human body, emits a sound that is something like speech. The sea's motion "Made constant cry, caused constantly a cry, / That was not ours although we understood, / Inhuman, of the veritable ocean."

The juxtaposition of the phrases "made constant cry" and "caused constantly a cry" is an example of the incremental modification of meaning by phrases in apposition I mentioned earlier as a basic rhetorical device in Stevens's poetry. On the one hand, phrases in apposition are implicitly equivalent, since they are alternative ways to fill out the same syntactic pattern making a sentence. On the other hand, they must be different, too, different ways of saying the same thing. What is the difference between saying the mimic motion of the sea "made constant cry" and saying that it "caused constantly a cry"? The changes move away from the almost overt personification in "made constant cry" to the more mediated and indirect "caused constantly a cry." In one case the sea makes a constant cry, as though it were some sentient thing crying. In the other case the impersonal movement of the waves causes a cry, as the movement of a tree's branches in the wind mechanically causes a creaking sound. The replacement of the first phrase by the second suggests that the second is the better formulation, as does the concluding assertion that the cry is "not ours" and is "inhuman." The cry is something it would be a mistake to anthropomorphize, even though such prosopopoeias are irresistible, as in calling the sea's sound a "cry" at all. We cannot carry on a conversation with the sea. Nevertheless, we "understood" the sea's cry and knew it was the sound of the veritable ocean, the real right thing, the *Ding an sich*. In the first section of "The Comedian as the Letter C," entitled "The World Without Imagination," Stevens uses the latter phrase to name the sea when nakedly confronted. The word "veritable" also appears there:

> Here was the veritable ding an sich, at last,
> Crispin confronting it, a vocable thing,
> But with a speech belched out of hoary darks
> Noway resembling his. (I, 69–72)

In articulating the subtle distinction between "made" and "caused," Stevens manifests in his own discourse the power human language has to differentiate itself through time, to make meaning by difference, whereas the sea can only go on "constantly" bringing about the same inhuman, undifferentiated cry over and over through time. For the sea all times are the same. Time, however, is the medium of articulation for human speech, for example, in the woman's song. This is made clear, "articulated," in the next section of the poem. Here Stevens begins to make an extremely careful and delicate adjudication between saying the woman's song is entirely independent of the sea and saying the woman's song is in one way or another a transformation into articulate language of the sea's song. It must, alogically, be both at once, for reasons Stevens gives. If the song is only the first, it would be factitious, artificial, without basis. If the second, the woman's song would be without originality. She would be no more than the medium through which the sea speaks, as in Arthur Rimbaud's theory of poetic inspiration in the "lettres du voyant."

Presumably Stevens means to avoid these extremes when he asserts that "The sea was not a mask. No more was she." A mask is an artificial face over a real face, disguising it. If the sea were a mask, it would be no more than a projection and covering over of the woman's face, or perhaps a mask over some personified spirit behind. If the woman were a mask, she would be no more than a face through which the sea might speak. The masks of ancient Greek tragedy, perhaps covertly alluded to in the image of "the ever-hooded, tragic-gestured sea" and in the "theatrical distances" of the sublime seascape, were also megaphones to amplify the voices of the actors in the large open space of the Greek theater. Neither the sea nor the woman was a mask for the other, a megaphone through which the other could speak, nor, apparently, a mask for any other thing either.

Nor is it the case that the song and water were "medleyed sound," the song and the cry inextricably mixed. Stevens insists that the two are immiscibly separate. This is true even though, as the poet says, "It may be that in all her phrases stirred / The grinding water and the gasping wind." All human speech or song may rise from the grinding and gasping mixture of liquid and air in the throat. In that sense human speech finds its origin in sea and air. Nevertheless, "even if what she sang was what she heard," even, that is, if her song was imitation of the sea's song, the two were not mixed in her song because "what she sang was uttered word by word." This would support the notion that the woman is a prosopopoeia for the idea of order. Order means differentiation as well as putting things in their places. The sea's song is all possible words uttered all together at once, over and over. The sounds of water and wind are therefore no more than "meaningless plungings." The woman, the idea of order, has sorted these potential words out and sings them one by one. This means that even if her song is related to the sea's song in the intimate sense that she does no more than distinguish and enunciate in sequence rather than all at once some of the words the sea iterates always, nevertheless she sings her own song rather than merely being the mouthpiece for the sea. As the poet firmly asserts, "it was she and not the sea we heard."

Nevertheless, the poet's voice in the recording he made of this poem emphasizes the way "she" is so close a sound to "sea," differing from it by the variation of a single phoneme: "It was *she* and not the *sea* we heard." Both those sounds are onomatopoeias for the hissing sound the wind makes or the sound the sea makes as a small wave crests and then flows to its limit up the beach. Though it was "she" and not "sea" we heard, the sound "she" as well as the sound "sea," it could be argued, are initially spoken as meaningless hisses by the grinding water and the gasping wind, whether in nature or in the human throat and mouth. Human speech proper is made by setting against one another two such minimally different sounds as "she" and "sea." Meaning arises from the difference between one sound and the other. The poet's words show this in action.

The basic distinction between the woman's song, by implication all human speech (for example, that of the poet in this poem, or my own in this chapter), on the one hand, and the speech of the sea, on the other, is articulated in an eloquent and beautiful passage a little later in the poem:

> If it was only the dark voice of the sea
> That rose, or even colored by many waves;
> If it was only the outer voice of sky
> And cloud, of the sunken coral water-walled,
> However clear, it would have been deep air,
> The heaving speech of air, a summer sound
> Repeated in a summer without end
> And sound alone. But it was more than that.

These lines enumerate the elements of a Key West seascape: the depths of the sea, dark but prismatically differentiated by its waves (in the pun on "rose" as "arose" and as a color, reinforced by "colored"), the more distant sky and clouds, the submerged coral reefs, the tropical weather of endless summer. The sketching out by naming its elements of an elementary site, locus of the genius of the sea, is made in passing, in the course of asserting that if the woman's song spoke only the voice of sea and sky it would have been, however clearly it might have been sung, one long inarticulate hum, buzz, or roar, meaningless noise rather than comprehensible speech. Meaning depends on division and differentiation, so one sound can be told from another. It also depends on syntactical and grammatical articulations, distinctive and distinguishable rhythms and pauses that establish the beginnings and ends of sentences, marking out the borders of words, phrases, sentences, paragraphs. The woman's song is not just "uttered word by word." It is also "sung," that is, modulated in pitch. Song adds to the rhythms and cadences of speech the articulations of melody.

The voices of sea and sky have no such divisions. They have no marked beginnings and endings. They are just one single, meaningless sound repeated endlessly in a summer without end. To call them "voices" is an inaccurate euphemism, another covert personification ascribing a voice to what in fact has none. The description Stevens gives of these voices shows how inappropriate the word "voice" is as a name for sounds that are more like the roar of William Carlos Williams's sea elephant ("Blouaugh!") than like anything properly to be called a voice. A few lines before, Stevens had drawn the most extreme conclusion from the radical distinction he makes between the woman's song and the "voices" of sea and wind. The former, he asserts, has nothing whatsoever to do with the latter. The woman, the idea of order, is herself the progenitor of her song, its only begetter and "maker," while "The ever-hooded, tragic-gestured sea / Was merely a place by which she walked to sing." To call the sea "ever-hooded" and "tragic-gestured" alludes back to the description of the sea as "Like a body wholly body, fluttering / Its empty sleeves." The sea is "ever-hooded" because its face is never uncovered.

"Tragic" is used in an odd way here, akin to its use in a passage from "Chocorua to Its Neighbor." Mt. Chocorua figures the star above him as "not man yet he was nothing else" (VIII, l. 2), and says that he vanishes within the mind, "taking there / The mind's own limits, like a tragic thing / Without existence, existing everywhere" (VIII, ll. 3–5). To be without discernible limits of one's own is to be tragically deprived, even if one exists everywhere. Stevens's sea in "The Idea of Order at Key West" is "tragic-gestured" because it is a body wholly body and cannot properly gesture at all.

A strong fear of the inhuman sea runs all through this poem. It is a tragic pity and terror for what exceeds the human. These emotions are properly tragic because they are pity and fear for what we may have been and what we might become, of what we even still are, in our kinship with the sea-matter muttering meaningless gaspings and grindings. Whatever the poet says about the power of song or other human artifacts to measure out the sea, to give it coordinates, to map it, the sea as named here to some degree always escapes such humanizing gestures, just as it does in "The Comedian as the Letter C." "C" is only a letter in the human alphabet, comic and superficial, with the lightness and inconsequentiality of a pun, the veritable sea turned into the innocent first letter of Crispin's name. The sea, on the other hand, is terrifyingly inhuman, a body wholly body, fluttering its empty sleeves. Human speech names both with the same sound. No idea can wholly reduce this dark monster to order.

I began my reading with a topographical paradigm, instigated by Stevens's word "genius." The genius of the sea should make empty undifferentiated space into a place, with borders, coordinates, and distinguishable locations. The generative spirit of the place ought to establish boundaries and lay down lines. The genius of this sea, however, does not seem to have done a very good job of that. Its chief self-expression is the meaningless "heaving speech of air," and the sea is limitless, without distinguishable marks except the vanishing horizon. The singing woman, however, does not seem to have done much better if the sea is no more than the place she happens to be when she walks and sings. Her song seems to have nothing to do with the sea, nor to be in any sense the spirit of the place where she sings.

Nevertheless, the woman's song seems to liberate some spirit or other. That leads the poet to ask an important question, perhaps the fundamental question of the poem: "Whose spirit is this?" This question is asked by the collective "we" for whom the poet is spokesperson. It is asked urgently, ready to be asked again, "because we knew / It was the spirit that we sought and knew / That we should ask this often as she sang." "Spirit" is another variant of "idea," "genius," "mind," and "voice." The question asserts that there is a spirit about the premises, a ghostly presence, generated somehow by the song and scene, palpable to the listeners, the "we" for whom the poet speaks. No one can doubt that there is a spirit in the place. The question is, *whose* spirit is this?

∼

"Whose spirit is this?" That seems an idiotic question to ask and go on asking, since the answer seems so obvious. We have been told that the woman sings beyond the genius of the sea. The only other spirit around would seem to be the singer's own consciousness. To see the poem as a celebration of the creative power of the solitary human imagination would be compatible with a standard reading of Stevens's poetry. Such a reading seems unequivocally confirmed by the affirmations that end the section of the poem dealing with the singer striding along the shore:

> She was the single artificer of the world
> In which she sang. And when she sang, the sea,
> Whatever self it had, became the self
> That was her song, for she was the maker. Then we,
> As we beheld her striding there alone,
> Knew that there never was a world for her
> Except the one she sang and, singing, made.

"Maker": the word is an English translation of the Greek word for poet: *poietes.* Along with "artificer" the word "maker" emphasizes the independence and sovereignty of the act of singing. Singing is making. It has an irresistible power to transform everything into a private, subjective structure. This structure is artifice in the sense of being the result of a fabricating power. To what is made by singing Stevens gives a traditional totalizing name: "world." Self and world come together in the song. They are made and made one by her singing: "there never was a world for her / Except the one she sang and, singing, made."

If this were the whole story there would be no problem, and Stevens's question "Whose spirit is this?" would be pointless. But things have been said earlier in the poem and are said later that forbid so univocal an answer. After having denied that "it [the spirit] was only the dark voice of the sea," the poet goes on to affirm that "it was more than that, / More even than her voice, and ours, among / The meaningless plungings of water and the wind." These lines are a crucial turning point of the poem. They assert that the act of singing and thereby making a world that seems free of place, not subservient to the genius of the place where the song is sung, liberates or projects a "spirit." This spirit is more than either the preexisting genius loci, on the one hand, or the creative conscious-ness of the singer, on the other. The spirit is also more than the voice of the listening and looking "we" for whom the poet speaks. He speaks the poem we are reading.

What kind of spirit can that be? "Whose spirit is this?" The im-portance of the question now begins to be clearer, though the an-swer does not seem to be given unequivocally anywhere in the poem. Certainly it is not given by the assertion that she was the single artificer of the world she sang and, singing, made. Sole maker though she is, her making creates or finds a special spirit, unique to that song. That spirit was not there before the song, neither as the genius of the sea nor as the poet's own preexisting self. Nevertheless, it absorbs both the seascape and the poet's consciousness into a new totalizing construct presided over by a new genius loci. This construct Stevens calls a "world."

Stevens, in lines we have not yet looked at hard enough, does not say the sea's self becomes the singer's self. He says, "And when she sang, the sea, / Whatever self it had, became the self / That was her song." The newly created or discovered spirit is neither the self of the sea nor the self of the maker but, in Stevens's careful formulation, "the self that was her song." The true subject of this poem is the power of song, poetry, or other artifacts to create or uncover a new integrating spirit, along with a new place to go with it. This new spirit is neither the genius of a place nor the genius of the poet but the genius of the song, poem, or other work. It is a *genius carminis*. That's whose spirit "it" "is": the spirit of the song. The song is inaugural, genetic, world-begetting. It also begets the self of the singer, in a double constitutive perlocution. The song is an act of genius, in the etymological sense of giving birth. "The Idea of Order at Key West" is a poem about the creating, ordering, measuring, totalizing, topographical, map-making power of language or other signs. One might say that the poem is a deconstruction of the concept of the genius loci and its replacement by the idea that signs make order.

To put this another way, "The Idea of Order at Key West" is a poem about the performative power of poetic language. Words and other signs can make something happen. In this case they bring about the magical appearance of a "world" with all its topographical attributes. This is a hyperbolic version of the way words may, for example, christen a ship or marry a couple. Such lesser performatives, Stevens's poem implies, take place in the context of a constantly iterated new start in poetry and its analogues. This endlessly repeated creative act makes the whole worldly context within which people can be married or ships christened. The topography of a place is not something there already, waiting to be described, constatively. It is made, performatively, by words or other signs, for example, by a song or a poem.

On the basis of this insight we can now understand an apparent contradiction in the poet's scrupulous formulations. On the one hand, the sea "Was merely a place by which she walked to sing." If it already had a "genius," this preexisting spirit was irrelevant to the inaugural making performed by the song. On the other hand, the song turns a mere place into a world. It does this with words that name the place. The song is a *locum tenens* in a quadruple sense. It holds the place, functions as a placeholder. It takes the place of the place, substituting itself for the place. It takes place in that place. And it takes the place or takes over the place, as we say, "They took the place by storm." This act of place taking brings into the open a new spirit, the spirit of the world the song has made out of sea and wind sounds.

This transformation of empty place into world is given a specific definition. Place taking puts sharp edges and definite measurements, both spatial and temporal, in place of the undifferentiated sea sound, that "summer sound / Repeated in a summer without end." As the poet says: "It was her voice that made / The sky acutest at its vanishing. / She measured to the hour its solitude." The hours of that summer without end have no solitude, since they are all promiscuously mixed up with one another. The song divides the hours from one another and measures each. It gives each hour its solitude, just as it imposes sharp lines on the undifferentiated expanse of the sea. The song even reverses the way distance blurs by making the sky "acutest at its vanishing." The sky becomes most distinct at the sharp line on the horizon where sea and sky meet without ever meeting.

∼

I said poetry *or other signs* have, for Stevens, an inaugural power. The lines addressing Ramon Fernandez tell why it is necessary to grant more than just words this order-imposing, order-finding power. The question posed to Fernandez is not "Whose spirit is this?" but "Why does this happen as it does happen?" The poet asks Fernandez why it is that the lights in the fishing boats at anchor off the town have the same world-establishing power as does the woman's song. This is another important turn in the poem. It extends what has been said about the song to human making generally. The lines have a grave majesty and stately cadence that is one recurrent note in Stevens's poetry:

> Ramon Fernandez, tell me, if you know,
> Why, when the singing ended and we turned
> Toward the town, tell why the glassy lights,
> The lights in the fishing boats at anchor there,

As the night descended, tilting in the air,
Mastered the night and portioned out the sea,
Fixing emblazoned zones and fiery poles,
Arranging, deepening, enchanting night.

Here, not language, but things made by man, the lights cast by
the fishing boats, as they tilt in the waves, have the same power as
the woman's song to make a neutral place (or non-place) into a
global topography. The boats' lights bring the scene to light. They
locate poles, divide the sea surface into temperate, arctic, and tropic
zones. The lights draw out all the arrangements and apportionings
that are inscribed on a nautical chart. Why is this? The boats affirm
mastery over the night by implicitly mapping it, as indeed fishing
boats do in the accumulated knowledge their owners have of where
fish, shore, currents, rocks, reefs, sandbars, islands, depths, and
shallows are. The fishing boats make the sea cease to be a wild,
sublime, unmasterable expanse. For fishermen the vast distances of
the sea are anything but an undifferentiated surface. Their boats
both "arrange" and "deepen" even the night sea. The boats' lights,
finally, in a brilliantly appropriate locution, are said to "enchant"
the night. The Latin word for lyric poetry, *carmen*, means not only
"chant" but also "incantation." The boats, like the woman's song,
exercise a magical power of enchantment over the scene, changing
mere space into a fully differentiated site governed by its own
genius of the place.

Human acts of building and making, such as the making of the
fishing boats, are a species of poetry. Or, it might be better to say,
poetry is only one example of the human power to construct
something, whether out of words or out of wood, metal, or stone.
This construction magically gathers space around it, by a kind of
performative enchantment, in one case by words, in other cases by
the building of a boat, a house, or a bridge. The means of a
performative act may be wood, metal, nails, and paint, as well as
the normal instrument of performative action, words.

I have mentioned a bridge as such an artifact, as well as the
fishing boats Stevens names. As I have shown in my discussion in

chapter 9 of Martin Heidegger's "Building Dwelling Thinking," Heidegger connects the Greek word *logos* (one synonym for "genius," "spirit," "measure," and "order," in Stevens's poem) with the Greek *legein*, to gather. Heidegger's essay is organized around the assertion that a genuine human topography gathers together and organizes what he calls the "fourfold one" of earth, sky, divinities, and mortals. This is an assemblage not too different from the elemental components of Stevens's poems: shore, sea, sky, singer, and spirit. Though Stevens and Heidegger are by no means saying the same thing, each may be taken as an implicit commentary on the other. Stevens's poem as much helps us to read Heidegger, to understand what he is getting at, as Heidegger helps with Stevens. Each is a bridge or a boat to the other. Heidegger asserts that "The Bridge *gathers* to itself *in its own way* earth and sky, divinities and mortals."[15] "In its own way": this is an important point. Just as each new bridge, according to Heidegger, gathers the space around it in a new and unprecedented way, so the woman's song and the fishing boats in Stevens's poem each make a unique topography of the surrounding shore, sea, sky, and harbor. Each poem, like each new act of building, is a new beginning, as all true performatives are. They make something happen that was not predictable from the elements that were there to start with, in this case sea, sky, and shore. They exceed the intentions of the builders or singers. Stevens's singer is not shown to be at all aware of the effect of her song on the poet and his companions. Her song instigates another performative discourse in Stevens's poetic commentary on it, just as Stevens's poem, in turn, gives rise to other new starts that he could not have anticipated. These are the essays written about the poem, for example, this one. Such a series of metaphorical displacements has no predetermined goal. It is governed by no ascertainable law, though in retrospect each element in it seems to be a response to an imperative demand.

The two examples, Heidegger's and Stevens's, of constructed things that have topographical power are not fortuitous. Each manufactured thing is a way to get from here to there. A boat or a bridge is a means of displacement, of traversing space, of *Übergang*.

Each is therefore a metaphor for metaphor itself as translation or carrying over. The etymology of the word "metaphor" supports this. The Greek *metafora* means "transport." A navigational chart tells you the way to get from here to there on the uncharted sea. It charts the uncharted and translates its distances and features into legible signs printed out on the surface of the paper.

The examples of the bridge and the boat tell us that the imposition of a new topographical order is an act of figuration, whatever Heidegger may say in denial of this. Topography substitutes the names of things for the things themselves. It then reorders those names in new structures of substitution and displacement, for example, by speaking in a topographical poem of the sea as "like a body wholly body, fluttering / Its empty sleeves." Both bridge and boat are also traditional figures for the temporal dimension of human life, that is, for the human journey from birth to death. Stevens does not speak in this poem of the fact that human beings are mortal, though elsewhere he writes with great power about death, for example, in "The Owl in the Sarcophagus." Heidegger, by contrast, as I have shown in chapter 9, in "Building Dwelling Thinking" makes the fact that human beings are mortal their essential characteristic. Heidegger's insistence on death, versus Stevens's omission of it, is one important difference between the two texts. Stevens emphasizes the forward-looking, affirmative, world-creating power of the woman's song. For Heidegger the whole topography around the bridge arises from the fact that human beings, and only human beings, can die.[16] The difference between Stevens and Heidegger on this point means an essential difference in the topography each text inscribes.

It could be argued, however, that death is there covertly in Stevens's poem, too, present in the never fully effaced threat the sea posed and continues to pose to all human ordering powers. If the veritable ocean is the inhuman origin of human speech, therefore of the human generally, it may also be its implicit end. The word "sea" in "The Idea of Order at Key West" is a placeholder or substitute for death, hiding it but also revealing again the fact that death, as Paul de Man puts it, "is a displaced name for a linguistic predicament."[17] This means, I take it, that the word "death" is another of the many catachreses for the unknown X that surrounds and pervades the clarity of cognition, as its origin, end, and underlying ground. The word "sea" is another such catachresis. It is a word we move in to cover our ignorance and to hide our fear of this unknowable and unnameable "something." But that covering and hiding are never wholly successful, as the dark undercurrent in this poem shows. That Stevens does not utter the word "death" here may indicate not that he has forgotten human beings are mortal but that he remembers it only too well and is trying, unsuccessfully, to forget it. To say "sea" instead is perhaps to say "death" anyway.

Identifying another essential difference between Heidegger and Stevens will help us to measure each. Heidegger's model in "Building Dwelling Thinking" is a single culture, perhaps even a national culture speaking a single language. Such a culture, Heidegger wants us to believe, has taken possession once and for all of a landscape and installed itself there. This installation invokes a special version of the fourfold one of sky, earth, divinities, and mortals. Heidegger's vision is, if the word may be allowed, "totalitarian." His stress is on the uniformity and continuity of an authentic culture, the sameness over the generations of behavior and belief shared by everyone living within that culture.[18]

For Stevens, on the other hand, in a way that seems more democratic and American, or perhaps Nietzschean, in its perspectivism, in any case not so totalizing or totalitarian, a given landscape opens itself to potentially limitless topographical mappings. There is at least one for each person, though even for a single person a given mapping is always provisional. Each mapping is "the cry of its occasion" ("An Ordinary Evening in New Haven," XII, l. 1). That means it is always good for that momentary occasion only. All the mappings are responses to "words of the sea," but these responses are almost infinitely variable, always open to revision. They can be thought of as superimposed on one another and on the landscape, like different navigations through a hypertext.[19] If for the woman who strides the beach at Key West "there never was a world for her / Except the one she sang and, singing, made," a new song sung by her or by another, it is implied, would make a new world. The poet and his companion(s) have a different world from her and another map, the one made by Stevens's poem. Any essay on the poem delineates yet another topography. It's a free country. Anyone can and does map the country in his or her own way, a way that is good only for that one time, in an always provisional act of performative naming. By stressing the imaginary aspect of this mapping, the way it is an act of consciousness or of language, Stevens, in a way after all not entirely different from Heidegger's evasions, bypasses the way American history is often a chronicle of (territorial) appropriation leading not just to the dispossession but to the death of those who were there first.

This ever-renewed, ever-unsatisfied making and mapping power is given a generalized name in the final lines of the poem, not yet cited or read. That power is called a "blessed rage for order." The phrase gives the poet's answer to the "Why?" he has posed to Ramon Fernandez a few lines earlier. The lights in the fishing boats at anchor master the night and portion out the sea because there is a general maker's rage for order exemplified by the fishing boats, the woman's song, or by Stevens's poem. "Rage": the word is a strong one. According to *Webster's New Collegiate Dictionary* (1949), it names "extreme vehemence of emotion or suffering, mastering the will" and "enthusiasm, excitement, or fervor." If "order" is rational, a matter of measurements, proportions, and outlines, the rage for order is irrational, instinctive, uncontrollable, not a matter of choice. It is perhaps a response to the terrifying indifference and formlessness of the sea. Rage to order what? Stevens's answer is unequivocal. The maker orders not the topographical features out there—shore, sea, sky, and horizon—but the words for them, that is, topography in the sense of landscape aspects already carried over into a generalized toponymy, the names of places. Even the lights of the fishing boats, it would seem, act to master the night and portion out the sea by the mediating power of words. But Stevens's words here must be scrutinized carefully. In his poems every word counts, like the fine print and small symbols on a nautical chart:

> Oh! Blessed rage for order, pale Ramon,
> The maker's rage to order words of the sea,
> Words of the fragrant portals, dimly-starred,
> And of ourselves and of our origins,
> In ghostlier demarcations, keener sounds.

Properly speaking, these lines are not a sentence. They are an exclamation followed by a noun with a series of subordinate clauses but no verb. The lines do what they say. The inarticulate cry of the "Oh!" is a direct expression of that rage for order. The rage for order is said to be "blessed." This may be taken in a weak or merely aesthetic sense, as when Henry James speaks of the "blest novella" as a literary form that he likes because it solves a lot of formal problems for him. Or the word may have a stronger sense connecting it with "genius" and "spirit" elsewhere in the poem. The rage for order may be blessed in the sense that it is the means whereby a spirit is installed in the place, a new genius of the sea invoked. The rage for order is blessed because it blesses. It makes the place hallowed, enghosted, inhabited by a spirit. A blessing is a kind of speech act, a performative with special rules and protocols.

After the exclamatory beginning that gives the reader an example of such a performative, a blessing addressed explicitly to or received from Ramon Fernandez, who is pale as a ghost and as silent as one, the remaining lines of this last section parade topographical names, the instruments of this blessing. They present a list of the things the words are words of: sea, "fragrant portals," dim stars, ourselves, our origins. But the phrase "words of the sea" has a particularly acute form of the ambiguity present in all such genitive phrases, for example "genius of the sea" in the first line of the poem. After the phrase "words of the sea," the word "of" is repeated three more times in the next two lines, as if to call attention to its enigma: "Words of the fragrant portals, dimly-starred, / And of ourselves and of our origins." Do words of the sea come from the sea, as their origin, according to the notion, presented earlier in the poem, that human language arises as the articulation and division of the gasping and grinding winds and waves? Hölderlin puts this forcefully in his translation of Creon's words in Sophocles' *Antigone*: "Der Ort sagt," "The place speaks"; or, as Derrida translates this, "C'est le lieu qui me dicte," "It is the place that speaks orders to me."[20] Or are words of the sea words that freely name in one language or another the sea and its various features, that is, are words of the sea imposed by human beings on the sea rather than coming from it? It cannot be decided which, though nothing here more urgently needs deciding. It can be neither without the shadow or ghost of the other. The urgency is both for the reader, who wants to do justice to the poem, and for Stevens, whose interminable poetic meditation was generated by an ever-renewed, ever-unsatiated desire to "get it right," to give credit where credit is due to the "imagination" and to "reality" in human makings.

What the maker's urge to order wants to do, the lines make clear. It wants to gather words for sea, sky, horizon, ourselves, and the origins of those selves together in a totalizing, all-including, integrating construct that makes a world distinguished by having "ghostlier demarcations, keener sounds"—ghostlier and keener than those words are in themselves, as a haphazard collection of words that happen to be there? Or ghostlier and keener than the sea and sky are before they are gathered together in a poetic act of naming? Or ghostlier and keener than previous word orders, as Stevens's poem may be sharper, more distinct, more carefully demarcated than the woman's song? The poem does not tell us which, another "either/or" that becomes an illogical "both/and." It is clear, however, that the poem places a high price on sharp divisions and fine tuning. One measure of these is the line that goes from the sea's grinding to the refined discriminations of such a poem as "The Idea of Order at Key West." Keener is better.

Why the demarcations are "ghostlier," we now know. The lines and divisions on a map, for example, lines of latitude and longitude, are not really there in nature. No pole marks the pole, no line is drawn around the earth at the equator, no boundary line separates Canada from the United States. Such demarcations are "ghostly." The demarcations are also "ghostlier" with each successive refinement because the enunciation of poetic words, words that make, brings a ghost, spirit, or genius to inhabit the place. The comparative in "ghostlier" and "keener" suggests an endless process of further refinement, making more spiritual and making keener.

This implication is reinforced by the beautiful phrase, echoing Emerson's "Seashore,"[21] for the distant sky over the sea toward the horizon: "fragrant portals, dimly-starred." This names the fragrance of the night air in Key West. The fragrant air seems to bring the distant near through one of the more intimate senses, just as do the dim stars shining over the distant sea. It also affirms that the starry night sky over the sea is not a definite border or horizon where everything stops, but "portals," doorways leading always beyond whatever distant place has been reached. If the figure of portals reaches out toward the indefinite future of ghostlier demarcations, keener sounds, the assertion that the maker has a rage to order also words "of ourselves and of our origins" incorporates both poet and the community for which he speaks into this act of ordering.

The poet and his community are created in the poem. This making also incorporates and recuperates their "origins," that is, the other temporal direction from the future toward which those "portals" open. The ordering rage of the poet gathers together origin and unreachable end, near and far, people and the sea around them, into one complex and highly differentiated whole. The earlier part of the poem suggests that our "origins," at least the origins of our language, therefore of our selves as they are made by language, may be the sea and seawind sounds: "It may be that in all her phrases stirred / The grinding water and the gasping wind." We rose from the sea with our words and are still implicitly tied to our origins. A proper order remains still a refinement of words "of our origins," of our *arché*.

~

Recalling the Greek word for "beginning" will allow me to come full circle back to the title of the poem and to gloss the somewhat enigmatic and multivalenced word "idea" there. An "idea of order" is almost a tautology, since "idea" in one way or another already includes the idea of an order received or imposed. Today the word most usually means a mental grasping, a concept, as when we might say, "I have good idea what 'idea' means," or, "That's a great idea." But the word "idea," as I have said, comes from the Greek *idein*, to see. An idea was a visual image, the image something made on our eyes and therefore on our power of seeing. This was according to an archaic notion of seeing as the transfer of little images of things from the things to our eyes, as when we see a small replica of ourselves in another person's eyes. But for Plato, the priority of thing over its idea was reversed. The idea came to be "seen" (in the sense of "conceived") as the origin of the thing, its archetype or celestial model, therefore as invisible. According to *Webster's New Collegiate Dictionary* (1949), an idea is "one of the archetypes, or patterns, of which existing things are imperfect copies," shadows on the cave's wall. To say that "she" is the idea of order may mean either that she is order made visible in the "idea" of it, that is, in its visible embodiment, or that she is the personification of the invisible idea of order, that is, of the nonphenomenal archetype on which all orders are modeled. Stevens, of course, plays on all these meanings in the phrase "the idea of order," as well as in the title of the book of poems in which this poem is placed: *Ideas of Order.* Stevens adds perhaps even a covert reference to the word "idea" as it is used by such a modern phenomenologist as Edmund Husserl in his major work *Ideen* (*Ideas*). Ideas, for Husserl, are intentional orientations of consciousness binding subject and object together.

When Stevens, at the beginning of "Notes Toward a Supreme Fiction," asks the "ephebe" reader, novice in seeing, to "Begin, ephebe, by perceiving the idea / Of this invention, this invented world, / The inconceivable idea of the sun" and says we must "see the sun again with an ignorant eye / And see it clearly in the idea of it" (I, ll. 1–3, 5–6), the emphasis is on the inventive power of human seeing. This power is as creative, almost, as Plato's archetypes, though the idea of the sun seems to be there already, ready to be glimpsed when we have washed heaven clean of previous mythological images of it, Phoebus Apollo and the rest. Yet we must not, like Platonic Christianity, "suppose an inventing mind as source /

Of this idea nor for that mind compose / A voluminous master folded in his fire" (I, ll. 7–9). This is another of Stevens's rejections of prosopopoeia. These lines may be taken as a retrospective gloss on "idea" in "The Idea of Order at Key West." The idea of order is the organizing principle, the archetype or originating pattern, of order, but it is not a personalized, conscious mind. It works without anybody's deliberate intent, not even the intent of a patriarchal deity. Anarchy is the opposite of order. The maker's rage for order is a rage to move from anarchy to a situation that is governed by an originating, patterning power that puts everything in its place and subordinates it to a single supervising spirit.

But just whose spirit is this? I have come back by a circuitous route and for the last time to a re-asking of the fundamental question posed by this poem. A final, unequivocal answer to this question would finish my reading with a satisfying click. The problem is that no unequivocal answer can be given, though we are now beginning to get an idea of why that is so and of why Stevens says the spirit of the place, invoked by the song, was not only more than the sound of sea and wind, but also "More even than her voice, and ours." The question is whether the spirit was there already or whether it is freely imposed by singer, fishing boats, or poet on an indifferent place. This question cannot be answered, for reasons that are evident. The song, the lights, the poem all share the fundamental undecidability of all performative speech acts, or, as the fishing boats or Heidegger's example of the bridge instruct us, of all construction of signs or significant artifacts that then make something happen.

On the one hand, such performatives use words or other signs that are already there, able to be repeated. They are a repetition in their present use. Their meaning depends on their iterability. Moreover, they presuppose the authority in the name of which they speak, whether that is the authority of a preexisting spirit, measure and measurer of the scene, or the authority of the spirit of the performer, his or her ordering ego. On the other hand, as Stevens clearly affirms, the spirit of the place that becomes apparent when the performative is uttered has no precedent either in an already latent genius, or in the mind of the one who utters the performative. It is an unpredictable and unprecedented new start, good only for that time and place, able to be repeated countless times with different words and with a different topographical effect.

Heidegger's formulations can help us here once more. Of the bridge, he says, as I have shown in chapter 9, that it both "admits" and "installs" the fourfold. Well, which is it? Whose spirit is this? It makes a lot of difference whose it is. If the act of building or making, constructing a bridge or a poem, "admits" the unity of the fourfold, that is, makes a site a coherent topography governed by a single spirit, then the spirit must have been there already waiting to be admitted. If the spirit and its topography are "installed," then they may be put there by the ungrounded and unauthorized act of making. The two verbs, *zulassen* and *einrichten*, contradict one another. Just as W. B. Yeats wavers in *Ideas of Good and Evil* between saying the spirit is "created" by poetry and saying it is "revealed" by poetry, and just as the word "invention," used by Stevens in the passage from "Notes Toward a Supreme Fiction" already quoted, means both "find" already there and "make up," so Heidegger cannot decide whether the act of building admits or installs the unity of the fourfold.

Nor can Stevens in "The Idea of Order at Key West" give an unequivocal answer to the question "Whose spirit is this?" This is no doubt why he has to ask the question often as she sings. All performative speech acts are undecidable in just this way. The ground validating the performative was not there before, but when it is there it seems to have been there already, waiting to be brought out into the open, for example, when a landscape becomes a topography. Stevens's singer depends upon and yet creates anew the genius of the sea. Such inaugural acts are by no means unequivocally positive. On the one hand, these acts of language have the effects they do have in the social, historical, and material realms. These effects may be considerable, even in the case of a poem, not to speak of a political speech act like the Declaration of Independence. On the other hand, there is an almost irresistible temptation after the fact to ascribe to these inaugurating acts a preexisting

foundation they lacked. Such forgetful mystifications are not innocent. Like all lies or self-deceptions they can lead to bad results, for
example, the claim to a bogus authority for unauthorized acts of
violence. On the other hand, it is extremely difficult to live from
moment to moment with a clear and distinct recognition of the
groundlessness of such initiating speech acts. To try to do so is one
of the main tasks today in the creation of new community forma-
tions, new kinds of national or group solidarity.[22]

All such performative acts of language are responses to a demand
that can only be identified when the responses have been uttered.
This is a curious kind of categorical imperative that implies a new
kind of ethical responsibility. It is responsibility to a law that is only
installed and made evident in our utterance. The woman's song in
Stevens's poem has the urgency of a response to an imperative
summons. His poem is a response to the singer's response, a
prolonged, meditative attempt to "get it right." My essay is a
response to the response to the response. No one and no identifiable spirit has demanded that I write about this poem, but when I
read the poem I have the sense that the poem needs my care,
demands my care. It cannot take place without my help. My own
discourse makes a space or site within which it takes place. Is that
constative or performative? Something of both. My essay, I hope,
gives knowledge of Stevens's poem. But it does more than that. It
creates its own new region of meaning, with its own locations and
coordinates. All three of these inaugural acts are "unsponsored,
free," as Stevens puts it in "Sunday Morning" (VIII, l. 7).

If we ask of Stevens's singing woman a version of the question the
narrator of Henry James's "The Figure in the Carpet" asks about
Hugh Vereker's novels, "Where did she get her tip?," no answer is
forthcoming, though her song transforms the seascape for the poet,
as the poet transforms it for the reader. This structure of singer and
listener is doubled by my relation as reader to the poem. All these
are relations of obligation. They are ethical obligations of a peculiar
sort. Each is an irresistible obligation, but one without clear directions except the demand to go beyond, as the singer "sang beyond
the genius of the sea." Such performatives are always blind. They

do not know where they are going or what they are going to create, though they appear in retrospect to be governed by the spirit that comes into view only when the speech act is enacted. The woman's song, it seems, is improvised. It is a free response to the place or even entirely detached from it, though it transforms the place. Stevens's poem too is constructed as a free meditation, following spontaneously the poet's lines of thought.

The same thing can be said of my chapter. I did not know where it was going to go when I began writing it. "Things," as they say, not only things in the poem itself, but things in my own living and making in one place or another, have become clearer, insights have flashed, "ah ha! moments" have occurred. Things have happened through the act of writing that no amount of simple thinking or silent reading could have achieved. Writing this chapter has transported me from here to there, like a bridge or a boat. It has taken me to a place I did not even know existed, much less intend to reach, before I started writing. Then portal after portal opened. Song, poem, and essay: each installs or admits a new topography in unpredictable inaugural events, new starts that display the ethics of topography.

§ 11 Derrida's Topographies

> about this place where I am going, I know enough
> to think, with a certain terror, that things are not
> going well there and that, considering everything,
> it would be better not to go there.
> —Jacques Derrida[1]

This chapter is about Derrida and literature. I use deliberately the blandest, most innocent, least question-begging conjunction. I want to put my remarks in the context of an ideological story that is making the rounds. Of course it does not have currency with you and me, dear reader. We know better. But the traces of this story's force are widely visible. A recent book by Jonathan Loesberg, *Aestheticism and Deconstruction: Pater, Derrida, de Man*[2] defends Derrida and de Man from the claim that they are ahistorical by arguing that neither is really interested in reading works of literature. Of Derrida, Loesberg says: "Because Derrida embeds his analysis of literary language within his analysis of foundational philosophy, it has as little relevance to the interpretation of actual literary works as his philosophical discussion has to the status of particular propositions" (106). Later he asserts categorically that "de Man's theory of literary language will no more produce practical criticism than does Derrida's" (116). Where did this strange contrary-to-fact story about Derrida's and de Man's lack of interest in doing literary criticism come from, and what is its ideological function?

Rodolphe Gasché was the first to argue in detail that Derrida is a technical philosopher in the wake of Husserlian phenomenology and that de Man, myself, and other American "deconstructionists" have falsified his work by using it in literary criticism.[3] We have

291

made it, so the story goes, into nothing more than a new New Criticism. In fact, the Yale group were more influenced by William Empson and Kenneth Burke than by John Crowe Ransom or Allen Tate. And they were by no means ignorant of Continental phenomenology. Derrida's teaching at Yale was spectacularly forceful and original, but it entered a context there that was far from foreign to it. Why then does Gasché's argument so much appeal still today to Loesberg and others, for example, to Jeffrey T. Nealon and to Mas'ud Zavarzadeh?[4] Gasché's reading is part of an ideological narrative that plays an essential part these days in the reassertion of thematic and mimetic readings of literature, in the return to "history," and in the reinstatement of traditional ideas about personal identity, agency, and responsibility. As Thomas Cohen has recognized in incisive diagnoses,[5] what has happened is the following: deconstruction or post-structuralism, some people have thought, has to be denigrated ("abjected" is Cohen's word) in order to justify certain ways of turning or returning to history, to thematic and mimetic interpretations of literature, to the social, to multiculturalism, to the widening of the canon, to cultural studies, and to "identity politics." This has by no means happened universally. Works by Judith Butler, Diane Elam, Alex Garcia Düttmann, and many others appropriate deconstruction for new work. Nevertheless, others have falsely identified deconstruction as nihilistic, as concerned only with an enclosed realm of language cut off from the real world, as destroying ethical responsibility by undoing faith in personal identity and agency, as ahistorical, quietistic, as fundamentally elitist and conservative. The Yale "Deconstructors" can then be dismissed as made-over New Critics who are presumed to have shared the politics of the Southern agrarians. The discovery of de Man's wartime writings doubly justifies writing him off. He has come to be seen as both a new New Critic *and* someone with a tainted past, however the early writings are read in relation to the later.

That leaves Derrida. To argue, as Loesberg does, following Gasché, that Derrida is really a philosopher, whose work has little or no relevance to literary studies, is to recuperate him from the "abjection" of American deconstruction. It is hard to make Derrida either a fascist or a New Critic, though his abiding interest in Heidegger puts him, for some people, under suspicion of the former, while his evident interest in reading works of literature puts him in danger of being seen as a strange, Continental, crypto–New Critic. Calling him a phenomenological philosopher in the tradition of Husserl avoids both bad names. But this recuperation is performed at the cost of neutralizing Derrida. It puts him out of literature departments and back in the philosophy department. So anyone in literature, anyone doing cultural studies, feminist studies, studies of popular culture, "new historicism," or multicultural studies can, if she or he wants to, breathe a sigh of relief, and say: "Thank God. I don't have to take Derrida seriously any more. He is just a philosopher, after all." Given what interests most members of American philosophy departments these days, the last thing most of them would be likely to take seriously is Derrida's theories about the contradictory founding moments of philosophical thinking.

This narrative, like all such ideologemes, like ideology in general, is extremely resistant to being put in question or refuted. It takes many forms and is used in aid of many different arguments, including those by people who consider themselves friendly to Derrida, such as Loesberg or Nealon. However cogently this story is shown to be a linguistic construct based on a whole set of radical misreadings, it is still likely to be unconsciously assumed, taken as a natural truth. It fits Althusser's definition of ideology as a set of unconscious assumptions that obscure one's real material conditions of existence or de Man's definition of ideology as "the confusion of linguistic with natural reality, of reference with phenomenalism."[6]

The result of this handy bit of ideological storytelling is to underwrite the return to unreflective mimetic, thematic, and biographical readings of literature so widespread today. One unfortunate result of this return is that wherever it is accepted it disables the crucially necessary political and intellectual work being attempted today in the name of a better democracy by cultural studies, women's studies, ethnic studies, studies in "minority discourse," and so on. The disabling might be defined by saying that the left, whenever it (perhaps unconsciously) reassumes the old, traditionalist ideological presuppositions of the right about mimesis, about the acting and responsible self, about thematic ways to read literature and other cultural forms, is cooperating in the return to a neoconservative and nationalist atmosphere that is occurring in many places now and that the "left" means to be trying to forestall and contest. Another way to put this is to say that a discourse that reaffirms these assumptions is unable to contest the power of what Marx called "bourgeois ideology" and what is today called "the hegemony of the dominant discourse" because it is, in its essence, bourgeois ideology all over again. This reaffirmation leaves the dominant discourse as dominant as ever because it is another form of it. It is vulnerable to the same critique Marx made of Feuerbach or of "German ideology" generally, that it is no more than a theoretical or mental rearrangement of the terms it challenges and has therefore no means of touching the material world. It is incapable of producing historical events. Only a materialist inscription can do that.

~

What about Derrida and literature, then? Take, for example, the following passage from Derrida's description of a crypt in "Fors: The Anglish Words [*mots anglés*] of Nicolas Abraham and Maria Torok": "Caulked or padded [*calfeutré ou capitonné*] along its inner partition, with cement or concrete [*ciment ou béton*] on the other side, the cryptic safe [*le for cryptique*] protects from the outside the very secret of its clandestine inclusion or its internal exclusion."[7]

Are these words literal or figurative, referential or fictional, philosophical or literary? What do these words name? How would one verify answers to these questions? This essay is an attempt to account for Derrida's language use in this sentence.

Calfeutré ou capitonné? *Ciment ou béton*? These words describe or name everyday objects, things ready to hand in our collective perceptual world. They belong to the technical vocabulary of the construction trades. A building contractor would order so many cubic yards of cement to pour the foundation for a new house, or, for that matter, to build a new crypt in a cemetery. Padding or caulking are also construction materials. To what strange use is Derrida putting these words here? The words do not seem to refer to any "real" cement, caulking, or padding. Could they be "literary"? What would that mean? How is the literary related to the topographical in Derrida's work?

A comparison may be made with the use made of words in works conventionally designated "literature." Examples would be the following two descriptions of other cryptic enclosures, secret places, like the crypt in "Fors," where something or someone both dead and alive is buried, where something has happened without having happened. The first is from Thomas Hardy's description of the Fawkes Fires on the top of Rainbarrow in *The Return of the Native*, the second from a translation of the opening description of the burrow in Franz Kafka's "The Burrow":

> It was as if these men and boys had suddenly dived into past ages, and fetched therefrom an hour and deed which had before been familiar with this spot. The ashes of the original British pyre which blazed from that summit lay fresh and undisturbed in the barrow beneath their tread. The flames from funeral piles long ago kindled there had shone down upon the lowlands as these were shining now. Festival fires to Thor and Woden had followed on the same ground and duly had their day.[8]

> I have completed the construction of my burrow and it seems to be successful. All that can be seen from the outside is a big hole; that, however, really leads nowhere; if you take a few steps you strike against natural firm rock.[9]

"Ashes," "barrow," "rock," "burrow": are these words used by Hardy and Kafka in the same way as Derrida uses *ciment* and *béton*? Derrida's writing, it would seem, is primarily philosophical and theoretical. It is only intermittently and contingently concerned with literature or written "as literature." It may be that literature enters into Derrida's work only when he "does literary criticism," that is, when he writes about one or another work generally assumed to be literature—Mallarmé, Joyce, or Baudelaire; Celan, Shakespeare, or Melville, and many others. Writing about literature could then be opposed to writing about philosophy, anthropology, political science, theology, architecture, and so on, but the stylistic texture of Derrida's own work would never be "literary." Its ground or starting place would certainly not be literature but philosophical reflection, as Gasché and Loesberg argue.

What, for Derrida, distinguishes a literary use of language from other uses, if indeed there is such a distinction, or if indeed such a thing as literature exists? I shall approach this question indirectly, by a roundabout route, namely by way of an attempt to map Derrida's topographies, or, more precisely, in order to account for that sentence I cited from "Fors."

"Derrida's topographies": this is an immense domain, requiring a virtually interminable mapping procedure for its full graphing. New topographies are constantly being added in new work, for example, Derrida's current seminars in Paris and at the University of California at Irvine (beginning in 1992) on "the secret and responsibility." Some invitation to the reader to place things and concepts within an imaginary space has been a feature of his work from the beginning, for example, in the early image of the "closure of metaphysics," or in the spatial figures indicated in the titles of *Marges, Parages,* or *Khôra,* or in the theory of invention, with its image of extrapolation in *Psyché: Inventions de l'autre,* or in the strange topography of "Fors," or in the geographical figures (if they *are* figures) of *L'Autre Cap,* or in the many places where the words "topography," "topology," "toponymy," "frontier," "places," "topoi," "margin," "limit," or the like appear. The immense, intertwined problematics of politics, of exemplarity, of nationalism, and of translation, not to speak of literature, in Derrida are inseparable from images of some definite place, "this place here" with all its geographical and social particularity.

The chief obstacle to a complete cartography of Derrida's topographies, however, is not the extent and complexity of the terrain but the presence within any place on his map—inside it, outside it, intestine, clandestine, deep buried, and yet on the surface—of a place that cannot be mapped. This place resists toponymy, topology, and topography, all three. Somewhere and nowhere in every

Derridean topography is a secret place, a crypt whose coordinates cannot be plotted. This place exceeds any ordinary topographical placement. What is the relation, for Derrida, between literature and the secret place-without-place hidden in every topography?

~

Far from being peripheral to Derrida's work, just one more topic approached from perspectives that are properly "philosophical," literature, it can be argued, is his main concern throughout. For Derrida, everything begins with the question of literature and is approached from that place. In "Ponctuations: Le Temps de la thèse" ("Punctuations: The Time of the Thesis"; written in 1980), Derrida recalls that about 1957 he had " 'deposited,' as they say," a thesis subject entitled "L'Idéalité de l'objet littéraire" ("The Ideality of the Literary Object"). A little later he indicates something of what that thesis might have contained. The title, he says, is to be understood in the context of Husserl's thought, much in the air in the fifties:

> It was a question, then, for me, to deploy, more or less violently, the techniques of transcendental phenomenology in the elaboration of a new theory of literature, of this very particular type of ideal object that is the literary object, an ideality "concatenated" [*enchaînée*], Husserl would have said, concatenated with so-called natural language, a non-mathematic or non-mathematizable object, but nevertheless different from music or works of plastic art, that is to say, from all the examples privileged by Husserl in his analyses of ideal objectivity. For I must recall a little globally and simply, my most constant interest, I would say even before the philosophical interest, if that is possible, went toward literature, toward the writing called literary.
>
> What is literature? And first of all, what is writing? How does writing come to upset even the question "What is?" [*Qu'est-ce que?*] and even "What does that mean?" [*Qu'est-ce que ça veut dire?*]. Put otherwise—and this is the putting otherwise that is important for me—when and how does inscription become literature and what happens then? To what and to whom does that return? [*À quoi et à qui cela revient-il?*] What happens between [*Qu'est-ce qui se passe entre*] philosophy and literature, science and literature, politics and litera-

ture, theology and literature, psychoanalysis and literature, there in the abstraction of its label is the most insistent question.[10]

If Derrida's most insistent question, reaffirmed here in a text of 1980, goes toward literature, and if science, politics, theology, psychoanalysis, and even philosophy are to be approached, for him, from the point of view of the question "What is literature?," much hangs, in comprehending his work, on understanding just what he means by literature or by saying "l'objet littéraire" is an "objet idéal."

Could it be that though Derrida never wrote that thesis, all his work from one end to the other, in all its amplitude and diversity, has been obliquely preliminary notes toward that unwritten thesis on "l'idéalité de l'objet littéraire"? These notes have often been based on readings of specific literary texts. Passages from three recent works, " 'This Strange Institution Called Literature': An Interview with Jacques Derrida," *Donner le temps* (*Given Time*), and *Passions*, give provisional answers to the question "What is literature?" In the first and third of these he says that literature is a modern institution that begins at a certain moment in history and is tied in complex ways to history, politics, law, and society. There could be and have been cultures with no concept of literature in the sense the modern West means the word. Literature, for example, cannot exist outside democracy and the complete freedom of speech permitted in principle in a democracy, though of course never yet fully permitted in fact. Democratic freedom guarantees the "*right to say everything.*"[11] Literature, that is, goes along with a certain irresponsibility. Democratic freedom of speech gives me the right to say anything and everything and not be held accountable for it, not to have to respond when questioned about it. This irresponsibility is the basis of the most exigent responsibility. Derrida in the interview is unequivocal on this last point:

> The writer can just as well be held to be irresponsible. He can, I'd even say that he must sometimes demand a certain irresponsibility, at least as regards ideological powers, of a Zhdanovian type for example, which try to call him back to extremely determinate responsibilities

before socio-political or ideological bodies. This duty of irresponsibility, or refusing to reply for one's thought or writing to constituted
powers, is perhaps the highest form of responsibility. To whom, to
what? That's the whole question of the future or the event promised by
or to such an experience, what I was just calling the democracy to
come. Not the democracy of tomorrow, not a future democracy which
will be present tomorrow but one whose concept is linked to the to-
come [*à-venir*, cf. *avenir*, future], to the experience of a promise
engaged, that is always an endless promise.[12]

Irresponsibility vis-à-vis constituted ideological powers is sometimes the only way to begin to fulfill an infinitely more exigent
responsibility toward the democracy to come. Our responsibility to
that democracy to come takes the form of a promise that is endless
because it can never be declared fulfilled. It always remains future.
This future makes the most imperative demands on our actions
today. For example, it requires our refusal under certain circumstances to accept responsibility before constituted authorities. But
just what does this freedom to say everything have to do with
literature? Why is this freedom enacted especially in literature?
What Derrida says in an important footnote in *Passions* will help
answer that question:

> Something literary [*Quelque chose de la littérature*] will have begun
> when it will not have been possible to decide if, when I speak of
> something [*quelque chose*] I speak of some thing, of the thing itself [*de
> la chose même*], this one here, for itself, or if I give an example, an
> example of something, or an example of the fact that I am able to
> speak of some thing, of my way of talking of something, of the
> possibility of speaking in general of something, or again of writing
> these words, etc. (89)

If literature is a historical phenomenon, an institution that
began at a certain moment in certain Western societies and that
could disappear entirely, literature is also a permanent and inalien-
able possibility in language, in signs generally, or in what Derrida
calls the "trace." The conditions of the possibility of literature have
always already been there, not only ever since there have been

human beings and language but even before that, in a preverbal realm.

About Derrida's idea of the preverbal there would be much to say.[13] His notion of the preverbal contradicts everything people think they know about Derrida and about so-called "deconstruction" generally. He and "it," we are told, give absolute priority to language. Deconstruction holds that language makes everything in the human world. For humankind, "it's all language." On the contrary, what Derrida calls literature paradoxically does not depend on letters or on language in the ordinary sense. The impossibility of deciding whether a sign or a trace is about something or is only an example of a word, sign, or trace begins already in animal gesture or play, for example, when a kitten pretends that a ball of paper is a mouse. What Derrida says about this is clear and without reservation: "What I have just said about something [*quelque chose*] does not need to wait for speech, that is to say discursive enunciation and its written transcription. It is valid already for every trace in general, even a preverbal one, for example, a mute pointing [*déictique muet*], or animal gestures or games" (*Passions*, 90).

As can be seen, the possibility of literature depends on the strange structure of exemplarity, on the fact that every example at one and the same time is just one example out of many, perhaps innumerable, examples of the same thing that might be given and is always at the same time the example of examples, the exemplary example, unique and singular.[14] To put this another way, it is impossible to tell when an example ceases to be an example and becomes something to be taken seriously, something for which the one who gives the example must take responsibility. The dependence of literature on the possibility of giving examples is evident not only in Derrida's formulations about when literature will have begun but also in the way it seems impossible to talk about this concept of literature without giving examples. You cannot talk about exemplarity except by way of examples, for example, my example of the playing kitten or Derrida's example of "un déictique muet, le geste ou le jeu animal," phrases introduced by Derrida with the words *par exemple*.

What does this have to do with the connection of literature and democracy, the fact that democracy, which accords the right to say everything, is a condition for literature to appear as an institution in history and in specific societies? The answer is given in what Derrida says about the "I" as an example of the literary. If literature begins when it is impossible to decide, when I speak of something, whether I am indeed speaking of something—this thing here—or whether I am giving an example of something or of the fact that I can speak of something, the same thing can be said of the "I" in any utterance. It is impossible to decide whether "I" am speaking for myself or whether I am giving an example of the possibility of using the word "I": "No one could seriously contradict me if I say (or write, etc.) that I do not write about me but about 'me,' about some other me [*un moi quelconque*] or about the me in general, by proposing an example: I am only an example or I am exemplary" (*Passions*, 89). If this is the case, then I can never be held responsible for anything "I" say because I can always claim it was not "I" speaking but that I was only giving an example of the possibility of saying whatever I said or indeed of saying anything at all. Another way to put this, as Derrida observes, is to say that literature is inseparable from irony. If the "I" can always be "literary," then I cannot be held responsible for what I say. I can always say what I have said is literature. Therefore everything can be said, irresponsibly. Democracy with its right to free speech is indeed the indispensable condition for the appearance of literature as an institution, with all its legal, social, and pedagogical circumstances, even though the conditions of possibility for literature to begin have always begun, even in the preverbal trace, even in the prehuman state, even in animal gesture or play, and even though the freedom to say everything has never in fact been granted in any democracy.

～

How does this conception of literature help us to understand, for example, "Fors," or, more particularly, the status of those words *calfeutré ou capitonné, ciment ou béton* in that one sentence in "Fors"? What is the relation of the ideality of the literary object to the crypt, to the secret, and to topography? If the words *calfeutré*, *capitonné, ciment,* or *béton* are "literary" in Derrida's sense of the word, then they designate ideal objects that can be approached only through these words or their iteration, though these objects exist separate from the words and would go on existing even if every copy of the text that contains those words were to be destroyed, just as, for example, the burial mound, a prehistoric barrow, described at the beginning of *The Return of the Native* exists only "in the novel," as we say, and cannot be visited anywhere else, even though it may have been "modeled" on a real barrow in Sussex, and just as the burrow made by Kafka's animal in "The Burrow" is an excavation that exists only in literature, only in the particular story Kafka wrote. Nevertheless, the ideal objects these words designate, the barrow, the burrow, do not depend on these words for their existence. They exist as ideal objects that we can approach through whatever copy of *The Return of the Native* or "The Burrow" we happen to be reading, even though as ideal objects they are not dependent on any one copy of those works or even on all of them collectively. This is an exceedingly sharp twisting in thought that makes an aporia. The ideal literary object is both constituted by the words on the page and shown by those words to have already been there, independent of the words that embody it.

The passage I have cited from "Fors" is part of a general topographical description of a crypt near the beginning of the essay. A crypt, says Derrida, is a strange locus in the mappable topography of a communal living space. The latter is organized around the forum, an open square within space. The communal space is itself limited by borders around the city, village, or commune as a whole. Such a topography presupposes frontiers, paths, roads, streets, fields, hills, gardens, buildings, and bridges enclosed by framing edges designating inside and outside. This topography is open to a complete cartography. This map allows the trained map reader to get from any one place within the designated borders to any other place without getting lost.

The forum or town square at the center is the place toward

which all roads lead. It is the place, as Derrida says, "where the free circulation and exchange of objects and speeches can occur" (Exiv; F12). The forum is open, exposed to everyone in the community. It is the marketplace where words and objects can be exchanged because they have a common measure establishing equivalents, for example, a common currency or a common language governed by shared codes and a shared "logos." The forum is the place of buying, selling, and exchange. It is no accident that the medieval trivium and quadrivium—grammar, rhetoric, and logic, along with arithmetic, geometry, astronomy, and music—were named with topographical terms that designate the place where roads come together in a forum. In that open space in the community, social intercourse is governed by a grammatical, rhetorical, and logico-dialectical language that allows the mastery of number, space, time, and musical intervals. Topography, the graphing of a place, presupposes arithmetic and geometry, and by implication, the rest of the seven liberal arts, too. The clarity and openness of the forum, the possibility of mapping it completely, is an effect of the trivium and quadrivium. The latter are the pedagogical institutionalizing of logocentrism. Topography is a logocentric practice through and through. It depends, for example, on the law of non-contradiction. A place is either there in a given place or not there, and no thing, a building, for example, can be in more than one place at once.

A crypt, says Derrida, upsets all the logic of this mapping. It is there and not there, neither inside nor outside, or both inside and outside at once. It cannot be located on any map. The avenues by which it might be approached confound the protocols of mapping:

> Within this forum . . . the crypt constructs another . . . forum like a closed . . . speaker's box, a *safe*: sealed [*clos*], and thus internal to itself, a secret interior within the public square, but, by the same token, outside it, external to the interior. Whatever one might write upon them, the crypt's parietal surfaces do not simply separate an inner forum from an outer forum. The inner forum is (a) safe, an outcast ouside inside the inside. [*Elles font du for intérieur un dehors exclu du dedans*]. (Exiv; F12–13)

The question, "Qu'est-ce qu'une crypte?" ("What is a crypt?"), as Derrida observes, is modeled on questions that, "ever since philosophy began," have been called "first": "What, originally, is the Thing [*La Chose*]? What is called Thinking?" (Exiii; F10). These questions may indeed go back to the origin of philosophy, but, in the form Derrida puts them, they are allusions to Martin Heidegger. They allude to such topographically organized essays by Heidegger as "The Thing," "Building Dwelling Thinking," or "What is Called Thinking?" "Fors" is, among other things, part of the never-ending reading and rereading of Heidegger that makes up such a large part of Derrida's work. Derrida's current seminars on the secret and responsibility are returning to the topographical question of the crypt's nature and location. The readings of Heidegger have continued in these seminars. Every secret, it might seem, is hidden in some kind of crypt. "Secret" is Crypt's middle name, along with "Death," and "Cipher," as Derrida observes of the latter two (Exiii; F11). The relation of the crypt to the secret, however, is not quite that simple.

But "Qu'est-ce qu'une crypte?" To claim, as Derrida does in "Fors," that this question will henceforth precede the original philosophical questions about the Thing and about thinking, questions that are central to Heidegger's thought, is to propose a major challenge to Heidegger and a reorientation of his thought. Instead of orienting thinking toward the Thing, as a map is "oriented" toward the east or toward sunrise, or toward the north pole, Derrida proposes that *Cryptonymie: Le Verbier de L'Homme aux loups* makes the question about the crypt more primordial, that about the Thing secondary, derived: "The Wolf Man's Verbarium . . . indicates that the Thing is to be thought out *starting from* the Crypt, the Thing as a 'crypt effect' " (Exiii; F10). Such a reorientation depends on the deplacements effected by psychoanalysis, but at the same time it displaces psychoanalysis, or at least displaces a certain common order of psychoanalysis. From now on all maps, topographies of the person or of communities, will be oriented by the question of the crypt. I say "question of the crypt" rather than "crypt" because the distinctive feature of any crypt is that, as

Derrida says, "No crypt presents itself" (Exiv; F12). In the to-pographical landscape of the self or of society, the crypt is both there and not there, both unreachably inside the inside and at the same time outside every border, beyond every horizon. It is here, there, everywhere, and nowhere in public and private space. It is there, motivating everything, but you cannot get there from here. It does not present itself.

I have said Derrida describes "*a* crypt," but there is already a contradiction in his formulations. The essay begins by asking, repeatedly, "Qu'est-ce qu'une crypte?" After an iteration of this question, Derrida goes on to ask another, a sort of question without question, since only the question mark at the end gives these phrases an interrogative tone: "Not *the* crypt [la *crypte*] *in general* but *this* one, in its singularity, the one I shall keep coming back to [*au bord de laquelle je reviendrai toujours*]?" (Exiii; F10). Exactly which crypt is it that Derrida here names *celle-ci*, the one in front of which he stands and on which he inscribes this preface? And what is the difference between "*la* crypte," in general, and this crypt here, this one? The answer to this question would seem to be easy to give. Or is it? Derrida, it would seem, is talking about the crypt described by Abraham and Torok as existing in the unconscious of the Wolfman. "Fors" is a preface to Abraham and Torok's *Cryptonymie: Le Verbier de L'Homme aux loups* (1976; translated as *The Wolf Man's Magic Word: A Cryptonymy*). That in turn is a commentary on Freud's "Wolfman," or, as it is properly called, in the English translation, "From the History of an Infantile Neurosis" (1918). Both of these are commentaries on the Wolfman's own text, that is, on the Wolfman as a series of symptoms, to a considerable degree verbal symptoms, that his succession of analysts must read and interpret. Derrida's "Fors" is a commentary on a commentary on a commentary on a commentary (not to mention the writings on the Wolfman by Ruth Mack Brunswick and by the Wolfman himself), each one trying to outdo the previous one in breaking into the hidden crypt in the Wolfman's unconscious.

But is it so clear that the crypt in question, "celle-ci, toute singulière, au bord de laquelle je reviendrai toujours," is the one the

Wolfman so successfully kept hidden for so long? "Fors" begins with some elaborate wordplay that holds in elliptic, cryptic compression the entire program of the essay. I engage myself to write, says Derrida, only on the title of Abraham and Torok's book, or rather, not even on the title, but on the first half of the first word, that is, on the *crypte* in *cryptonymie*, or rather, not even on a word but on a broken word, "on [*sur*] the first detachable fragment of a title, on its broken symbol or its truncated column." He will write on a half word, or rather not even on a broken word but on a thing or on a word-thing: "What if I vaulted to a stop [*Si je tombais en arrêt*], immobilizing myself and you, reader, in front of a word or a thing, or rather in front of the place of a word-thing" (Exii; F9). When Derrida says he writes *sur* the crypt, he means, of course, both that he writes "about" it and that he literally writes on it. "Fors" is graffiti defacing a tomb. When Derrida says "Je tombais en arrêt," he means not only that he "vaults to a stop," as Barbara Johnson's translation has it, but that he "falls," as one might drop dead, into a tomb. The word *arrêt* ("stop" or "stopping") vibrates with all the resonances connecting it to death that Derrida gives the word in his commentaries on Blanchot's *L'Arrêt de mort* (*Death Sentence*).

About what it might mean to confront a word that is also a thing, a word that has been reduced back to its material components and thereby has become a place of substitutions, alliterations, and assonances exceeding meaning and taking place at the level of preverbal sound or inscription, the essay later on has much to say, as it does about the new "anasemic" notion of the symbol. The anasemic sense of "symbol" transforms and transgresses the Greek sense of the word. For the Greeks a symbol was the broken half of a whole object, for example, a broken stick or stone, that signals a compact or engagement between two persons when the broken halves are joined. When Derrida says he engages himself he is referring to the use of a symbol as a way of sealing a contract or making a promise. In the anasemic symbol, however, the other half is permanently and irrevocably missing. It is hidden in that inaccessible crypt. Nevertheless, the broken symbol, the half word that is not a word but a word-thing, is the only testimony we have that the crypt exists. It is also our only way of knowing anything about the cryptic enclosure as a place that is not a place, a place-no-place where events take place without taking place. As Derrida says in a footnote later on in the essay, the wordplay, the odd syntax, the alogical language, even before being described through the bizarre turns of phrase in such formulations as these, are not play but necessity: "This is not mere wordplay, or syntax twisting, not a gratuitous contamination of meanings; only the constraints of this singular topography [*cette topique singulière*]. This topography has already produced the *necessity* of this language, even before being written in its bizarre turns of phrase, its syntactical equivocations, its outward resemblances [*ses dehors ressemblants*]" (E118n9; F21). By *dehors ressemblants* I take it Derrida means the figurative or tropological surface of the language necessary to talk about the crypt, for example, his own language about cement and caulking. It is the preverbal *topique singulière* that necessitates such deviations from proper language. At the same time these deviations are the signs of the cryptic topography, just as strange perturbations in star clusters may be the signs of an invisible black hole.

At this point, at this place in our trajectory across the face of one small part of Derrida's topographies, we begin to have a glimpse of the linguistic status of those phrases about cement, padding, and caulking. Derrida is not writing about the *Cryptonymy* of Abraham and Torok, nor about Freud, nor about the Wolfman. He uses those previous writers as a pretext for the construction of a crypt of his own out of words. Abraham and Torok aim to show that Freud was fundamentally wrong in his reading of the Wolfman. They want to substitute their quite different analysis for his. In an analogous way, Derrida is discreetly critical of Abraham and Torok, for example, of what they say about introjection and incorporation, crucial concepts in understanding the cryptic enclosure in their reading of it. Derrida substitutes his *Bau* for theirs.

∼

But what does the cryptic structure have to do with literature? It would seem that the ideal literary object would harbor no secrets.

It would always be wholly accessible by way of the words. In this it would be parallel to the geometric ideal object as defined by Husserl and as commented on in Derrida's 1962 introduction to his translation into French of Husserl's *Der Ursprung der Geometrie*, *The Origin of Geometry*. Nothing could, so it appears, be more open and without secrets than a triangle or a square. Insofar as the ideality of the literary object is like the ideality of the geometric object, literature would seem to be without secrets, too, even though literature is *enchaînée* in ordinary language.

Derrida's language about the crypt, however, the language that he produced as a result of his engagement to write on the first half of the first word of Abraham and Torok's title, is, when you come to think of it, "literary" in at least one way. Of Derrida's language about his burrow, crypt, or construction one cannot decide whether it is referential in the normal sense or whether he is giving an example of the possibility of using words in this way, the possibility of saying "Calfeutré ou capitonné sur sa paroi intérieure, ciment ou béton sur l'autre face," or of pointing toward something by saying "I mean this one here." When Derrida says, "*this* crypt here" (as opposed to saying "*a* crypt"), this locution can also, like any deictic gesture, be literature. He may be giving an example of how you can say this or he may be pointing to the crypt of Abraham and Torok, or to his own crypt, the one the words of his essay embody. The reader cannot be sure. The impossibility of deciding whether what Derrida writes is referential or exemplary is a feature of the contortions of language necessitated by the strange *topique* of the crypt. This is another way of saying that the crypt is an "ideal literary object" in the sense in which Derrida uses that term.

Derrida's current way of saying this is to argue that all literature harbors a secret. The secret is an essential feature of literature. How can this be? A passage in the fourth chapter of *Given Time* (1991) gives the answer. We normally think of a secret as in principle discoverable. It is hidden from me or from others, but someone knows the secret and could "give it away," perhaps even be forced by interrogation or by torture to give it away against his or her will.

Even if the secret is not being kept by anyone in particular but is something hidden in nature, a secret motherlode of gold in a mountain, for example, the secret could in principle be brought out into the open. For Derrida, however, just as a true gift, if there is such a thing, cannot be given in recompense for another gift and cannot in any way be repaid, so a true secret, if there is such a thing, cannot ever, by any means, be revealed.

Literature is exemplary of this feature of the secret. Derrida's example is the way it is eternally impossible to find out whether the friend in Baudelaire's "La Fausse Monnaie" ("The Counterfeit Money") gave the beggar a counterfeit coin or a real one. There is nowhere to go behind the smilingly enigmatic words on the page, no authority to whom to appeal, not even to the author, in order to decide this question, even though the decision is essential to our reading of Baudelaire's text. Literature is not like a prisoner who may be forced by torture to tell all. It is not like a mountain whose mineral secrets may be exposed. Literature eternally keeps its secrets, and the secret is an essential feature of literature. If on the one hand the secret tells us something essential about literature, literature on the other hand tells us something essential about the secret. It tells us that the true secret, if there is such a thing, is not hidden somewhere, in some place from which it might in principle be wrested, recovered, uncovered. A true secret is all on the surface. This superficiality cannot by any hermeneutic procedures, material or linguistic, be gone behind. A literary text (and any text may be taken as literary) says what it says. It cannot be forced to say more than it says. Speaking of the characters in Baudelaire's "The Counterfeit Money," Derrida says, "These fictional personages having no consistency, no depth beyond their literary phenomenality, the absolute inviolability of the secret they carry follows primarily from the essential superficiality of their phenomenality [*phénoménalité*] from the too-evident [*trop-évident*] of what they offer to our vision [*de ce qu'ils donnent à voir*]."[15] The phrase "too-evident" may be an oblique reference to the hiding in the open of the incriminating letter in Poe's "The Purloined Letter."

The word *phénoménalité* here links with Derrida's early, quasi-

Husserlian concept of the ideality of the literary object (but he is no more, strictly speaking, Husserlian than he is Heideggerian). The phenomenality of literature is a strange presence without presence or present. It is a landscape, topic, or topography that can only be reached in one or another of its embodiments in some copy of the text in question, even though it exceeds them as much as the ideal triangle does any visible embodiment of it. Literature is a phenomenality without phenomenality, just as the dead-alive body in the crypt in "Fors" can never be faced directly as a phenomenal object because it is the result of an event that took place without ever having taken place. Evidence of its existence is given only by the anasemic symbols of it. These are broken word-things whose missing half can never be found. To say literature is an ideal object is the same thing as to say it always hides an inviolable secret because it is always a matter of a surface without depth. The reader cannot go behind it, or beneath it, or before and after it. Literature keeps its secret, but on the surface. It is irresponsible. It is unresponsive. It does not respond. Like Bartleby in Melville's "Bartleby the Scrivener," one of Derrida's points of reference in the current seminars on the secret, a work of literature, when we demand that it answer our questions, says, "I would prefer not to."

This would seem to distinguish the secret essentially from the crypt. The crypt is cunningly created of walls and surfaces, blind alleys, labyrinthine windings. A crypt is a matter of a depth so deep that all approach to it is baffled, while a true secret, the literary secret, is all on the surface, a surface with no depth. Nevertheless these two forms of hiding, it is easy to see, come in the end to the same thing, or are versions of the same structure. To say the secret is all on the surface is to say that it generates the illusion of hiding a secret at some fathomless depth. The crypt, by contrast, is hidden by being placeless, by being everywhere and nowhere at once, outside the inside and inside the outside. It is an error to imagine it as hidden beneath some definite spot in the landscape. If in my initial citation from "Fors" Derrida uses the word "secret" to define a crypt ("le for cryptique protège contre le dehors même le secret de son exclusion intestine ou de son inclusion clandestine"), in *Given*

Time he uses the word "crypt" to define a secret: "The interest of 'The Counterfeit Money' lies in the constructed enigma [*l'énigme construite*] of the crypt that allows one to read what will remain eternally unreadable [*donne à lire ce qui restera éternellement illisible*], absolutely indecipherable, refusing every promise of decipherment or of hermeneutic" (F193). It might be best to think of the crypt as one case among many of the secret, since the secret—for example, as Derrida defines it toward the end of *Passions*—is the more inclusive topic and includes the cryptic structure as a special case.

I claim to have shown the convergence in Derrida's thinking of the themes of topography, the crypt, the secret, and literature, even though I have given no more than a sketch-map of the unmappable. A virtually interminable work would be necessary to fill in the details of this map. Even then the most important thing would still escape mapping. But to sketch out this terrain does more than just indicate what it might mean to say that Derrida has always been obsessed with the question "What is literature?" Nor is it enough to say that the question "What is literature?" turns out to be another way of saying "What is a crypt?" or "What is a secret?" since the literary is indissociable from the cryptic secret. No, one must say that Derrida's writing is itself open to being taken as literature, just as what is written about irony can always be taken as ironical. Derrida writes literature in the sense that he writes "on" the secret crypt about the cryptic secret. This will be misunderstood, however, unless we remember that literature is the most serious and responsible form of writing, the form that is responsible to the democracy to come. Whatever is written on the crypt is absorbed into the cryptic structure. Derrida's discourse too keeps its inviolable secret. Another way to put this is to say that whatever Derrida writes "on," whether it is Plato or Mallarmé, Hegel or Genet, it is impossible to decide whether the discourse that results is "about" Plato or Mallarmé, Hegel or Genet, or whether it uses them as examples of the possibility of using language in such and such a way. Without ceasing to respect the specificity of philosophy, psychoanalysis, theology, juridical discourse, and the rest, Derrida brings into the open in each the possibility of reading it as literature, since literature, that is, the trace, the secret, is the condition of possibility of each of these discourses. Derrida's own writing does not escape this necessity. To write in a way that reveals what is literary in every discourse, however, is the best way to try to fulfill in the most responsible way the promise to the *à-venir*. On the one hand, any text can be read as literature, that is, read by suspending its reference to a "transcendental referent." This means, on the other hand, that there is no text that is intrinsically literary, essentially literary.[16] Derrida has for many years been tirelessly exploring the consequences of this permeating of all language by the possibility of being taken as literature. But what Derrida says of texts in general must also apply to what he writes. It is an unavoidable necessity of Derrida's topographies that what he writes must be open to being taken as literature. The secret and the crypt can only be named in language that suspends and is suspended from the referential dimension of language.[17] What Derrida writes in "Fors" can be taken as literature in the specific sense that he uses straightforwardly referential language about wall building to compose performative catachreses, anasemic symbols, of the inviolable secret.

To turn whatever is written "on" into literature, in the particular way in which Derrida associates literature with undecidability, inviolable secrecy, and the irresponsibility that is the most exigent responsibility, might even be said to be the deconstructive move par excellence. Deconstruction "is" the operation that brings into the open the possibility in any trace that it might be taken as literature. Deconstruction, it can be said, if there is such a thing, is the exposure of the literary in every utterance, writing, or graphic mark. But this exposure can only be performed through literature, that is, through a use of language about which it cannot be decided whether it is referential or only an example of using language referentially, whether it is performative or only an example of what an efficacious performative would be like. A salient example is furnished by the phrases about the *ciment*, *béton*, and *calfeutre* of the cryptic enclosure that I began by citing. They are written on a crypt and they constitute a crypt. Whether they are to be taken literally or are only an example of anasemic language cannot be told. The sentence remains cryptic. It guards a secret that is indecipherable. This secrecy, this suspension, in both senses of the word, of and from referentiality, is the condition of possibility for language or other signs to function performatively, to do something for which the one who does it must take responsibility, even though he or she cannot know whether the performative will be efficacious or exactly what it will make happen.

~

What does that mean for the question of whether or not Derrida takes literature seriously? In one way or another both Derrida and de Man hold that the performative aspect of literature, philosophy, and criticism, of language and other signs generally, makes history. The distinction between cognitive statements and performative speech acts is well known, as is the recognition that the separation can never be made absolute. There is always a cognitive side to performatives, and vice versa. Nevertheless, the performative side of language is not something that can be known. That is what Derrida means in recent seminars when he says "the gift, if there is such a thing," "the secret, if there is such a thing," "witnessing, if there is such a thing." Since the gift, the secret, and witnessing are kinds of performatives, they are not the objects of a possible, certain cognition. They must remain a matter of "if." De Man's way of putting this was to say that the performative force of language, its power to make something happen in history and society, is linked to its materiality, that is, to a non-referential, non-cognitive side of language. In the lecture "Kant and Schiller," speaking of the sequence in Kant's third *Critique* from a "cognitive discourse as trope" to "the materiality of the inscribed signifier," de Man argues that it is only the later that is historical, that can be a historical event. The regressive misreading of Kant initiated by Schiller is not historical, not a series of historical events. There is in Kant, said de Man, "a movement from cognition, from acts of knowledge, from states of cognition, to something which is no longer a cognition but which is to some extent an occurrence, which has the materiality of something that actually happens, that actually occurs . . . , that does something to the world as such. . . . There is history from the moment that words such as 'power' and 'battle' and so on emerge on the scene; at that moment things happen, there is occurrence, there is event. History [has to do with] the emergence of a language of power out of the language of cognition."[18] This conception of the materiality of inscription is worked out in "Shelley Disfigured," in "Aesthetic Formalization: Kleist's *Über das Marionettentheater*," and in "Hypogram and Inscription," as well as in the essays on Kant and Hegel.[19] Derrida's allegiance to literature is another version of this recognition of the performative, constitutive efficacy of the "literary" dimension of language. For Derrida this feature of language and other signs creates and discovers—invents—the ideal objects that are essential to the movement toward the democracy to come.

A major contribution that so-called "deconstruction" (for example, Derrida's current writing and seminars) can make to today's frontier work in cultural studies, women's studies, historicism, and minority discourse is just in this area. What is needed is as clear as possible a recognition of a potential performative, history-making power in language, including the language of literature, philosophy, and, yes, even "practical criticism." This potential power may or may not be actualized or effective in a given case. It would be a foolhardy person who would claim that what he or she writes is a historical event. It is in any case not on the order of cognition. Nevertheless, a purely mimetic, cognitive, referential view of cultural artifacts will reaffirm just the conservative ideology that cultural studies, women's studies, and the rest want to contest. To put this in de Manian terms, the "linguistics of literariness" includes the performative dimension of literary language. Understanding it will help account for the occurrence of ideological aberrations, but knowing those aberrations will not change them. Only the performative, material, "word-thing" side of language will do that. Transforming and, most of all, using performatively this insight of deconstruction is a chief task of the humanities today. That would be another example of the way the act of reading, registered in the most responsible critical terms, may actively liberate a past text for present uses. This new act is not engineered by a previously existing, self-conscious "I." It is constitutive of the "I" that enunciates it. Walter Benjamin describes in somewhat consonant terms in the seventeenth of the "Theses on the Philosophy of History" the way a "historical materialist" sees "a revolutionary chance in the fight for the oppressed past" when he finds a way to "blast [*herauszusprengen*] a specific era out of the homogeneous course of history—blasting a specific life out of the era or a specific work out of the lifework."[20] *Herauszusprengen* names here a performative speech act that has potential effects on the future, not a historical cognition that tells something true about the past.

§ 12 Border Crossings, Translating Theory: Ruth

Bless thee, Bottom, thou art translated!
—*A Midsummer Night's Dream*

In concluding this book of topographies, I turn from a concern for topography in novels, poems, and philosophical works to the question of what happens when literary theory itself is translated and crosses national or cultural boundaries.

"Translation": the word means, etymologically, "carried from one place to another," transported across the borders between one language and another, one country and another, one culture and another. This, of course, echoes the etymology of "metaphor." A translation is a species of extended metaphorical equivalent in another language of an "original" text. The German words for "translation" mean the same thing: *Übertragung, Übersetzung,* "carried over" and "set over," as though what is written in one language were picked up, carried over, and set down in another place.

A work is, in a sense, "translated," that is, displaced, transported, carried across, even when it is read in its original language by someone who belongs to another country and another culture or to another discipline. In my own case, what I made, when I first read it, of Georges Poulet's work and, later on, of Jacques Derrida's work was no doubt something that would have seemed more than a little strange to them, even though I could read them in French. Though I read them in their original language, I nevertheless "translated" Poulet and Derrida into my own idiom. In doing so I made them useful for my own work in teaching and writing about English literature within my own particular American university context. This context was quite different from the European intellectual contexts within which Poulet and Derrida write. If what I did with their work would have seemed strange to them could they have known about it, something not quite what they had in mind when they wrote the works in question, I might feel the same if I could know what those who read my work in a language I do not know, for example, Chinese or Romanian, are making of it. Any words in any language, but perhaps especially, within literary studies, works of theory, may be translated in this way to a different context and be appropriated there for new uses. Just how this can be and what it means for literary theory is itself a difficult theoretical question.

The most important event of the last thirty years in North American literary study is no doubt the assimilation, domestication, and transformation of European theory. This includes theory of many kinds: phenomenological, Lacanian, Marxist, Foucauldian, Derridean, and so on. This crossing of borders has been an interdisciplinary event through and through. This event has fundamentally transformed literary study in the United States from what it was when I began such study forty-five years ago. Now the same thing is happening throughout the world, with both European and North American literary theory. This happening is in many ways extremely problematic. Just what is involved? Is it a good thing or a bad thing? These days, in the fields of literary and cultural studies, theory "travels" everywhere, to allude to the title of an essay by Edward Said: "Travelling Theory." In a recent lecture given at the Humanities Research Institute of the University of California, located in Irvine, he has spoken eloquently of another example, the influence of Lukács on Fanon.[1] *The Wretched of the Earth*, says Said, would not be what it is without Fanon's reading of Lukács, though Lukács did not at all have the Algerian struggle for independence in mind when he wrote *The History of Class Consciousness*. North American and European theoretical works are being translated and assimilated within many different languages and cultures: in the Far East, in Latin America, in Russia and other parts of Eastern Europe, in Australia, in Africa, and in India. In each place, of course, such translation takes place in a different way, at a different pace, and according to different protocols.

Just why it should be literary theory that seems to be carried over so easily, that crosses borders with such facility, is not immediately clear. Nor is it quite clear what it means that literary theory originally developed in Europe and the United States should now be traveling everywhere in the world, often by way of its North American versions. Why is this happening? Is it because theory is conceptual and generalized, therefore applicable in any context and to works in any language and within the local topography of any culture and time? Theory would, it might seem, in this differ from pedagogical techniques or specific readings of specific works. The latter are tied to particular sites and situations. Therefore they do not translate well or "travel" well, as they say of certain delicate wines that are best drunk where they are made. Literary theory, on the other hand, is like the vacuum-sealed box wines that travel anywhere and keep for a long time even after they are opened.

But, metaphorical joking aside, what, exactly, literally, is literary theory anyway? We all think we know what it is, but this may be a mistake, possibly even a theoretical mistake. Even though we all think we know what theory is, it may be the essence of literary theory to resist definition. As Paul de Man puts this in a rather chilling formulation: "the main theoretical interest of literary theory consists in the impossibility of its definition."[2] What in the world does this mean? Why cannot literary theory, like almost anything else, be defined? If it were true that theory cannot be defined, it would not be altogether certain that literary theory could be institutionalized in scholarship and pedagogical practice so easily and so successfully as seems to have been the case in the United States with Continental theory, and as seems to be the case around the world now with North American literary theory. If it is not theory that is spreading everywhere, what is it that masquerades under that name? What I have elsewhere called the "triumph of theory" may be the triumph of mystified misunderstandings of the theories in question. That would make the triumph of theory another unconscious form of the resistance to theory. This different form would not be the loud and uncomprehending hostility to theory by those who have never read it that is so evident in American journalism today, but rather an unintentional betrayal of theory by those who have the warmest feelings toward it, who teach courses about it and attempt to "apply" it in teaching and writing. Just what that possibility might mean for the translation and assimilation of Western theory in non-Western countries is not immediately clear. This chapter tries to confront that question.

It is conceivable that true literary theory, the real right thing, may be impossible to teach or to use in practical criticism. Theory may be impossible to translate in all the senses of that word, that is, impossible to transfer to another context, for example, another language. *Traduttore, traditore*: this (untranslatable)[3] Italian saying may be "true in spades," as they say, for literary theory, to use another perhaps untranslatable idiom. To translate theory is to traduce it, to betray it. Nevertheless, something called theory is now being translated from the United States all over the world. How does this happen?

The analogy between the exportation of theory and the spread of Western technology is appealing, but does the analogy hold? Technology is tied to the culture of its country of origin in quite a different way from the way literary theory is tied to its sources. There can be no doubt that technological innovations transform cultures. Walter Benjamin has argued this persuasively for photography and film in a famous essay, "Das Kunstwerk im Zeitalter seiner technischen Reproduzierbarkeit" ("The Work of Art in the Age of Mechanical Reproduction").[4] Photography and cinema have been followed by transistor radios, television, jet planes, tape players, CD's, VCR's, and personal computers as potent agents of cultural change. It sometimes seems as if we are rapidly moving toward a single, worldwide culture of blue jeans, portable radios, and tape players, in which everyone is tied to everyone else by FAX machines and electronic mail.[5] Such a single, universal culture might have the good effect of ultimately making nationalist wars obsolete, though we might have to wait a long time for that. But having a single, worldwide technological culture is likely to have bad effects, too. Benjamin defined one of these as a loss of "aura" in the artwork in modern times. We might generalize the effect of modern communication technologies as the weakening and up-rooting of local cultural differences everywhere, as much in my New England or California as, for example, in Taiwan or Brazil. Such technologies are exported to non-Western countries to transform them into the West's own semblance, even though those non-Western countries, like Taiwan or Japan, may outdo the United States in innovative skill in the development of these technologies.[6]

Does literary theory participate in this uprooting and hasten it? Is literary theory no more than another Western technological device, like the jet engine, television and computer technology, or the atomic bomb? I do not think so. Even though television and computer technology, for example, to some degree determine the uses that are made of them, as Benjamin argued for photography and film, nevertheless they are also in another sense neutral. They can be used in many different ways within a local culture, turning it into new forms of itself, no doubt, but still into forms of itself. It is to some degree adventitious that these technologies come bringing Western popular music, films, and videos to non-Western countries. They can also be used, and are being used, for local filmmaking or for recording the popular or traditional music of non-Western countries. Literary theory, on the other hand, in spite of its high degree of apodictic generalization, is tied, perhaps even inextricably tied, to the language and culture of its country of origin. Though theory might seem to be as impersonal and universal as any technological innovation, in fact it grows from one particular place, time, culture, and language. It remains tied to that place and language. Theory, when it is translated or transported, when it crosses a border, comes bringing the culture of its originator with it. Quite extraordinary feats of translation are necessary to disentangle a given theoretical formulation from its linguistic and cultural roots, assuming anyone should wish to do that. In fact, it may be impossible to do it. Those who seek to assimilate a foreign theory and put it to new, indigenous uses may have imported something like a Trojan horse or something like one of those computer viruses that turn resident programs to their own alien and disruptive uses. Just because a literary theory is *not* like a Western technological innovation, it may be more dangerous, not just one more tool of industrialization but a bringer of an even more profound cultural change.

~

How may it be that theory cannot be translated? Paul de Man, after having said that literary theory is impossible to define, goes on a couple of pages later in the same essay not so much to define literary theory as to identify the conditions under which it arises. Though theory may not be defined, one thing about it is sure, according to de Man: it arises not through abstract speculation, but in concrete, empirical situations. It arises from a certain way of "approaching" specific literary texts. Literary theory is born, that is, from a certain kind of reading. It arises from reading that attends not to themes and meanings but to the question of how themes and meaning come to be. "Literary theory," says de Man, "can be said to come into being when the approach to literary texts is no longer based on non-linguistic, that is to say historical and aesthetic, considerations or, to put it somewhat less crudely, when the object of discussion is no longer the meaning or the value but the modalities of production and of reception of meaning and of value prior to their establishment—the implication being that this establishment is problematic enough to require an autonomous discipline of critical investigation to consider its possibility and its status."[7] Whatever literary theory may be, according to de Man, it focuses on the power language has to generate meaning and value. "Meaning" here goes with "historical," while "aesthetic" goes with "value." The generation of meaning by literature is a historical event. The ascription of value is an aesthetic event. Literature is made of words and of nothing but words. Whatever power it has to reflect social and material reality or to make something happen in individual and social life arises from some potency in language or transmitted through language. It follows that literary theory must be language about language, in one way or another a branch of rhetoric, though rhetoric must be taken here to include also rhythmic and material aspects of language, as well as overt tropes. The focus of literary theory, to put this another way, must be on the performative powers of language, not on non-linguistic, that is to say historical and aesthetic, considerations. De Man does not say historical and aesthetic considerations are not worthy of investigation. He just says literary theory should concern itself with the way literature generates these, not take them as givens to be explored in themselves. If literature, as one cultural artifact among many others, is to be approached theoretically, then theory must concern itself with the way specific literary works use words to change history, society, and individual lives, that is, to generate "meaning" and "value."

I have said that literary theory may be untranslatable because it cannot be detached from the local topographies of its source. Two forms of this cultural specificity or idiomatic quality of literary theory may be identified. One is the untranslatability of the conceptual words that form the core of the given theory. Examples would be the word "allegory" as Samuel Taylor Coleridge, Friedrich Schlegel, John Ruskin, Walter Pater, Marcel Proust, Walter Benjamin, Paul de Man, and I use it, or the word *Erscheinung* as used by Benjamin, or the words "parasite" and "host" as I use them in "The Critic as Host." Each of these words has a long history within Western culture and cannot easily be detached from that history. That history is the history of chief previous uses of the word. *Erscheinung*, for example, means in German "appearance," or, more literally, "shining forth." "Appearance" can be said in more or less any language. But the word *Erscheinung* also carries with it, for example, the uses made of it by Hegel in his *Lectures on Aesthetics*. To use the word may be to make an allusion to the concept of art within Romanticism. My use of the word "parasite" echoes the complex uses of that word by Shelley. The word "allegory" has a long genealogy, not only the sequence of its uses within Romanticism and post-Romanticism indicated by the authors I have cited, but, before that, a manifold history going back to the Greeks and the Christian exegetes of the Bible. Every influential work of contemporary Western literary theory turns on such complex conceptual words, words that carry with them a silent history.

But Western literary theory is tied to its cultural and linguistic origins in another quite different and apparently opposite way. There is no work of theory without examples. The examples are essential to the theory. The theory cannot be fully understood without the examples. These examples tie the theory not just to a specific language and culture, but to particular works within that culture. These works were themselves rooted in a particular time and place. To put this another way, literary theory is always a reading of some specific work or works. The relation of theory to reading is itself a difficult theoretical question. Though there is no theory without reading, theory and reading are asymmetrical. Reading always alters, disqualifies, or puts in question the theory used to read it, while being essential to that theory's formulation. The examples J. L. Austin gives in the course of developing his theory of performative speech acts in *How to Do Things with Words* qualify and even undermine his theoretical formulations, though the distinction Austin makes between performative and constative language cannot be understood without the examples. When the work of Jacques Derrida and Paul de Man, or my own work, is reduced to abstract theoretical formulations, it is often forgotten that those formulations in every case are attained by an act of reading. Derrida's reading of Mallarmé, for example, is the essential context of his notion of "dissemination," just as his reading of Paul Celan is the essential context of his theory in *Schibboleth* of what in a given language may not be translated. De Man's reading of Rousseau's *Julie* is essential to his mature notion of allegory. His reading of the word "fall" in Keats's *The Fall of Hyperion* is essential to his theoretical positings in "The Resistance to Theory." Passages from Thackeray, Shelley, and others are essential for my notion that the relation of parasite to host may figure the relation of critic to text. What I shall say later on here about the Book of Ruth in the Bible is essential to the theoretical argument I am making in this chapter. To understand what Derrida means by dissemination you must read Mallarmé or at least read carefully Derrida's reading of Mallarmé. To understand what de Man means by allegory you must read de Man's reading of Rousseau. To understand what I mean by saying the critic is a "host," you must take into account what I say about my examples, even though I read them in relation to general theoretical clarifications to which the act of reading might lead. To understand this chapter you must take into account what I say about the Book of Ruth.

Does this mean that works of theory cannot be translated, cannot be transported across the borders into a new country and a new language or into a new discipline to be effective there? On the contrary, I think such translation is entirely possible. It happens every day. I certainly hope it will happen with work of mine translated into various languages. Just as I can get on a jet plane in Los Angeles and find myself a few hours later almost anywhere in the world, in Taipei, Jerusalem, or Brasília, without much sensation of crossing a border, so works of theory nowadays are often translated and the translation published even before they appear in their original languages. But the difficulty of understanding just what is at stake in such translation should not be underestimated. The fact that border crossings and translations happen so rapidly nowadays may mislead us about what happens in translation. This is particularly the case when what is in question is translation into a language so rich, so different from English, and with such a splendid literary and intellectual tradition as, for example, Chinese.

～

How does this translation happen? How do works of theory get a new start in a new language and within a new culture? Just how does this transfer "take place"? How does a work of theory cross borders, occupy a new territory, and make a new place for itself in a new language? I shall try to explain this by telling a story. It is not my story but a very old one from the Hebrew Bible and the Christian Old Testament, the story of Ruth. The story will serve as an example of what I am talking about, since it has been translated into many different languages and cultures. As it happens, I can read it only in translation, not in the original Hebrew. Though it might persuasively be argued that this disqualifies me from saying anything valuable about the Book of Ruth, the fact that I try to do so anyway is an example of my theme: the possibility of translating texts, including theoretical ones, from one language, culture, or discipline to another. No translation can carry over all the subtleties of alliteration, anagrammatic echo, and repetition of words, motifs, and episodes, that organize this text in itself and also tie it by allusion to other parts of the Bible. All of the proper names in Ruth, for example, have conceptual meaning. The story also contains many references to Jewish law and custom, for example, the law of levirate marriage, or the custom that allowed the poor to gather stalks of corn left behind by the gleaners, though only two at a time. Ruth has been read in innumerable different ways over the centuries by millions of people. It is read aloud in synagogues on Shavuoth (Pentecost). Ruth carries with it, like every other book of the Bible, an immense history of interpretation and commentary in both the Jewish and Christian traditions.[8] I propose to see it, somewhat playfully, as an allegory of the traveling of theory from one cultural site to another, one language to another. To propose this allegorical reading adds one reading more to all the readings and translations that have gone before. Taking what in Protestantism is called "latitude of interpretation," I add another allegorical or, to use a more biblical word, "parabolic" reading to all the readings of Ruth. In doing that, you will note, I "translate" or transpose the text once more into a different context, that of my own theoretical research. There is much precedent within Christianity for parabolic or allegorical readings of texts from the Hebrew Bible or Old Testament, though not, of course, for quite the one I shall propose. A parabolic meaning by no means hollows out the historical, referential, or "realistic" meaning. Rather the allegory depends on the literal meaning.

The Book of Ruth tells a story of assimilation, the assimilation, one might almost say, the "translation," of a Moabite woman into Israelite culture during the time of the judges. This was some time in the latter part of the second millennium before Christ. Though every verse of this admirably economical and circumstantial text counts, the story can be quickly told. A famine has led a man of Bethlehem-Judah, Elimelech, to leave the land of Judah for the country of Moab. He dies and his two sons, Mahlon and Chilion, die, leaving his wife, Naomi, alone with two Moabite daughters-in-law. The famine passes and one of the daughters-in-law, Ruth, chooses to follow Naomi back home to Bethlehem. She utters the famous promise that forswears her Moabite citizenship, so to speak, and decides for Israelite citizenship. I cite the King James translation, the one with most resonance for me: "Intreat me not to leave thee, or to return from following after thee: for whither thou goest, I will go; and where thou lodgest, I will lodge: thy people shall be my people, and thy God my God: where thou diest, will I die, and there will I be buried: the Lord do so to me, and more also, if ought but death part thee and me" (Ruth 1:16–17). Ruth's promise is an oath of allegiance. It is a powerful speech act dividing her life in two. She swears by the new God under whose judgment her speech act places her. Nothing is said about the language in which this promise is uttered. Hebrew and Moabite were apparently so similar as to be essentially the same language. Nevertheless, there may have been differences in pronunciation that would have marked Ruth as an alien.[9] She was, in any case, submitting herself proleptically to the laws and customs of a new country. To be able to make a promise or swear an oath within a new culture is already to have changed oneself into another person.

In Judah Ruth goes then, again on her own initiative, to glean in barley and wheat fields belonging to Boaz, a powerful kinsman of her father-in-law. Boaz notices her. He encourages her to go on working in the fields, feeds her, and protects her from being "touched" by the young men who are harvesting: "Have I not charged the young men that they shall not touch thee?" (2:9). Harvest was a time when young men and women worked together in the fields and therefore a time of possible sexual license, as it still was in Thomas Hardy's England. Finally, after the harvest is over, following her mother-in-law's advice, Ruth uncovers Boaz's feet as he lies sleeping on the threshing floor "at the end of a heap of corn" (3:7) after a day of winnowing barley. She places herself at his uncovered feet. Later in the night, he wakes up, finds her, and promises to take her into his keeping.

The English version and the Midrashic and Rabbinical commentaries seem to agree that Ruth and Boaz do not sleep together, even though he does do what she asks: "spread therefore thy skirt over thine handmaid; for thou art a near kinsman" (3:9). The text says she rose up before they could recognize one another, that is, while it was still dark: "And she lay at his feet until the morning: and she rose up before one could know another. And he said, Let it not be known that a woman came into the floor" (3:14).

The next day, before ten elders of the city, Boaz offers, as by custom he must, to a still nearer kinsman of Elimelech the chance to "redeem" Elimelech's land, making it clear that this will mean also taking responsibility for Ruth. Here the law of levirate marriage (Deuteronomy 25:5–10) is implicitly invoked. This law declared that if a married man dies, his brother must marry his widow in order to keep his line or "inheritance" alive, to "raise up his seed." If not the brother, then another near kinsman. The other kinsman is Ruth's father-in-law's brother, her dead husband's uncle, while Boaz is one step further removed, that is, Ruth's father-in-law's nephew, her dead husband's cousin. This other kinsman, who is called only "so and so" (*Peloni Almoni* in Hebrew), refuses, so Boaz buys the land and Ruth along with it.

The transfer of land is confirmed when Boaz (or perhaps the kinsman) takes off his shoe and gives it to the kinsman.[10] Apparently by the time the story was written down, the custom was already archaic, since the text has to explain it: "Now this was the manner in former time in Israel concerning redeeming and concerning changing, for to confirm all things; a man plucked off his shoe, and gave it to his neighbour: and this was a testimony in Israel. Therefore the kinsman said unto Boaz, Buy it for thee. So he drew off his shoe. And Boaz said unto the elders, and unto all the people, Ye are witnesses this day, that I have bought all that was Elimelech's, and all that was Chilion's and Mahlon's, of the hand of Naomi. Moreover, Ruth the Moabitess, the wife of Mahlon, have I purchased to be my wife, to raise up the name of the dead upon his inheritance, that the name of the dead be not cut off from among his brethren, and from the gate of his place: ye are witnesses this day" (4:7–10). The shoe here functions as a kind of silent speech act sealing the bargain. It may have signified the power to pace out the land being transferred, measuring it by the foot, so to speak, but it has further curious resonances and implications. It is an act of graceful obeisance. To take off one shoe and give it away renders you less capable of walking, more vulnerable, just as a cowboy in a Western film is vulnerable when he takes off his gun holster when entering a saloon. To give a person one of your shoes to seal a bargain is somewhat analogous to a familiar idiom in English: "I'd give you the shirt off my back." A "symbol" for the Greeks was originally an object broken and divided between two people that would confirm some commitment when the two halves were again fitted together ("thrown together," in the literal meaning of *symbolon*). In a somewhat similar way, dividing a pair of shoes between two persons confirms a bond between them. The shoe, a means of walking safely from one place to another, becomes the sign of the transfer of property from one person to another, its "changing," as the Bible says, or its "translation," as we might almost say.

The Hebrew term for Boaz's repossessing of Elimelech's land for its proper family is translated as "redeem." As any member of a farming family knows, a field is a most precious possession. Its transfer from one family to another is a major event. Such a transfer is analogous to the expansion of the territorial borders of a nation or to the change of a person from one citizenship to another. As Ruth ceases to be a Moabitess and becomes an Israelite, so Elimelech's land is redeemed for Elimelech's inheritance, and so Elimelech's genealogical line is maintained through Ruth's marriage to Boaz. Topographical distinctions are powerful carriers of meaning in this story: Moab as against Judah; Boaz's fields as against other fields; Elimelech's land unredeemed and then redeemed. The story is organized around the crossing of borders and the establishment of territorial rights. Movements of going, crossing borders, returning, and transferring tie one aspect of the story to others and underlie it as a structural matrix.

Ruth then marries Boaz and becomes the mother of Obed. Naomi "becomes nurse" to the child. It is in effect a child of her own, a son to carry on Elimelech's family after the death of her two sons. The last verses of Ruth tell the reader why the birth of Obed is important. They give the clue as to why this story became part of sacred scripture: "And Obed begat Jesse, and Jesse begat David" (4:22). The assimilation of Ruth the Moabitess into Israelite society was essential to the carrying on of Elimelech's bloodline. More important, it was essential to the sequence of generations that led first to King David, an essential actor in the Old Testament or Hebrew Bible story, and, for a Christian, ultimately to Jesus himself. Jesus came of the house of Jesse and David, as the elaborate genealogy at the beginning of Matthew specifies. Without Ruth, the alien, the Moabitess, there would have been no David and no Jesus, so her story must be told.

As Sir Edmund Leach has argued in a brilliant article about the genealogies in the Old Testament, far from being a somewhat boring series of adventitious "begats," these genealogies have a crucial function.[11] They testify to the continuity of Israelite culture. Its unbroken tradition is demonstrated by the continuity of its bloodlines. Beyond that, the genealogies show that there has been just the right balance of endogamy and exogamy. Too much endogamy or intermarriage is a kind of incest, leading to a weakening of the bloodlines. Too much exogamy or miscegenation would cause the purity of Israelite blood to thin out and vanish. Moabites, from the Israelite point of view, were outlandish barbarians, infamous for having refused to feed the Israelites when they were returning from Egypt to the promised land. To assimilate a Moabitess into the lineage of Israelite kings was no small thing. There must be just the right amount of marriage outside the tribe, just enough and no more, just as there must be at certain crucial points in Old Testament history something approaching incest. The commentators on the Book of Ruth often see Ruth as parallel to Leah and Rachel, also to Tamar, following the lead of Ruth 4:11–12, in which the witnesses say to Boaz: "The Lord make the woman that is come into thine house like Rachel and like Leah, which two did build the house of Israel. . . . And let thy house be like the house of Pharez, whom Tamar bare unto Judah, of the seed which the Lord shall give thee of this young woman." Just as Jacob was tricked by Laban into marrying Leah in addition to Rachel, thereby becoming father of the twelve tribes of Israel, so Tamar, disguised as a harlot, seduced her father-in-law, Judah, thereby becoming the mother of Pharez, direct ancestor of Boaz, therefore of David and, for Jews, of the Messiah to come, for Christians, of Jesus of Nazareth (Genesis 29:20–28; Genesis 38).

The story of Ruth is a strong confirmation of Leach's theory. For a time, before Ruth crossed the border from Moab into Israel, the whole of sacred history hung in the balance. Unless Ruth had made her decision and uttered her promise, "whither thou goest, I will go," that history could not have gone forward. Nevertheless, Ruth can hardly have made her decision in order to become the great-grandmother of King David and the many times great-grandmother of Jesus. A parallel would be the way Leda, in Yeats's "Leda and the Swan," could not know, as Zeus presumably did, that her rape would lead to two great cycles of stories in Greek mythology, the Trojan war and the story of Agamemnon. Yeats poses this as a question: "Did she put on his knowledge with his power . . . ?" The answer, if the question is taken literally, must be "no," though in the violence done to her by the intervention of the god's power she certainly learned something of what future Greek history would be like. Ruth's ignorance of the future when she makes her oath of allegiance to Naomi exemplifies an important feature of performative speech acts. In them, knowing and doing are never congruent. A speech act makes something happen, all right. It is a way of doing things with words, but just what will happen can never be clearly and exactly foreseen.

⁓

The story of Ruth can be taken as a parable of the translation of theory. In such a parabolic reading, Ruth the Moabitess is a figure of traveling theory. Whatever her original language and culture may have been, she can cross the border into Israel and be assimilated there only by translating herself, so to speak, or being translated, into the idiom of the new culture. She becomes a proper wife and mother among the Israelites. Nevertheless, she brings something of her own, something that resists full translation and assimilation. The decision to follow Naomi was her own. She shows great enterprise in putting herself in Boaz's way. Much of the initiative that makes the story happen is her own. Ruth is shown as an attractively strong-willed young woman, with a mind of her own. She is someone very much in charge of her own life. Whatever the commentators say, she does not seem simply the passive instrument of a historical or divine purpose that exceeds her and that makes use of her to gain its own ends. In a similar way, literary theory has its own stubborn and recalcitrant particularity. Its reliance on examples and its pivoting on the reinscription of conceptual words that have a long history tie it to its language and culture of origin. Nevertheless, it opens itself to assimilation within other cultures and languages. Like Ruth, it is prepared to say, "whither thou goest, I will go." Naomi, nevertheless, as Ziva Ben-Porat has observed,[12] plays an important role in the story. She serves as the mediator introducing Ruth to a new country and a new life. She tells Ruth how to behave in approaching Boaz. In my parabolic reading she would represent the necessary transmitter of theory, the teacher or translator who turns the alien theory into something that can be understood, transformed, and assimilated in the new place.

In a new country a theory, like Ruth, is put to new uses that cannot be foreseen. These uses are an alienation of the theory, its translation into a new idiom, and its appropriation for new, indigenous purposes. Ruth's story is told from an Israelite point of view. What matters to those in Judah is the continuity and vitality of their own cultural heritage. They assimilate the alien, making the different into the same, but at the same time changing that same, in order to ensure that vitality, just as works of traveling theory are transformed in the new country or in a new discipline. In the new place a theory is made use of in ways the theory never intended or allowed for, though it also transforms the culture or discipline it enters. When theory crosses borders it is translated in the sense that

Puck fits Bottom out with an ass's head in Shakespeare's *A Midsummer Night's Dream.* When theory travels it is disfigured, deformed, "translated."

To figure theory as the feminine within a strongly patriarchal culture reverses the usual gender ascription that sees theory as the product of a male will to mastery, even as the product of a Western white male will to mastery over women, minorities, and the subject peoples of "other" cultures. My reversal of that is congruent with my claim that theory is in a complex relation to reading and to a given nation's cultural projects, a relation that might better be figured as the relation of woman to man, rather than that of man to woman. That the issues of gender and gender relations should arise in a discussion of something that initially seems to have nothing to do with them is in accordance with a general law. All our thinking is in one way or another gendered, even when it seems most removed from gender questions.

I have said that when theory travels it is deformed, "translated." This can be seen not only in Ruth's story but in what has happened to the text of Ruth. Ruth is itself a theoretical text. It exemplifies in schematic narrative form a set of theoretical presuppositions about Israelite culture at that time: the form and function of promises, oaths, and non-verbal gestures like removing and giving a shoe; the subservience of women to the function of keeping a name and an inheritance alive, so that a woman can be "purchased" and has value just as a piece of land on which barley or wheat can be grown has value; certain complex assumptions about endogamy and exogamy in relation to the vitality and persistence through history of Israelite culture; a strong sense of territoriality. Theory here goes with example, but the example always exceeds and is to some degree incongruent with the theory, just as the independence and individual enterprise of Ruth, the pathos of her story, exceeds and to some degree contradicts the theoretical assumptions about genealogy and inheritance the story was written to exemplify. In a similar way my account of Ruth exceeds the theoretical uses to which I put my reading and to some degree goes counter to them.

If Ruth's story is a narrative of alienation and assimilation that can exemplify theoretical propositions about the travel of theory, what has happened to the text of Ruth (as opposed to what happens within the story) is also exemplary of the fate of theory. This book of the Hebrew Bible has been alienated from itself, translated from itself. It has been put to entirely new uses, uses by no means intended by the original authors or scribes. The first and most significant alienation (after all the changes that made the story of Ruth a sacred text in the Hebrew Bible) was, of course, the assimilation of Ruth into the Christian Bible in all its subsequent translations, first into the pre-Christian Greek Septuagint, then into the Latin Vulgate, then into almost innumerable vernacular languages. The original writer or writers of Ruth had no intention of using it as a means of legitimating the claim of Jesus to be the Messiah. That, nevertheless, is its "theoretical" function in the Christian Bible. In coming to perform this function Ruth has been alienated from itself. It has been translated in the strong sense of that word. Harold Bloom's way of putting this is to say that the New Testament in its relation to the Hebrew Bible is the most outrageous example of "misprision" in the history of the West, that is, of "mistakings" or takings amiss, translation as mistranslation.

Ruth is a powerful text. Like a strong theoretical insight, it sticks in the mind and invites further applications. Ruth has opened itself to many other striking but less historically decisive misprisions. I shall mention only two.

One is the English folk tradition of *Sortes Sanctorum* (Latin for Oracles of the Holy Writings) on Valentine's Day, described in detail in chapter 13 of Hardy's *Far from the Madding Crowd*. In this folk practice of divination by Bible and key, a young woman balances a Bible open at the first chapter of Ruth on a long house key and repeats the verses beginning "whither thou goest, I will go," while thinking about the man who attracts her. If the Bible moves, then she will come to marry that man. This is a mistranslation if there ever was one. The verses from the Bible are Ruth's speech expressing her fidelity to Naomi, her mother-in-law. They have nothing to do with her marriage to Boaz, except by unintentional prolepsis, since she has not even met him or perhaps even heard of him yet. But the words can be displaced with uncanny appropriateness to a new context in which they fit perfectly. There they can have a new performative function. This transposition is analogous to the way the "Wellerisms" in Dickens's *Pickwick Papers* are forms of words that will have meaning in wildly different social contexts. It is also analogous to the way a theoretical formulation developed in the course of reading some specific work, such as Derrida's idea of untranslatability in its relation to his reading of Celan, may have a new effective function in an entirely new context. In the new context it may assist in reading a work in a different language and social situation. "Whither thou goest, I will go; and where thou lodgest, I will lodge: thy people shall be my people, and thy God my God": this is just what a young woman should say when she joins herself to her husband, even though the words in their original context did not mean that at all.

Another mistranslation or violent appropriation of Ruth is the hauntingly beautiful lines in Keats's "Ode to a Nightingale." Keats heard the nightingale in a garden in Hampstead, a suburb of London. The poem speaks of the nightingale's song as something that has sounded the same in many different places and at many different times over the centuries. The nightingale's song ties Keats's own place and time to innumerable other places, times, and situations in which the nightingale's song has been heard. Thinking of this expands the poet's attention away from his preoccupation with his own suffering, limitation, and mortality to give him a virtual kinship with people in all those other places and times who have heard the nightingale. Hearing the nightingale is a momentary escape from the imminence of death, though also a way to experience the desire for death. Along with "ancient days" when the bird could be heard by "emperor and clown," and "magic casements, opening on the foam / Of perilous seas, in faery lands forlorn," as sites where the nightingale might have been heard, Keats includes Ruth gleaning barley in Boaz's field: "Perhaps the self-same song that found a path / Through the sad heart of Ruth, when, sick for home, / She stood in tears amid the alien corn" (ll. 64–70). This is very moving. It associates Ruth with Keats's general presentation of the human situation as forlorn, derelict, haunted by death, even "half in love with easeful Death" (l. 52). This pathos of alienation, however, has no biblical precedent. It is all Keats's invention. It is his translation, or mistranslation, of the story of Ruth for his own quite different purposes. Ruth in the Bible is not shown to have suffered one pang of homesickness for the country of Moab, nor to have dropped a single tear. In fact, her mind seems to be charmingly fixed on getting herself the best possible new husband in the new country. No nightingale is mentioned in Ruth. But just as a work of theory may be translated and put to entirely new uses, so the book of Ruth yields without apparent resistance to what Keats does with it.

I propose therefore what might be called the "Wellerism theory of traveling theory," taking the term from Dickens's *Pickwick Papers*. (Wellerisms are discussed in chapter 4, above.) Just as "I'm pretty tough" fits Tony Weller's description of himself as a father contemplating the marriage of his son, but also might just as well be something "the wery old turkey remarked wen the farmer said he wos afeerd he should be obliged to kill him for the London market,"[13] so theoretical insights, though they are always generated in local acts of reading and have no use except in relation to acts of reading, can be transferred from their initial sites to innumerable other moments of reading in any language or discipline. But it is important to keep in mind the essential distortion involved in this translation, however scrupulously and accurately the theory is rendered in the new language. A theoretical formulation is a positing that can be effectively posited again or repositioned in many different situations and applied to many different texts or works in many media.

Theory's openness to translation is a result of the fact that a theory, in spite of appearances, is a performative, not a cognitive, use of language. The word "theory," which means "clear-seeing," seems to promise knowledge. Works of theory are nevertheless potent speech acts. A theory is a way of doing things with words, namely facilitating (or sometimes inhibiting) acts of reading. The performative words of the Christian marriage ceremony, "I pronounce you man and wife," are functional only in a given, unique marriage situation. They join just this man and this woman. Nevertheless, the same words can be used innumerable times to marry innumerable couples. In a similar way, though the formulations of literary theory originated in a unique act of reading, they can be effective in unpredictable new contexts. In those new contexts they enable, or perhaps distort, new acts of reading, even readings of works in languages the originator of the theory did not know. At the new site, giving an impetus to a new start, the theory will be radically transformed, even though the same form of words may still be used, translated as accurately as possible into the new language. If the theory is transformed by translation, it also to some degree transforms the culture or discipline it enters. The vitality of theory is to be open to such unforeseeable transformations and to bring them about as it crosses borders and is carried into new idioms.

The somewhat disturbing openness of theory to translation, its promiscuity, so to speak, reveals something essential about the original theory. Far from being a definitive expression of some way language or another kind of sign works, a theoretical formulation is always provisional and idiomatic, never wholly clear and never wholly satisfactory. The evidence for that is the way the formulation is amenable to having quite different effects in different contexts. A theoretical formulation never quite adequately expresses the insight that comes from reading.[14] That insight is always particular, local, good for this time, place, text, and act of reading only. The theoretical insight is a glimpse out of the corner of the eye of the way language works, a glimpse that is not wholly amenable to conceptualization. Another way to put this is to say that the theoretical formulation in its original language is already a translation or mistranslation of a lost original. This original can never be recovered because it never existed as anything articulated or able to be articulated in any language. Translations of theory are therefore mistranslations of mistranslations, not mistranslations of some authoritative and perspicuous original. This ought to cheer up those who translate theory and then use it performatively in a new situation. "Getting it right" no longer has the same urgency when it is seen to be impossible, though that by no means means we should not try our utmost to do so.

Notes

Notes

Introduction

1. Marcel Proust, *À la recherche du temps perdu* (Paris: Gallimard, 1954), 1: 388–89; *Remembrance of Things Past*, trans. C. K. Scott Moncrieff and Terence Kilmartin (New York: Vintage, 1982), 1: 422. For a discussion of Proust's Cratylism, see Roland Barthes, "Proust et les noms," *To Honor Roman Jakobson* (The Hague: Mouton, 1967), 150–58.

2. From *Webster's New Collegiate Dictionary* (Springfield, Mass.: G. & C. Merriam Co., 1949).

3. Ibid.

Chapter 1

1. *La Vérité en peinture* (Paris: Flammarion, 1978), 94; *The Truth in Painting*, trans. Geoff Bennington and Ian McLeod (Chicago: University of Chicago Press, 1987), 81–82: "Everything will flower at the edge of a deconsecrated tomb."

2. In a letter to Henry Church, April 4, 1945, apropos of his "Description Without Place," *Letters of Wallace Stevens*, ed. Holly Stevens (New York: Knopf, 1966), 494.

3. "Coole Park and Ballylee, 1931," in *The Poems, A New Edition*, ed. Richard J. Finnerman (New York: Macmillan, 1983), 244.

4. Heidegger's thinking through of what is at stake in the outlines man makes in building and dwelling has formed the instigation for Maurice Blanchot, both in his criticism and in those strange *récits* showing anonymous men and women living in placeless hotel rooms, moving

from one room to another in unmappable itineraries. I have discussed Blanchot's *L'Arrêt de mort* in *Versions of Pygmalion* (Harvard, 1990).

5. Martin Heidegger, "Der Ursprung des Kunstwerkes," *Holzwege* (Frankfurt am Main: Vittorio Klostermann, 1972), 58. Martin Heidegger, "The Origin of the Work of Art," *Poetry, Language, Thought*, trans. Albert Hofstadter (New York: Harper and Row, 1971), 70. The English translations of "Building Dwelling Thinking" (*Bauen Wohnen Denken*) and "The Thing" (*Das Ding*) will be cited from the latter volume, the German from *Vorträge und Aufsätze*, 2 (Pfullingen: Neske, 1954). Numbers refer to pages in these volumes.

6. Thomas Hardy, *The Return of the Native* (London: Macmillan, 1974), 33. Further references will be to this edition by page numbers in the text.

7. A dialect word for a wooden mask to frighten people, with cow's horns and hair, and a movable jaw.

8. Small lizards or newts.

9. Dialect word for skeleton or carcass.

10. F. E. Hardy, *The Life of Thomas Hardy* (London: Macmillan, 1965), 220.

11. The Greeks used for both Dionysus and the sun the contradictory epithets *enorchos* ("betesticled") and *pseudenor* ("unmanly"). See Peter Sacks, *The English Elegy* (Baltimore: The Johns Hopkins University Press, 1985), 1–37 for a discussion of the "paradoxical blend of absence and presence, of weakness and strength" (34) in the solar fertility gods that are a major figurative resource of elegy.

12. In "the most consistent conclusion," the conclusion Hardy never wrote except in a footnote of 1912, the conclusion truest to the solar trajectory of the action, Diggory "disappear[s] mysteriously from the heath, nobody knowing whither—Thomasin remaining a widow" (author's note, 413).

Chapter Two

1. Plato, *Protagoras*, trans. W. K. C. Guthrie, *Collected Dialogues*, ed. Edith Hamilton and Huntington Cairns, Bollingen Series 71 (Princeton: Princeton University Press, 1963), 311e–12a. Further references will be identified by the traditional section numbers and letters in this translation, abbreviated *CD*.

2. My reading of Henry James's *What Maisie Knew* in the second chapter of *Versions of Pygmalion* (Cambridge, Mass.: Harvard University

Press, 1990) established analogies among the acts of the author, the narrator, the protagonist, and the reader. Those analogies, however, worked to leave the reader somewhat dismayingly on his or her own, without a clear ethical command to follow: "Do this," or "Don't do that." Another way to put this is to say that an implicit question still remained at the end of my exploration of *What Maisie Knew*. The question might be posed in this way: What is gained, after all, in turning to actual stories to learn about the ethics of reading, as opposed, say, to staying with texts like those prefaces, philosophical treatises on ethics, and works of literary theory I discussed in *The Ethics of Reading*? If we really need stories for their ethical teaching, we really need stories and not just various examples of talking about stories, even talk by the authors of those stories. Why is that? Why do we need the stories themselves not only to understand the ethics of reading but also to make ethical decisions?

3. In what I say about the *Protagoras* I am much indebted to a brilliant long essay by Thomas Cohen on the dialogue, "Hyperbaton." A shorter version of this essay is forthcoming in Cohen's *Anti-Mimesis*, to be published by Cambridge University Press. Cohen's essay is a comprehensive reading of the *Protagoras* in the context of Plato's other dialogues and in the context of the complex history of interpretations of the *Protagoras*. I concentrate on the topic of prosopopoeia in the dialogue in its relation to the function of storytelling as a reading of ethics and as a demonstration of the ethics of reading.

4. See Tzvetan Todorov, *The Poetics of Prose* (Ithaca: Cornell University Press, 1977), 73. Todorov quotes Borges, as Hilary Schor, in an essay on *Cranford*, observes: "On this night, the king hears from the queen's mouth her own story. He hears the initial story, which included all the others, which—monstrously—includes itself. . . . If the queen continues, the king will sit still and listen forever to the truncated version of the *Arabian Nights*, henceforth infinite and circular."

5. Ludwig Wittgenstein, "The Brown Book," *The Blue and Brown Books* (New York: Harper & Row, 1965), 162–63. I have discussed this section of "The Brown Book" in more detail in *Ariadne's Thread* (New Haven: Yale University Press, 1992).

6. W. B. Yeats, *The Complete Poems* (New York: Macmillan, 1958), 265.

Chapter 3

1. Cambridge: Cambridge University Press, 1987.

2. Heinrich von Kleist, *The Marquise of O— and Other Stories*, trans.

Notes to Pages 85–90

Martin Greenberg (New York: Frederick Ungar Publishing Co., 1973), 246, henceforth E, followed by the page number of the citation.

3. Heinrich von Kleist, *Sämtliche Werke und Briefe*, ed. Helmut Sembdner, II (Munich: Carl Hanser Verlag, 1985), 9. Citations from this volume will henceforth be identified by "G," followed by the page number.

4. This is the "Nachricht von Hans Kohlhasen, einem Befehder derer Chur-Sächsischen Lande. Aus Petri Haftitii geschriebener Märckischer Chronic," from the third volume of *Diplomatische und curieuse Nachlese der Historie von Ober-Sachsen und angrentzenden Ländern*, by Christian Schöttgen und George Christoph Kreysig (Dresden, 1731). See G, 895–96, for this reference.

5. See Paul de Man's formulation of this, apropos of Kleist's plays. The observation comes in passing during a reading of Rousseau's *Profession de foi*: "A text such as the *Profession de foi* can literally be called 'unreadable' in that it leads to a set of assertions that radically exclude each other. Nor are these assertions mere neutral constations; they are exhortative performatives that require the passage from sheer enunciation to action. They compel us to choose while destroying the foundations of any choice. They tell the allegory of a judicial decision that can be neither judicious nor just. As in the plays of Kleist, the verdict repeats the crime it condemns" ("Allegory of Reading," *Allegories of Reading* [New Haven: Yale University Press, 1979], 245). De Man shows the way the temptation of "theism," in the *Profession de foi*, is at once condemned as intellectually foolish and at the same time shown to be in some form inevitable. The text demands that we make a judgment of what it says and about what it says, while showing that such judgment is necessarily groundless. My reading of Kleist's allegory of justice in "Michael Kohlhaas" also sees the situation of the reader as analogous to that of the protagonist, but while not denying the rigor of the narrow place in which Rousseau's *Profession de Foi*, de Man's essay, and Kleist's "Michael Kohlhaas" in their different ways put their readers, I glimpse the possibility of a new justice and a new taking of responsibility for acts and judgments made in this narrow place. If we must judge and act, we must also say of these acts and judgments, as Kohlhaas and the signers of the Declaration of Independence in different ways did of what they had done: "Yes, I did it, and I take responsibility for it, even though it was unjust in the sense of not being based on an ascertainable prior ground of justice within the political order I inhabited. I declare my act and judgment to be the basis of a new justice." A

work of literature lays down the law, I am arguing, in a way analogous to these acts and judgments.

6. Immanuel Kant, *Grundlegung zur Metaphysik der Sitten, Werkausgabe* (Frankfurt am Main: Suhrkamp Verlag, 1982), 28, my translation. I have discussed this sentence and its surrounding context in Kant in "Reading Telling: Kant," *The Ethics of Reading* (New York: Columbia University Press, 1987), 13–39, esp. 26–30. The paperback edition of 1989 rectifies an error in translation in the first edition. Hardy E. Jones, in *Kant's Principle of Personality* (Madison: University of Wisconsin Press, 1971), defines Kant's idea of the relation between moral agency and lawmaking in a way that parallels what I am saying about "Michael Kohlhaas" the story and Michael Kohlhaas the person. For Kant, says Jones, "a person is a moral agent with an autonomous will by virtue of his law-making capacity—his power of self-legislation. Kant says that rational agents are subject to laws arising from their self-legislating will: they are required to obey only those rules of which they themselves are sources. This is something which is essential to their freedom and without which they could not be rightly regarded as morally responsible beings" (131). I owe this citation to Paul Privateer. Jones in the passage I cite does not signal, as Kleist does, the social disorder or violence that might follow if each citizen were to obey only laws of which he or she was the source, nor does he signal what is problematic about that word "source." What faculty or agency within me is the source of the laws I establish with my "self-legislating will"? Kant's books of moral philosophy are attempts to answer this question, or rather to explain why it cannot be answered, why we cannot ever confront the moral law within us face to face, though its imperative command over us is categorical.

7. Jacques Derrida has written brilliantly on this paradox of a performative masking as a constative statement in two essays, "Declarations of Independence," *Otobiographies* (Paris: Galilée, 1984), 13–32, and "Admiration de Nelson Mandela ou Les Lois de la réflexion," *Psyché: Inventions de l'autre* (Paris: Galilée, 1987), 453–75.

8. The actual letter Luther sent has not survived. It is lost to history.

9. The work of diplomacy, says Benjamin, "wie der Umgang von Privatpersonen [like the intercourse of private persons]" is "jenseits aller Rechtsordnung und also Gewalt [beyond all legal systems and therefore beyond violence]" (Walter Benjamin, "Zur Kritik der Gewalt," *Gesammelte Schriften*, ed. Rolf Tiedemann and Hermann Schweppenhäuser, I:1 [Frankfurt am Main: Suhrkamp, 1977], 195; "Critique of Violence,"

Reflections, trans. Edmund Jephcott [New York: Harcourt Brace Jovano-vich, 1978], 293).

10. Benjamin, in the essay cited earlier, "Zur Kritik der Gewalt," observes that the "great" criminal characteristically commands such paradoxical respect and admiration from the people. He is the law-breaker who nevertheless reveals something essential about the violence involved in all lawmaking, even if his punishment is accepted as neces-sary to maintaining law and order (German ed., 183; English ed., 281).

11. In the body of this paper my lips must remain sealed, since the meaning of the story depends on the fact that the Elector's future is not revealed there. In this footnote, however, separated from the "body" of the paper as neatly as Kohlhaas's head is separated from *his* body, I append the following. The Elector of Saxony from 1532 to 1547, that is, at the time of the story, was John Frederick I, der Grossmütige or Magnani-mous (1503–54), the last Elector of the Ernestine branch of the house of Wettin. He was wounded and taken prisoner by Charles V's victorious army at the battle of Mühlberg (April 24, 1547). Though a sentence of death was not carried out, in the capitulation of Wittenberg, May 10, 1547, the Elector renounced the electoral lands to his second cousin, Maurice, duke of Saxony from 1541, of the Albertine line of the Wettins. Presumably the gypsy woman's prophecy contains these facts. As the Elector fears, he is the last of his line to rule Electoral Saxony. My source, by the way, the *Encyclopaedia Britannica,* says nothing at all about Kohl-haas in the entry for John Frederick I, much less about the gypsy woman. There is a three-volume life of John Frederick I have not yet seen. Ich muß es nachlesen.

Chapter 4

1. Citations are by page number from the Penguin edition of *Pickwick Papers* (Harmondsworth: Penguin Books, 1972).

2. J. L. Austin, *How to Do Things with Words,* ed. J. O. Urmson and Marina Sbisà, 2d ed. (Oxford: Oxford University Press, 1980), 9.

3. Ruth Webb Lee, *A History of Valentines* (New York: The Studio Publications, Inc., 1952), 16. Subsequent references to this work will be cited in the text by author's name and page.

4. Thomas Hardy, *Far from the Madding Crowd* (New York: Norton, 1986), 78. Further references will be to this edition by page number.

5. Frank Staff, *The Valentine and Its Origins* (New York: Frederick A.

Praeger, 1969), 43. Subsequent references to this work will be cited in the text by author's name and page.

6. Jacques Derrida, *Limited Inc*, ed. Gerald Graff, trans. Samuel Weber and Jeffrey Mehlman (Evanston: Northwestern University Press, 1988), 18.

7. Ibid., 30–31.

8. The word appears in the first sentence of Sam's valentine. It is prominent both because of its apparent incongruity in context and because Sam cannot read what he has written over a blot. That illegibility generates a controversy between Sam and his father over whether "circumscribed" or "circumwented" is the better word. Sam has written: "I feel myself ashamed and completely circumscribed in a dressin' of you" (540). A little dialogue follows:

> "That ain't as good a word as circumwented, Sammy," said Mr Weller, gravely.
>
> "Think not?" said Sam.
>
> "Nothin' like it," replied his father.
>
> "But don't you think it means more?" inquired Sam.
>
> "Vell p'raps it is a more tenderer word," said Mr Weller, after a few moments' reflection. (540)

This is, of course, sublimely comic and slightly condescending nonsense, condescending to the uneducated lower classes who use big words wrongly and have foolish linguistic theories. One word does not mean more than another. It means something different. Neither word in this case seems quite right, at least at first glance. On the other hand, Sam *is* "circumscribed" in his valentine writing, not only in the sense that he is hemmed in, coerced by his feelings and by his sense of inferiority to Mary, ashamed of his temerity in addressing her, but also in the literal sense that he is "written around," narrowly enclosed on all sides by conventions of language and the specific conventions of courtship and valentine sending that constrain him to write in certain ways, even though he feels himself ashamed by the fact that she is such a "lovely creetur" (540). "Circumscribed" is uncannily the right word after all, a much better word than "circumwented." It does mean more—in its context.

9. Derrida's chief work on performatives, *Limited Inc*, is cited above. De Man's most radical appropriation and reworking of the theory of performatives is the chapter on Rousseau's *Confessions*, "Excuses," in

Allegories of Reading (New Haven: Yale University Press, 1979). See, for example, the following passages: "Writing always includes the moment of dispossession in favor of the arbitrary power play of the signifier and from the point of view of the subject, this can only be experienced as a dismemberment, a beheading, or a castration" (296); "Far from seeing language as an instrument in the service of a psychic energy, the possibility now arises that the entire construction of drives, substitutions, repressions, and representations is the aberrant, metaphorical correlative of the absolute randomness of language, prior to any figuration or meaning. It is no longer certain that language, as excuse, exists because of a prior guilt but just as possible that since language, as a machine, performs anyway, we have to produce guilt (and all its train of psychic consequences) in order to make the excuse meaningful. Excuses generate the very guilt they exonerate, though always in excess or by default" (299).

10. Ibid., 301.

11. Or even gives meaning to what apparently has none. The stone Pickwick finds with letters in some unknown language (+BILST/UM/PSHI/S.M./ARK) is, when blanks are put in the right place, a perfectly readable series of English words: +BIL[L] STUMPS HIS MARK (217). The words are, as it happens, a classic example of the way a non-word can function as a performative. A cross is put by an illiterate person in place of a signature and then ratified through an explanatory note by someone who can write certifying who made the cross. The cross works as well as a signature to bind the one who makes it.

Chapter 5

1. W. H. Auden, "Introduction," *A Selection from the Poems of Alfred, Lord Tennyson* (Garden City, N.Y.: Doubleday, 1944), x.

2. See his *Tennyson and the Text: The Weaver's Shuttle* (Cambridge: Cambridge University Press, 1992).

3. Hallam Tennyson, *Alfred Lord Tennyson: A Memoir*, 2 vols., II (London: Macmillan, 1897), 127. Further citations will be by author and page number in the text.

4. *The Poems of Tennyson*, ed. Christopher Ricks (London: Longmans, 1969), 784–86. Further citations will be from this edition, by line for poetry, by editor and page for prose.

5. What is a "bygone memory"? It is an odd phrase, by no means the same in nuance as "memory of the bygone."

6. Cited in Ricks, 785, from *Nineteenth Century* 33 (1893): 170.

7. On this aspect of tears, see Jacques Derrida, *Memoirs of the Blind: The Self-Portrait and Other Ruins,* trans. Pascale-Anne Brandt and Michael Naas (Chicago: University of Chicago Press, 1993) 122–29.

8. Samuel Taylor Coleridge, *Lay Sermons,* ed. R. J. White, *The Collected Works* VII, Bolligen Series (London: Routledge and Kegan Paul, 1972), 29–30.

Chapter 6

1. Gerard Manley Hopkins, "The Wreck of the Deutschland," ll. 9–12, from *The Poems,* 4th ed., ed. W. H. Gardner and N. H. MacKenzie (London: Oxford University Press, 1970). All poetry citations are to this edition. The following books by Hopkins are also cited in this chapter: *The Journals and Papers of Gerard Manley Hopkins,* ed. Humphry House and Graham Storey (London: Oxford University Press, 1959) (*J*); *The Sermons and Devotional Writings of Gerard Manley Hopkins,* ed. Christopher Devlin (London: Oxford University Press, 1959) (*S*); *Letters of Gerard Manley Hopkins to Robert Bridges,* ed. C. C. Abbott (London: Oxford University Press, 1935) (*L*); *Correspondence of Gerard Manley Hopkins and Richard Watson Dixon,* ed. C. C. Abbott (London: Oxford University Press, 1935) (*C*).

2. J. L. Austin, *How to Do Things with Words,* 2d ed., ed. J. O. Urmson and Marina Sbisà (Oxford: Oxford University Press, 1980), 56–66.

3. Jacques Derrida gives another example of this contamination of constative by performative language: " 'He promises' is not an explicit performative and cannot be one unless an 'I' is presupposed, for example: 'I swear to you that he promises,' etc." (*Ulysse gramophone: Deux mots pour Joyce* (Paris: Galilée, 1987), 129, my trans. Pages 123–29 of this book admirably identify the problematic of the "yes." What I say about saying yes in Hopkins is a way of saying yes to these pages.

4. See Jonathan Culler's admirable essay, "Apostrophe," *Diacritics* 7, no. 4 (Winter 1977): 59–69.

5. *How to Do Things with Words,* 22, Austin's italics.

6. "But how didst Thou speak? In the way that the voice came out of the cloud, saying, This is my beloved Son? For that voice passed by and passed away, began and ended; the syllables sounded and passed away, the second after the first, the third after the second, and so forth in order, until the last after the rest, and silence after the last. Whence it is

abundantly clear and plain that the motion of a creature expressed it, itself temporal, serving Thy eternal will. And these Thy words, created for time, the outward ear reported to the intelligent soul, whose inward ear lay listening to Thy Eternal Word. But she compared these words sounding in time, with that Thy Eternal Word in Silence, and said, "It is different, far different. These words are far beneath me, nor are they, because they flee and pass away; but the Word of my Lord abideth above me for ever" (*The Confessions of St. Augustine*, trans. Edward B. Pusey [New York: Pocket Books, Inc., 1951], 219–20). Later references to Augustine will be given in the text, by page number to this edition. See Paul Ricoeur's discussion of Augustine's analysis of time and language in *Time and Narrative*, I, trans. Kathleen McLaughlin and David Pellauer (Chicago: University of Chicago Press, 1984), 5–30.

7. See Jacques Derrida, *Limited Inc*, ed. Gerald Graff, trans. Samuel Weber and Jeffrey Mehlman (Evanston: Northwestern University Press, 1988).

8. See Derrida, *Ulysse gramophone*, 126.

9. Compare Derrida, *Ulysse gramophone*, 126: "But I believe, yes, that, to say it in a classic philosophic code, *yes* is the transcendental condition of every performative dimension" (my trans.). My "yes," like Derrida's *oui*, is the indication of an affirmative answer to one of the questions I posed at the beginning. Is there a performative dimension to my own discourse or that of others *about* performatives? Yes, I affirm, there is.

Chapter 7

1. For a bilingual version of the lectures on ancient rhetoric and an English translation of "On Truth and Lies in an Extramoral Sense," see *Friedrich Nietzsche on Rhetoric and Language*, ed. and trans. Sander L. Gilman, Carole Blair, and David J. Parent (New York: Oxford University Press, 1989). Readers should be aware that this edition must be used with circumspection. For a challenge to its accuracy and scholarship see Anton Bierl and William M. Calder, III, "Friedrich Nietzsche: 'Abriss der Geschichte der Beredsamkeit': A New Edition," *Nietzsche-Studien* 21 (1992): 363–89. For convenience I have used it, however. Further citations from it will appear in the text, by "E" or "G" and page number. For an annotated French version of Nietzsche's early writings on rhetoric, see Friedrich Nietzsche, "Rhetoric et langage," ed. and trans. Jean-Luc Nancy and Philippe Lacoue-Labarthe, *Poétique* 5 (1971): 99–142. For the

German of "Über Wahrheit und Lüge," I have used the bilingual German and French edition: Friedrich Nietzsche, *Das Philosophenbuch/Le Livre du philosophe*, trans. Angèle K. Marietti (Paris: Aubier-Flammarion, 1969). Page references to this edition are given in the text by "G" and the page number.

2. See Bierl and Calder, "Nietzsche," 364.

3. For an account of Aristotelian epistemology, I have learned much from a brilliant unpublished paper by Jonathan Cohen. See also Jonathan Leer, *Aristotle: The Desire to Understand* (Cambridge: Cambridge University Press, 1988).

4. See Martin Stingelin, "Nietzsches Wortspiel als Reflexion auf Poet(olog)ische Verfahren," *Nietzsche-Studien* 17 (1958): 346–49, and Anthonie Meijers and Martin Stingelin, "Konkordanz zu den Wörtlichen Abschriften und Übernahmen von Beispielen und Zitaten aus Gustav Gerber: *Die Sprache als Kunst* (Bromberg 1871)," in "Nietzsches Rhetorik-Vorlesung und in 'Über Wahrheit und Luge im Außermoralischen Sinne,'" *Nietzsche-Studien* 17 (1958): 350–68.

5. For accounts of Nietzsche's relation to Gerber and to Jena Romanticism, see Ernst Behler, "Friedrich Nietzsche et la philosophie du langage du romantisme d'Iéna," *Philosophie* 27 (1990): 57–75; Ernst Behler, "Selbstkritik der Philosophie in der dekonstruktiven Nietzschelektüre," *Krisis der Metaphysik*, ed. Günter Abel and Jörg Salaquarda (Berlin: Walter de Gruyter, 1989), 283–306; Anthonie Meijers, "Gustav Gerber und Friedrich Nietzsche: Zum historischen Hintergrund der sprachphilosophischen Auffassungen des frühen Nietzsche," *Nietzsche-Studien* 17 (1988): 369–90. See also Paul de Man, "Rhetoric of Tropes (Nietzsche)," *Allegories of Reading* (New Haven: Yale University Press, 1979), 103–18, especially pp. 104–6 on Nietzsche's early rhetorical writings and their relation to Gerber and to "Gerber's own antecedents in German Romanticism, especially in Friedrich Schlegel and Jean Paul Richter" (106).

6. See Jacques Derrida, "White Mythology: Metaphor in the Text of Philosophy," in *Margins of Philosophy*, trans. Alan Bass (Chicago: University of Chicago Press), 216–19; Paul de Man, "Anthropomorphism and Trope in the Lyric," *The Rhetoric of Romanticism* (New York: Columbia University Press, 1984), 239–43; Philippe Lacoue-Labarthe, "Le détour," *Le Suject de la philosophie* (Paris: Flammarion, 1979); Andrzej Warminski, "Towards a Fabulous Reading: Nietzsche's 'On Truth and Lie in the Extramoral Sense,'" *Graduate Faculty Philosophy Journal*, New School for

Social Research (1991); J. Hillis Miller, "The Disarticulation of the Self in Nietzsche," *Monist* 64 (April 1981): 247–61. Lacoue-Labarthe's essay is a comprehensive discussion of Nietzsche's early writing on rhetoric. It was first published in the issue of *Poétique* cited above in note 1.

7. Another way to formulate this, as Steven Mailloux reminds me, would be to say that the initial distinction between literal and metaphorical language breaks down, leaving a single realm of language that is neither literal nor figurative. But that distinction underwrites the possibility of answering a question about what something *is*: "Was ist also Wahrheit?" In the disappearance of the distinction between literal and figurative language, the possibility of answering in literal language questions about what something is also vanishes. It is replaced by a potentially endless series of catachreses for an unknown X. Since that X remains forever unknown, it cannot ever be literally named. What is truth? Well, I cannot give you an answer to that in so many literal words. I can only answer in one or another catachresis. Truth is a mobile army. Truth is a worn coin.

8. See Meijers and Stingelin, "Konkordanz," 352–60.

9. For exceptions, see Martin Heidegger, "Wer ist Nietzsche's Zarathustra," *Vorträge und Aufsätze* (Pfullingen: Neske, 1967), trans. as "Who is Nietzsche's Zarathustra," trans. Bernd Magnus, *The New Nietzsche*, ed. David B. Allison (New York: Dell, 1977), 64–79; Bernard Pautrat, "Retour à l'est," *Versions du Soleil* (Paris: Seuil, 1971), 329–61.

10. Friedrich Nietzsche, *Werke*, ed. Karl Schlechta (Munich: Carl Hanser, 1966), 2: 447, henceforth "ZG." *The Portable Nietzsche*, ed. Walter Kaufmann (New York: Viking, 1959), 312, henceforth "ZE." References will be given in the text.

11. I have approached this question from a different direction in "Gleichnis in Nietzsche's *Also Sprach Zarathustra*," *International Studies in Philosophy* XVII, 2 (1985), 3–15, reprinted in *Theory Now and Then* (London: Harvester Wheatsheaf; Durham: Duke University Press, 1991), 277–91.

12. See Charles Singleton, "In Exitu Israel de Aegypto," *Dante: A Collection of Critical Essays*, ed. John Freccero (Englewood Cliffs, N.J.: Prentice Hall, 1965), 102–21; Paul de Man, *Allegories of Reading*, 205: "The paradigm for all texts consists of a figure (or a system of figures) and its deconstruction. But since this model cannot be closed off by final reading, it engenders, in its turn, a supplementary figural superposition which narrates the unreadability of the prior narration. As distinguished

from primary deconstructive narratives centered on figures and ultimately always on metaphor, we can call such narratives to the second (or third) degree *allegories.*"

13. Sigmund Freud, *Beyond the Pleasure Principle,* trans. James Strachey (New York: Bantam, 1967), 110. "The Book" is presumably the Koran.

14. Friedrich Nietzsche, *Die Geburt der Tragödie, Werke,* ed. Karl Schlechta, I, 12. The translation is by Carol Jacobs, who quotes this passage as one of the epigraphs to her brilliant essay, "Nietzsche: The Stammering Text: The Fragmentary Studies Preliminary to *The Birth of Tragedy,*" *The Dissimulating Harmony* (Baltimore: Johns Hopkins University Press, 1978), 3–22.

Chapter 8

1. In *Lenin and Philosophy and Other Essays,* trans. Ben Brewster (New York: Monthly Review Press), 160. Other references to this essay will be given by page number in the text.

2. Paul de Man, *The Resistance to Theory* (Minneapolis: University of Minnesota Press, 1986), 11.

3. William Faulkner, *Light in August* (New York: The Modern Library, 1950), 386.

4. William Faulkner, *Absalom, Absalom!* (New York: Vintage Books, 1972), 8. Further references will be identified by page numbers from this edition.

5. Althusser, in "A Letter on Art in Reply to André Daspré" (April 1966), allows for this possibility but makes a problematic distinction between seeing and knowing: "I believe that the peculiarity of art is to 'make us see' [*nous donner à voir*], 'make us perceive,' 'make us feel' something which *alludes* to reality. . . . What art makes us *see,* and therefore gives to us in the form of '*seeing,*' '*perceiving,*' and '*feeling*' (which is not the form of '*knowing*') is the ideology from which it is born, in which it bathes, from which it detaches itself as art, and to which it *alludes.* . . . When we speak of ideology we should know that ideology slides into all human activity, that it is identical with the 'lived' experience of human existence itself: that is why the form in which we are '*made to see*' ideology in great novels has as its content the '*lived*' experience of individuals. . . . If I wanted to use Spinoza's language again here, I could say that art makes us 'see' 'conclusions without premises,'

whereas knowledge makes us penetrate into the mechanism which produces the 'conclusions' out of the 'premisses.' This is an important
distinction, for it enables us to understand that a novel on the 'cult,'
however profound, may draw attention to its 'lived' effects but *cannot
give an understanding of it*; it may put the question of the 'cult' on the
agenda, but it cannot *define the means* which will make it possible to
remedy these effects" (Louis Althusser, *Lenin and Philosophy and Other
Essays*, 222–24). I owe this citation to discussions of it in an excellent
unpublished dissertation by Byron Caminero-Santangelo, "Failing the
Test: Narration and Legitimation in Conrad's Short Fiction" (University
of California, Irvine, 1993) and in an unpublished paper by David
McClemont, "Just You and I: Addressing the Reader in Althusser and
Eliot" (1992), as well as to a brilliant discussion of ideology in Althusser
in an unpublished paper by Thomas Albrecht, "Ideology as a Literary
Form: On Aesthetic Ideology in Althusser." I agree with Caminero-
Santangelo that what Althusser says appears to be absurdly condescending to art. Surely novels can, and in fact in some cases conspicuously do,
give rigorous knowledge of the mechanisms that produce ideologies.
Moreover, Althusser's distinction between seeing and knowing seems
difficult if not impossible to maintain. If you "see" something you also
"know" it, at least according to an association of seeing and knowing that
goes in our tradition back to Aristotle.

6. In several remarkable pages in *The German Ideology* (Karl Marx
and Frederick Engels, *Collected Works*, V [New York: International Publishers, 1976], 41–45; Karl Marx, *Die Deutsche Ideologie*, in his *Die
Frühschriften*, ed. Siegfried Landshut [Stuttgart: Alfred Kröner, 1971],
354–59; cited hereafter as "E" and "G"), Marx (who was evidently the
sole author of these pages) attempts to show a world-historical progression whereby the human race separated itself from the animals as consciousness, language, society, and the division of labor gradually developed toward the production of ideology. Marx apparently wants to show
how ideology, something detached from matter, from human beings'
actual material conditions of existence, was born out of materiality, the
materiality of nature, of animal life, of the body, even out of the materiality of language and consciousness, or of language as the material
embodiment of consciousness, inseparable from consciousness, as well as
out of the concrete material conditions of production, circulation, and
exchange. In trying to do this, Marx shows, perhaps in spite of himself,
that you cannot detach ideology from materiality. Over and over, at each

stage of the universal historical progression he sketches out, he shows (1) that you cannot see how to get from one stage to the next, or think the transition, though (2) the transition does nevertheless occur, by a species of unfathomable or unintelligible leap, while nevertheless (3) a leap is not necessary because all the later stages were always already there from the beginning. These three things are asserted at once in undialectizable contradiction. The different "moments" (*Momente*), to use Marx's word, are not each negations of the previous ones, but related in a different way, as new configurations of a non-synthesizable "contradiction" (*Widerspruch*). Every new stage that is reached turns out to be materiality all over again, not free, detached, ineffective superstructure, as ideology is supposed to be for Marx, something without purchase on the real world because it is wholly disembodied, as Marx does seem to assert. The most striking case of the impossibility of freeing ideology from materiality comes toward the end of the passage, when he comes to the stage of ideology proper. He identifies this with the appearance of priests. Since priests are celibate they do not participate in the productive division of labor in the sex act, said by Marx to be the primal and originary example of the division of labor. A little later in the passage, ideology, for example, nationalist ideology, turns out to be "muck" and then "trash," in the German, *Dreck*. *Dreck* is not just mud, refuse, trash, but also dung, feces. Ideology, this passage asserts, is not the free-floating spirit of superstructure, but the residue or remainder left over after the material process of eating, consumption, digestion, and defecation. Ideology, far from being the highest, is the lowest, the most material thing of all, a leftover, remainder, or residue. Ideology is, literally, materially, *Dreck*, in the English vernacular, "shit." So ideology is matter, a particularly low, disgusting, useless (except for fertilizer) kind of matter. Once more the process of history, even at its most advanced stage, the stage of industrial capitalism, has not advanced beyond its starting point in materiality. If you begin with materiality, you cannot get beyond it. Materiality is a beginning that does not begin and yet is abundantly productive. It produces history, by a process whereby it is continually starting and making things happen without ever getting anywhere beyond itself. A careful reading of this passage in the original German would be necessary to show in detail the way it continuously advances through stages, from *Moment* to *Moment*, without ever succeeding in leaving materiality behind. Consciousness (*Bewußtsein*), for example, appears to arise quite late in the development of social man from the animals, but consciousness is still and always has been materialized in language, from which it cannot be distinguished. Language is the material "outering" of consciousness for social relations, but language is not added later to a consciousness already there. "Language is as old as consciousness" ("Die Sprache ist so alt wie das Bewußtsein") (E44; G357). The whole passage about language and consciousness puts this assertion in context. It is an extremely important passage for understanding Marxism: "Only now, after having considered four moments [*Momente*], four aspects of primary historical relations, do we find that man also possesses 'consciousness.' But even from the outset this is not 'pure' consciousness ['*reines*' *Bewußtsein*]. The 'mind' ['*Geist*'] is from the outset afflicted with the curse [*den Fluch*] of being 'burdened' ['*behaftet*'] with matter ['*der Materie*'], which here makes its appearance in the form of agitated layers of air, sounds, in short, of language [*der Sprache*]. Language is as old as consciousness, language is practical, real consciousness that exists for other men as well, and only therefore does it exist for me; language, like consciousness, only arises from the need, the necessity, of intercourse [*des Verkehrs*] with other men. Where there exists a relationship [*ein Verhältnis*], it exists for me: the animal does not '*relate*' ['verhält'] itself to anything, it does not '*relate*' itself at all" (E43–44; G356–57). The same moving forward through history to a higher abstraction and differentiation that does not leave matter behind, that remains essentially materialized, is repeated a little later in the passage about modern nationalist ideology I have referred to above. The ideology of nationalism is "muck" (these phrases are not in the German edition, but the word was possibly *Dreck*), not pure spirit, but dung. It seems to a given nation that the contradiction between a national and a general or international consciousness is entirely internal: "since this contradiction [*Widerspruch*] appears to exist only as a contradiction within the national consciousness, it seems to this nation that the struggle too is confined to this national muck, precisely because this nation represents this muck as such. Incidentally, it is quite immaterial [*ganz einerlei*] what consciousness starts to do on its own: out of all this trash [*aus diesem ganzen Dreck*] we get only the one inference that these three moments, the productive forces, the state of society and consciousness, can and must come into contradiction with one another" (E45; G, only in part, 358). Ideology, what consciousness starts out to do on its own, is not *Geist* but *Dreck*, the material remainder of a material historical process resulting from a division of labor, "which was originally nothing but the division of labor in the sexual act" ("die Teilung der Arbeit im Geschlectsakt") (E44; G58). Or, rather, the *Geist* and the *Dreck* go inextricably together, like consciousness and its necessary materialization in language. The *Dreck* of ideology takes the form of abstract or idealist "mental expressions," which are concomitant images of material constraints. Ideology and matter are intertwined indissolubly, just as are consciousness and language. "It is self-evident, moreover," says Marx at the end of this section, "that 'spectres,' 'bonds,' 'the higher being,' 'concept,' 'scruples' ['*Gespenster*,' '*Bande*,' '*höheres Wesen*,' '*Begriff*,' '*Bedenklichkeit*'], are merely idealist, speculative, mental expressions [*Ausdruck*], the concepts apparently of the isolated individual, the mere images of very empirical fetters and limitations [*die Vorstellung von sehr empirischen Fesseln und Schranken*), within which move the mode of production of life, and the form of intercourse coupled with it [*zusammenhängende Verkehrsform*]" (E45; G359).

Chapter 9

1. See Werner Hamacher, "Amphora (Extracts)," *Violence: Space*, ed. Mark Wigley, guest issue of *assemblage: A Critical Journal of Architecture and Design Culture* 20 (1993): 40–41, for an admirably succinct and penetrating discussion of Heidegger's notion of place and space in the context of Aristotle, Celan, and others.

2. M. Heidegger, "Bauen Wohnen Denken," *Vorträge und Aufsätze*, 2 (Pfullingen: Neske, 1954): 19; *Poetry, Language, Thought*, trans. Albert Hofstadter (New York: Harper & Row, 1971), 145. Further references will be to these texts, identified as "G" and "E."

3. Brian Ingraffia, in a brilliant book forthcoming from Cambridge University Press, discusses this in detail from the perspective of biblical theology. The book is based on his dissertation, "Vanquishing God's Shadow: Postmodern Theory, Ontotheology, and Biblical Theology," University of California, Irvine, 1993.

4. "Das Ding," *Vorträge und Aufsätze*, 2: 59; "The Thing," *Poetry, Language, Thought*, 186. Further references will be to these texts, identified as "G" and "E."

5. Paul de Man, "The Resistance to Theory," *The Resistance to Theory*, (Minneapolis: University of Minnesota Press, 1986), 11.

6. See the entry on the Indo-European root *bheu* in *The American Heritage Dictionary*. Two, or more, can play Heidegger's game of etymology hunting.

7. The translator of "Bauen Wohnen Denken," Albert Hofstadter, obscures this issue by adding a phrase and a sentence in the translation not present at all in Heidegger's German. Heidegger says "Das althochdeutsche Wort für bauen, 'buan' [The Old High German word for building, *buan*]" (G20). Hofstadter's translation says: "The Old English and High German word for building, *buan*" (E146). Hofstadter adds: "The neighbor is in Old English the *neahgebur*; *neah*, near, and *gebur*, dweller." This sentence does not exist in the German original. Adding this sentence is by no means an innocent clarification. It bypasses the problem of translation by trying to persuade the reader that what works for the German language works for the English language, too. The historical context for this move includes, for example, the nineteenth- and twentieth-century justification for the study of Anglo-Saxon in English and American universities. This justification goes by way of a claim that English is, after all, a Germanic language. The study of Anglo-Saxon will put the student in connection with the roots of our culture, for example, the roots of democracy in the Germanic "Thing," or legislative and deliberative gathering of the men of the tribe. Gerald Graff discusses this in *Professing Literature: An Institutional History* (Chicago: University of Chicago Press, 1987). The meaning of "Thing" as formal gathering of community leaders is also mentioned by Heidegger as part of his argument supporting the idea that things like bridges gather.

8. See Karl Marx and Frederick Engels, *The German Ideology, Collected Works* (New York: International Publishers, 1976), 41–45; Karl Marx, *Die Deutsche Ideologie*, in his *Die Frühschriften*, ed. Siegfried Landshut (Stuttgart: Alfred Kröner, 1971), 354–59.

9. Just as Heidegger uses questions as a fundamental part of his rhetorical strategy, so I have used questions to a somewhat different purpose in my reading of his essay. That raises the question of the question. Heidegger's use of the question is another form of the double bind of the parable. You must already know the answer in order to ask the question: "as long as we do not bear in mind that all building is in itself dwelling, we cannot even adequately *ask* [*zureichend* fragen], let alone properly decide, what the building of buildings might be in its nature" (E148; G22–23). My questions, on the other hand, are a form of ironic detachment that is meant to sustain the interrogation of what Heidegger says. My questions are apotropaic, a way of trying to ward off the great force of Heidegger's rhetoric.

10. A passage in *Unterwegs zur Sprache* (*On the Way to Language*)

explicitly associates man's unique ability to experience death with his unique ability to speak, and therefore, presumably, to listen to the silence as language speaks through him: "Mortals are they who can experience death as death. Animals cannot do so. But animals cannot speak either. The essential relation between death and language flashes up before us, but remains still unthought [*ist aber noch ungedacht*]" (*Unterwegs zur Sprache* [Pfullingen: Günther Neske, 1959], 215; *On the Way to Language*, trans. Peter D. Hertz [New York: Harper & Row, 1971], 107). See Jacques Derrida, *Aporias*, trans. Thomas Dutoit (Stanford: Stanford University Press, 1993), for an extended discussion of the motif of death in Heidegger's work.

11. Deborah Esch, in a brilliant, unpublished essay, has discussed the problematic of examples by way of the example of the way the entry on "example" in the *O.E.D.* disobeys the basic ordering principle of entries in the *O.E.D.*, that is, the assumption that the historical sequence of uses is also a logical sequence tracing developing meanings of the word from initial literal meanings to later figurative ones. That logic is in the entry on "example" disturbed by the aporias of exemplification. The literal meaning of any example of example is already figurative, since an example is a synecdoche, and presupposes the validity of what it at the same time puts in question.

12. Does this mean that all modern mappings, since they are "scientific" in their use of coordinates and projections, presupposing an underlying neutral geometrical space, are a falsification? Yes, unless it is recognized that the making of a map according to various conventions is also a form of building, a way of letting things be or come into presence.

13. Martin Heidegger, *Sein und Zeit* (Tübingen: Max Niemeyer, 1967), 367; *Being and Time*, trans. John Macquarrie and Edward Robinson (London: SCM Press, 1962), 418.

14. The story here links up to the one in "The Origin of the Work of Art" about the so-called peasant shoes in Van Gogh's painting.

15. Heidegger's *Die Frage nach dem Ding* (*The Question of the Thing*) takes this up at length, mostly by way of a discussion of Kant (*What Is a Thing*, trans. W. B. Barton, Jr., and Vera Deutsch [Chicago: Henry Regnery, 1967]; *Die Frage nach dem Ding* [Tübingen: Max Niemeyer, 1975]).

16. A. N. Whitehead's idea of "prehension" posits a somewhat similar ubiquity. Everything, says Whitehead, in a sense is everywhere in the universe at all times (*Science and the Modern World* [New York: Free Press,

1967], 69–72). But for Heidegger this being everywhere is much more limited and individual, special to a single social group. One might even say Heidegger's conception of space is nationalistic. Moreover, for Heidegger ubiquity is a unique feature of Dasein, whereas for Whitehead a stone is as much everywhere at once as a person. Heidegger's attempt to support what he is saying by analogy to the way modern physics represents "the spatial medium of cosmic space as a field-unity determined by body as dynamic center" (E156) seems spurious, since in the end it is not the bridge as body but the bridge as product of man's building that, so he claims, is an *Ort* that determines a *Stätte* that enspaces. That is not at all the same thing. It is an analogy, a figurative substitution, and a false one at that.

17. Darmstadt, where the lecture was initially presented.

Chapter 10

1. Frank Lentricchia, *Ariel and the Police: Michel Foucault, William James, Wallace Stevens* (Madison: University of Wisconsin Press, 1988).

2. Wallace Stevens, *The Collected Poems* (New York: Alfred A. Knopf, 1954), 125.

3. This chapter has benefited greatly from opportunities to present earlier versions to audiences in Taipei, Jerusalem, Zurich, Lausanne, and Irvine. For their sponsorship or for helpful comments that have led to changes or additions, I thank especially Shan Te-hsing, Lee Yu-cheng, Sanford Budick, Emily Budick, Lawrence Besserman, Judith Besserman, Peter Hughes, Christa Knellwolf, Peter Halter, Catherine Gallagher, and Georgia Albert.

4. I have discussed Stevens's "A Primitive Like an Orb" in "When Is a Primitive Like an Orb?," *Tropes, Parables, Performatives* (London: Harvester Wheatsheaf, 1990; Durham: Duke University Press, 1991), 227–44.

5. Further unidentified citations come from this poem.

6. See James Longenbach, "The Idea of Disorder at Key West," *Raritan* 11, no. 1 (Summer 1991), 104–5.

7. Kimon Friar and John Malcolm Brinnin, eds., *Modern Poetry* (New York: Appleton-Century Crofts, 1951), 538.

8. See Ramon Fernandez, *Messages* (Paris: Gallimard, 1926); *Messages*, trans. Montgomery Belgion (New York: Harcourt, Brace, 1927).

9. Longenbach, "Idea," 110.

10. On the basis of the presence of the battleship *Wyoming* and other

naval ships at anchor off Key West when Stevens visited in 1934, Longen-bach argues for a complex political context and meaning for the poem (ibid., 92–114). There can be no quarrel with the project of establishing a political context for Stevens's life and work. Stevens's next volume, *Parts of a World*, ends with a poem making explicit reference to war: "Exam-ination of the Hero in a Time of War." Unfortunately for Longenbach's hypothetical reading of "The Idea of Order at Key West," however, there is no reference in it, that I can see, to the U.S. Navy. The only boats named are, in so many words, "fishing boats at anchor there," just what one would expect in Key West harbor. It seems to me exceedingly unlikely that "fishing boats" is a euphemism for battleships and de-stroyers. That is not Stevens's kind of word play.

11. See Ken Frieden, *Genius and Monologue* (Ithaca: Cornell Univer-sity Press, 1985).

12. *The American Heritage Dictionary* (1969).

13. Wordsworth, "Nutting," ll. 54–56.

14. See Friedrich Nietzsche, *Das Philosophenbuch/Le Livre du phi-losophe*, ed. Angèle K. Marietti (Paris: Aubier-Flammarion, 1969), 188; trans. David J. Parent, *Friedrich Nietzsche on Rhetoric and Language* (New York: Oxford University Press, 1989), 252.

15. Martin Heidegger, "Bauen Wohnen Denken," *Vorträge und Auf-sätze*, 2 (Pfullingen: Neske, 1967), 26, 27; *idem*, "Building Dwelling Thinking," *Poetry, Language, Thought*, trans. Albert Hofstadter (New York: Harper & Row, 1971), 152, 153.

16. This, by the way, would mean that a cat or a dog or a fish cannot have a "world," an exceedingly problematic assumption.

17. "Autobiography as De-Facement," *The Rhetoric of Romanticism* (New York: Columbia University Press, 1984), 81.

18. I have discussed the political implications of Heidegger's topo-graphical ideas in chapter nine.

19. I have been helped here by Terence Harpold's brilliant unpub-lished essay, "The Contingencies of the Hypertext Link."

20. Jacques Derrida, *Psyché* (Paris: Galilée, 1991), 271.

21. See Ralph Waldo Emerson, "Seashore," *Poems, Complete Works*, Concord edition, 9 (Boston: Houghton, Mifflin and Company, n.d.), 242. The sea speaks: "Then I unbar the doors: my paths lead out / The exodus of nations: I disperse / Men to all shores that front the hoary main."

22. For characteristically rigorous formulations of the failure of orig-

ination to have a ground for its leverage and the consequences of this, see the following two statements by Paul de Man, one from 1966, the other from 1983. The first is from the essay on Blanchot's reading of Mallarmé in *Blindness and Insight*, 2d ed. (Minneapolis: University of Minnesota Press, 1983), 66: "The poet can only start his work because he is willing to forget that this presumed beginning is, in fact, the repetition of a previous failure, resulting precisely from an inability to begin anew. When we think that we are perceiving the assertion of a new origin, we are in fact witnessing the reassertion of a failure to originate." The second is a passage about the coherence of his own work from the preface to *The Rhetoric of Romanticism* (New York: Columbia University Press, 1984), viii: "This apparent coherence *within* each essay is not matched by a corresponding coherence *between* them. Laid out diachronically in a roughly chronological sequence, they do not evolve in a manner that easily allows for dialectical progression or, ultimately, for historical totalization. Rather, it seems that they always start again from scratch and that their conclusions fail to add up to anything."

Chapter 11

1. "Ponctuations: Le Temps de la thèse," *Du droit à la philosophie* (Paris: Galilée, 1990), 442–43. Translations in this chapter are my own unless otherwise noted.

2. Princeton: Princeton University Press, 1991.

3. Rodolphe Gasché, *The Tain of the Mirror: Derrida and the Philosophy of Reflection* (Cambridge, Mass.: Harvard University Press, 1986). See, for example, the categorical statements in the introduction: "Moreover, deconstructionist criticism is the offspring of a heritage that has little in common with that of Derrida's thought. Deconstructionist criticism must be understood as originating in New Criticism; it is a continuation of American-bred literary scholarship" (3). Gasché's book is invaluable for its investigation of Derrida's relation to European phenomenology, but it is too lacking in detail in its treatment of American literary criticism to be persuasive in its claim that American deconstructionists are doing something that has little in common with what Derrida is doing. The question-begging genetic figures in "offspring of a heritage," "originating," and "American-bred" ignore the fact that the influence of phenomenology on American literary criticism, including, among many others, three members of the so-called Yale School (de

Man, Hartman, and myself), had already made a decisive break in the continuity of American New Criticism in the 1950's, prior to any influence of Derrida in America.

4. See Jeffrey Nealon, "The Discipline of Deconstruction," *PMLA* 107, no. 5 (October 1992), 1266–79, and Mas'ud Zavarzadeh, "Pun(k)deconstruction and the Postmodern Political Imaginary," *Cultural Critique*, vol. 14, no. 22 (Fall 1992): 5–47.

5. In the introduction to *Anti-Mimesis*, forthcoming from Cambridge University Press, and in "Diary of a Deconstructor Manqué: Reflections on Post 'Post-Mortem de Man,'" forthcoming in *Minnesota Review*.

6. Paul de Man, "The Resistance to Theory," *The Resistance to Theory* (Minneapolis: University of Minnesota Press, 1986), 11.

7. Jacques Derrida, "Fors," in Nicolas Abraham and Maria Torok, *Cryptonymie: Le Verbier de L'Homme aux loups* (Paris: Aubier Flammarion, 1976), 13. Jacques Derrida, "Fors: The Anglish Words of Nicolas Abraham and Maria Torok," foreword to Nicolas Abraham and Maria Torok, *The Wolf Man's Magic Word: A Cryptonymy*, trans. Nicholas Rand (Minneapolis: University of Minnesota Press, 1986), xiv. Further references will be indicated in the text by "F" and "E," respectively, followed by the page numbers. In places, I have altered the translation to more directly reflect the original.

8. Thomas Hardy, *The Return of the Native* (London: Macmillan, 1974), 44–45.

9. Franz Kafka, "The Burrow," *The Great Wall of China*, trans. Willa and Edwin Muir (New York: Schocken, 1948), 79.

10. Jacques Derrida, "Ponctuations," 443.

11. *Passions* (Paris: Galilée, 1993), 65. Later citations will be given by page number in the text.

12. "'This Strange Institution Called Literature': An Interview with Jacques Derrida," *Acts of Literature*, ed. Derek Attridge (New York: Routledge, 1992), 38.

13. See, for example, "Fors": "It is in fact precisely *because* the verbal instance is only a derivative effect that the word-thing [*mot-chose*] could constitute itself as such, re-become a kind of thing after the repression that cast it out. It is the topographical possibility [*possibilité topique*] of the crypt, the line of demarcation that it institutes between the process of introjection and the fantasy of incorporation, which would account for, but is not restricted to, the verbal function." (Exxxix; F58.)

14. For an exemplary discussion of the structure of exemplarity in

Derrida's work, see Michael B. Naas's brilliant introductory essay to the English translation of Derrida's *L'Autre Cap*, "Introduction: For Example," in Jacques Derrida, *The Other Heading*, trans. Pascale-Anne Brault and Michael B. Naas (Bloomington: Indiana University Press, 1992), vii–lix.

15. Jacques Derrida, *Donner le temps: I. La fausse monnaie* (Paris: Galilée, 1991), 194. Jacques Derrida, *Given Time: I. Counterfeit Money*, trans. Peggy Kamuf (Chicago: University of Chicago Press, 1992). Later page references to *Donner le temps* will be given in the text, with F to indicate the French edition, in my translation.

16. A passage in " 'This Strange Institution Called Literature' " uses phenomenological terms to express this with suitable nuance, guarding against various dangers of misunderstanding what it means to say that any text can be read as literature, while no text is in itself literary: "A philosophical, or journalistic, or scientific discourse, can be read in a 'nontranscendent' fashion. 'Transcend' here means going beyond interest for the signifier, the form, the language (note that I do not say 'text') in the direction of the meaning or referent (this is Sartre's rather simple but convenient definition of prose). One can do a nontranscendent reading of any text whatever. Moreover, there is no text which is literary *in itself.* Literarity is not a natural essence, an intrinsic property of the text. It is the correlative of an intentional relation to the text, an intentional relation which integrates in itself, as a component or an intentional layer, the more or less implicit consciousness of rules which are conventional or institutional—social, in any case. Of course, this does not mean that literarity is merely projective or subjective—in the sense of the empirical subjectivity or caprice of each reader. The literary character of the text is inscribed on the side of the intentional object, in its noematic structure, one could say, and not only on the subjective side of the noetic act. There are 'in' the text features which call for a literary reading and recall the convention, institution, or history of literature." (44.)

17. See the following passage in " 'This Strange Institution Called Literature' " for Derrida's expression of this equivocation: "There is no literature without a *suspended* relation to meaning and reference. *Suspended* means *suspense*, but also *dependence*, condition, conditionality." (48.)

18. "Kant and Schiller," unpublished manuscript, 5, 7.

19. Paul de Man, "Shelley Disfigured," *The Rhetoric of Romanticism*

(New York: Columbia University Press, 1984), 93–123; "Aesthetic Formalization: Kleist's *Über das Marionettentheater,*" *The Rhetoric of Romanticism*, 263–90; "Hypogram and Inscription," *The Resistance to Theory*, 3–20; "Sign and Symbol, in Hegel's Aesthetics," *Critical Inquiry* 8, no. 4 (Summer 1982): 761–75; "Hegel on the Sublime," *Displacement: Derrida and After*, ed. Mark Krupnik (Bloomington: Indiana University Press), 139–53; "Phenomenality and Materiality in Kant," *Hermeneutics: Questions and Prospects*, ed. Gary Shapiro and Alan Sica (Amherst: University of Massachusetts Press, 1984), 121–44.

20. Walter Benjamin, *Illuminations*, trans. Harry Zohn (New York: Schocken, 1969), 263; Walter Benjamin, *Illuminationen* (Frankfurt am Main: Suhrkamp, 1955), 278.

Chapter 12

1. "Travelling Theory," in *The World, the Text, and the Critic* (Cambridge, Mass.: Harvard University Press, 1983), 226–47; the later lecture has been revised and published as "Travelling Theory Reconsidered," in *Critical Reconstructions: The Relationship of Fiction and Life*, ed. Robert M. Polhemus and Roger B. Henkle (Stanford: Stanford University Press, 1994), 251–63.

2. Paul de Man, "The Resistance to Theory," *The Resistance to Theory* (Minneapolis: University of Minnesota Press, 1986), 3. Mentioning de Man perhaps incurs a responsibility to say something about de Man's wartime writings. I have elsewhere said in some detail what I have to say about those writings. (See "Paul de Man's Wartime Writings" and "An Open Letter to Jon Wiener," *Theory Now and Then* [London: Harvester Wheatsheaf, 1990; Durham: Duke University Press, 1991], 359–84.) De Man's later writings, far from being continuous with the wartime writings, repeatedly attack just those positions—for example, assumptions about literature and national identity—he held in the writings for *Le Soir*.

3. What is untranslatable is the contingent and intrinsically meaningless fact that in Italian changing a "u" to an "i" and making the "t" single rather than double changes "translate" into "traduce."

4. Walter Benjamin, *Illuminationen* (Frankfurt am Main: Suhrkamp, 1955), 148–84; *Illuminations*, trans. Harry Zohn (New York: Schocken Books, 1969), 217–51. My reference to this essay is an example of what I am discussing. Benjamin's essay has been widely influential in the United

States. It is often cited and commented on. It has generated much new work in "cultural criticism." It may have been read more often in English than in the German original.

5. It is characteristic of our present cultural situation that this chapter in a preliminary form was sent by FAX halfway around the world, from Maine to Taipei, as soon as it was finished.

6. I have argued this in more detail in "The Work of Cultural Criticism in the Age of Digital Reproduction," in *Illustration* (London: Reaktion Press, 1992; Cambridge, Mass.: Harvard University Press, 1992).

7. De Man, "Resistance to Theory," 7.

8. Some preliminary sense of this tradition can be gained from the entry on Ruth and *Ruth Rabbah* (the aggadic Midrash on the Book of Ruth) in the *Encyclopedia Judaica*. See also the entry by Jack Sasson on Ruth in *The Literary Guide to the Bible*, ed. Robert Alter and Frank Kermode (Cambridge, Mass.: Harvard University Press, 1987), 320–28; Yehoshua Bachrach, *Mother of Royalty: An Exposition of the Book of Ruth in the Light of the Sources*, trans. Leonard Oschry (Jerusalem: Feldheim, 1973); Edward F. Campbell, Jr., *Ruth: A New Translation with Introduction, Notes, and Commentary*, Anchor Bible series (Garden City, N.Y.: Doubleday, 1975); Jack M. Sasson, *Ruth: A New Translation with a Philological Commentary and a Formalist-Folklorist Interpretation* (Baltimore: Johns Hopkins University Press, 1979); Evelyn Strouse and Bezalel Porten, "A Reading of Ruth," *Commentary* (February 1979), 63–67; Shmuel Yerushalmi, *The Book of Ruth: MeAm Lo'ez*, trans. E. van Handel (New York: Maznaim, 1985); *The Book of Ruth; Megillas Ruth: A New Translation with Commentary Anthologized from Talmudic, Midrashic, and Rabbinic Sources*, trans. and compiled by Meir Zlotowitz (New York: ArtScroll Tanach Studios, 1976). For an excellent discussion of some medieval Christian commentary on Ruth in relation to Chaucer's references to it, see Ellen E. Martin, "Chaucer's Ruth: an Exegetical Poetic in the Prologue to the *Legend of Good Women*," *Exemplaria* 3, no. 2 (October 1991): 467–90.

9. I owe this knowledge to a conversation with Professor Moshe Greenberg of the Hebrew University of Jerusalem and to a helpful letter sent by Dr. Esther Beith-Halahmi of Bar-Ilan University in Israel. I cite part of Dr. Beith-Halahmi's letter for the interest of its details: "according to the only epigraphic 'document' from Moab we have, the Stelle of Mesha King of Moab (2 Kings 3, Amos 2:1, and 2 Chronicles 20), which

was found in Ancient Dibon by Samuel Klein in 1868 and whose fragments were bought by Charles Clermont-Ganneau for France in 1870, the language of Moab was almost indistinguishable from Hebrew. This Stelle in basalt stone, in which King Mesha immortalized his uprising against Israel, is inscribed in ancient Hebrew letters, and though we cannot know what the exact pronunciation was, it differs in spelling and vocabulary only slightly, containing a few words whose meaning differs and some others which do not appear in the Bible. In fact, after learning the ancient Hebrew alphabet, our students in Bible at Bar-Ilan read the text in class almost as easily as any ancient Hebrew text. This is not conclusive evidence of the language spoken by the Moabites since it could be argued that they might have inscribed the Stelle in the language of the enemy, but there is other evidence to support the thesis. See W. F. Albright in *The Archaeology of Palestine* (Harmondsworth: Penguin Books, 1949), 130–36; 177–203, esp. 180. Albright writes that 'the ancient Semitic tongues, outside Accadian, were so closely related to one another in grammar and pronunciation (phonetics) that each dialect had much in common with all its neighbors'; and the articles of Jacob Liver and of Hayim Rabin on Mesha (in Hebrew) and on Moab in *Encyclopaedia Biblia*, IV (Jerusalem: Bialik Institute, 1962), 707–22, esp. 716–18 on Moab; and 921–29 (esp. 925–29) on Mesha and his Stelle."

10. At least I think it is Boaz, not the kinsman, who takes off his shoe to seal the bargain. The referent of the "he" is ambiguous, and the commentators disagree.

11. The essay is included in Michael Lane, ed., *Structuralism: A Reader* (London: Jonathan Cape, 1970).

12. In response to an oral presentation of this chapter at a conference in Brasília.

13. Charles Dickens, *Pickwick Papers* (Harmondsworth: Penguin Books, 1972), 539.

14. This may be a form of the resistance of theory to itself and of the asymmetry of theory and reading of which de Man speaks at the end of "The Resistance to Theory": "To the extent however that they are theory, that is to say teachable, generalizable and highly responsive to systematization, rhetorical readings, like the other kinds, still avoid and resist the reading they advocate. Nothing can overcome the resistance to theory since theory *is* itself this resistance" (19).

Index

In this index an "f" after a number indicates a separate reference on the next page, and an "ff" indicates separate references on the next two pages. A continuous discussion over two or more pages is indicated by a span of page numbers, e.g., "57–59." *Passim* is used for a cluster of references in close but not consecutive sequence.

MERIDIAN

Crossing Aesthetics

Library of Congress
Cataloging-in-Publication Data

Miller, J. Hillis (Joseph Hillis)
Topographies/J. Hillis Miller.
p.   cm.—(Meridian)
Includes bibliographical references (p.) and index.
ISBN 0-8047-2378-8 (cl.)—ISBN 0-8047-2379-6 (pbk.)
1. Geography in literature.   I. Title.   II. Series.
PN56.G48M55   1995
809'.9332—dc20
94-25351
CIP

⊗ This book is printed on acid-free, recycled paper.
It was typeset in Adobe Garamond and Lithos
by Keystone Typesetting, Inc.